IT'S LONELY AT THE CENTRE OF THE EARTH

this book is for someone, somewhere.

Zoe xx

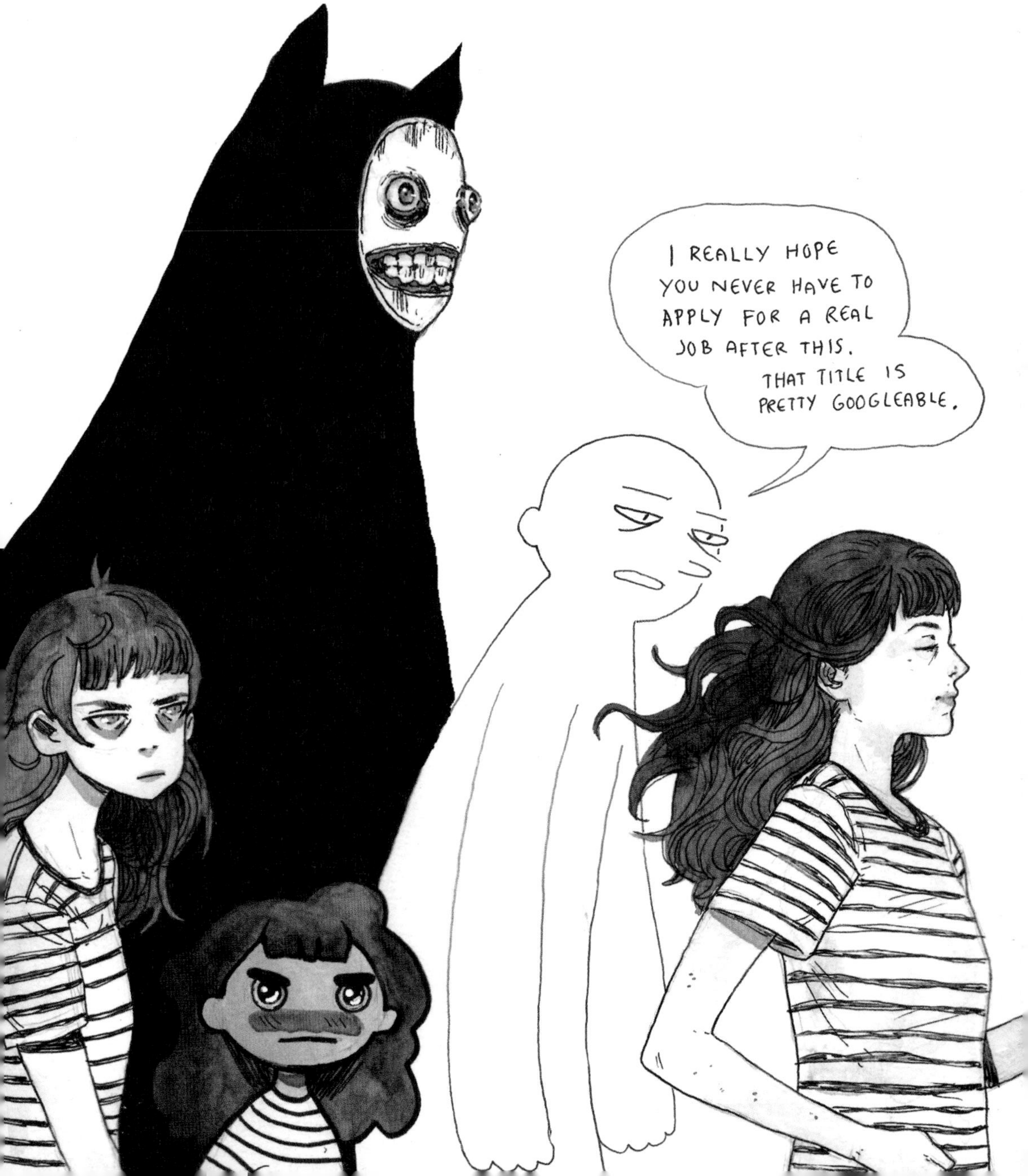
I REALLY HOPE YOU NEVER HAVE TO APPLY FOR A REAL JOB AFTER THIS.
THAT TITLE IS PRETTY GOOGLEABLE.

This book includes personal discussion and depiction
of suicide and self harm. While I hope this book may
serve as a comfort to some, its content may be
triggering. Make sure you are in a comfortable
place before reading, and remember that the sun
always rises on a new day. Thank you.

- Zoe

IMAGE COMICS, INC. · Robert Kirkman: Chief Operating Officer · Erik Larsen: Chief Financial Officer · Todd McFarlane:
President · Marc Silvestri: Chief Executive Officer · Jim Valentino: Vice President · Eric Stephenson: Publisher / Chief
Creative Officer · Nicole Lapalme: Vice President of Finance · Leanna Caunter: Accounting Analyst · Sue Korpela: Accounting
& HR Manager · Matt Parkinson: Vice President of Sales & Publishing Planning · Lorelei Bunjes: Vice President of Digital
Strategy · Dirk Wood: Vice President of International Sales & Licensing · Ryan Brewer: International Sales & Licensing Manager
Alex Cox: Director of Direct Market Sales · Chloe Ramos: Book Market & Library Sales Manager · Emilio Bautista: Digital
Sales Coordinator · Jon Schlaffman: Specialty Sales Coordinator · Kat Salazar: Vice President of PR & Marketing · Deanna
Phelps: Marketing Design Manager · Drew Fitzgerald: Marketing Content Associate · Heather Doornink: Vice President of
Production · Drew Gill: Art Director · Hilary DiLoreto: Print Manager · Tricia Ramos: Traffic Manager · Melissa Gifford:
Content Manager · Erika Schnatz: Senior Production Artist · Wesley Griffith: Production Artist · Rich Fowlks: Production Artist ·
IMAGECOMICS.COM

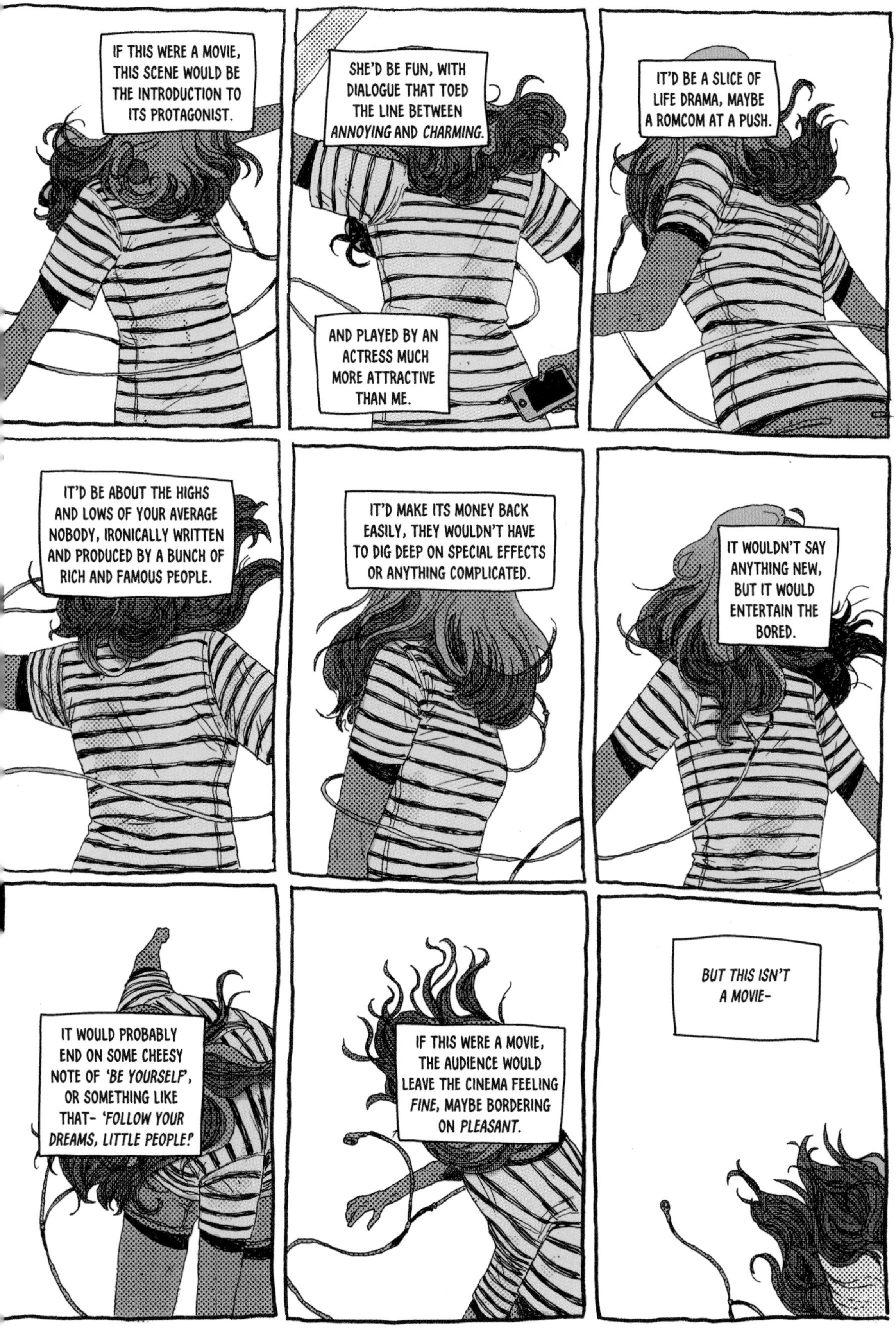
IF THIS WERE A MOVIE, THIS SCENE WOULD BE THE INTRODUCTION TO ITS PROTAGONIST.
SHE'D BE FUN, WITH DIALOGUE THAT TOED THE LINE BETWEEN *ANNOYING* AND *CHARMING*.
AND PLAYED BY AN ACTRESS MUCH MORE ATTRACTIVE THAN ME.
IT'D BE A SLICE OF LIFE DRAMA, MAYBE A ROMCOM AT A PUSH.
IT'D BE ABOUT THE HIGHS AND LOWS OF YOUR AVERAGE NOBODY, IRONICALLY WRITTEN AND PRODUCED BY A BUNCH OF RICH AND FAMOUS PEOPLE.
IT'D MAKE ITS MONEY BACK EASILY, THEY WOULDN'T HAVE TO DIG DEEP ON SPECIAL EFFECTS OR ANYTHING COMPLICATED.
IT WOULDN'T SAY ANYTHING NEW, BUT IT WOULD ENTERTAIN THE BORED.
IT WOULD PROBABLY END ON SOME CHEESY NOTE OF *'BE YOURSELF'*, OR SOMETHING LIKE THAT- *'FOLLOW YOUR DREAMS, LITTLE PEOPLE!'*
IF THIS WERE A MOVIE, THE AUDIENCE WOULD LEAVE THE CINEMA FEELING *FINE*, MAYBE BORDERING ON *PLEASANT*.
BUT THIS ISN'T A MOVIE-

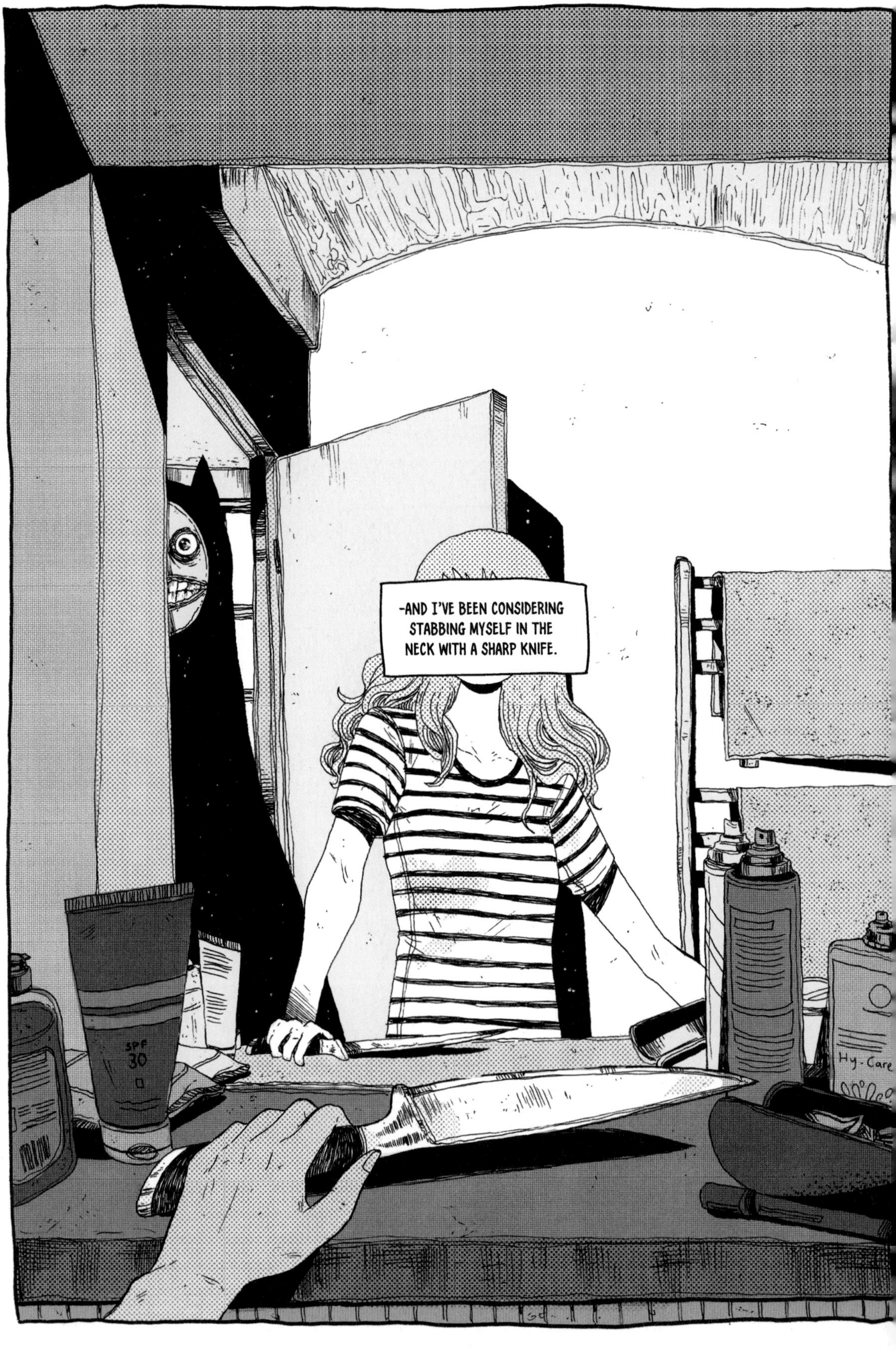

-AND I'VE BEEN CONSIDERING STABBING MYSELF IN THE NECK WITH A SHARP KNIFE.
SPF 30
Hy-Care

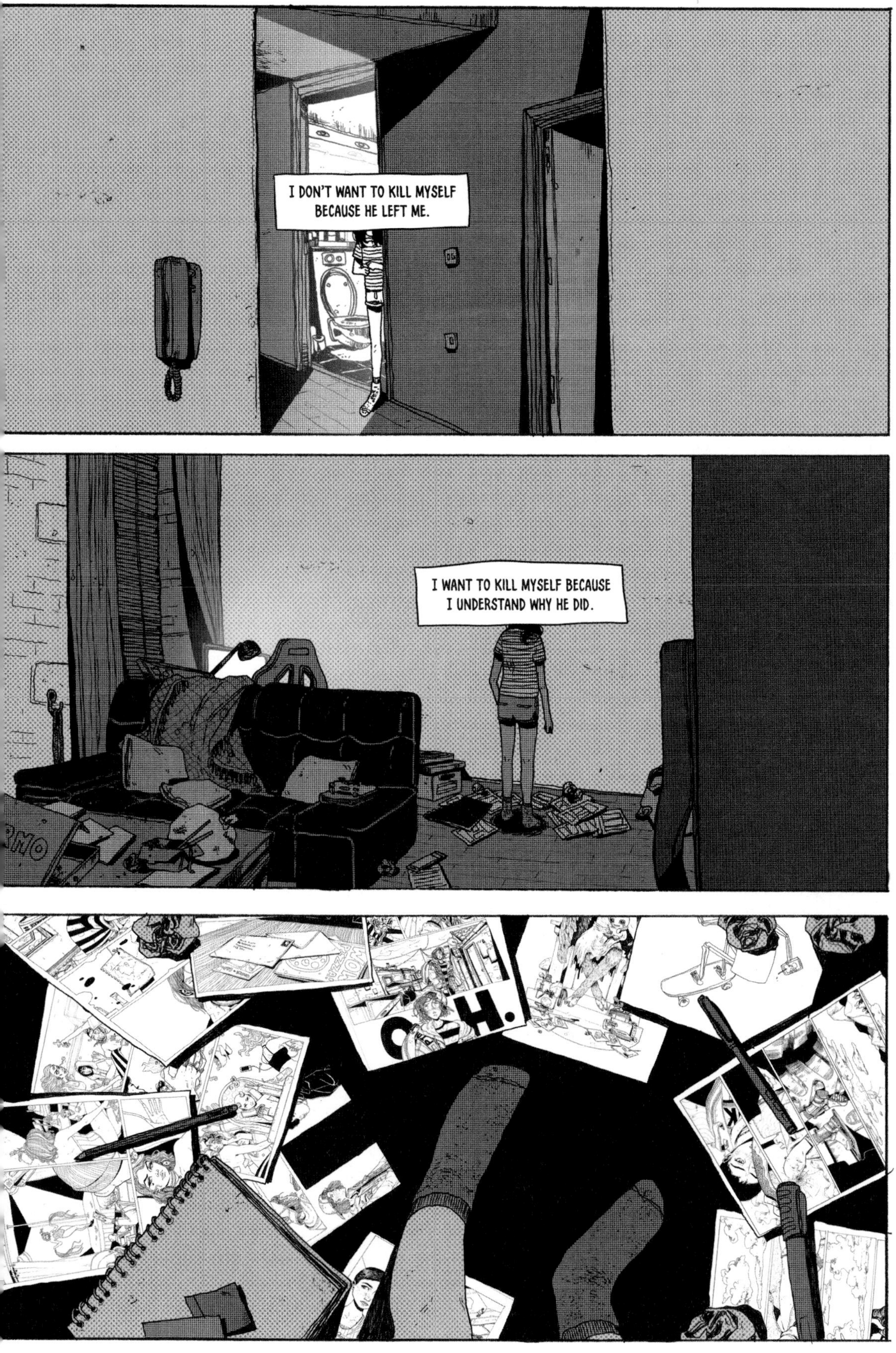
I DON'T WANT TO KILL MYSELF BECAUSE HE LEFT ME.
I WANT TO KILL MYSELF BECAUSE I UNDERSTAND WHY HE DID.

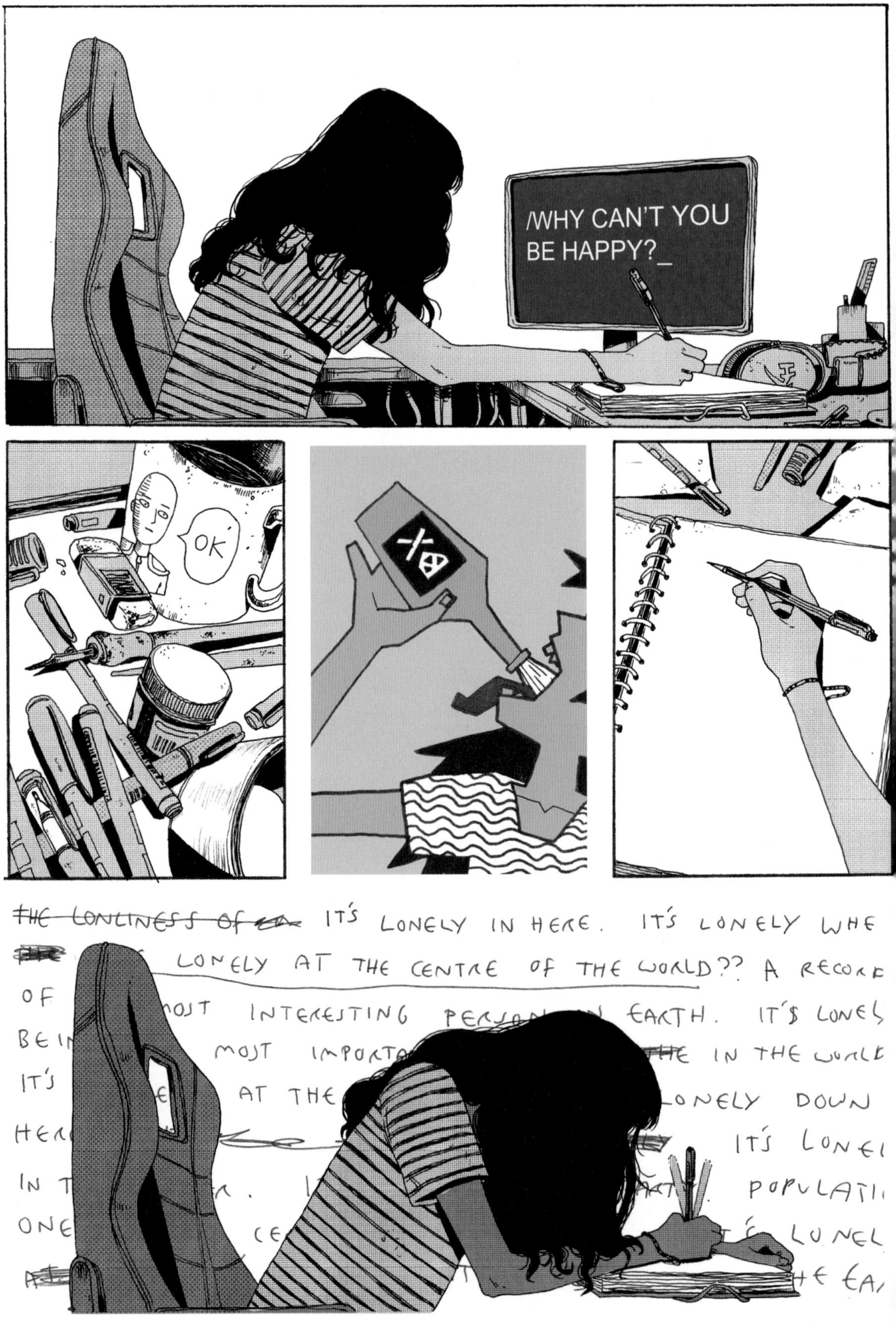
/WHY CAN'T YOU BE HAPPY?_
OK
~~THE LONLINESS OF~~ IT'S LONELY IN HERE. IT'S LONELY WHE
LONELY AT THE CENTRE OF THE WORLD?? A RECORD
OF
INTERESTING
EARTH. IT'S LONEL
MOST
IN THE WORLD
IT'S
AT THE
LONELY DOWN
IT'S LONEL
POPULATI
ONE

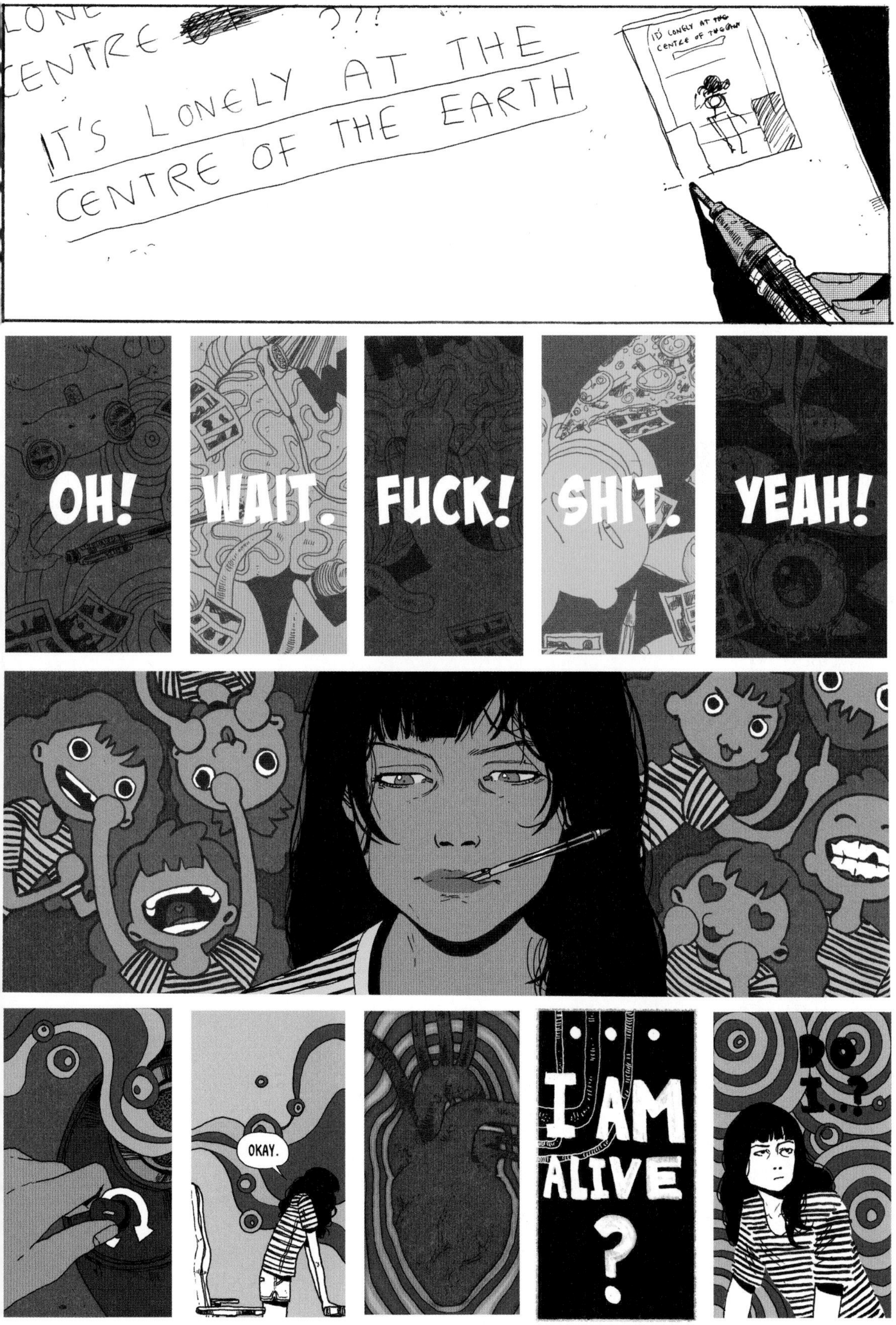

IT'S LONELY AT THE CENTRE OF THE EARTH
OH!
WAIT.
FUCK!
SHIT.
YEAH!
OKAY.
I AM ALIVE
?
DO I...?

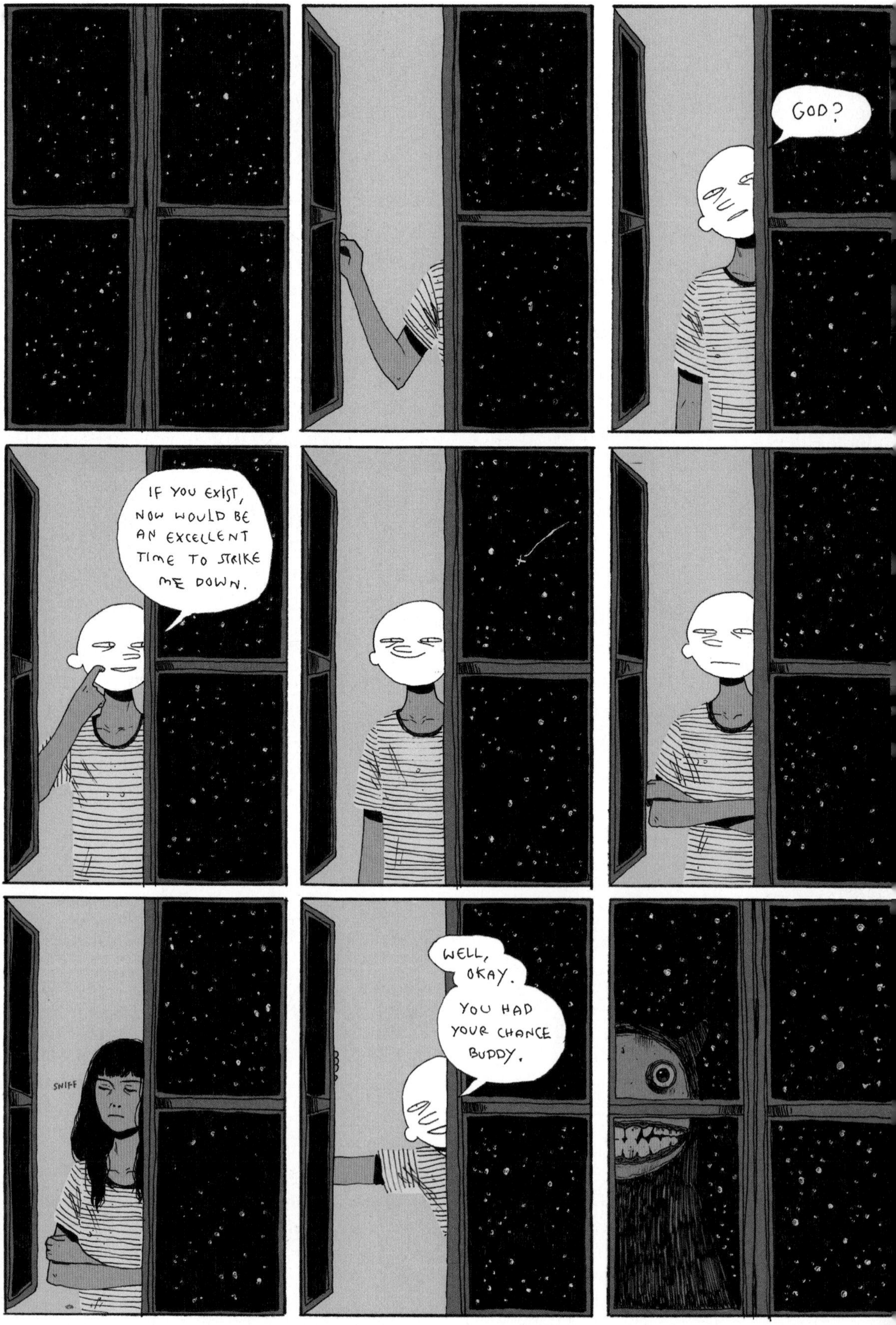
GOD?
IF YOU EXIST, NOW WOULD BE AN EXCELLENT TIME TO STRIKE ME DOWN.
SNIFF
WELL, OKAY.
YOU HAD YOUR CHANCE BUDDY.

ZOE THOUGHT THAT MAYBE
SHE NEVER REALLY
WANTED TO KILL HERSELF,
SOMETIMES IT FELT LIKE
A PERFORMANCE, A
PERFORMANCE FOR NO
AUDIENCE, BUT IT FELT LIKE
ACTING NONETHELESS.
SHE COULD STOP WRITING
THIS, SHE COULD PUT DOWN
THE PAINTBRUSH AND CHOOSE
TO LIVE OUTSIDE OF HER OWN
HEAD.

BUT THAT WOULD REQUIRE HER
TO THINK ABOUT SOMETHING
OTHER THAN HERSELF FOR A
CHANGE.

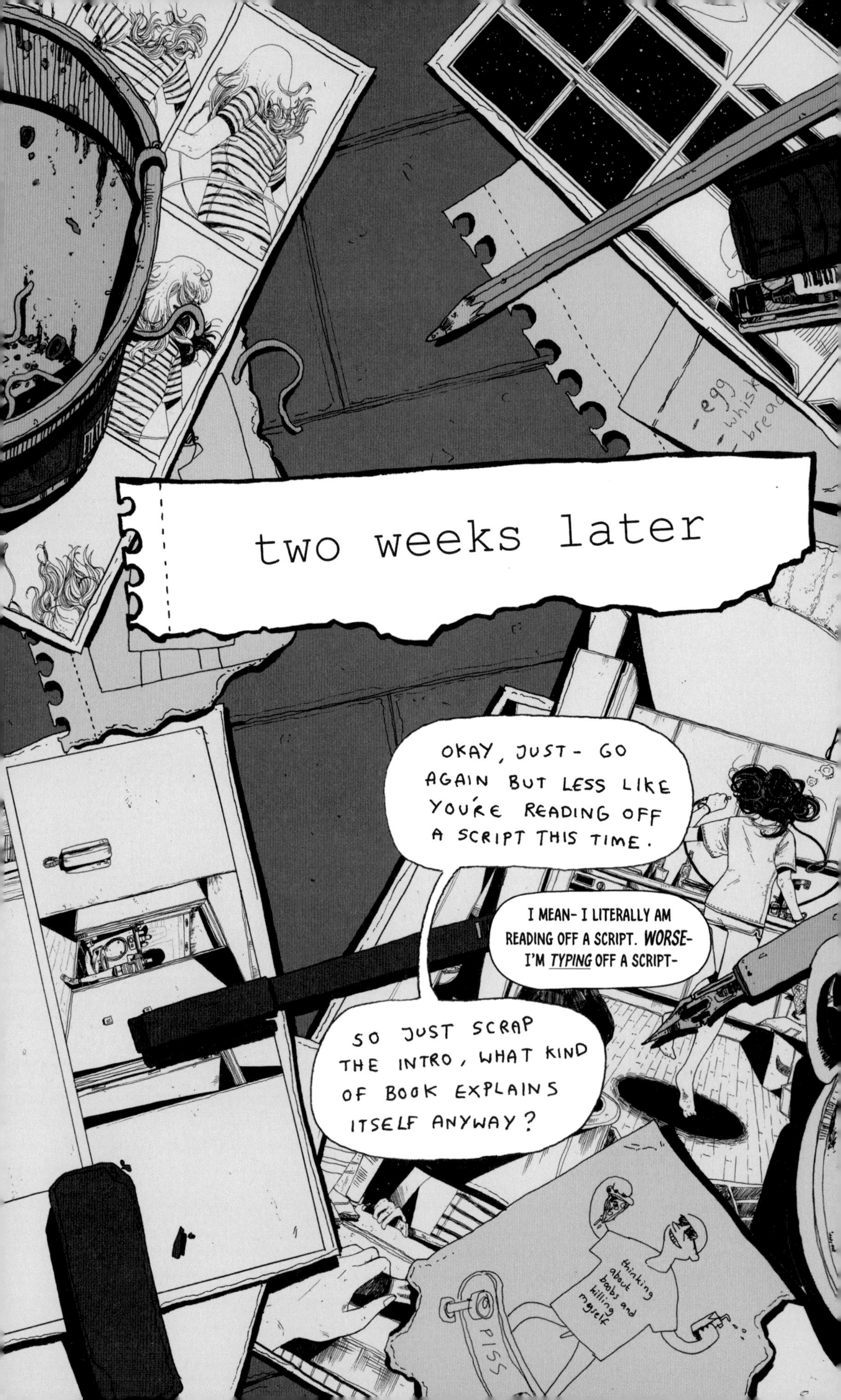

two weeks later
OKAY, JUST- GO AGAIN BUT LESS LIKE YOU'RE READING OFF A SCRIPT THIS TIME.
I MEAN- I LITERALLY AM READING OFF A SCRIPT. WORSE- I'M TYPING OFF A SCRIPT-
SO JUST SCRAP THE INTRO, WHAT KIND OF BOOK EXPLAINS ITSELF ANYWAY?
thinking about boobs and killing myself
PISS

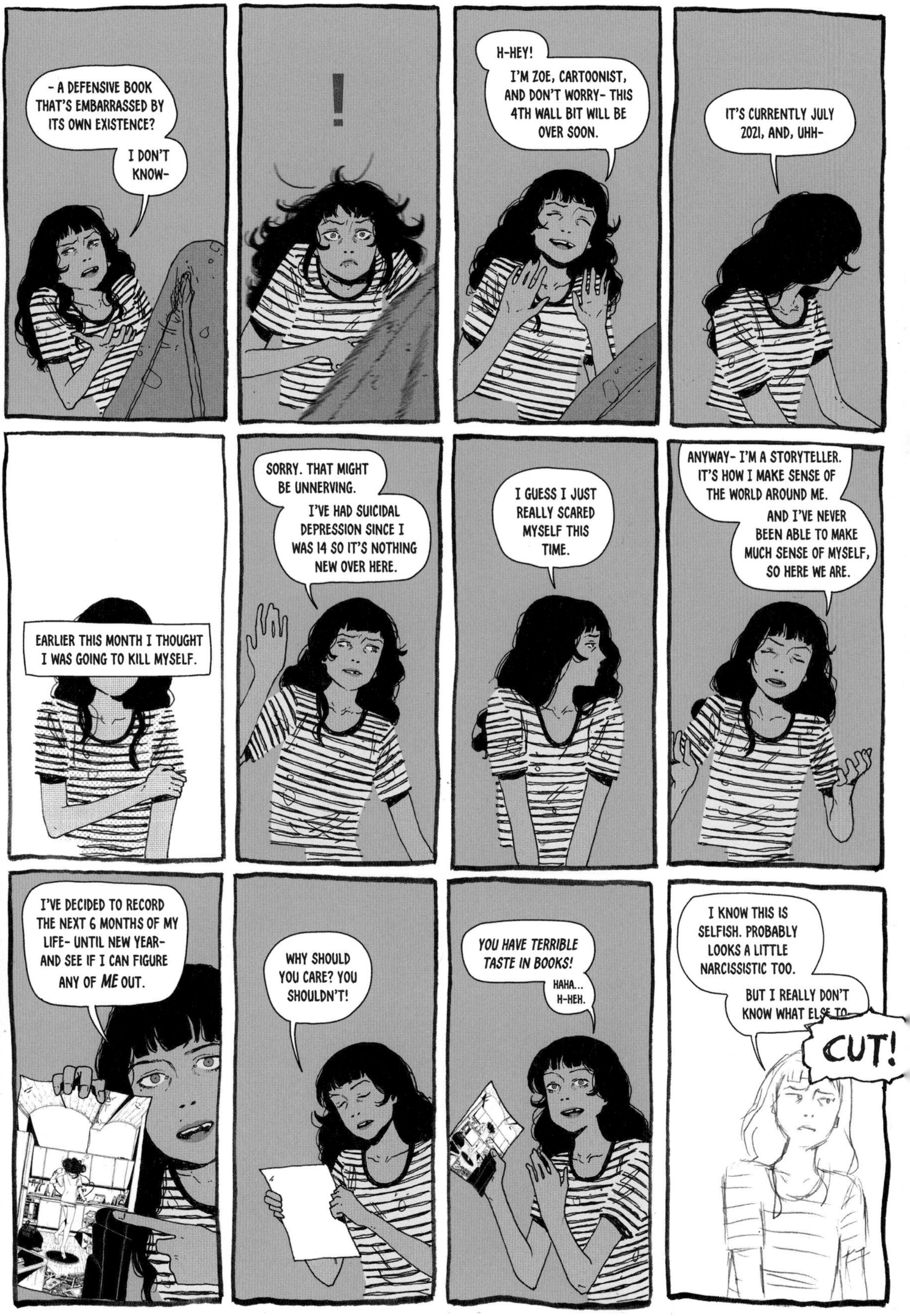
- A DEFENSIVE BOOK THAT'S EMBARRASSED BY ITS OWN EXISTENCE?
I DON'T KNOW-
!
H-HEY!
I'M ZOE, CARTOONIST, AND DON'T WORRY- THIS 4TH WALL BIT WILL BE OVER SOON.
IT'S CURRENTLY JULY 2021, AND, UHH-
EARLIER THIS MONTH I THOUGHT I WAS GOING TO KILL MYSELF.
SORRY. THAT MIGHT BE UNNERVING.
I'VE HAD SUICIDAL DEPRESSION SINCE I WAS 14 SO IT'S NOTHING NEW OVER HERE.
I GUESS I JUST REALLY SCARED MYSELF THIS TIME.
ANYWAY- I'M A STORYTELLER. IT'S HOW I MAKE SENSE OF THE WORLD AROUND ME.
AND I'VE NEVER BEEN ABLE TO MAKE MUCH SENSE OF MYSELF, SO HERE WE ARE.
I'VE DECIDED TO RECORD THE NEXT 6 MONTHS OF MY LIFE- UNTIL NEW YEAR- AND SEE IF I CAN FIGURE ANY OF *ME* OUT.
WHY SHOULD YOU CARE? YOU SHOULDN'T!
YOU HAVE TERRIBLE TASTE IN BOOKS!
HAHA... H-HEH.
I KNOW THIS IS SELFISH. PROBABLY LOOKS A LITTLE NARCISSISTIC TOO.
BUT I REALLY DON'T KNOW WHAT ELSE TO-
CUT!

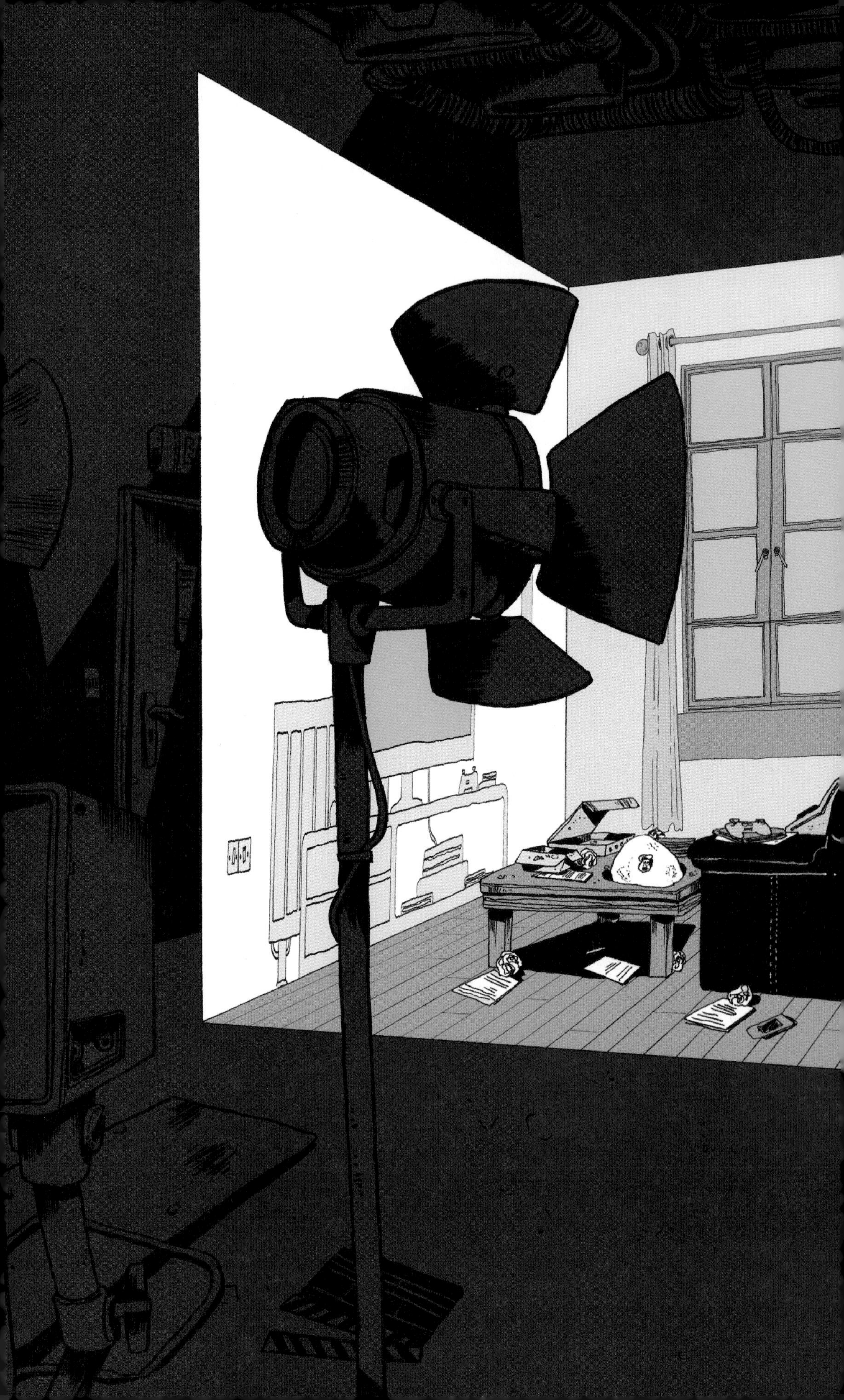

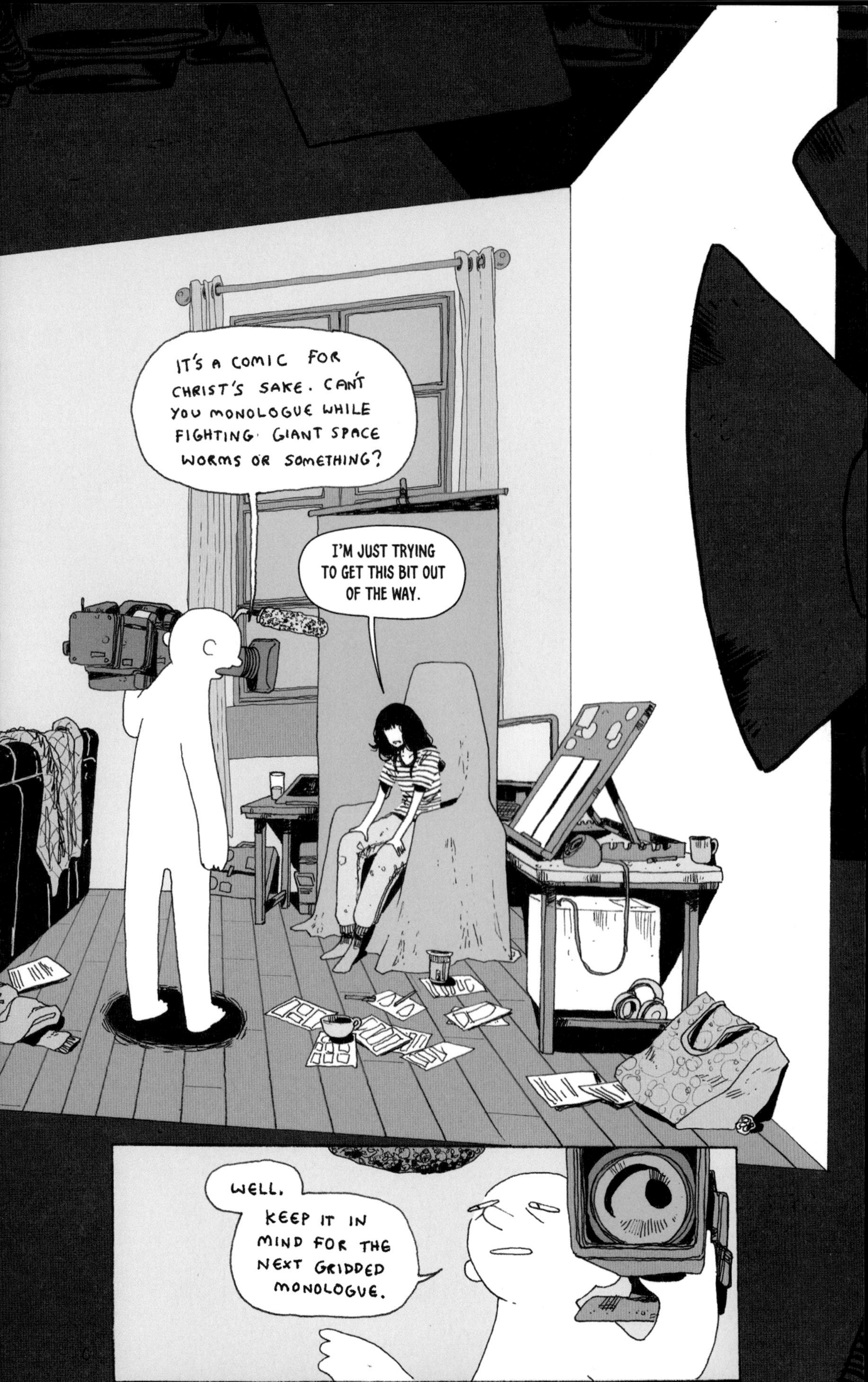
IT'S A COMIC FOR CHRIST'S SAKE. CAN'T YOU MONOLOGUE WHILE FIGHTING GIANT SPACE WORMS OR SOMETHING?
I'M JUST TRYING TO GET THIS BIT OUT OF THE WAY.
WELL. KEEP IT IN MIND FOR THE NEXT GRIDDED MONOLOGUE.

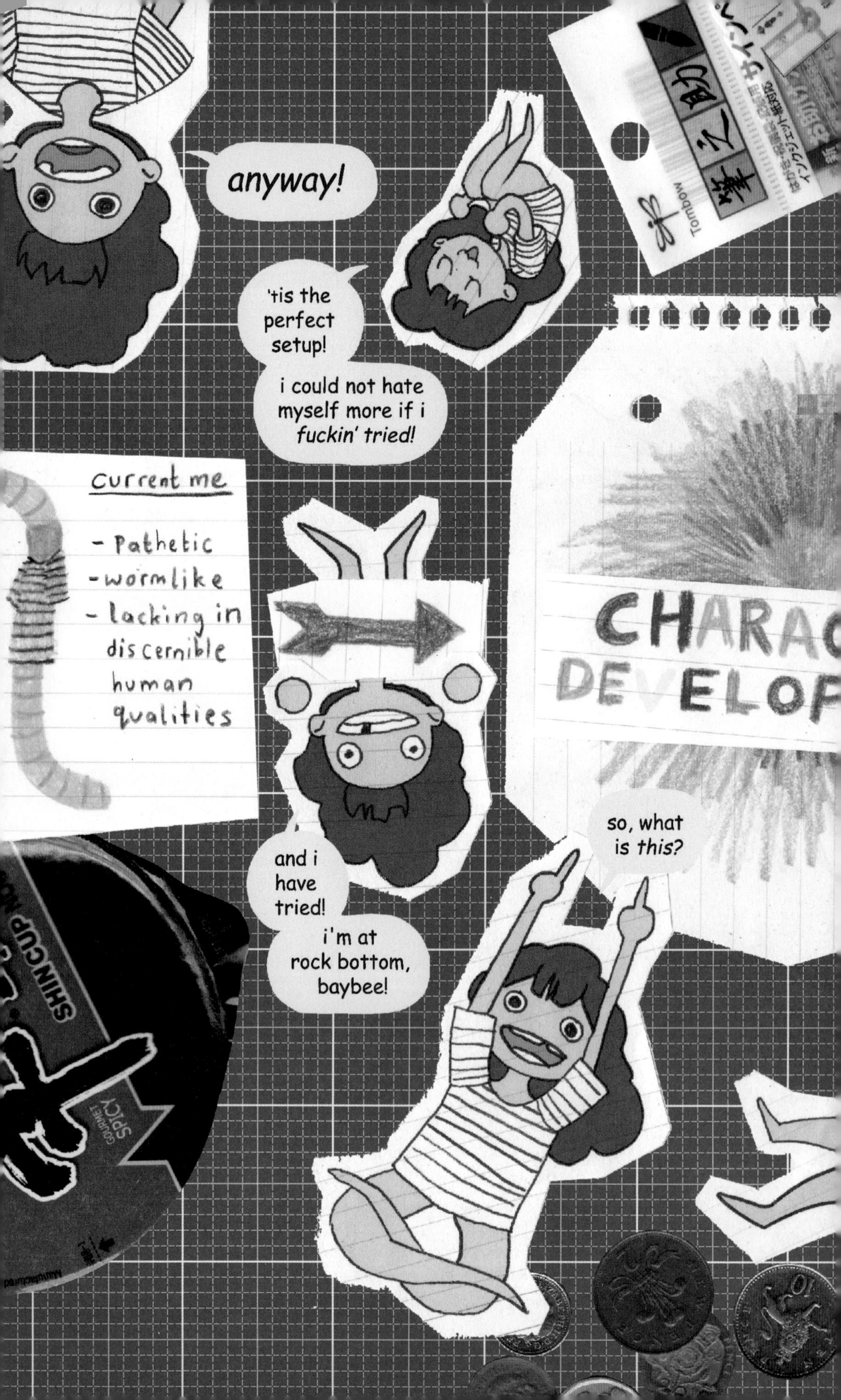
anyway!
'tis the perfect setup!
i could not hate myself more if i fuckin' tried!
current me
- Pathetic
- wormlike
- lacking in discernible human qualities
and i have tried!
i'm at rock bottom, baybee!
CHARAC
DEVELOP
so, what is this?
Tombow
SHIN CUP
GOURMET SPICY

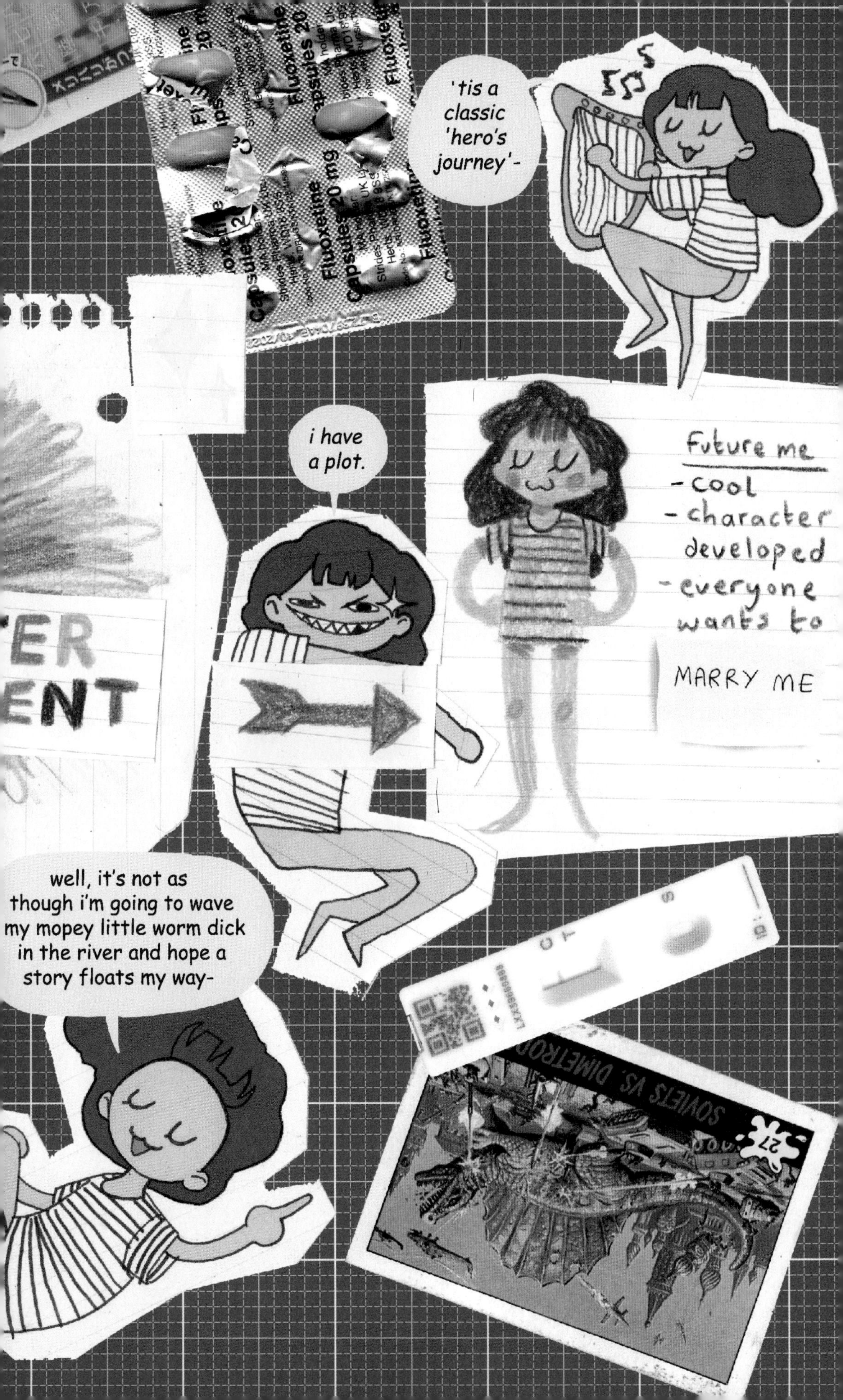

Fluoxetine Capsules 20 mg
'tis a classic 'hero's journey'-
i have a plot.
Future me
- cool
- character developed
- everyone wants to
MARRY ME
well, it's not as though i'm going to wave my mopey little worm dick in the river and hope a story floats my way-

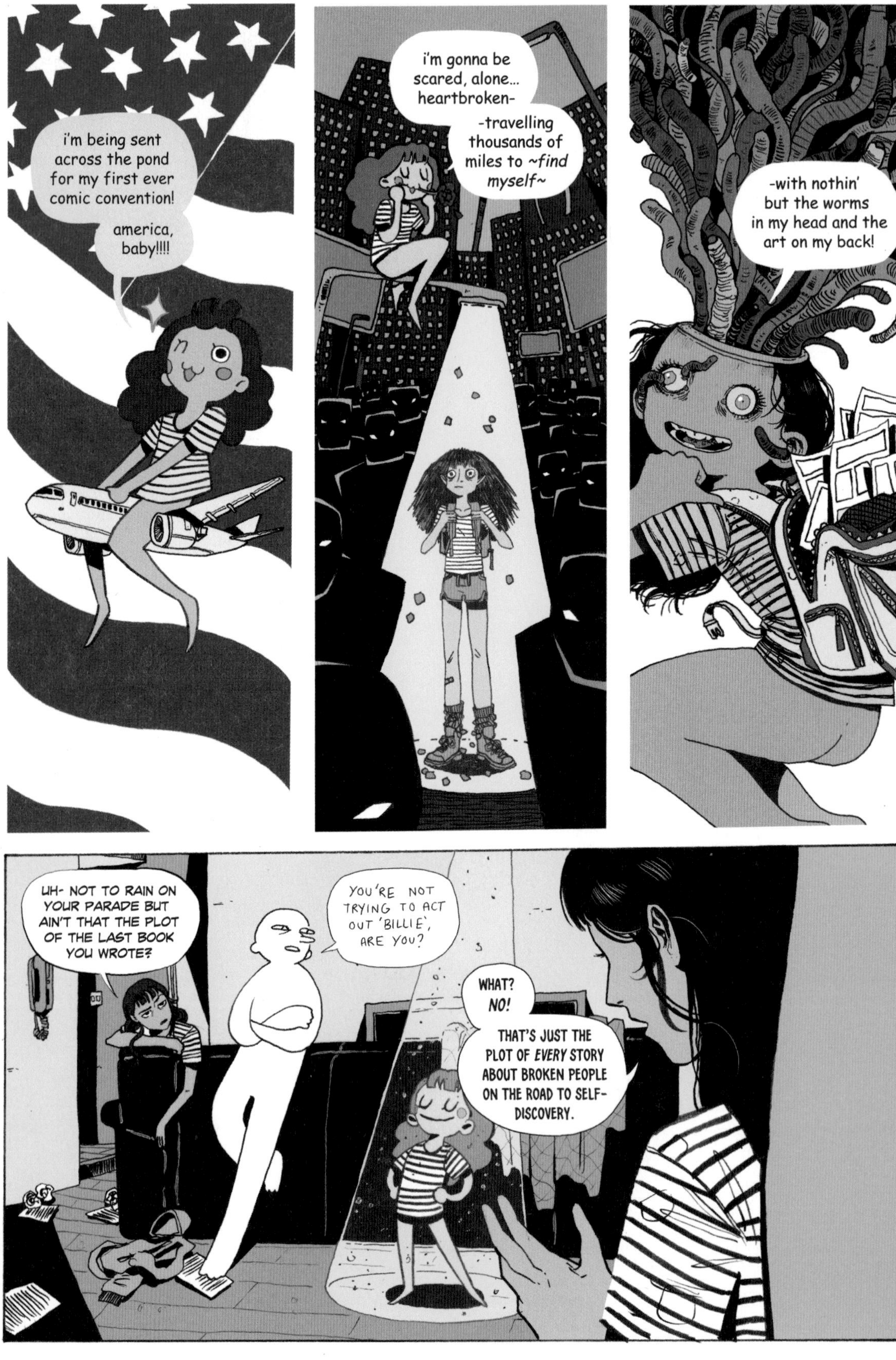

i'm being sent across the pond for my first ever comic convention!
america, baby!!!!
i'm gonna be scared, alone... heartbroken-
-travelling thousands of miles to ~*find myself*~
-with nothin' but the worms in my head and the art on my back!
UH- NOT TO RAIN ON YOUR PARADE BUT AIN'T THAT THE PLOT OF THE LAST BOOK YOU WROTE?
YOU'RE NOT TRYING TO ACT OUT 'BILLIE', ARE YOU?
WHAT? *NO!*
THAT'S JUST THE PLOT OF *EVERY* STORY ABOUT BROKEN PEOPLE ON THE ROAD TO SELF-DISCOVERY.

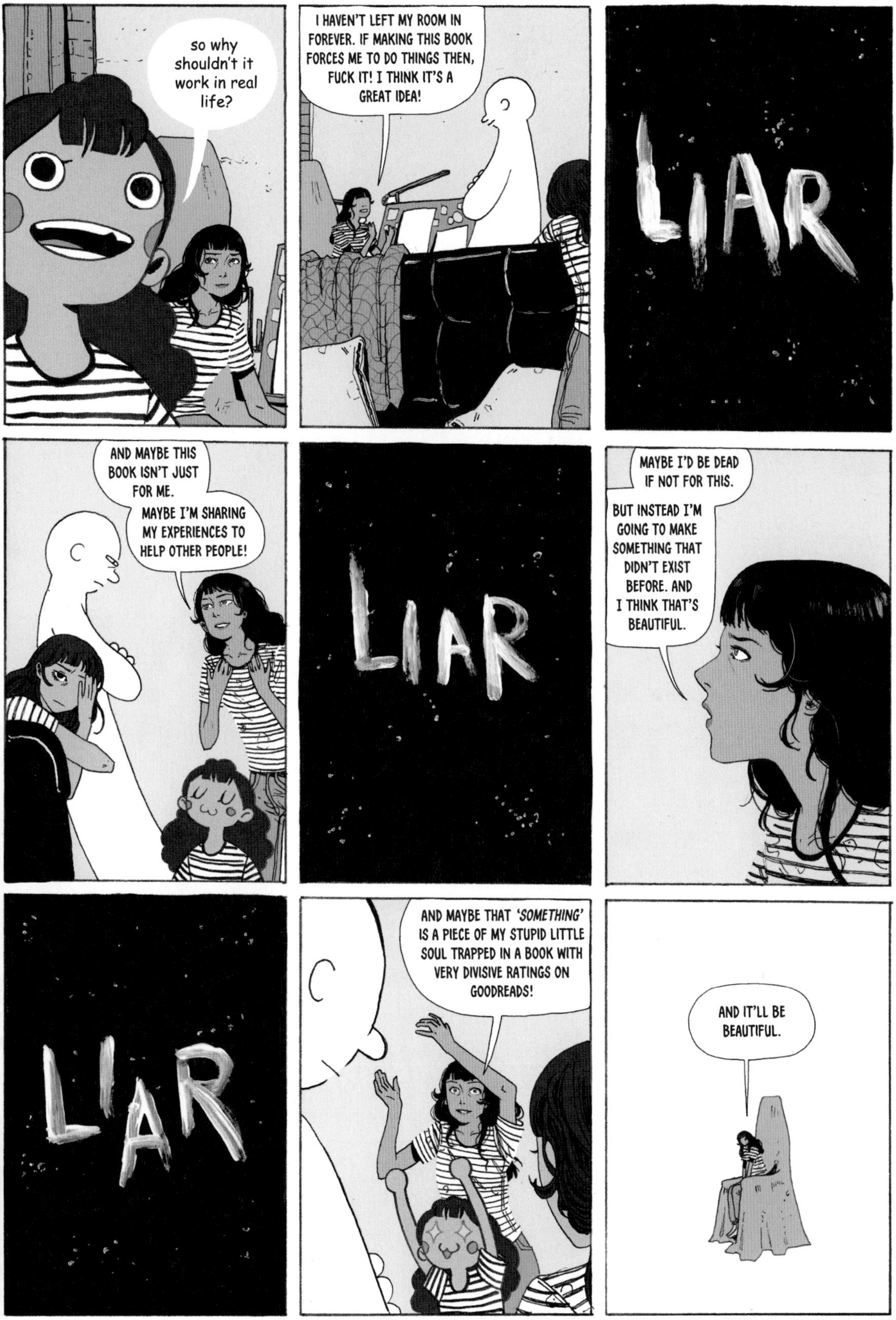
so why shouldn't it work in real life?
I HAVEN'T LEFT MY ROOM IN FOREVER. IF MAKING THIS BOOK FORCES ME TO DO THINGS THEN, FUCK IT! I THINK IT'S A GREAT IDEA!
LIAR
AND MAYBE THIS BOOK ISN'T JUST FOR ME.
MAYBE I'M SHARING MY EXPERIENCES TO HELP OTHER PEOPLE!
LIAR
MAYBE I'D BE DEAD IF NOT FOR THIS.
BUT INSTEAD I'M GOING TO MAKE SOMETHING THAT DIDN'T EXIST BEFORE. AND I THINK THAT'S BEAUTIFUL.
LIAR
AND MAYBE THAT *'SOMETHING'* IS A PIECE OF MY STUPID LITTLE SOUL TRAPPED IN A BOOK WITH VERY DIVISIVE RATINGS ON GOODREADS!
AND IT'LL BE BEAUTIFUL.

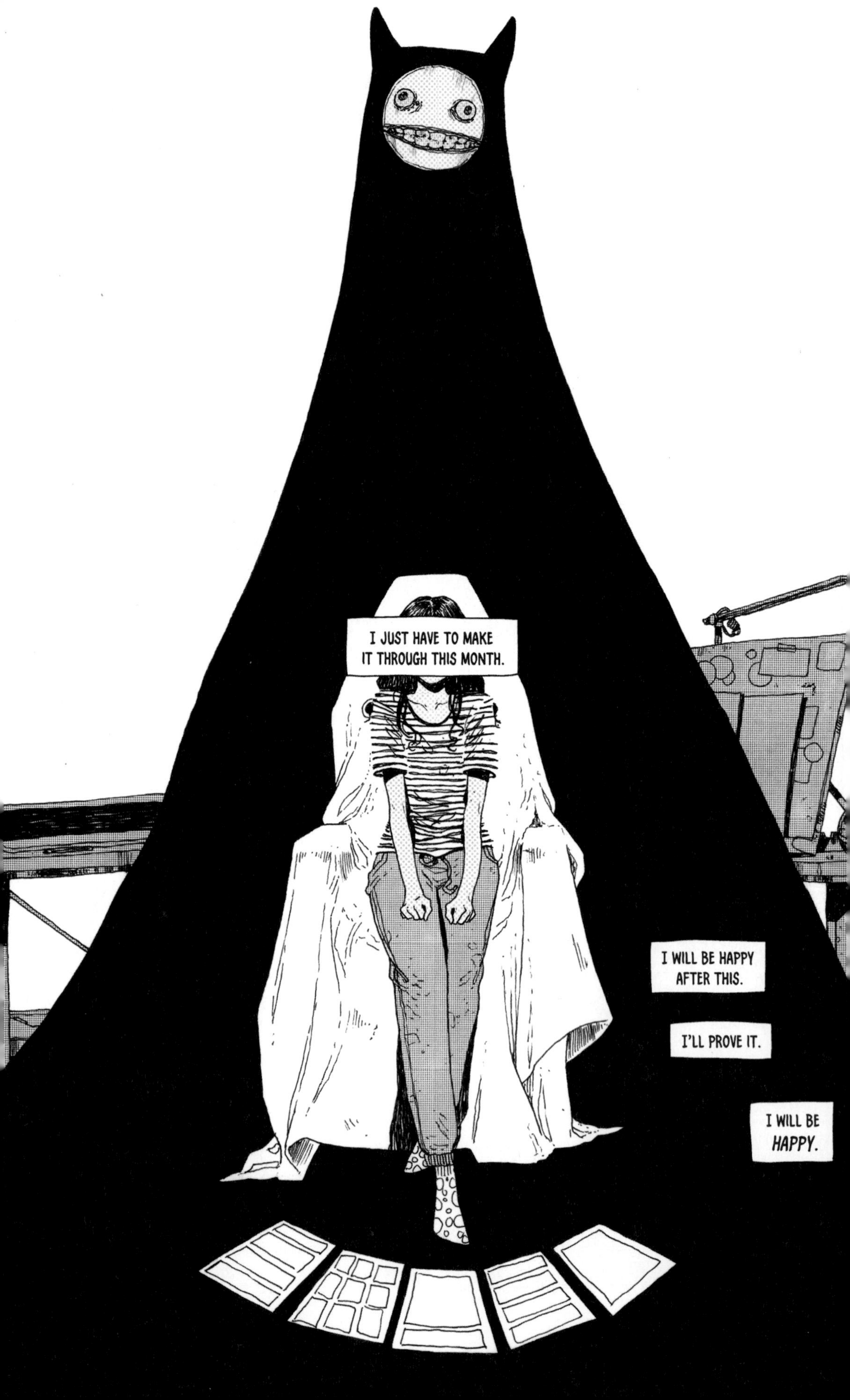
I JUST HAVE TO MAKE
IT THROUGH THIS MONTH.
I WILL BE HAPPY
AFTER THIS.
I'LL PROVE IT.
I WILL BE
HAPPY.

2013

AGE 14

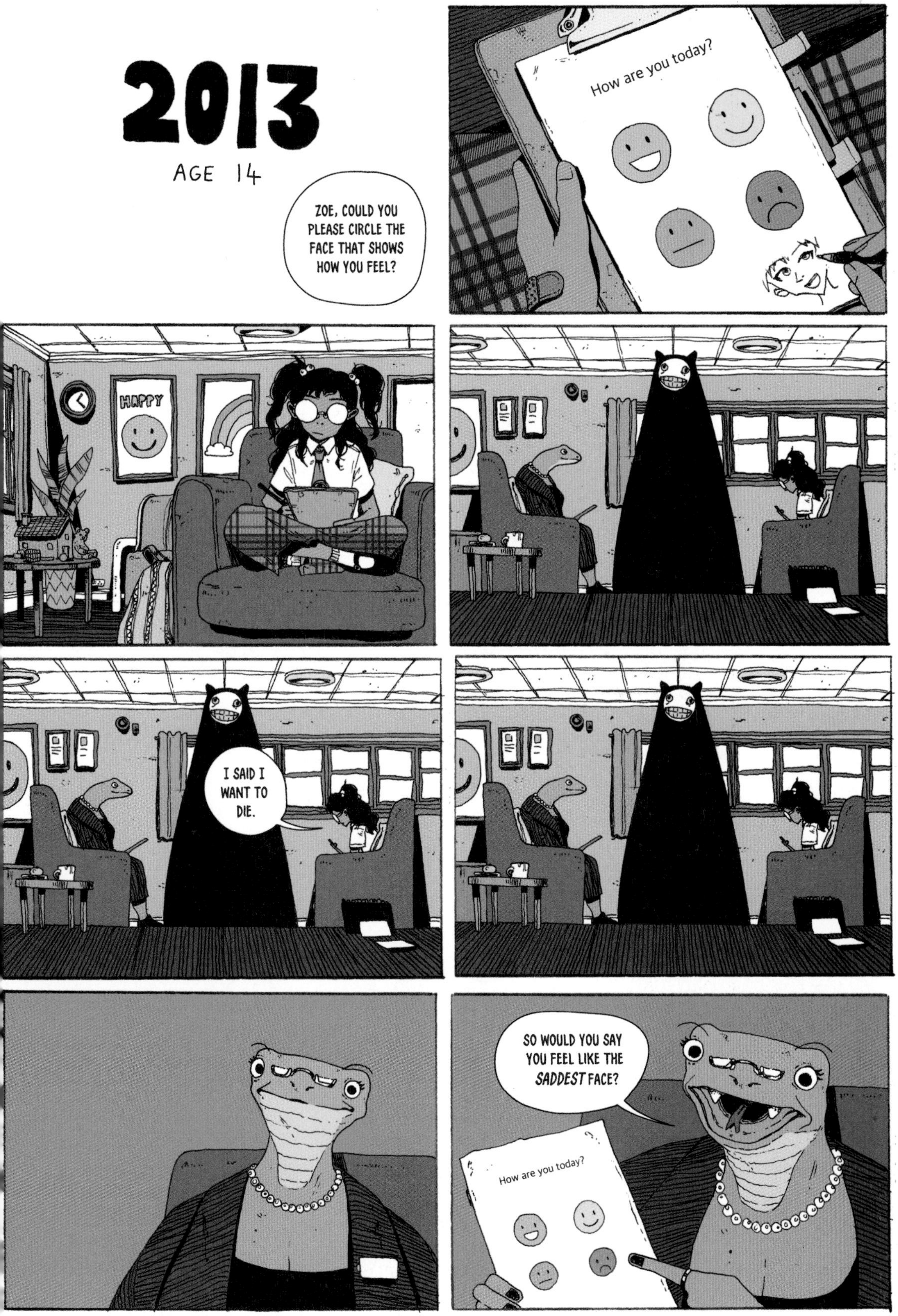

ZOE, COULD YOU PLEASE CIRCLE THE FACE THAT SHOWS HOW YOU FEEL?
How are you today?
HAPPY
I SAID I WANT TO DIE.
SO WOULD YOU SAY YOU FEEL LIKE THE *SADDEST* FACE?
How are you today?

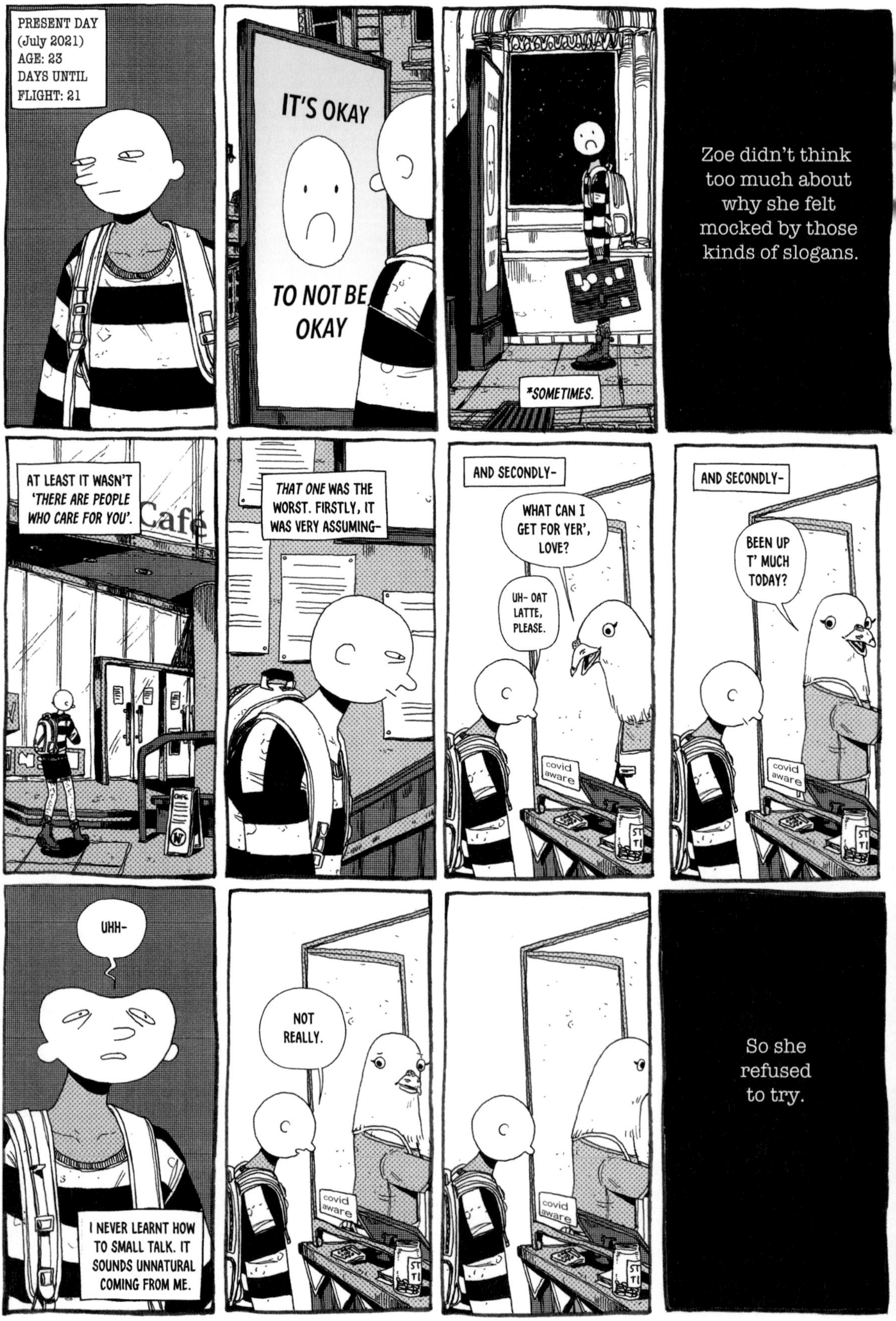

PRESENT DAY
(July 2021)
AGE: 23
DAYS UNTIL
FLIGHT: 21
IT'S OKAY
TO NOT BE
OKAY
*SOMETIMES.
Zoe didn't think too much about why she felt mocked by those kinds of slogans.
AT LEAST IT WASN'T '*THERE ARE PEOPLE WHO CARE FOR YOU*'.
Café
THAT ONE WAS THE WORST. FIRSTLY, IT WAS VERY ASSUMING-
AND SECONDLY-
WHAT CAN I GET FOR YER', LOVE?
UH- OAT LATTE, PLEASE.
covid aware
AND SECONDLY-
BEEN UP T' MUCH TODAY?
covid aware
UHH-
I NEVER LEARNT HOW TO SMALL TALK. IT SOUNDS UNNATURAL COMING FROM ME.
NOT REALLY.
covid aware
covid aware
So she refused to try.

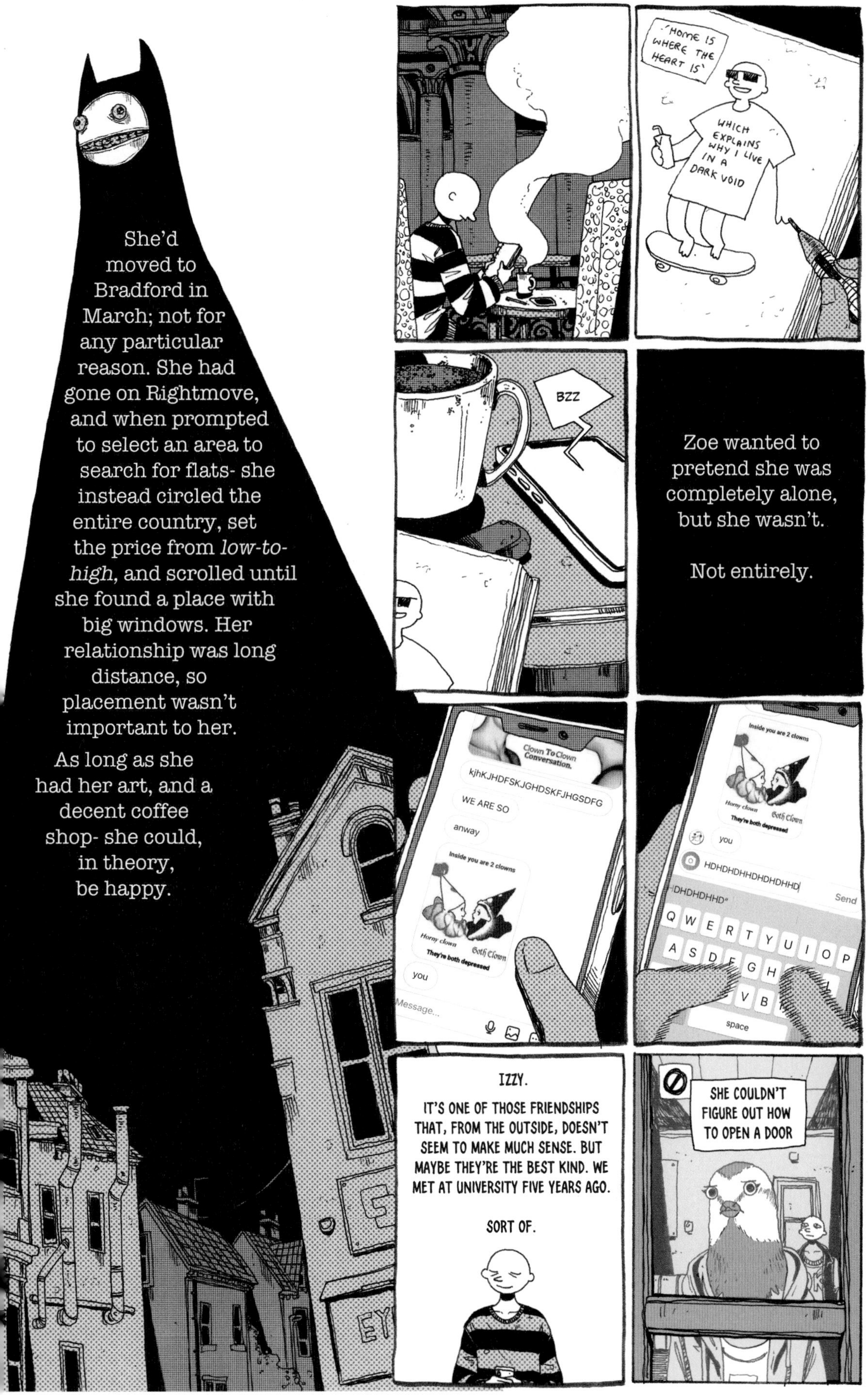

She'd moved to Bradford in March; not for any particular reason. She had gone on Rightmove, and when prompted to select an area to search for flats- she instead circled the entire country, set the price from *low-to-high*, and scrolled until she found a place with big windows. Her relationship was long distance, so placement wasn't important to her.
As long as she had her art, and a decent coffee shop- she could, in theory, be happy.
'HOME IS WHERE THE HEART IS'
WHICH EXPLAINS WHY I LIVE IN A DARK VOID
BZZ
Zoe wanted to pretend she was completely alone, but she wasn't.
Not entirely.
Clown To Clown Conversation.
kjhKJHDFSKJGHDSKFJHGSDFG
WE ARE SO
anway
Inside you are 2 clowns
Horny clown
Goth Clown
They're both depressed
you
Message...
Inside you are 2 clowns
Horny clown
Goth Clown
They're both depressed
you
Send
space
IZZY.
IT'S ONE OF THOSE FRIENDSHIPS THAT, FROM THE OUTSIDE, DOESN'T SEEM TO MAKE MUCH SENSE. BUT MAYBE THEY'RE THE BEST KIND. WE MET AT UNIVERSITY FIVE YEARS AGO.
SORT OF.
SHE COULDN'T FIGURE OUT HOW TO OPEN A DOOR

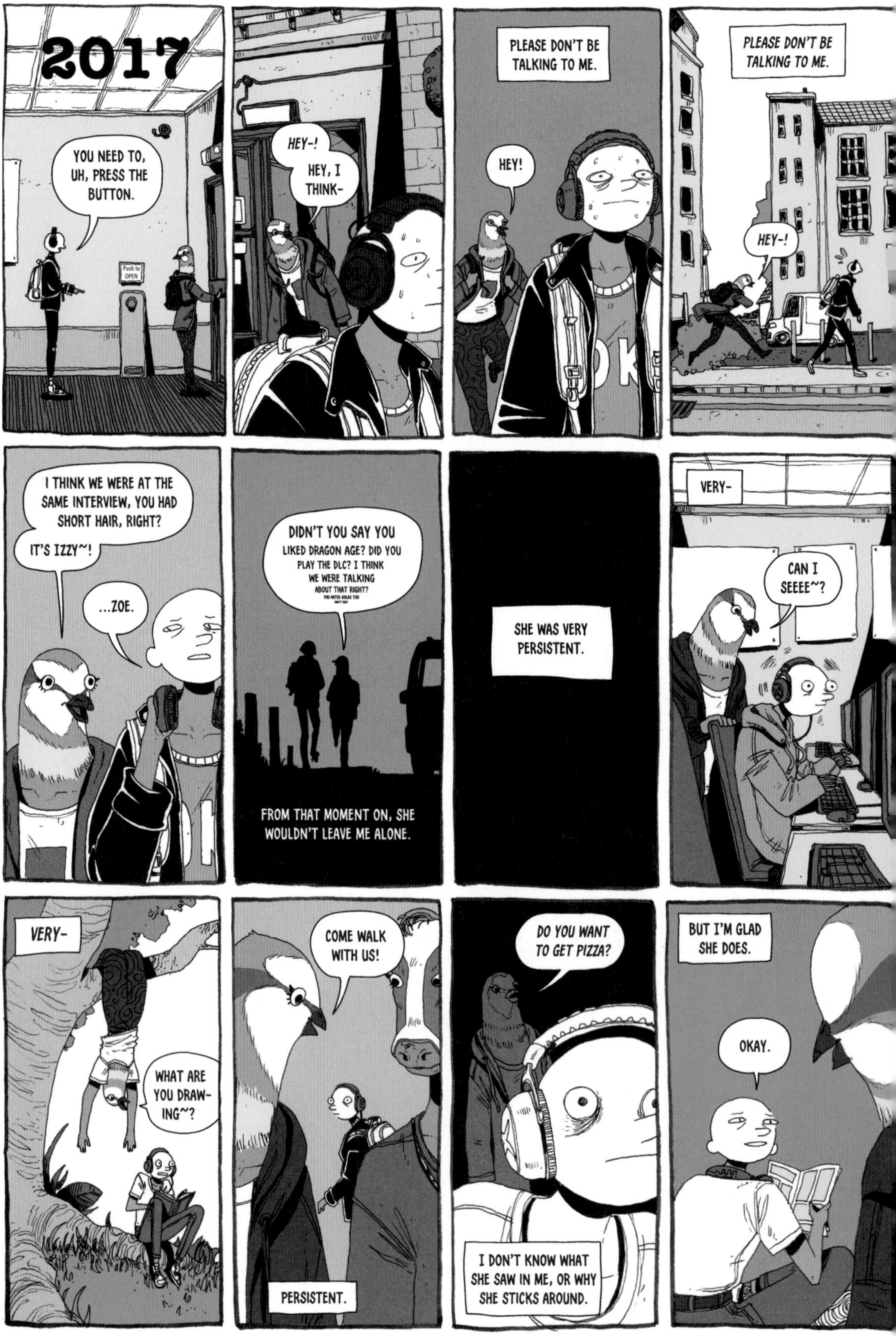
2017
YOU NEED TO, UH, PRESS THE BUTTON.
Push to OPEN
HEY-!
HEY, I THINK-
PLEASE DON'T BE TALKING TO ME.
HEY!
PLEASE DON'T BE TALKING TO ME.
HEY-!
I THINK WE WERE AT THE SAME INTERVIEW, YOU HAD SHORT HAIR, RIGHT?
IT'S IZZY~!
...ZOE.
DIDN'T YOU SAY YOU LIKED DRAGON AGE? DID YOU PLAY THE DLC? I THINK WE WERE TALKING ABOUT THAT RIGHT?
YOU HATED SOLAS TOO
FROM THAT MOMENT ON, SHE WOULDN'T LEAVE ME ALONE.
SHE WAS VERY PERSISTENT.
VERY-
CAN I SEEEE~?
VERY-
WHAT ARE YOU DRAW-ING~?
COME WALK WITH US!
PERSISTENT.
DO YOU WANT TO GET PIZZA?
I DON'T KNOW WHAT SHE SAW IN ME, OR WHY SHE STICKS AROUND.
BUT I'M GLAD SHE DOES.
OKAY.

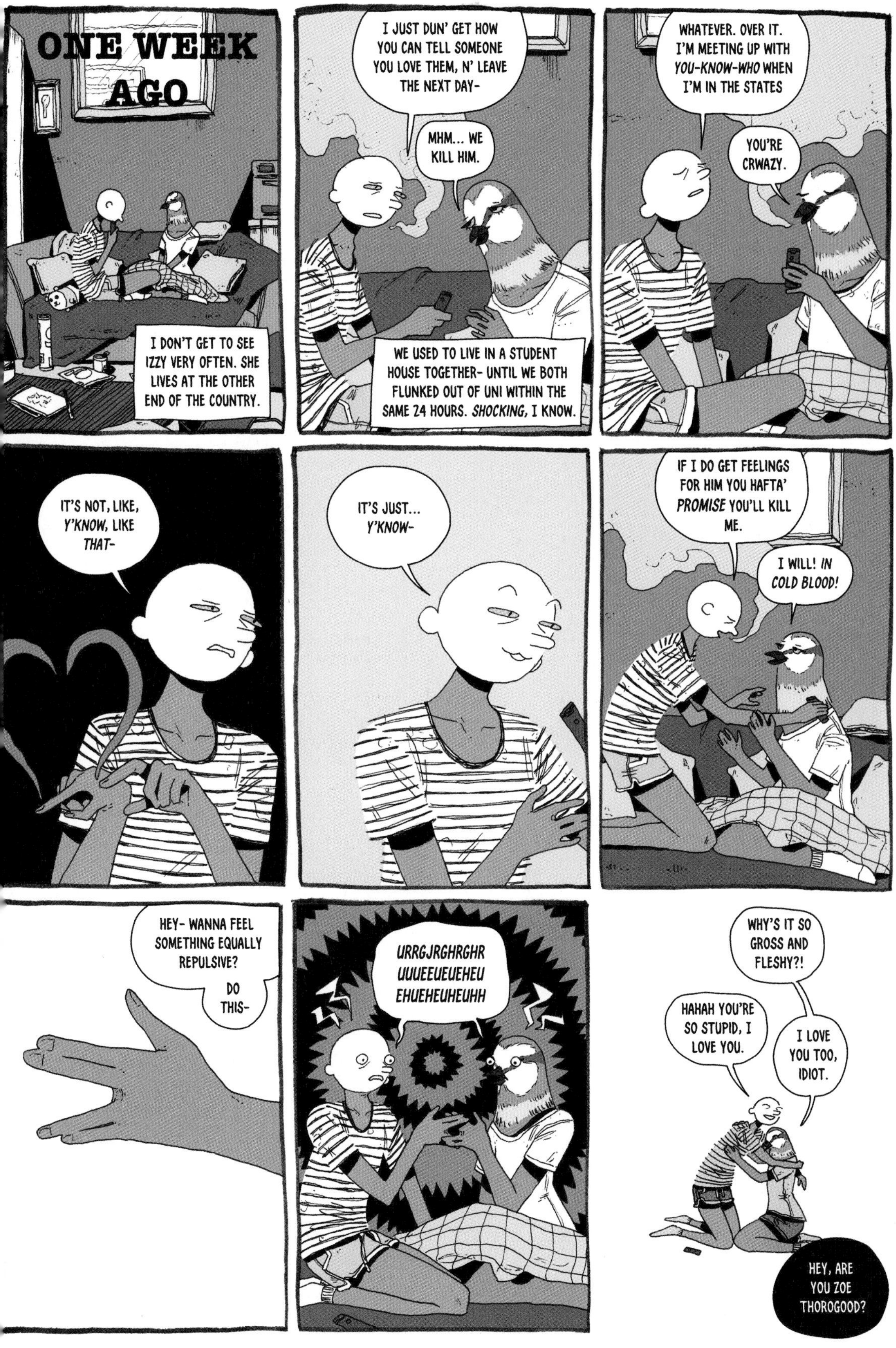
ONE WEEK AGO
I DON'T GET TO SEE IZZY VERY OFTEN. SHE LIVES AT THE OTHER END OF THE COUNTRY.
I JUST DUN' GET HOW YOU CAN TELL SOMEONE YOU LOVE THEM, N' LEAVE THE NEXT DAY-
MHM... WE KILL HIM.
WE USED TO LIVE IN A STUDENT HOUSE TOGETHER- UNTIL WE BOTH FLUNKED OUT OF UNI WITHIN THE SAME 24 HOURS. *SHOCKING*, I KNOW.
WHATEVER. OVER IT. I'M MEETING UP WITH *YOU-KNOW-WHO* WHEN I'M IN THE STATES
YOU'RE CRWAZY.
IT'S NOT, LIKE, *Y'KNOW*, LIKE *THAT*-
IT'S JUST... *Y'KNOW*-
IF I DO GET FEELINGS FOR HIM YOU HAFTA' *PROMISE* YOU'LL KILL ME.
I WILL! *IN COLD BLOOD!*
HEY- WANNA FEEL SOMETHING EQUALLY REPULSIVE?
DO THIS-
URRGJRGHRGHR UUUEEUEUEHEU EHUEHEUHEUHH
WHY'S IT SO GROSS AND FLESHY?!
HAHAH YOU'RE SO STUPID, I LOVE YOU.
I LOVE YOU TOO, IDIOT.
HEY, ARE YOU ZOE THOROGOOD?

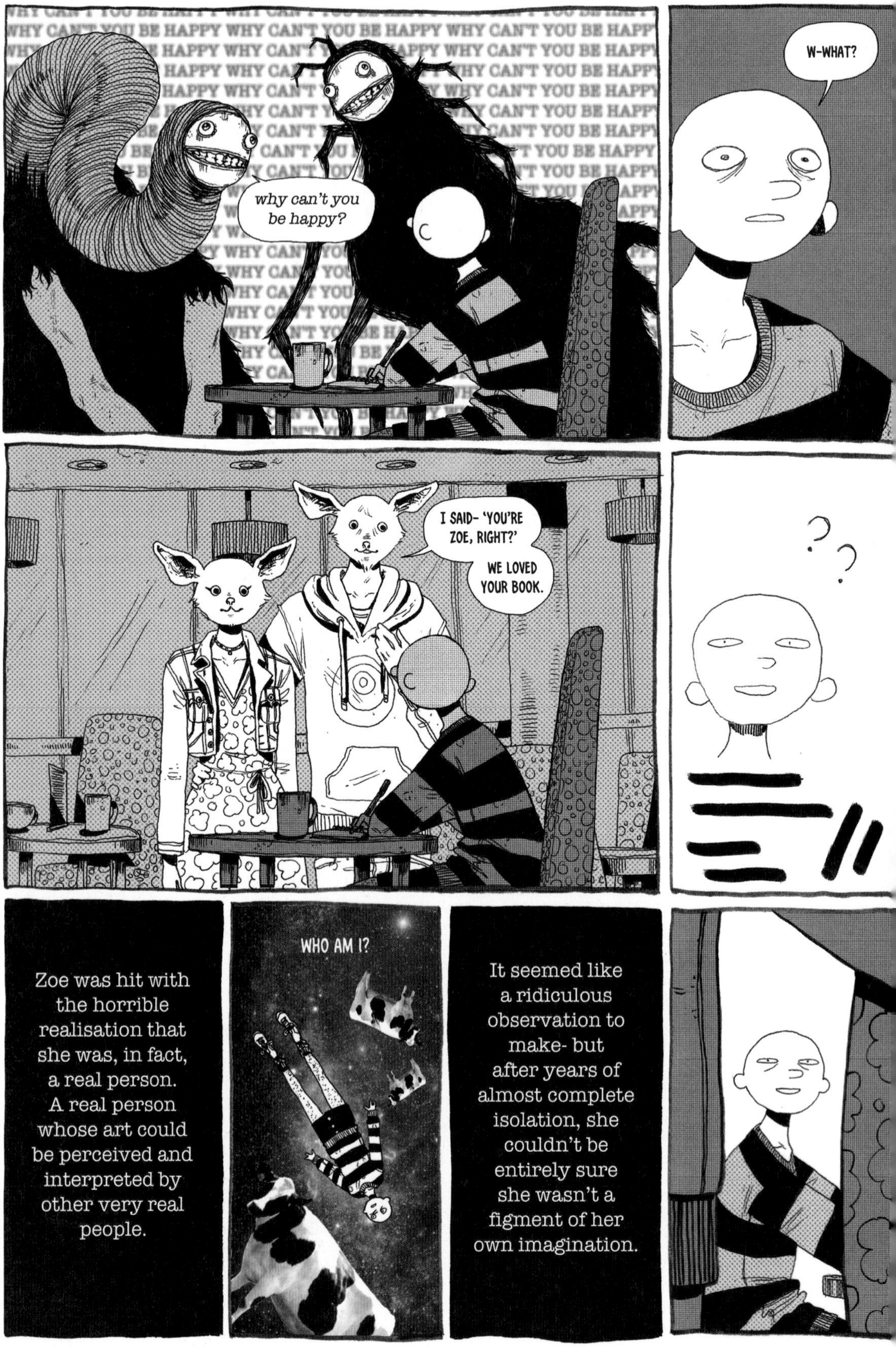

WHY CAN'T YOU BE HAPPY WHY CAN'T YOU BE HAPPY WHY CAN'T YOU BE HAPPY
why can't you be happy?
W-WHAT?
I SAID- 'YOU'RE ZOE, RIGHT?'
WE LOVED YOUR BOOK.
Zoe was hit with the horrible realisation that she was, in fact, a real person. A real person whose art could be perceived and interpreted by other very real people.
WHO AM I?
It seemed like a ridiculous observation to make- but after years of almost complete isolation, she couldn't be entirely sure she wasn't a figment of her own imagination.

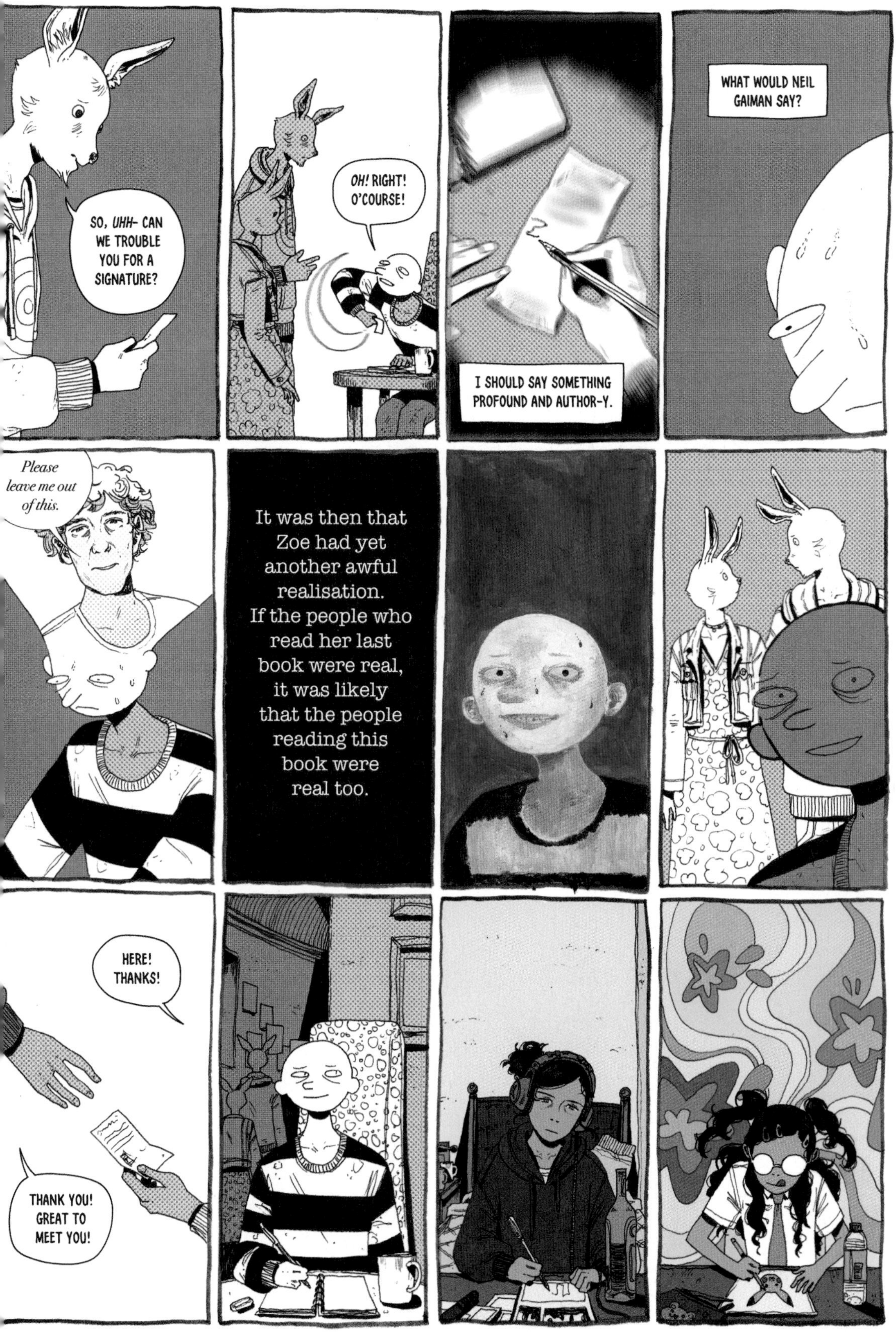
SO, UHH- CAN WE TROUBLE YOU FOR A SIGNATURE?
OH! RIGHT! O'COURSE!
I SHOULD SAY SOMETHING PROFOUND AND AUTHOR-Y.
WHAT WOULD NEIL GAIMAN SAY?
Please leave me out of this.
It was then that Zoe had yet another awful realisation. If the people who read her last book were real, it was likely that the people reading this book were real too.
HERE! THANKS!
THANK YOU! GREAT TO MEET YOU!

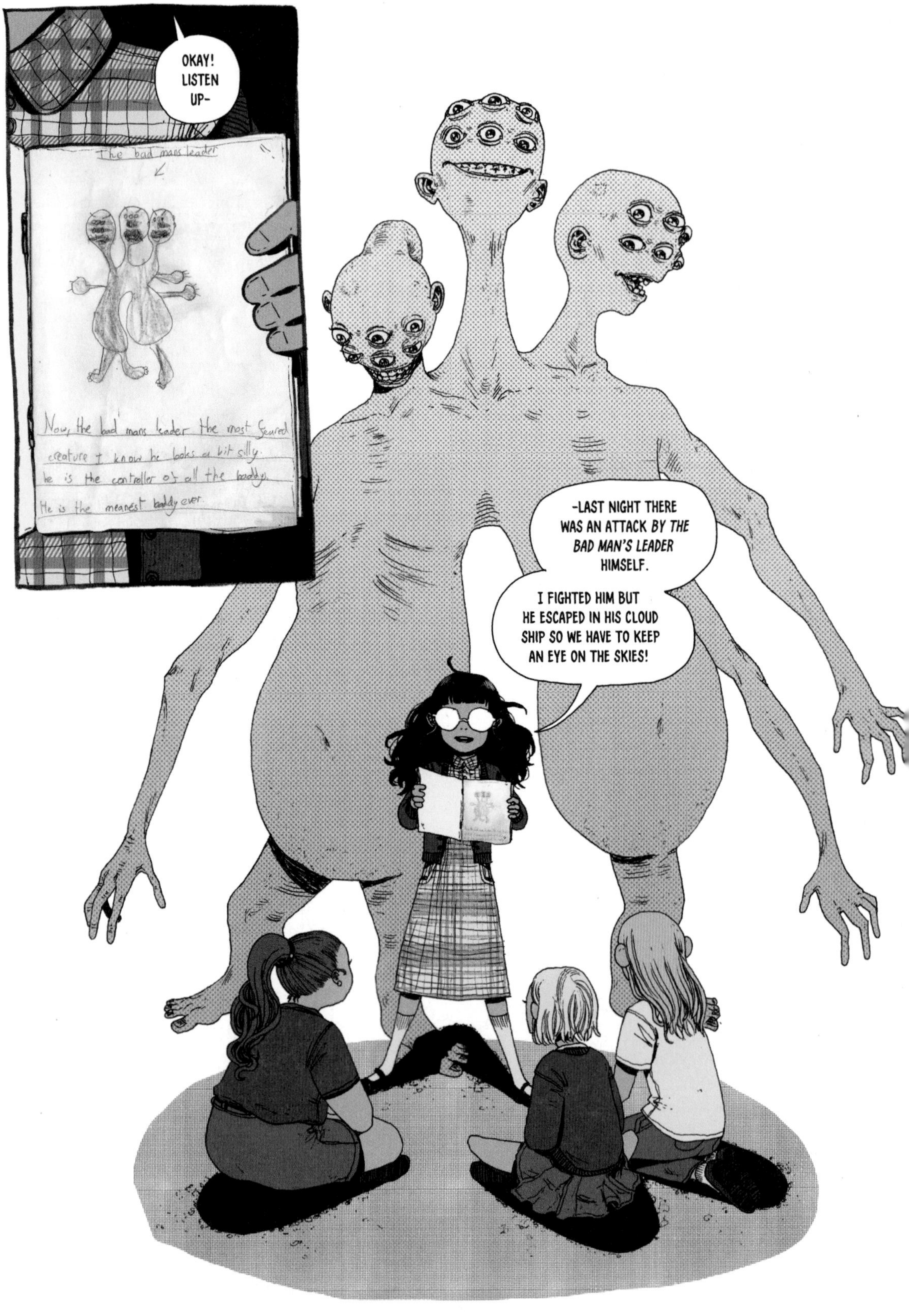
OKAY! LISTEN UP-
The bad mans leader
Now, the bad mans leader the most feared creature I know he looks a bit silly. he is the controller of all the baddys. He is the meanest baddy ever.
-LAST NIGHT THERE WAS AN ATTACK *BY THE BAD MAN'S LEADER* HIMSELF.
I FIGHTED HIM BUT HE ESCAPED IN HIS CLOUD SHIP SO WE HAVE TO KEEP AN EYE ON THE SKIES!

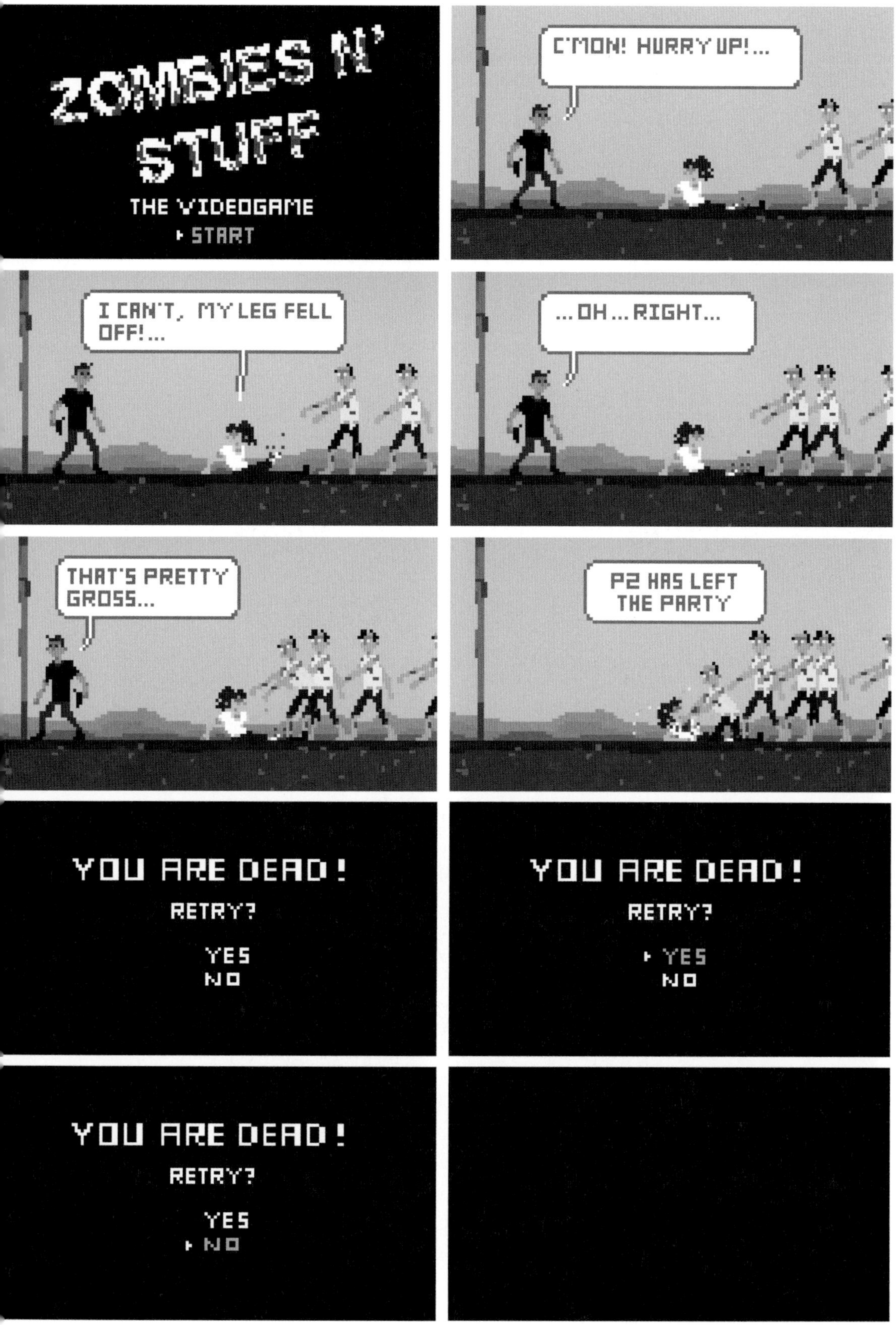
ZOMBIES N' STUFF
THE VIDEOGAME
START
C'MON! HURRY UP!...
I CAN'T, MY LEG FELL OFF!...
...OH... RIGHT...
THAT'S PRETTY GROSS...
P2 HAS LEFT THE PARTY
YOU ARE DEAD!
RETRY?
YES
NO
YOU ARE DEAD!
RETRY?
YES
NO
YOU ARE DEAD!
RETRY?
YES
NO

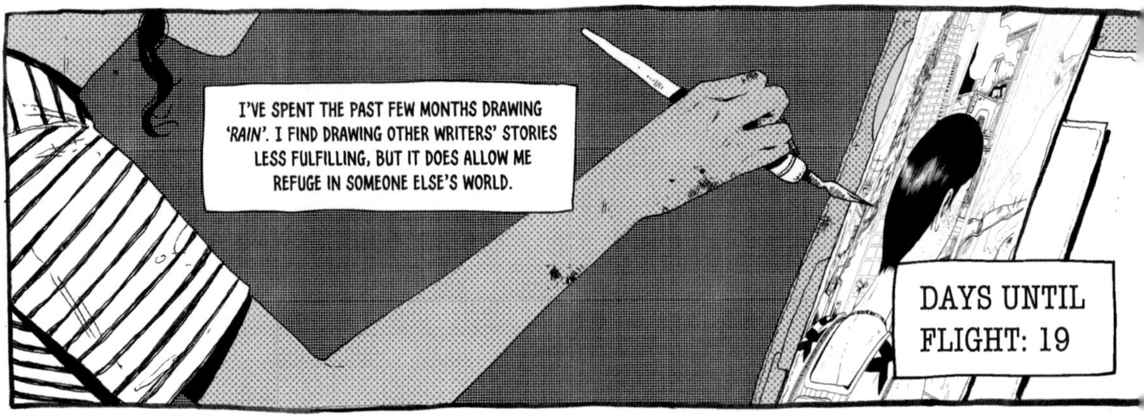
I'VE SPENT THE PAST FEW MONTHS DRAWING 'RAIN'. I FIND DRAWING OTHER WRITERS' STORIES LESS FULFILLING, BUT IT DOES ALLOW ME REFUGE IN SOMEONE ELSE'S WORLD.
DAYS UNTIL FLIGHT: 19

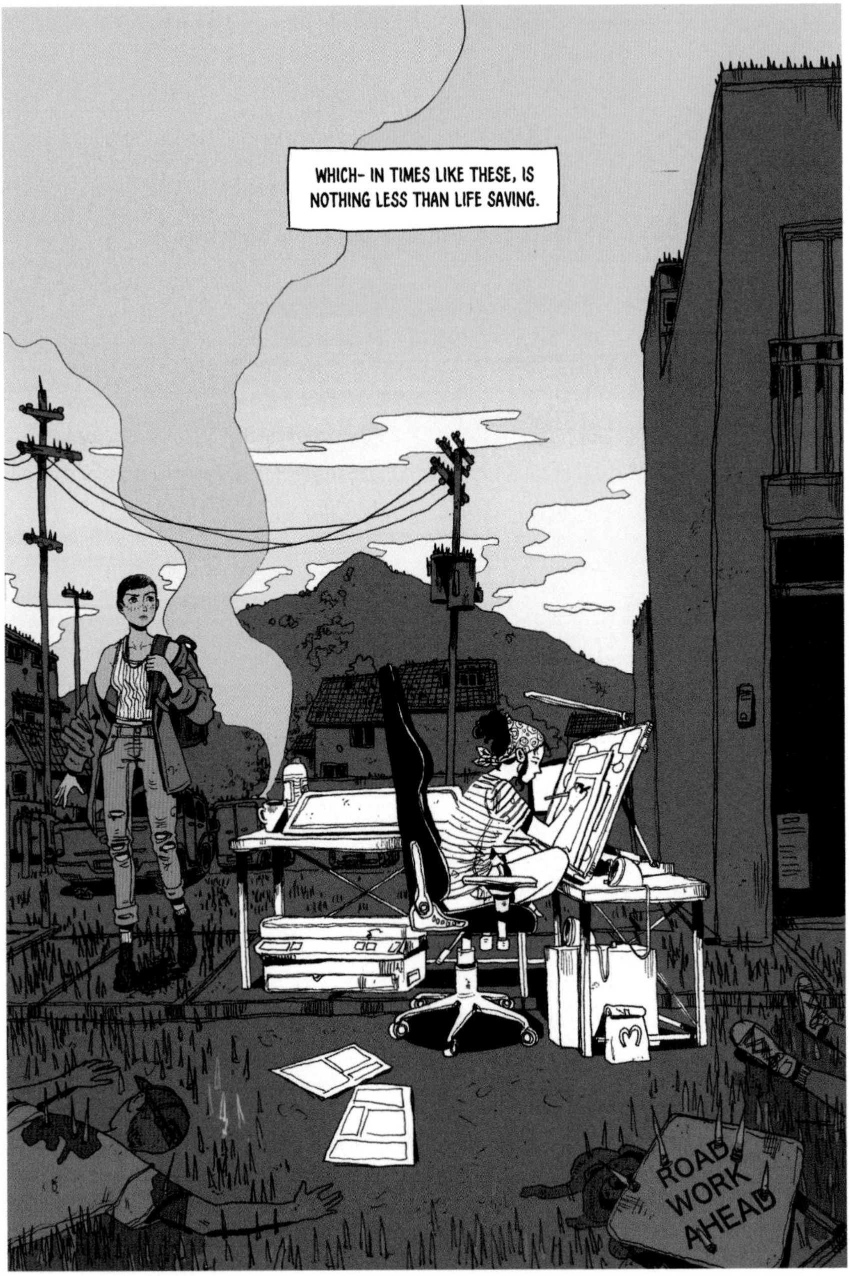
WHICH- IN TIMES LIKE THESE, IS NOTHING LESS THAN LIFE SAVING.
ROAD WORK AHEAD

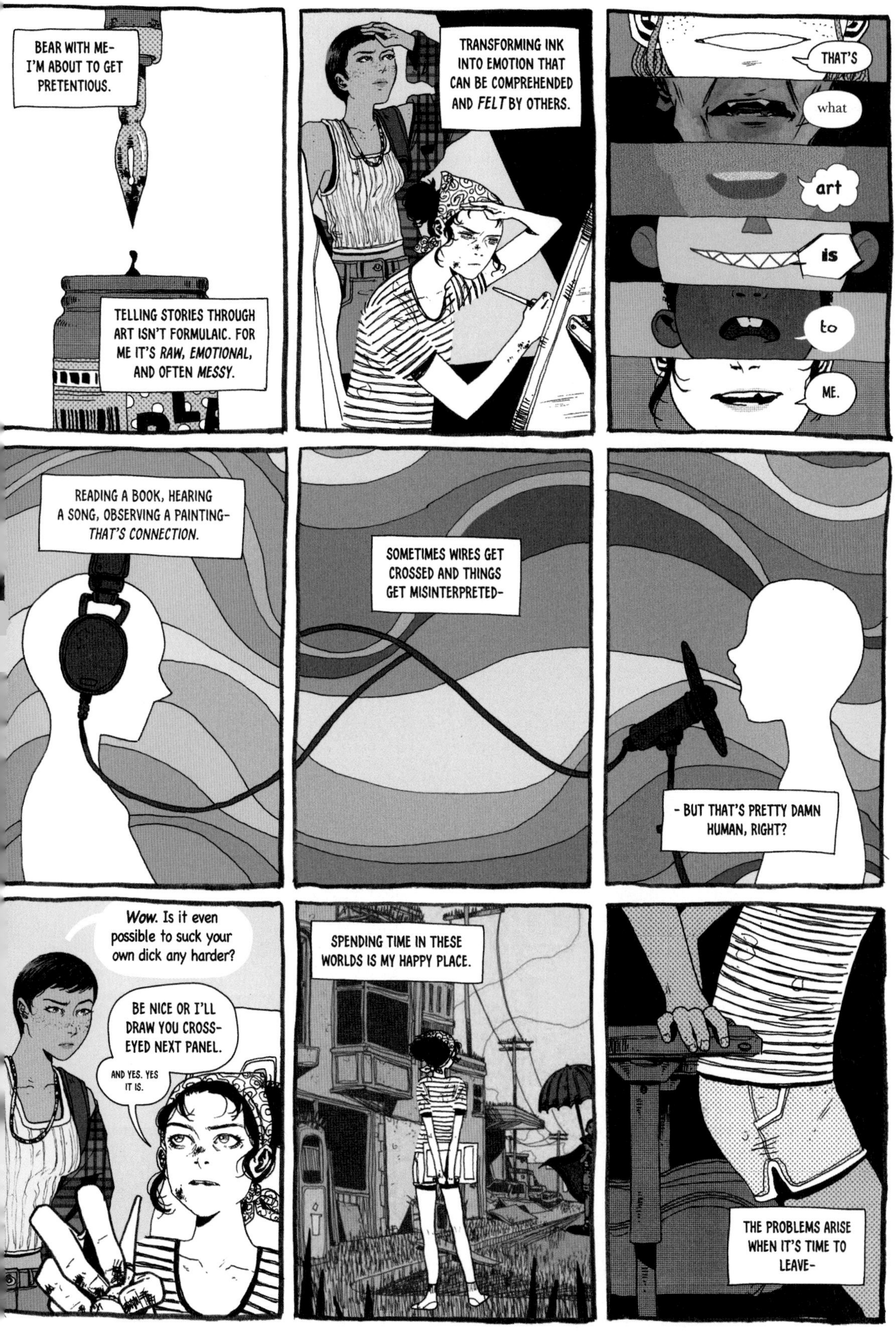
BEAR WITH ME- I'M ABOUT TO GET PRETENTIOUS.
TELLING STORIES THROUGH ART ISN'T FORMULAIC. FOR ME IT'S *RAW, EMOTIONAL,* AND OFTEN *MESSY*.
TRANSFORMING INK INTO EMOTION THAT CAN BE COMPREHENDED AND *FELT* BY OTHERS.
THAT'S
what
art
is
to
ME.
READING A BOOK, HEARING A SONG, OBSERVING A PAINTING- *THAT'S CONNECTION.*
SOMETIMES WIRES GET CROSSED AND THINGS GET MISINTERPRETED-
- BUT THAT'S PRETTY DAMN HUMAN, RIGHT?
Wow. Is it even possible to suck your own dick any harder?
BE NICE OR I'LL DRAW YOU CROSS-EYED NEXT PANEL.
AND YES. YES IT IS.
SPENDING TIME IN THESE WORLDS IS MY HAPPY PLACE.
THE PROBLEMS ARISE WHEN IT'S TIME TO LEAVE-

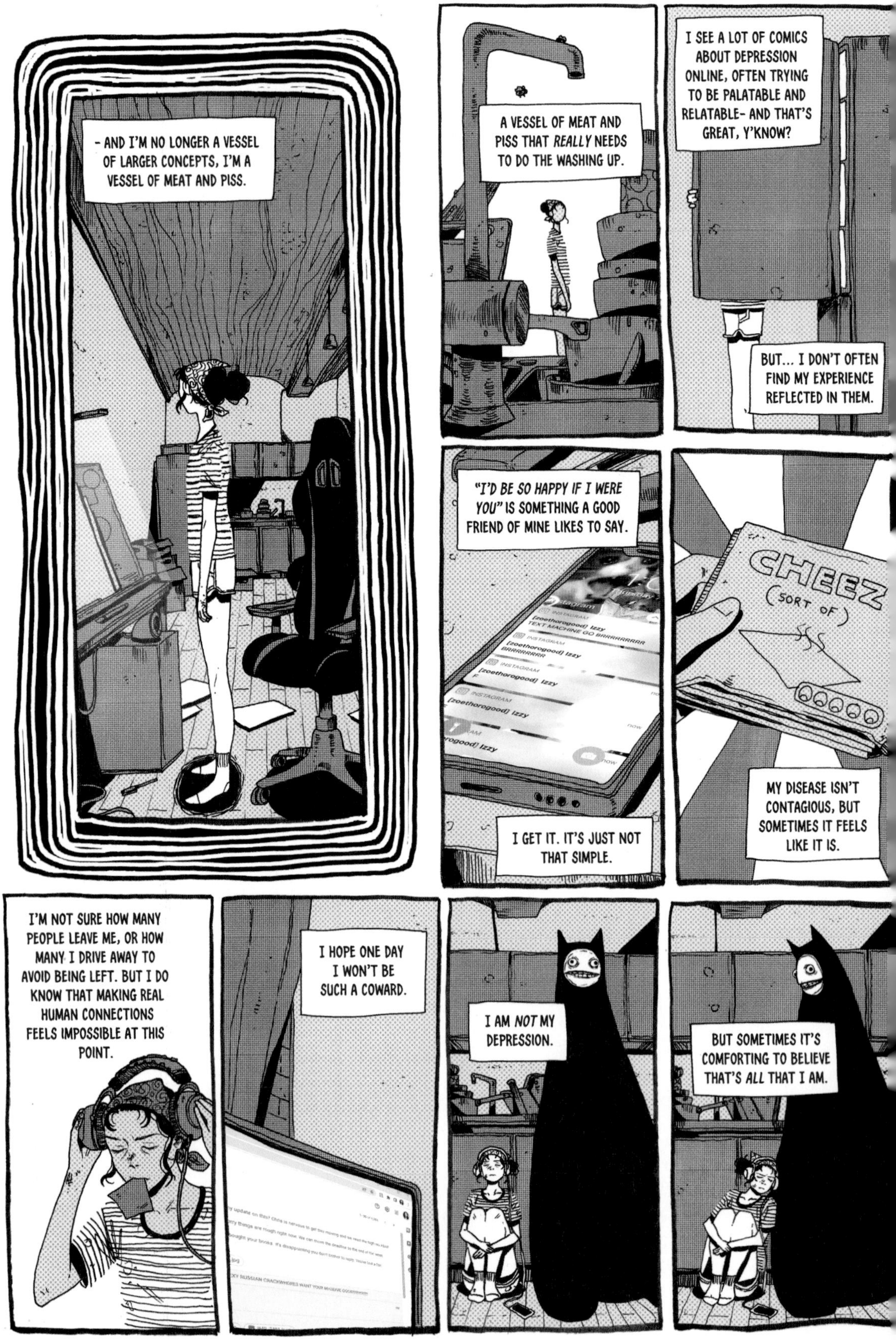
- AND I'M NO LONGER A VESSEL OF LARGER CONCEPTS, I'M A VESSEL OF MEAT AND PISS.
A VESSEL OF MEAT AND PISS THAT *REALLY* NEEDS TO DO THE WASHING UP.
I SEE A LOT OF COMICS ABOUT DEPRESSION ONLINE, OFTEN TRYING TO BE PALATABLE AND RELATABLE- AND THAT'S GREAT, Y'KNOW?
BUT... I DON'T OFTEN FIND MY EXPERIENCE REFLECTED IN THEM.
"I'D BE SO HAPPY IF I WERE YOU" IS SOMETHING A GOOD FRIEND OF MINE LIKES TO SAY.
[zoethorogood] Izzy
TEXT MACHINE GO BRRRRRRRRR
I GET IT. IT'S JUST NOT THAT SIMPLE.
CHEEZ
(SORT OF)
MY DISEASE ISN'T CONTAGIOUS, BUT SOMETIMES IT FEELS LIKE IT IS.
I'M NOT SURE HOW MANY PEOPLE LEAVE ME, OR HOW MANY I DRIVE AWAY TO AVOID BEING LEFT. BUT I DO KNOW THAT MAKING REAL HUMAN CONNECTIONS FEELS IMPOSSIBLE AT THIS POINT.
I HOPE ONE DAY I WON'T BE SUCH A COWARD.
I AM *NOT* MY DEPRESSION.
BUT SOMETIMES IT'S COMFORTING TO BELIEVE THAT'S *ALL* THAT I AM.

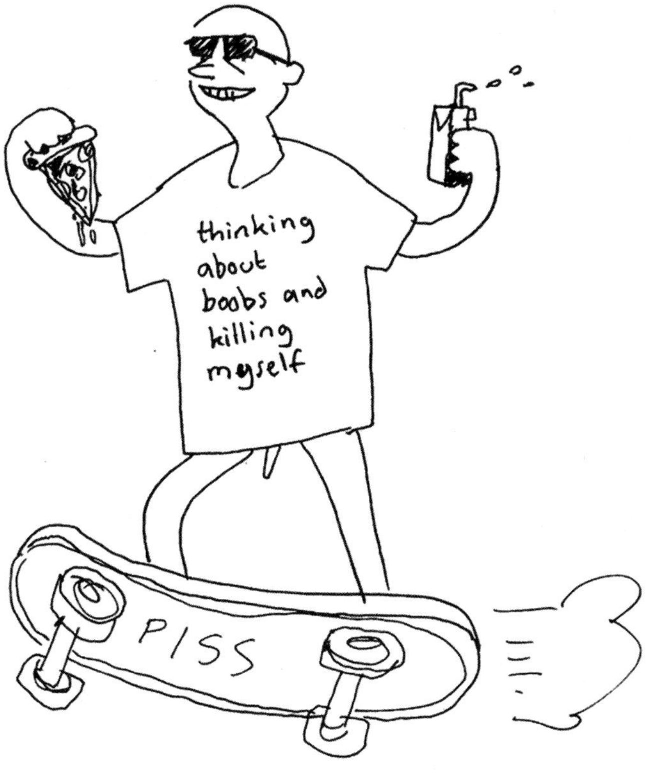
thinking
about
boobs and
killing
myself
PISS

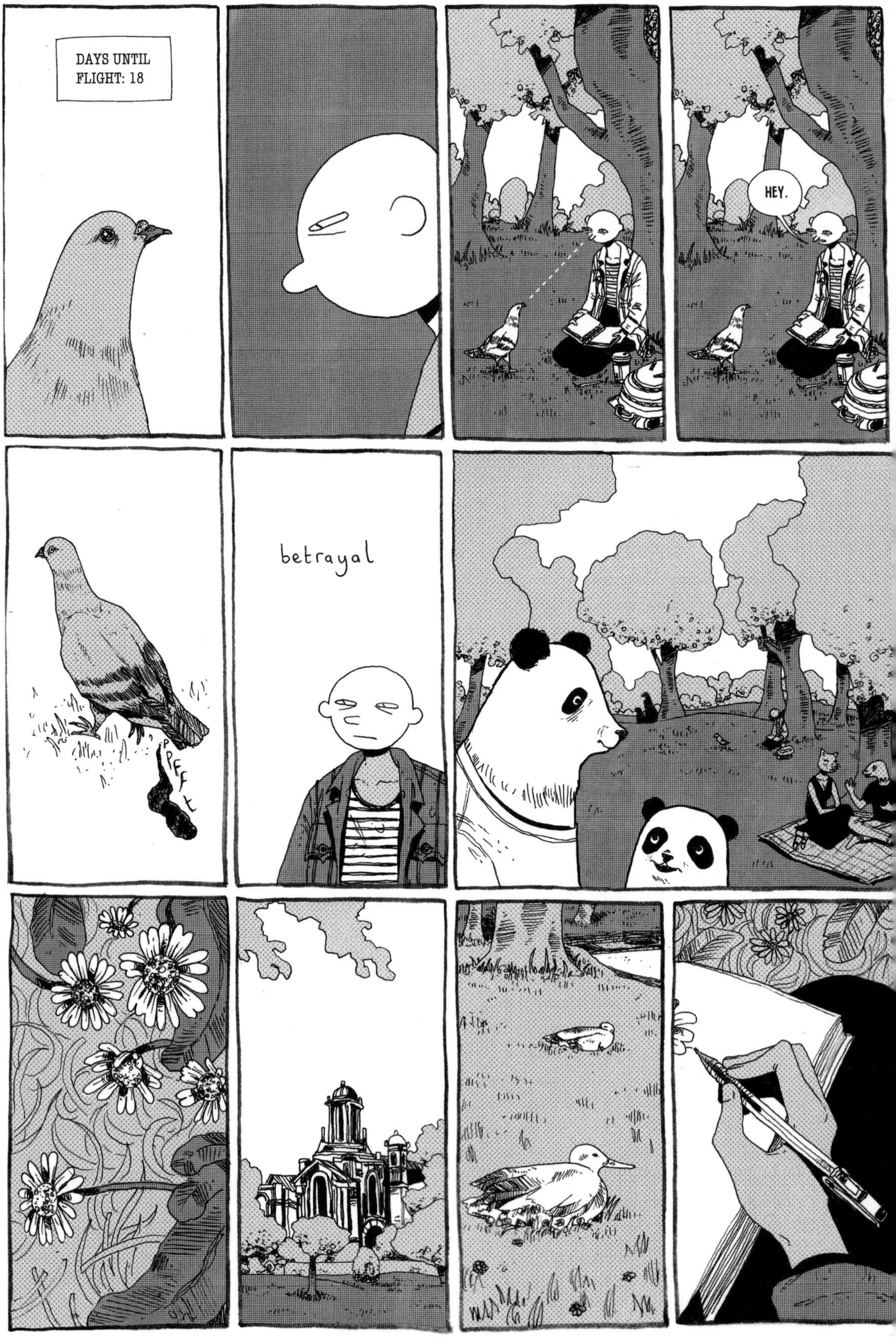
DAYS UNTIL
FLIGHT: 18
HEY.
PFFFt
betrayal

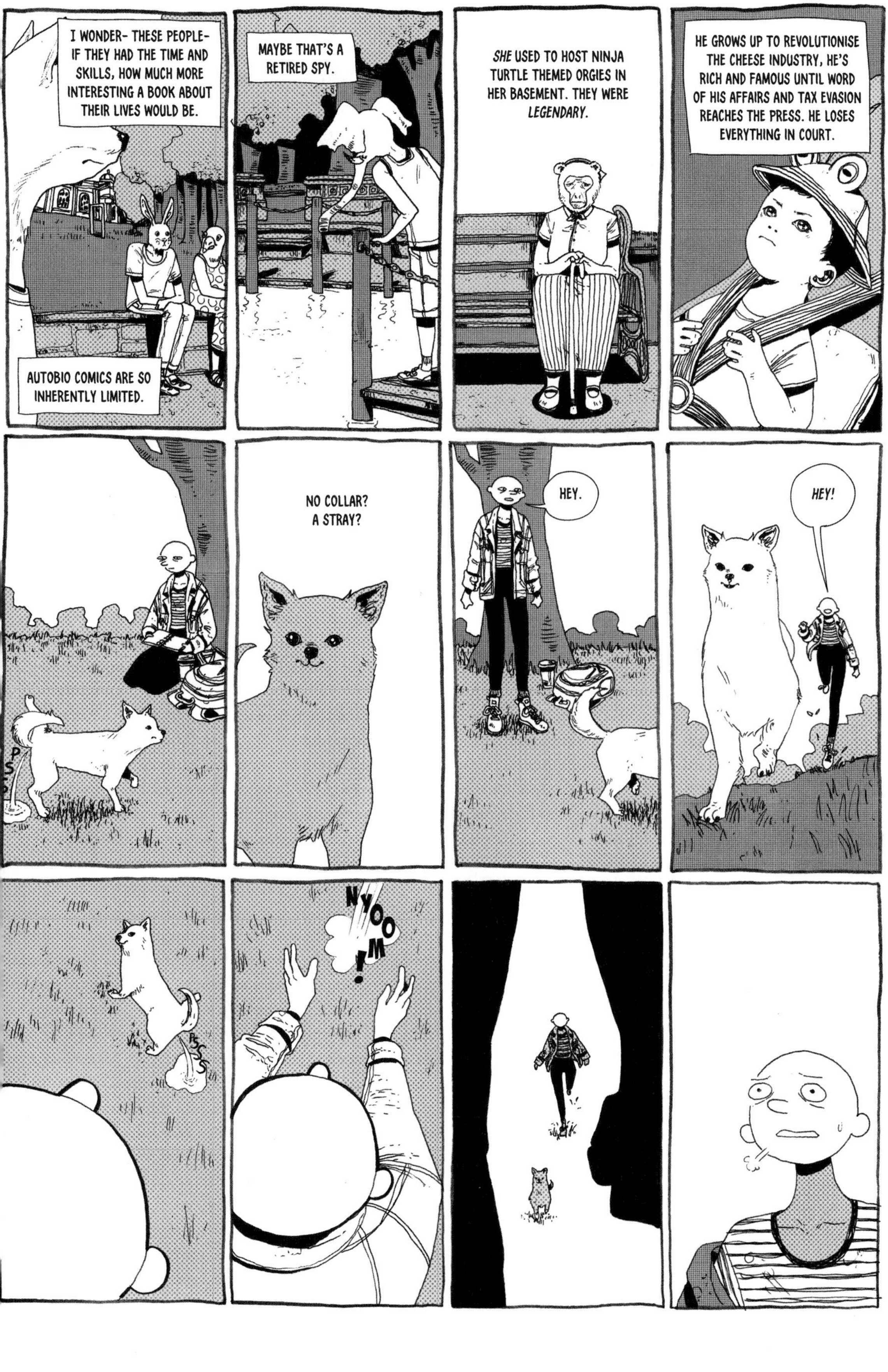
I WONDER- THESE PEOPLE- IF THEY HAD THE TIME AND SKILLS, HOW MUCH MORE INTERESTING A BOOK ABOUT THEIR LIVES WOULD BE.
AUTOBIO COMICS ARE SO INHERENTLY LIMITED.
MAYBE THAT'S A RETIRED SPY.
SHE USED TO HOST NINJA TURTLE THEMED ORGIES IN HER BASEMENT. THEY WERE *LEGENDARY*.
HE GROWS UP TO REVOLUTIONISE THE CHEESE INDUSTRY, HE'S RICH AND FAMOUS UNTIL WORD OF HIS AFFAIRS AND TAX EVASION REACHES THE PRESS. HE LOSES EVERYTHING IN COURT.
PSS
NO COLLAR? A STRAY?
HEY.
HEY!
PSSS
NYOOM!

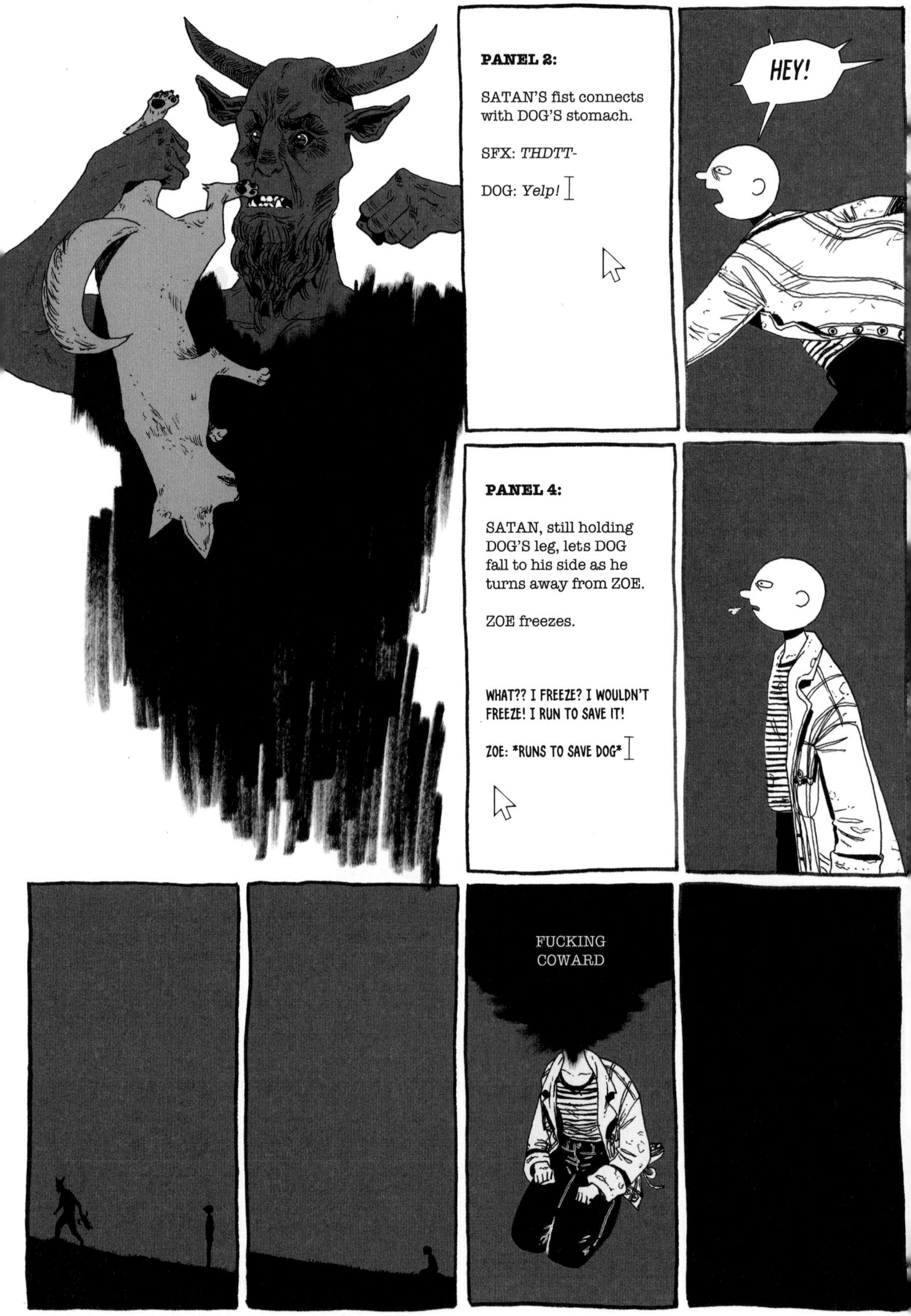
PANEL 2:
SATAN'S fist connects with DOG'S stomach.
SFX: *THDTT-*
DOG: *Yelp!*
HEY!
PANEL 4:
SATAN, still holding DOG'S leg, lets DOG fall to his side as he turns away from ZOE.
ZOE freezes.
WHAT?? I FREEZE? I WOULDN'T FREEZE! I RUN TO SAVE IT!
ZOE: *RUNS TO SAVE DOG*
FUCKING COWARD

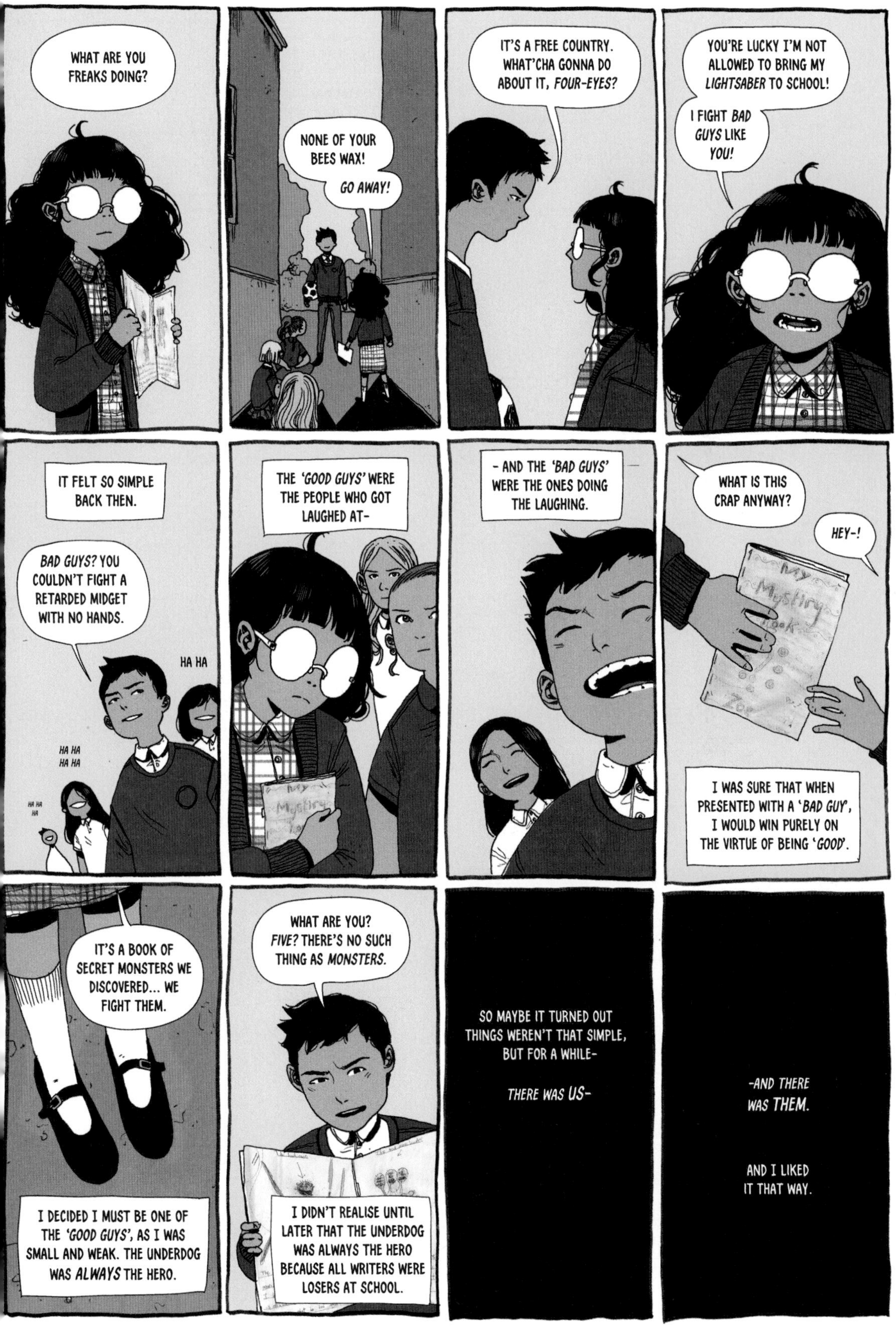
WHAT ARE YOU FREAKS DOING?
NONE OF YOUR BEES WAX!
GO AWAY!
IT'S A FREE COUNTRY. WHAT'CHA GONNA DO ABOUT IT, *FOUR-EYES?*
YOU'RE LUCKY I'M NOT ALLOWED TO BRING MY *LIGHTSABER* TO SCHOOL!
I FIGHT *BAD GUYS* LIKE *YOU!*
IT FELT SO SIMPLE BACK THEN.
BAD GUYS? YOU COULDN'T FIGHT A RETARDED MIDGET WITH NO HANDS.
HA HA
HA HA HA HA
HA HA HA
THE *'GOOD GUYS'* WERE THE PEOPLE WHO GOT LAUGHED AT-
My Mystery
- AND THE *'BAD GUYS'* WERE THE ONES DOING THE LAUGHING.
WHAT IS THIS CRAP ANYWAY?
HEY-!
My Mystery Book
I WAS SURE THAT WHEN PRESENTED WITH A *'BAD GUY'*, I WOULD WIN PURELY ON THE VIRTUE OF BEING *'GOOD'*.
IT'S A BOOK OF SECRET MONSTERS WE DISCOVERED... WE FIGHT THEM.
I DECIDED I MUST BE ONE OF THE *'GOOD GUYS'*, AS I WAS SMALL AND WEAK. THE UNDERDOG WAS *ALWAYS* THE HERO.
WHAT ARE YOU? *FIVE?* THERE'S NO SUCH THING AS *MONSTERS.*
I DIDN'T REALISE UNTIL LATER THAT THE UNDERDOG WAS ALWAYS THE HERO BECAUSE ALL WRITERS WERE LOSERS AT SCHOOL.
SO MAYBE IT TURNED OUT THINGS WEREN'T THAT SIMPLE, BUT FOR A WHILE-
THERE WAS US-
-AND THERE WAS THEM.
AND I LIKED IT THAT WAY.

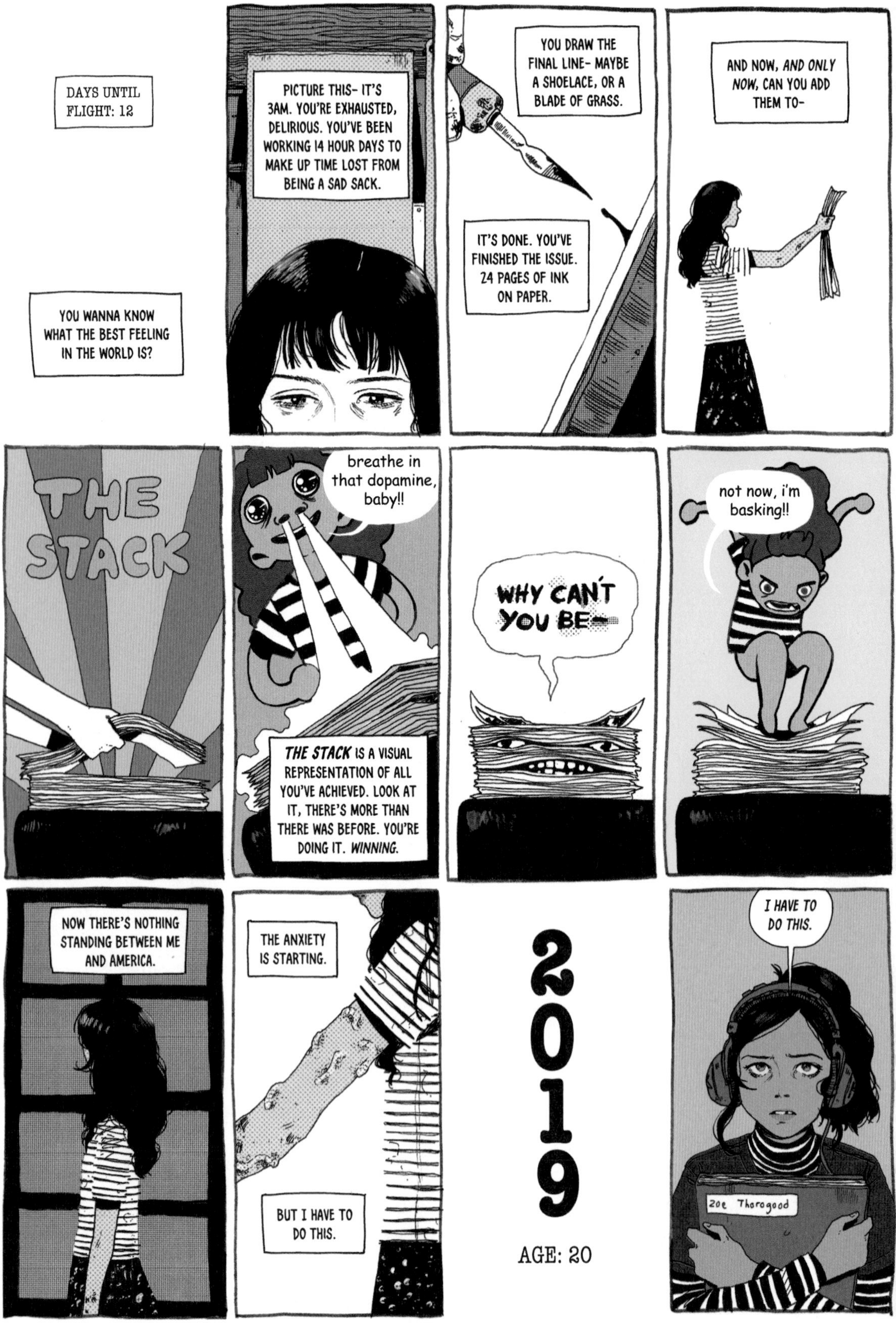
DAYS UNTIL FLIGHT: 12
YOU WANNA KNOW WHAT THE BEST FEELING IN THE WORLD IS?
PICTURE THIS- IT'S 3AM. YOU'RE EXHAUSTED, DELIRIOUS. YOU'VE BEEN WORKING 14 HOUR DAYS TO MAKE UP TIME LOST FROM BEING A SAD SACK.
YOU DRAW THE FINAL LINE- MAYBE A SHOELACE, OR A BLADE OF GRASS.
IT'S DONE. YOU'VE FINISHED THE ISSUE. 24 PAGES OF INK ON PAPER.
AND NOW, AND ONLY NOW, CAN YOU ADD THEM TO-
THE STACK
breathe in that dopamine, baby!!
THE STACK IS A VISUAL REPRESENTATION OF ALL YOU'VE ACHIEVED. LOOK AT IT, THERE'S MORE THAN THERE WAS BEFORE. YOU'RE DOING IT. WINNING.
WHY CAN'T YOU BE-
not now, i'm basking!!
NOW THERE'S NOTHING STANDING BETWEEN ME AND AMERICA.
THE ANXIETY IS STARTING.
BUT I HAVE TO DO THIS.
2019
AGE: 20
I HAVE TO DO THIS.
Zoe Thorogood

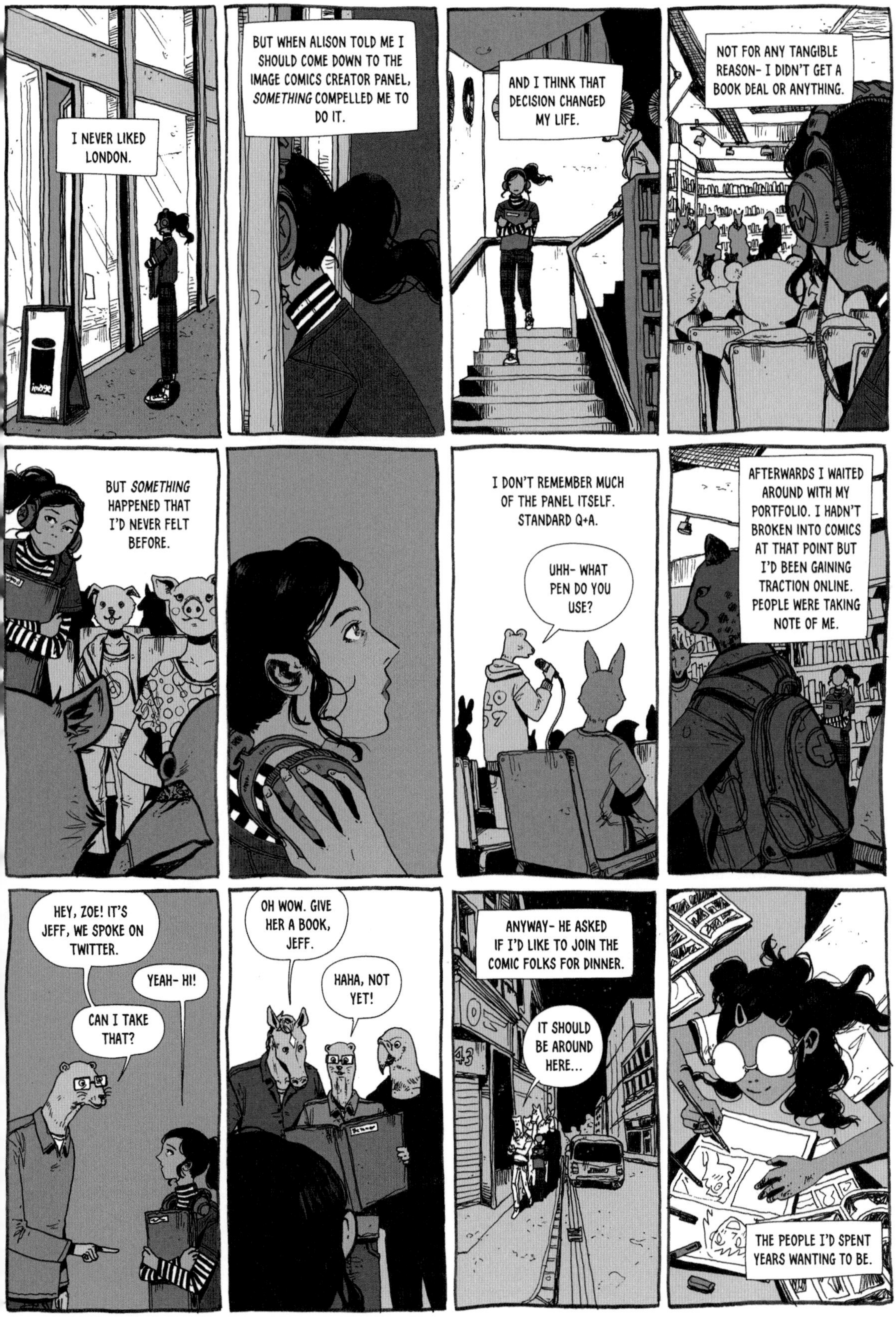
I NEVER LIKED LONDON.
image
BUT WHEN ALISON TOLD ME I SHOULD COME DOWN TO THE IMAGE COMICS CREATOR PANEL, *SOMETHING* COMPELLED ME TO DO IT.
AND I THINK THAT DECISION CHANGED MY LIFE.
NOT FOR ANY TANGIBLE REASON- I DIDN'T GET A BOOK DEAL OR ANYTHING.
BUT *SOMETHING* HAPPENED THAT I'D NEVER FELT BEFORE.
I DON'T REMEMBER MUCH OF THE PANEL ITSELF. STANDARD Q+A.
UHH- WHAT PEN DO YOU USE?
AFTERWARDS I WAITED AROUND WITH MY PORTFOLIO. I HADN'T BROKEN INTO COMICS AT THAT POINT BUT I'D BEEN GAINING TRACTION ONLINE. PEOPLE WERE TAKING NOTE OF ME.
HEY, ZOE! IT'S JEFF, WE SPOKE ON TWITTER.
YEAH- HI!
CAN I TAKE THAT?
OH WOW. GIVE HER A BOOK, JEFF.
HAHA, NOT YET!
ANYWAY- HE ASKED IF I'D LIKE TO JOIN THE COMIC FOLKS FOR DINNER.
43
IT SHOULD BE AROUND HERE...
THE PEOPLE I'D SPENT YEARS WANTING TO BE.

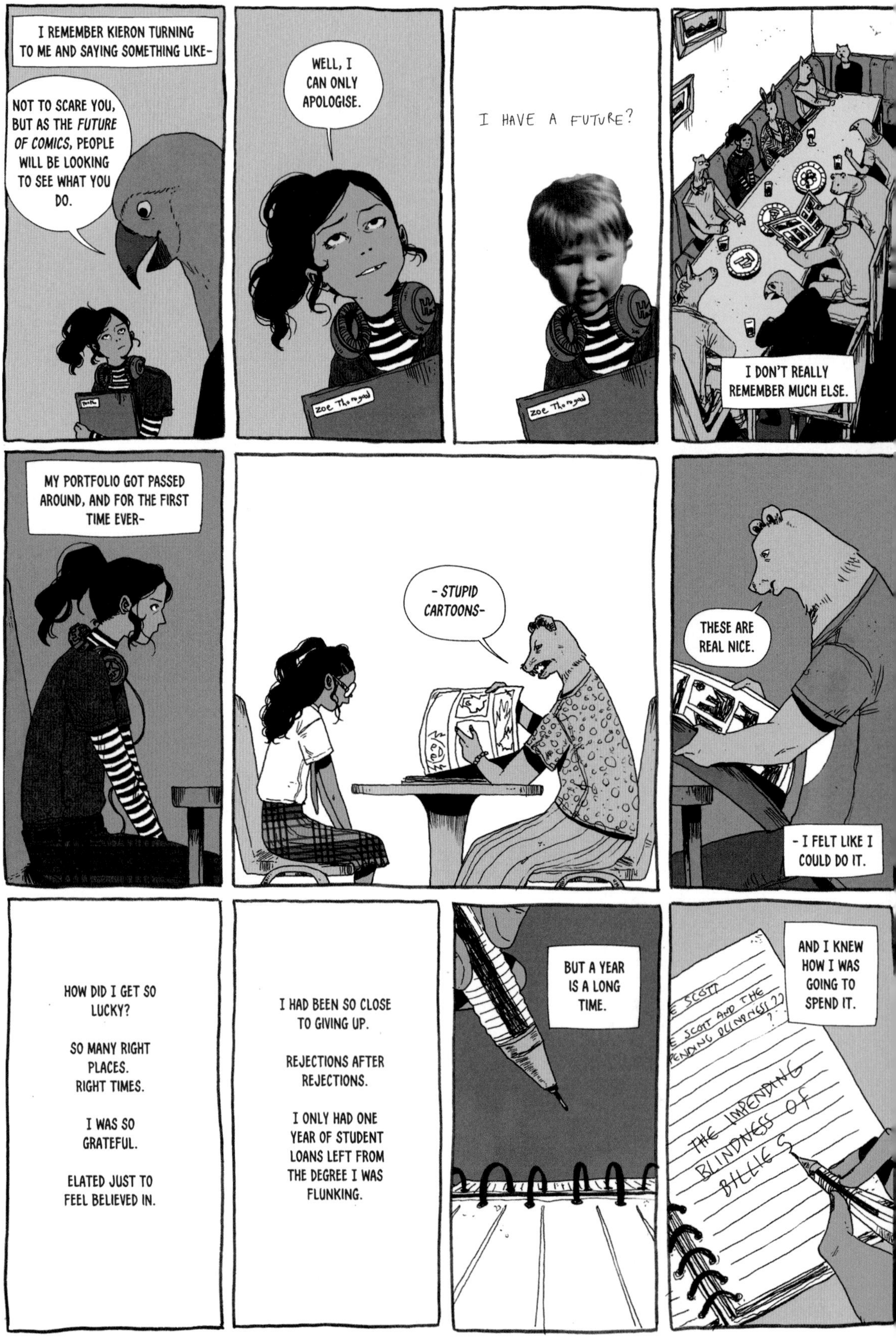

I REMEMBER KIERON TURNING TO ME AND SAYING SOMETHING LIKE-
NOT TO SCARE YOU, BUT AS THE *FUTURE OF COMICS*, PEOPLE WILL BE LOOKING TO SEE WHAT YOU DO.
WELL, I CAN ONLY APOLOGISE.
zoe Thorogood
I HAVE A FUTURE?
zoe Thorogood
I DON'T REALLY REMEMBER MUCH ELSE.
MY PORTFOLIO GOT PASSED AROUND, AND FOR THE FIRST TIME EVER-
-STUPID CARTOONS-
THESE ARE REAL NICE.
-I FELT LIKE I COULD DO IT.
HOW DID I GET SO LUCKY?
SO MANY RIGHT PLACES.
RIGHT TIMES.
I WAS SO GRATEFUL.
ELATED JUST TO FEEL BELIEVED IN.
I HAD BEEN SO CLOSE TO GIVING UP.
REJECTIONS AFTER REJECTIONS.
I ONLY HAD ONE YEAR OF STUDENT LOANS LEFT FROM THE DEGREE I WAS FLUNKING.
BUT A YEAR IS A LONG TIME.
AND I KNEW HOW I WAS GOING TO SPEND IT.
THE IMPENDING BLINDNESS OF BILLIE S

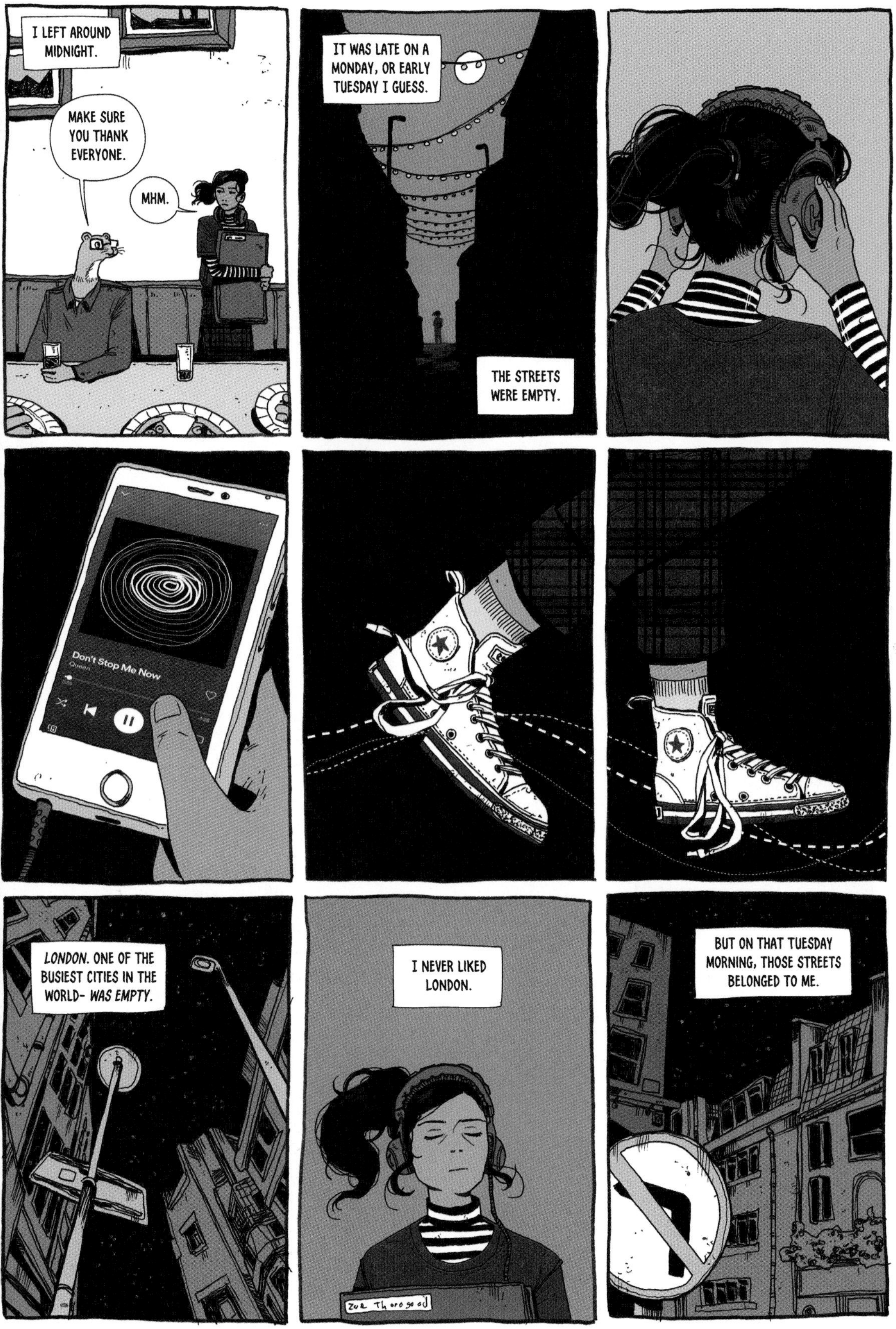
I LEFT AROUND MIDNIGHT.
MAKE SURE YOU THANK EVERYONE.
MHM.
IT WAS LATE ON A MONDAY, OR EARLY TUESDAY I GUESS.
THE STREETS WERE EMPTY.
Don't Stop Me Now
Queen
LONDON. ONE OF THE BUSIEST CITIES IN THE WORLD- *WAS EMPTY*.
I NEVER LIKED LONDON.
Zoe Thorogood
BUT ON THAT TUESDAY MORNING, THOSE STREETS BELONGED TO ME.

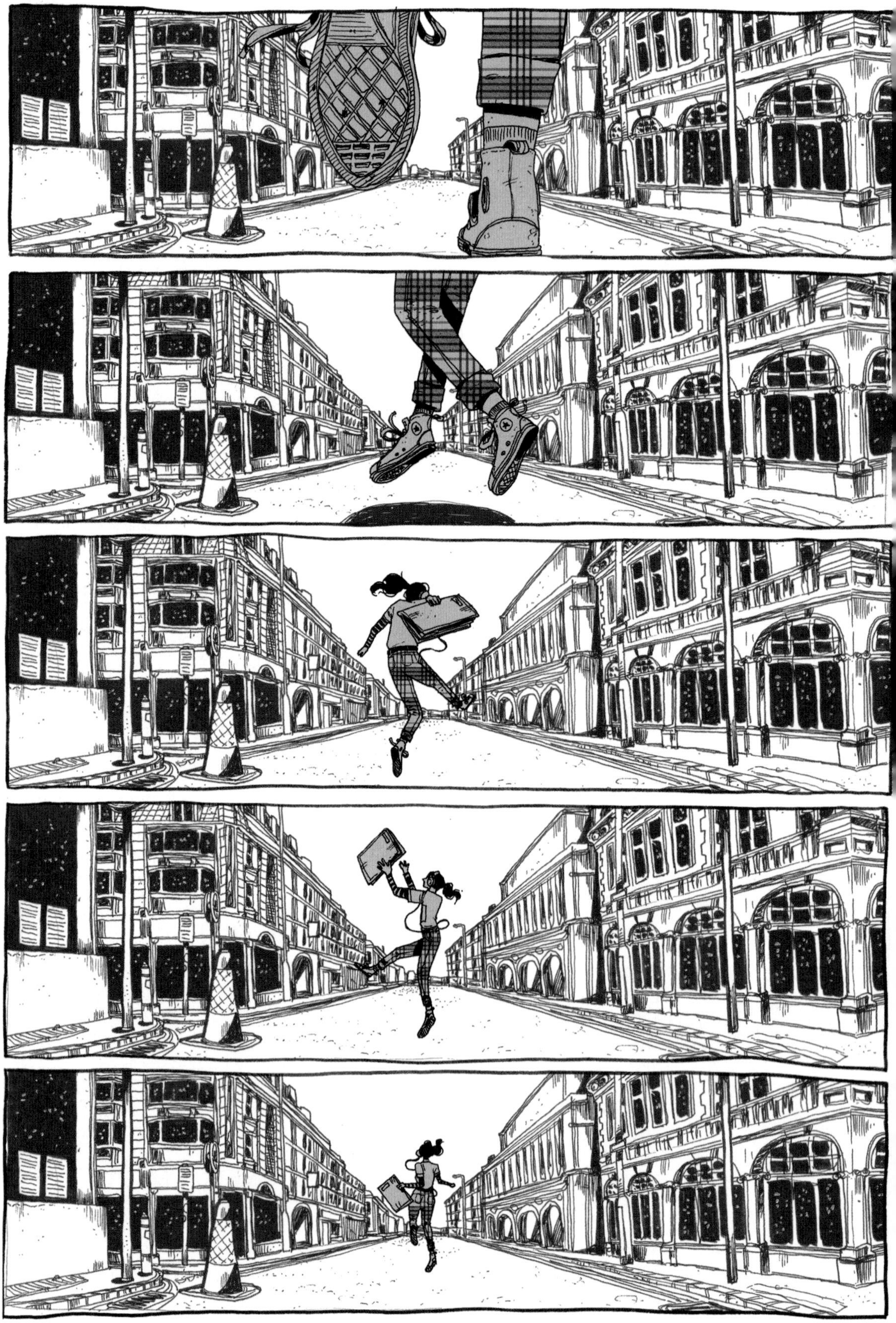

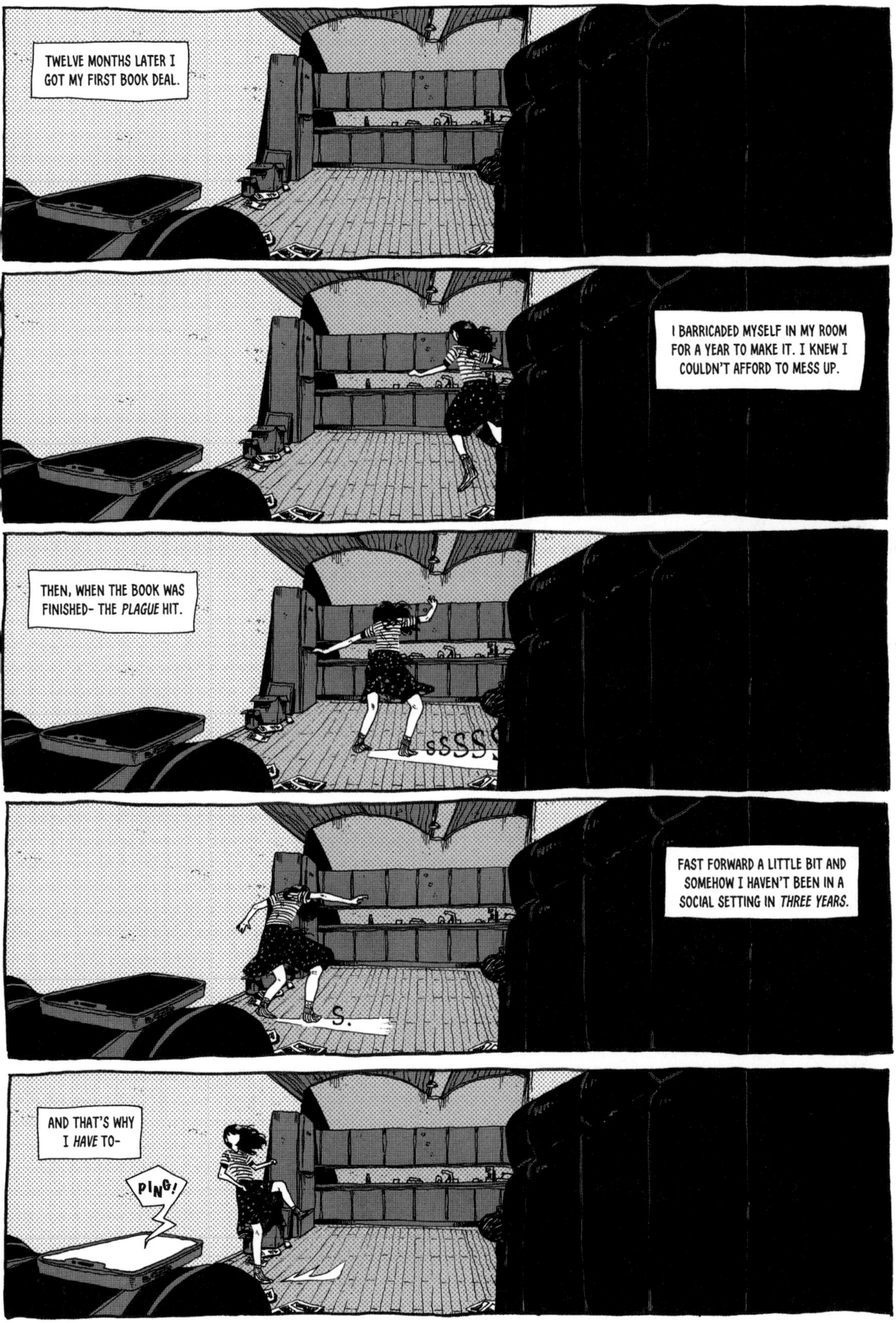
TWELVE MONTHS LATER I GOT MY FIRST BOOK DEAL.
I BARRICADED MYSELF IN MY ROOM FOR A YEAR TO MAKE IT. I KNEW I COULDN'T AFFORD TO MESS UP.
THEN, WHEN THE BOOK WAS FINISHED- THE *PLAGUE* HIT.
sSSS
FAST FORWARD A LITTLE BIT AND SOMEHOW I HAVEN'T BEEN IN A SOCIAL SETTING IN *THREE YEARS*.
S.
AND THAT'S WHY I *HAVE* TO-
PING!

Hey Zoe, unfortunately your flight's been cancelled due to covid. We'll get you over next year don't worry, things will be better by then.

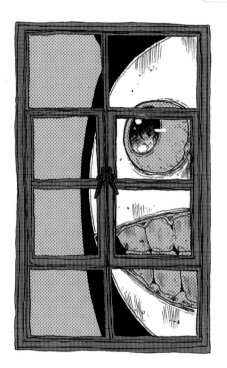

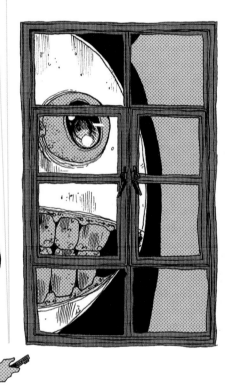

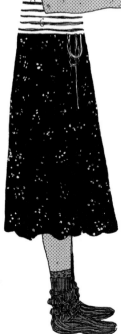

ZOE skids to a stand still.

ZOE (INNER): Fast forward a little bit and somehow I haven't been in a social setting in *three years.*

PANEL 5:

ZOE's phone flashes with a message we can't yet see.

ZOE (INNER): And that's why I have to-

SFX: PING

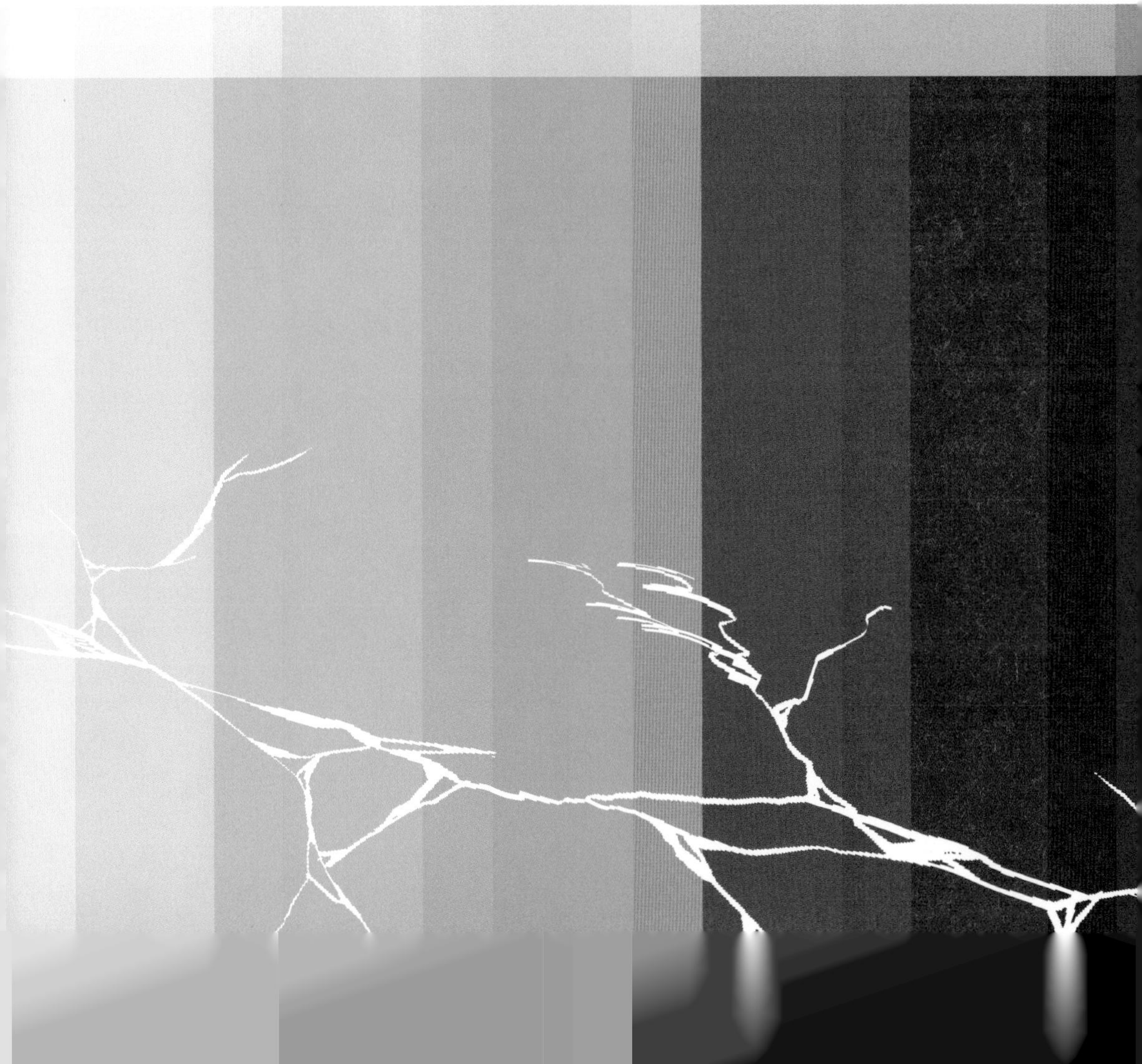

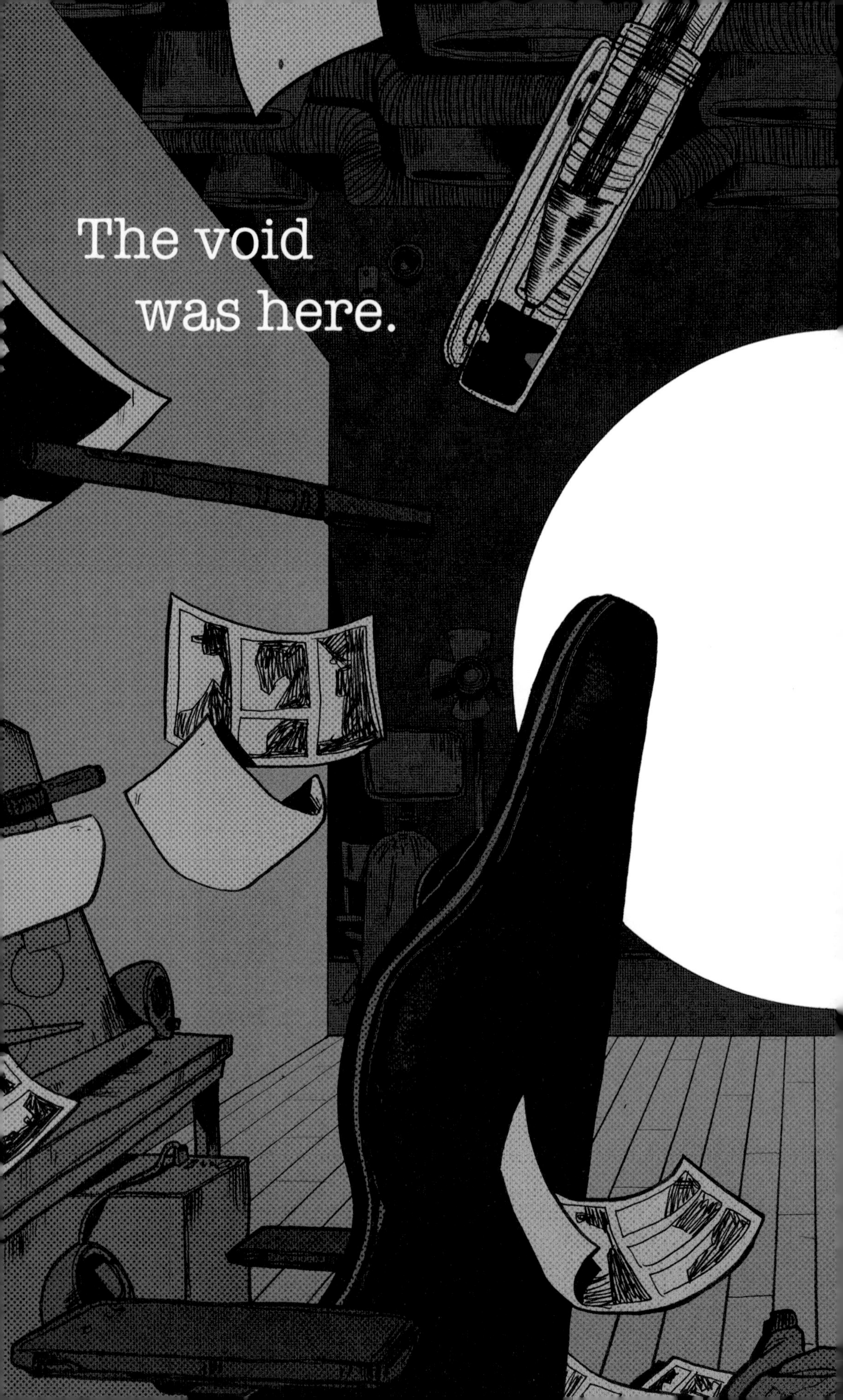
The void
was here.

FILMING IN PROGRESS

And it was
beautiful.

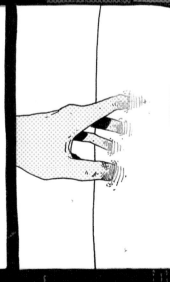

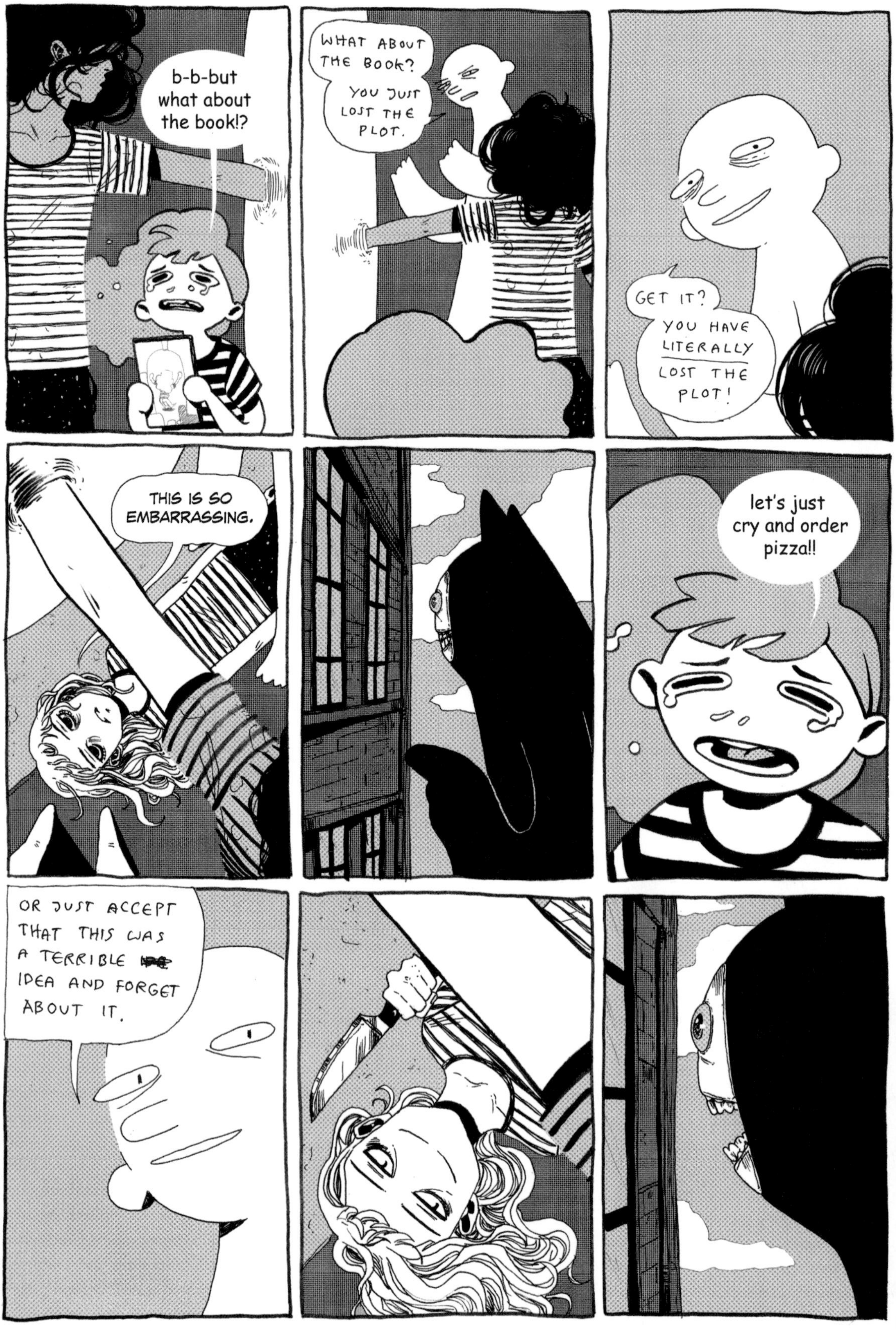

b-b-but what about the book!?
WHAT ABOUT THE BOOK?
YOU JUST LOST THE PLOT.
GET IT?
YOU HAVE LITERALLY LOST THE PLOT!
THIS IS SO EMBARRASSING.
let's just cry and order pizza!!
OR JUST ACCEPT THAT THIS WAS A TERRIBLE IDEA AND FORGET ABOUT IT.

that's the problem with flirting with the idea of something, sometimes you fall in

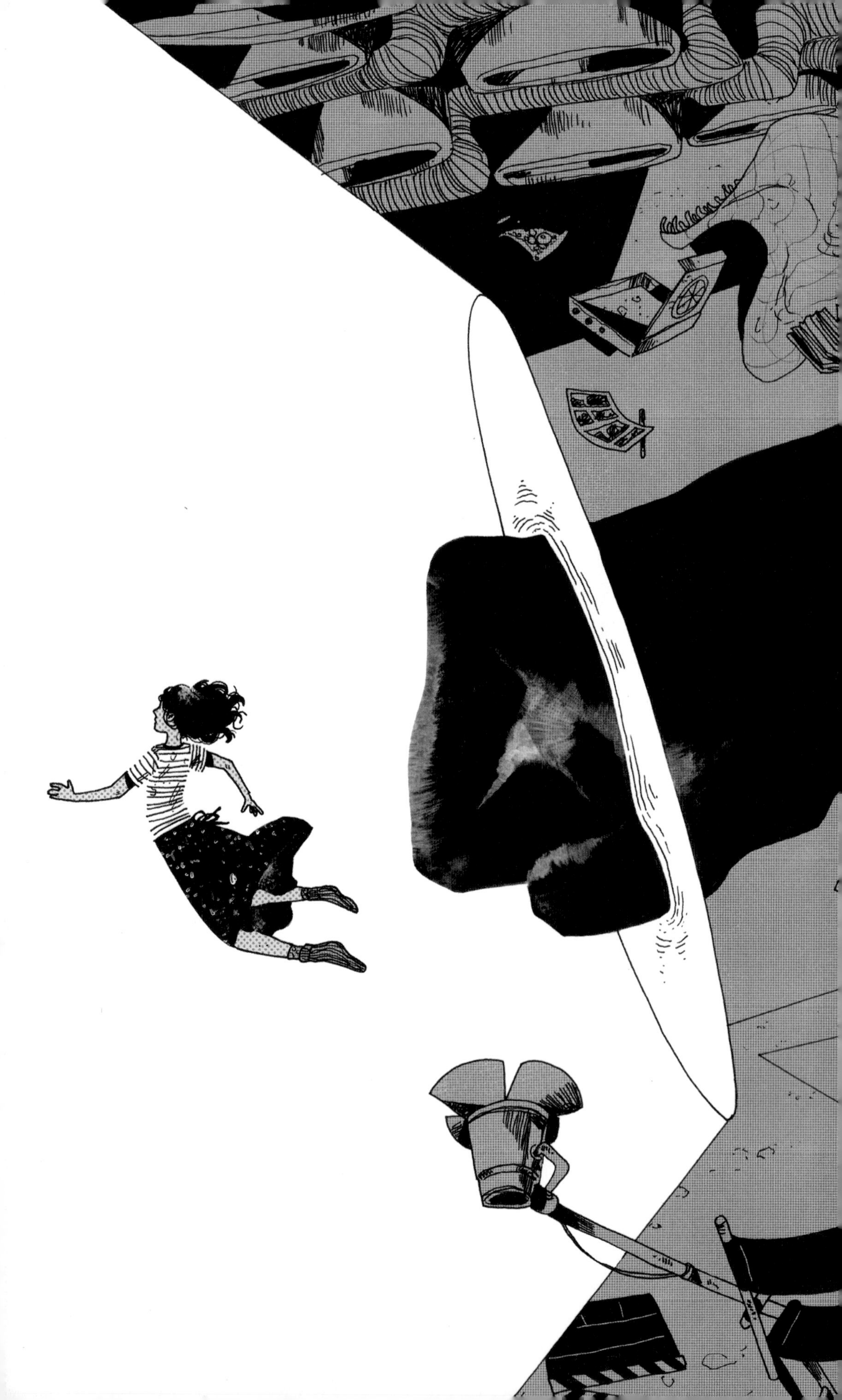

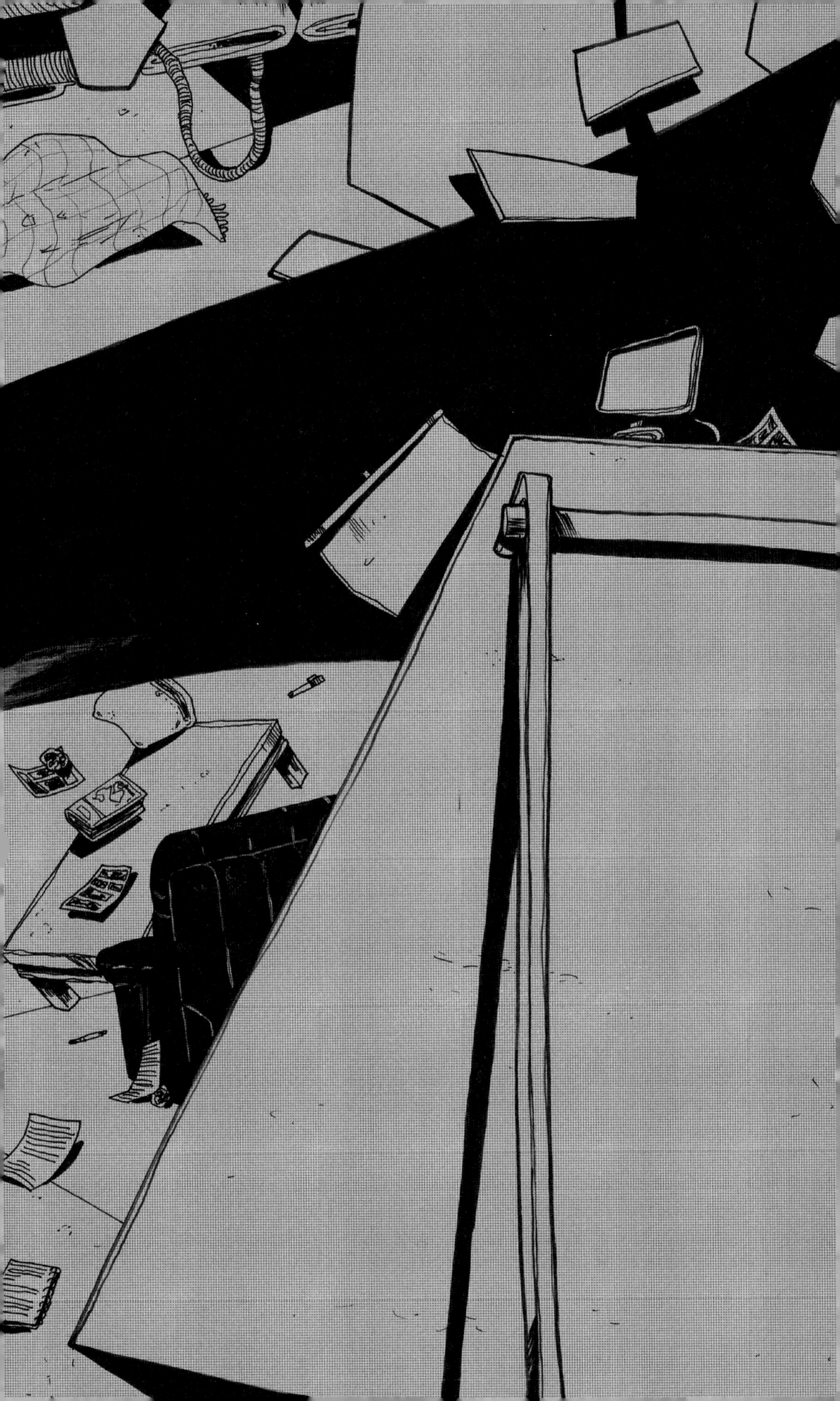

Hey...

can you hear me?

Nod if you can hear me

oh, right, I guess I'm just words on a page haha, why would you nod at that?

I hate being in the void. Nothing makes any sense down here

Whenever I read stories about it, y'know, nihilism and stuff, the answer is always 'human connection', which leaves me feeling so empty.

I wish I could connect to people, I feel like I'm always stuck behind a glass wall or a page turn or something, there but never really seen

Do you know me yet?

I guess not.

This is just a story. I don't know how much of me exists in these pages

But it's always been my belief that stories make us human

Do u wanna hear a funny story? I guess you can skip this section if you don't. It's pretty funny though.

So, when I was 18 I tried going to uni to study 3D game art. I lived in a student flat with 4 strangers, and this ENTIRE year I never used the kitchen because I didn't want to interact with the people I lived with.

(I'm sure they were lovely.)

Anyway, one day I decide I'm gonna be brave and treat myself to a microwaved sweet potato. So I walk out my room with the potato, but as I walk to the kitchen, I see people in it, and they've seen me, so I have to keep walking past so it doesn't look weird, but the only thing past the kitchen is the door to our flat

So I walk out the flat, the door closes and LOCKS automatically, and I haven't got my key

So im stuck outside my flat, bare foot in my pjs, hair wet cause I'd just washed it, holding an uncooked potato

And then hear people walking up the stairs, so im like OMG I BETTER LOSE THIS POTATO FAST!! (For some reason the potato was the thing I was most worried about them seeing)

So I call the elevator, put the potato in it, and send it up to the top floor

Anyway after nearly pissing myself I finally knock on the door so my flat mates can let me back in. While im barefoot, and dripping wet, in my pjs. Potatoless.

Sorry, I'm rambling.

Listen- I've been talking about myself so much I wasn't thinking about you

I don't know how long I'll be here for. Take a few pages for yourself, I promise I won't tell anyone what you do with them

I wish I could tell you what you need to hear. But this is all I can really do from this place

I'll try get back to the book now. I hope we get to talk again

IT'S LONELY AT THE
CENTRE OF THE EARTH

by Zoe Thorogood and ....

(your name here)

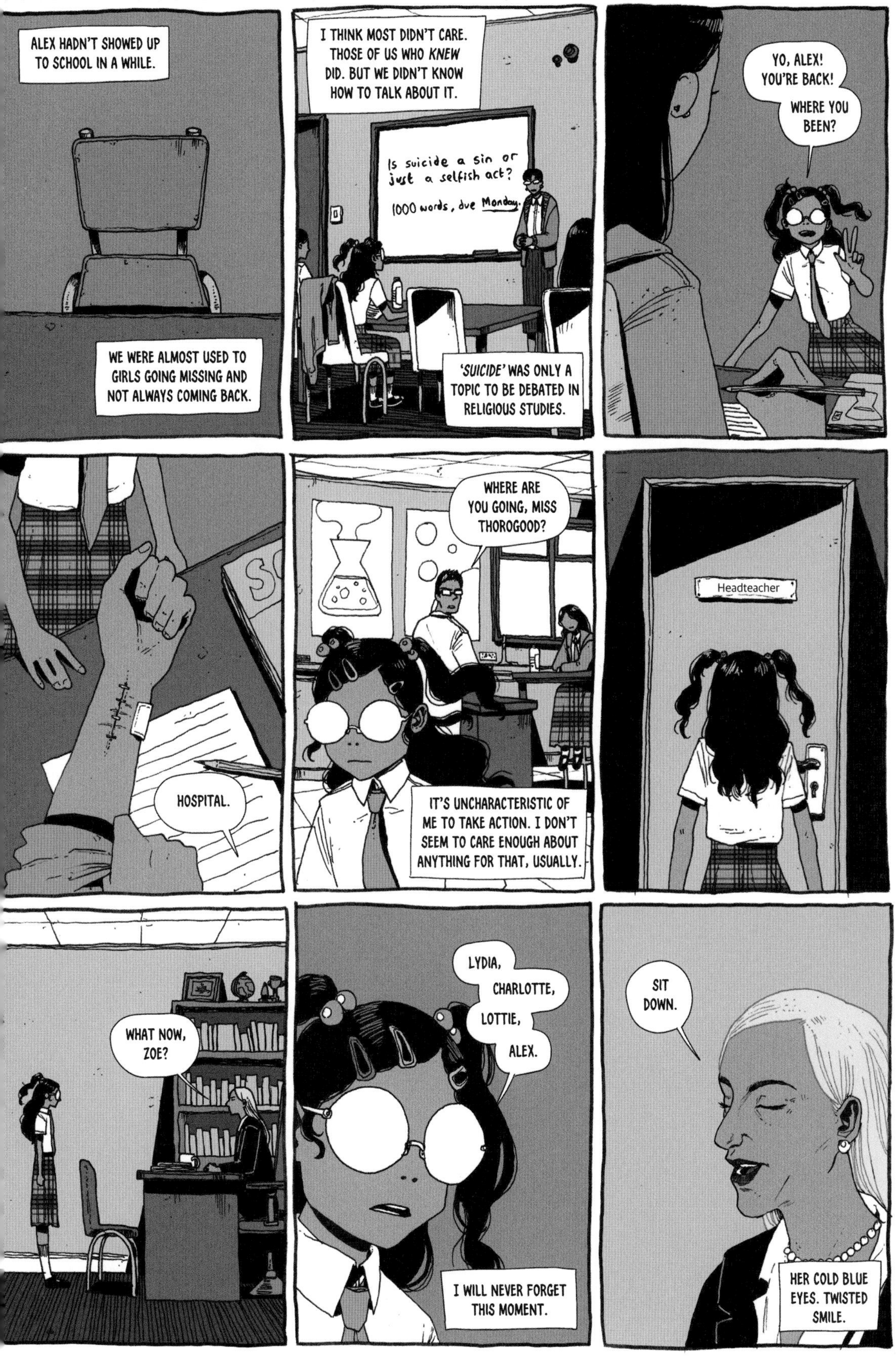
ALEX HADN'T SHOWED UP TO SCHOOL IN A WHILE.
WE WERE ALMOST USED TO GIRLS GOING MISSING AND NOT ALWAYS COMING BACK.
I THINK MOST DIDN'T CARE. THOSE OF US WHO *KNEW* DID. BUT WE DIDN'T KNOW HOW TO TALK ABOUT IT.
Is suicide a sin or just a selfish act?
1000 words, due Monday.
'*SUICIDE*' WAS ONLY A TOPIC TO BE DEBATED IN RELIGIOUS STUDIES.
YO, ALEX! YOU'RE BACK!
WHERE YOU BEEN?
HOSPITAL.
WHERE ARE YOU GOING, MISS THOROGOOD?
IT'S UNCHARACTERISTIC OF ME TO TAKE ACTION. I DON'T SEEM TO CARE ENOUGH ABOUT ANYTHING FOR THAT, USUALLY.
Headteacher
WHAT NOW, ZOE?
LYDIA,
CHARLOTTE,
LOTTIE,
ALEX.
I WILL NEVER FORGET THIS MOMENT.
SIT DOWN.
HER COLD BLUE EYES. TWISTED SMILE.

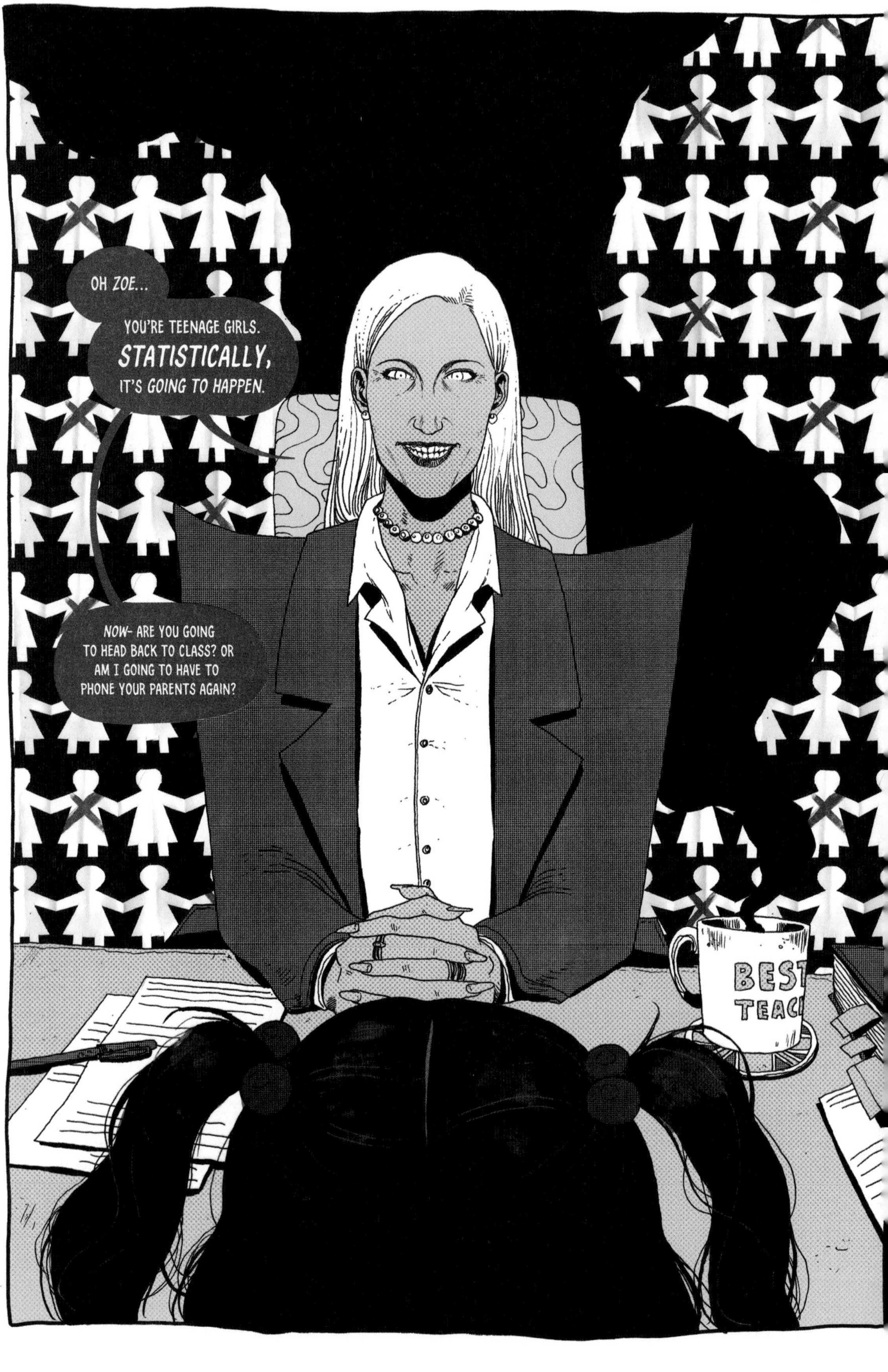
OH ZOE...
YOU'RE TEENAGE GIRLS. STATISTICALLY, IT'S GOING TO HAPPEN.
NOW- ARE YOU GOING TO HEAD BACK TO CLASS? OR AM I GOING TO HAVE TO PHONE YOUR PARENTS AGAIN?
BEST TEAC

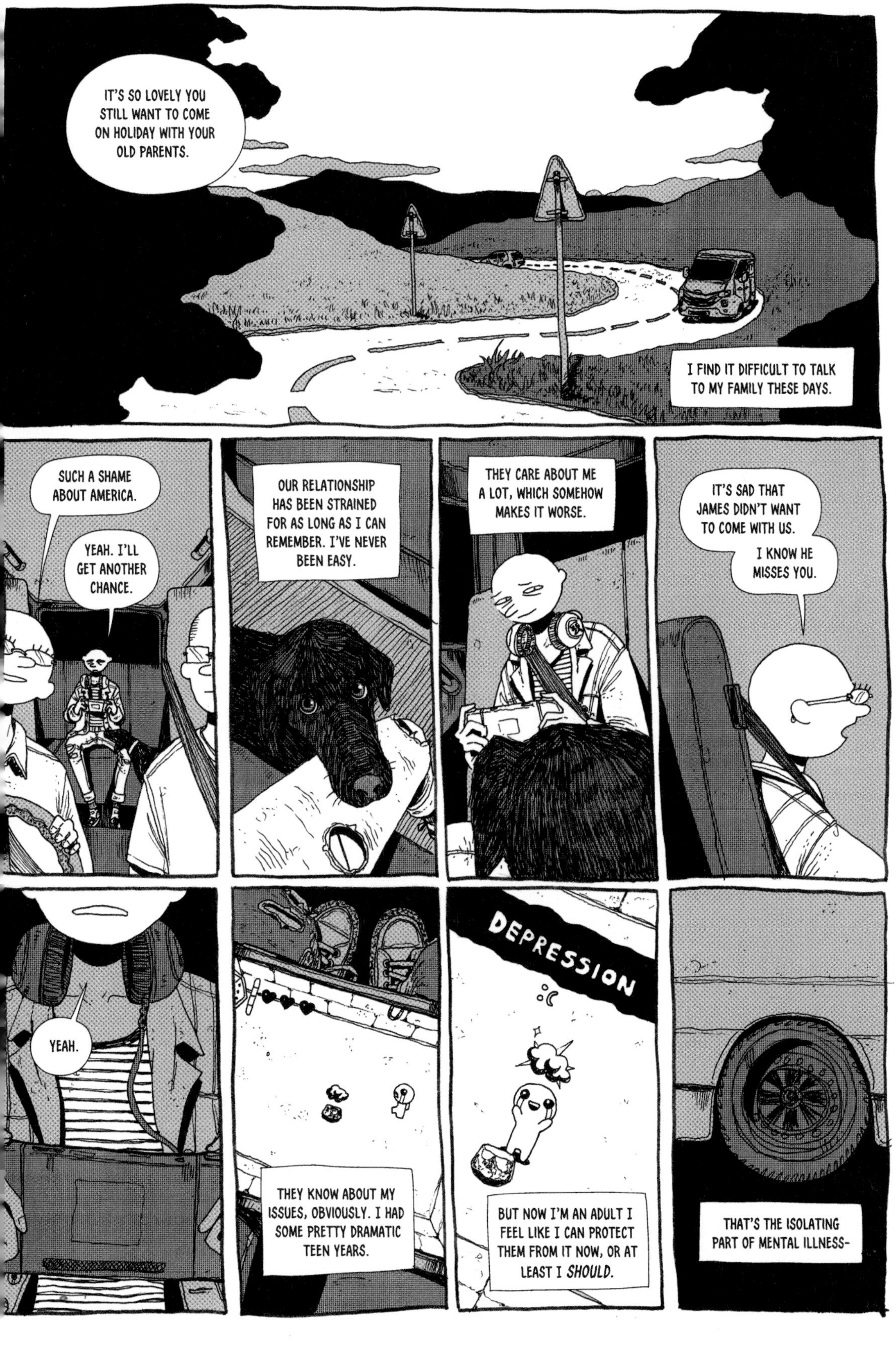
IT'S SO LOVELY YOU STILL WANT TO COME ON HOLIDAY WITH YOUR OLD PARENTS.
I FIND IT DIFFICULT TO TALK TO MY FAMILY THESE DAYS.
SUCH A SHAME ABOUT AMERICA.
YEAH. I'LL GET ANOTHER CHANCE.
OUR RELATIONSHIP HAS BEEN STRAINED FOR AS LONG AS I CAN REMEMBER. I'VE NEVER BEEN EASY.
THEY CARE ABOUT ME A LOT, WHICH SOMEHOW MAKES IT WORSE.
IT'S SAD THAT JAMES DIDN'T WANT TO COME WITH US.
I KNOW HE MISSES YOU.
YEAH.
THEY KNOW ABOUT MY ISSUES, OBVIOUSLY. I HAD SOME PRETTY DRAMATIC TEEN YEARS.
DEPRESSION
BUT NOW I'M AN ADULT I FEEL LIKE I CAN PROTECT THEM FROM IT NOW, OR AT LEAST I *SHOULD.*
THAT'S THE ISOLATING PART OF MENTAL ILLNESS-

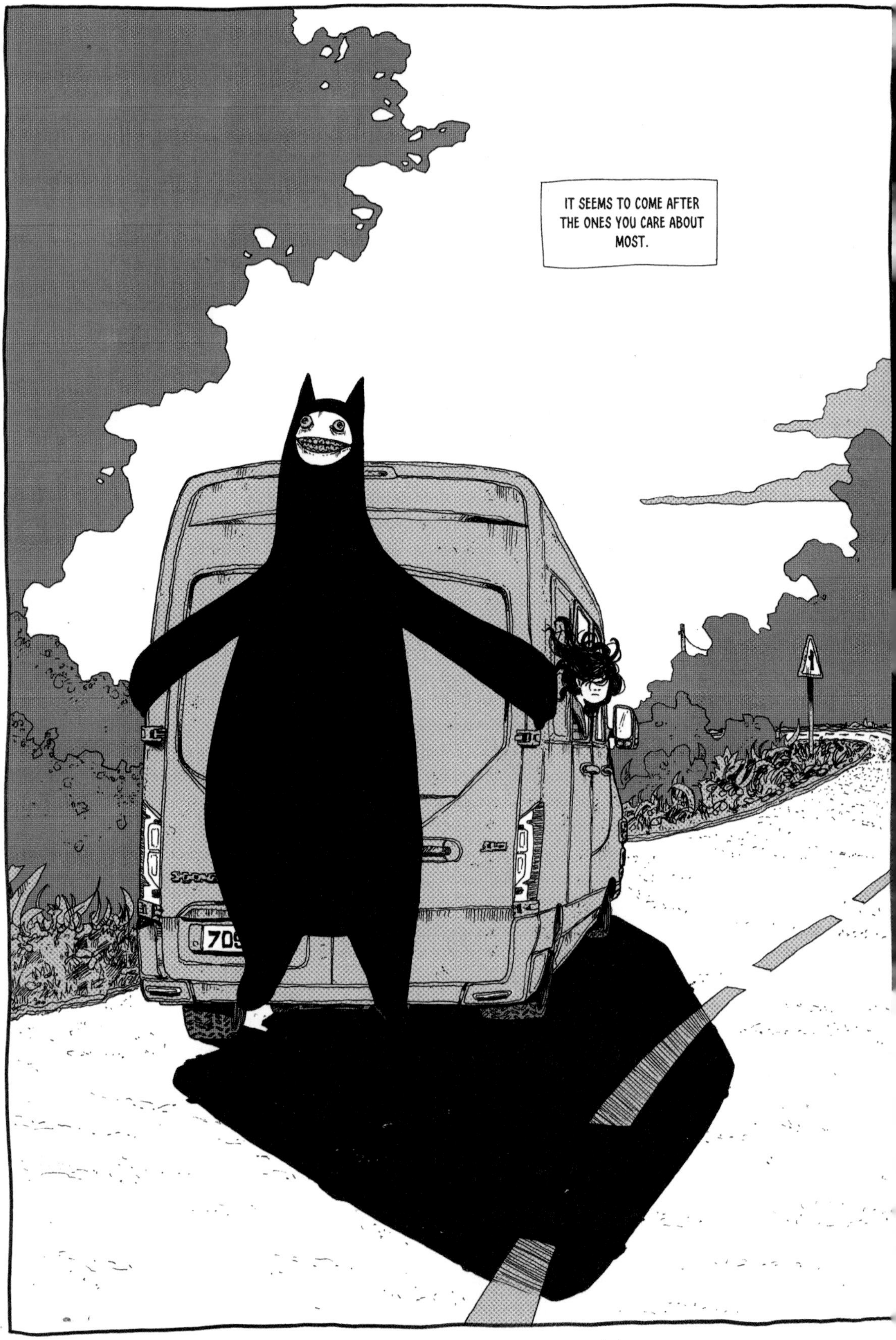
IT SEEMS TO COME AFTER
THE ONES YOU CARE ABOUT
MOST.

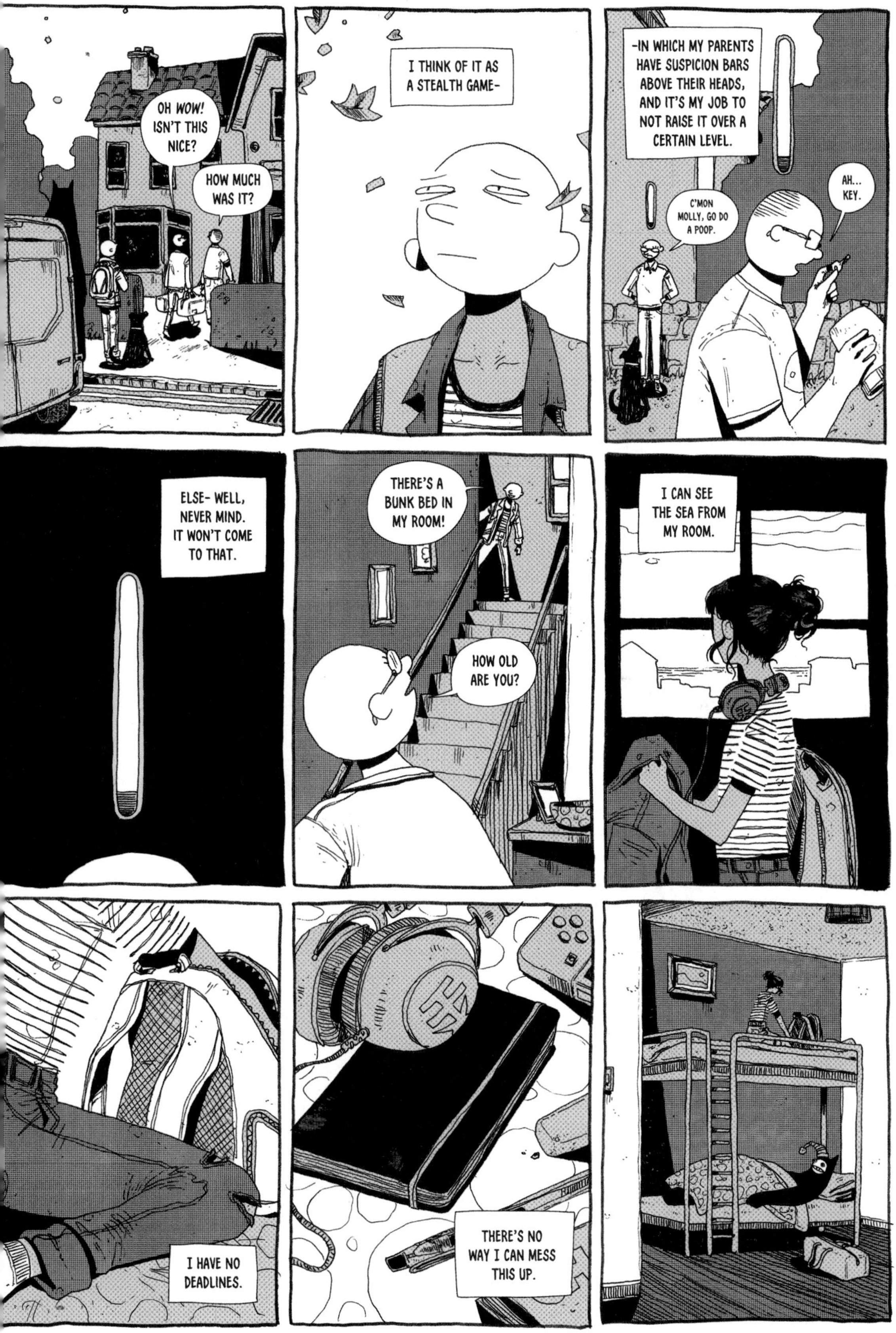
OH WOW! ISN'T THIS NICE?
HOW MUCH WAS IT?
I THINK OF IT AS A STEALTH GAME-
-IN WHICH MY PARENTS HAVE SUSPICION BARS ABOVE THEIR HEADS, AND IT'S MY JOB TO NOT RAISE IT OVER A CERTAIN LEVEL.
C'MON MOLLY, GO DO A POOP.
AH... KEY.
ELSE- WELL, NEVER MIND. IT WON'T COME TO THAT.
THERE'S A BUNK BED IN MY ROOM!
HOW OLD ARE YOU?
I CAN SEE THE SEA FROM MY ROOM.
I HAVE NO DEADLINES.
THERE'S NO WAY I CAN MESS THIS UP.

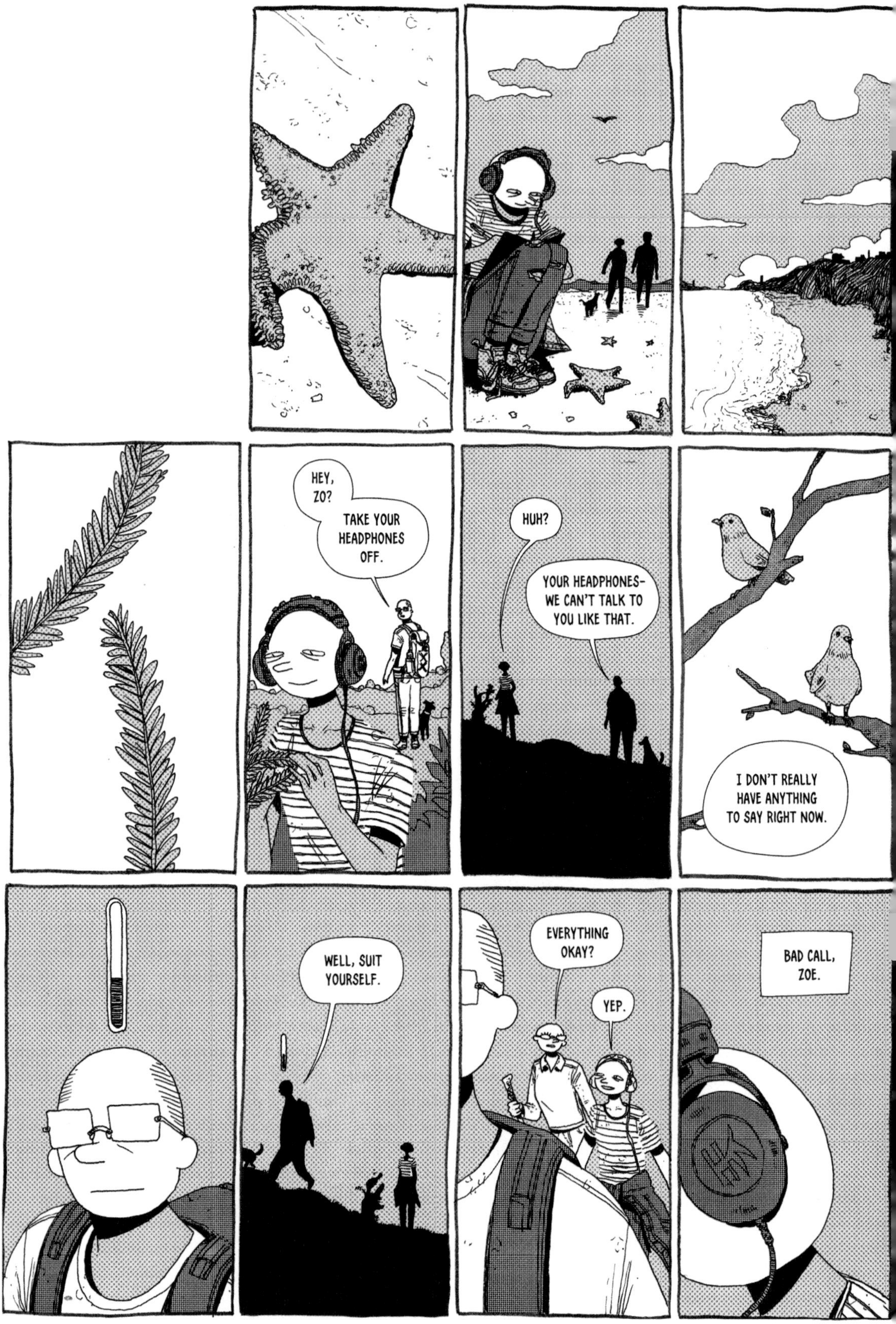
HEY, ZO?
TAKE YOUR HEADPHONES OFF.
HUH?
YOUR HEADPHONES- WE CAN'T TALK TO YOU LIKE THAT.
I DON'T REALLY HAVE ANYTHING TO SAY RIGHT NOW.
WELL, SUIT YOURSELF.
EVERYTHING OKAY?
YEP.
BAD CALL, ZOE.

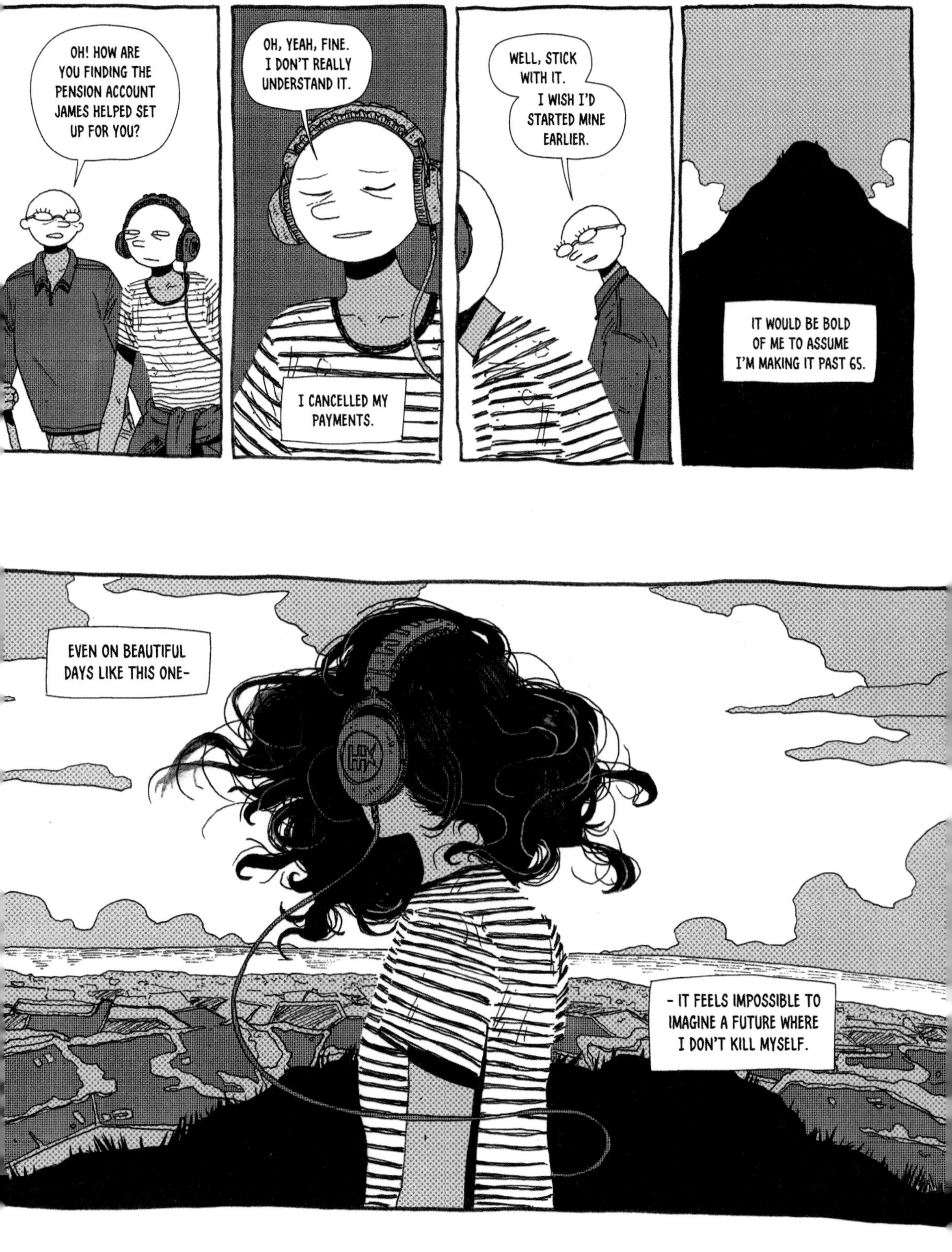
OH! HOW ARE YOU FINDING THE PENSION ACCOUNT JAMES HELPED SET UP FOR YOU?
OH, YEAH, FINE. I DON'T REALLY UNDERSTAND IT.
I CANCELLED MY PAYMENTS.
WELL, STICK WITH IT.
I WISH I'D STARTED MINE EARLIER.
IT WOULD BE BOLD OF ME TO ASSUME I'M MAKING IT PAST 65.
EVEN ON BEAUTIFUL DAYS LIKE THIS ONE-
- IT FEELS IMPOSSIBLE TO IMAGINE A FUTURE WHERE I DON'T KILL MYSELF.

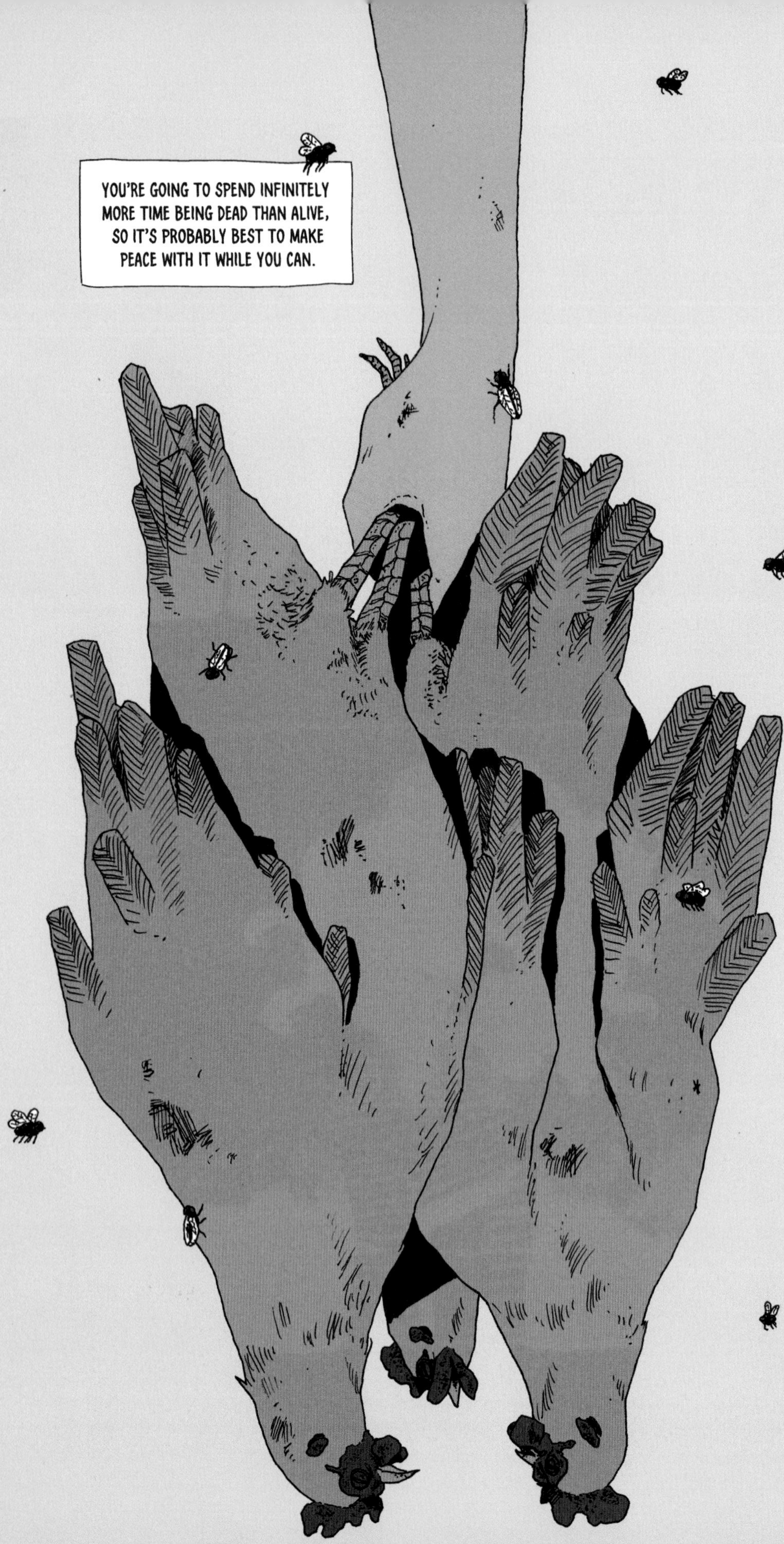
YOU'RE GOING TO SPEND INFINITELY MORE TIME BEING DEAD THAN ALIVE, SO IT'S PROBABLY BEST TO MAKE PEACE WITH IT WHILE YOU CAN.

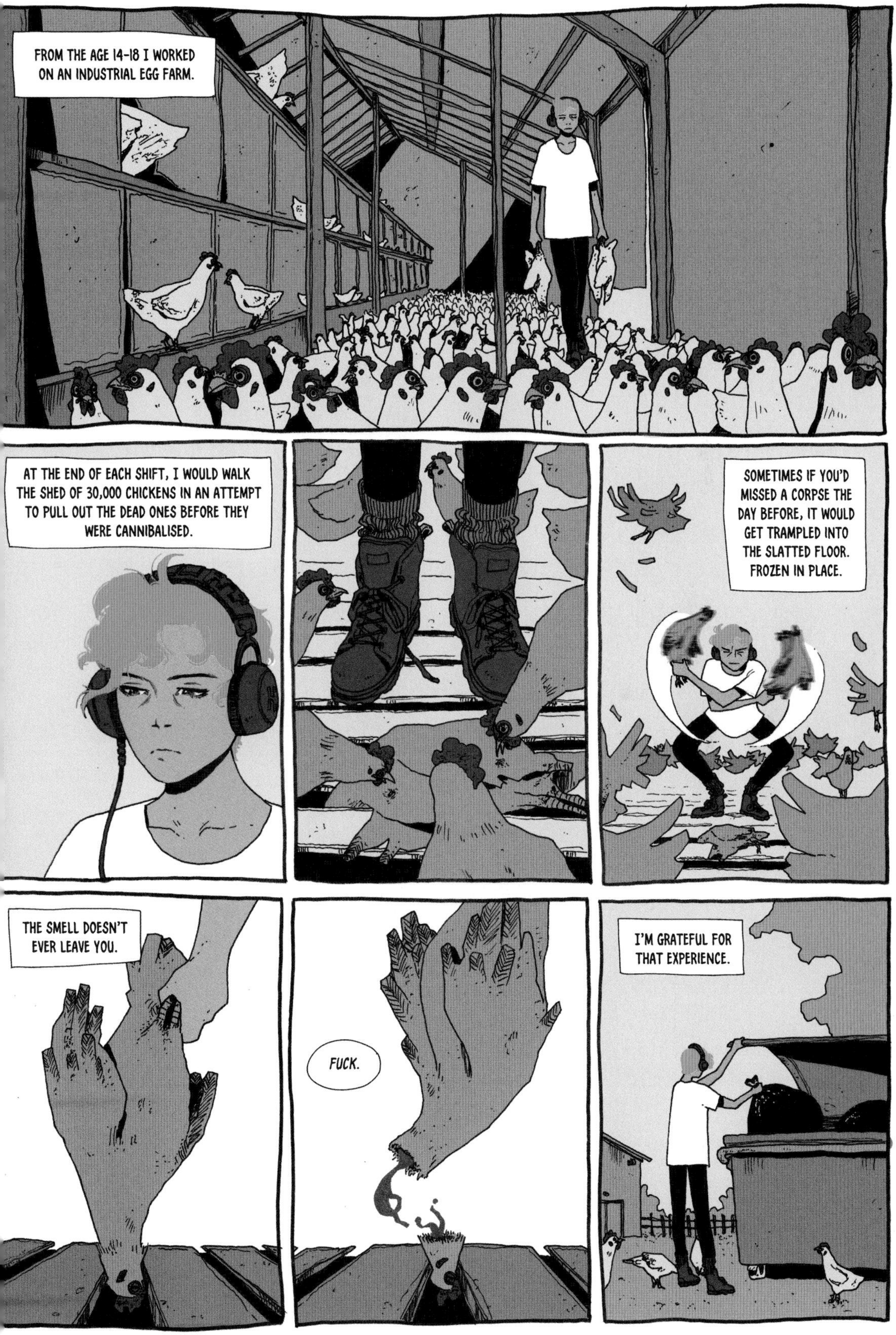
FROM THE AGE 14-18 I WORKED ON AN INDUSTRIAL EGG FARM.
AT THE END OF EACH SHIFT, I WOULD WALK THE SHED OF 30,000 CHICKENS IN AN ATTEMPT TO PULL OUT THE DEAD ONES BEFORE THEY WERE CANNIBALISED.
SOMETIMES IF YOU'D MISSED A CORPSE THE DAY BEFORE, IT WOULD GET TRAMPLED INTO THE SLATTED FLOOR. FROZEN IN PLACE.
THE SMELL DOESN'T EVER LEAVE YOU.
FUCK.
I'M GRATEFUL FOR THAT EXPERIENCE.

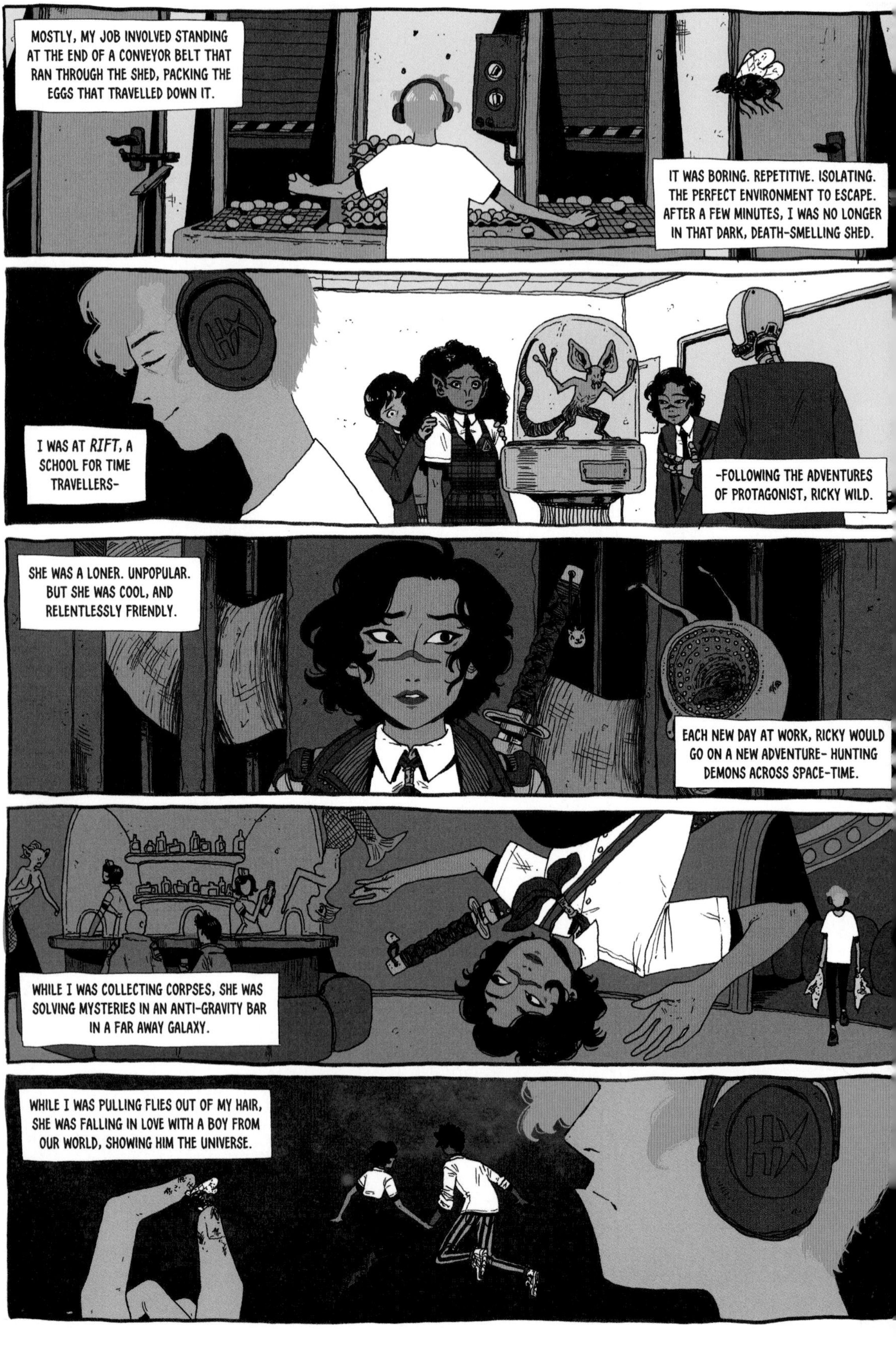
MOSTLY, MY JOB INVOLVED STANDING AT THE END OF A CONVEYOR BELT THAT RAN THROUGH THE SHED, PACKING THE EGGS THAT TRAVELLED DOWN IT.
IT WAS BORING. REPETITIVE. ISOLATING. THE PERFECT ENVIRONMENT TO ESCAPE. AFTER A FEW MINUTES, I WAS NO LONGER IN THAT DARK, DEATH-SMELLING SHED.
I WAS AT *RIFT*, A SCHOOL FOR TIME TRAVELLERS-
-FOLLOWING THE ADVENTURES OF PROTAGONIST, RICKY WILD.
SHE WAS A LONER. UNPOPULAR. BUT SHE WAS COOL, AND RELENTLESSLY FRIENDLY.
EACH NEW DAY AT WORK, RICKY WOULD GO ON A NEW ADVENTURE- HUNTING DEMONS ACROSS SPACE-TIME.
WHILE I WAS COLLECTING CORPSES, SHE WAS SOLVING MYSTERIES IN AN ANTI-GRAVITY BAR IN A FAR AWAY GALAXY.
WHILE I WAS PULLING FLIES OUT OF MY HAIR, SHE WAS FALLING IN LOVE WITH A BOY FROM OUR WORLD, SHOWING HIM THE UNIVERSE.

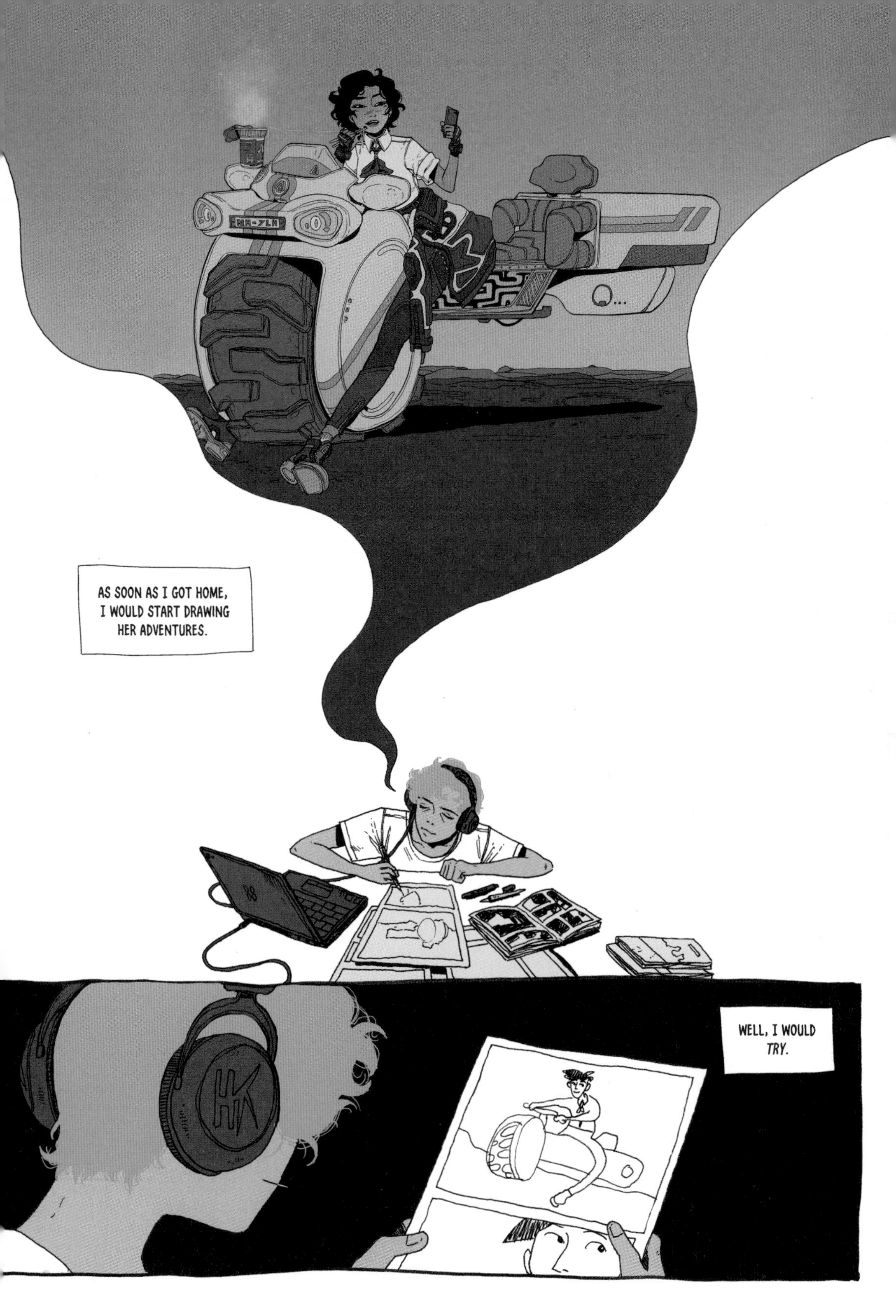

AS SOON AS I GOT HOME, I WOULD START DRAWING HER ADVENTURES.
WELL, I WOULD *TRY*.

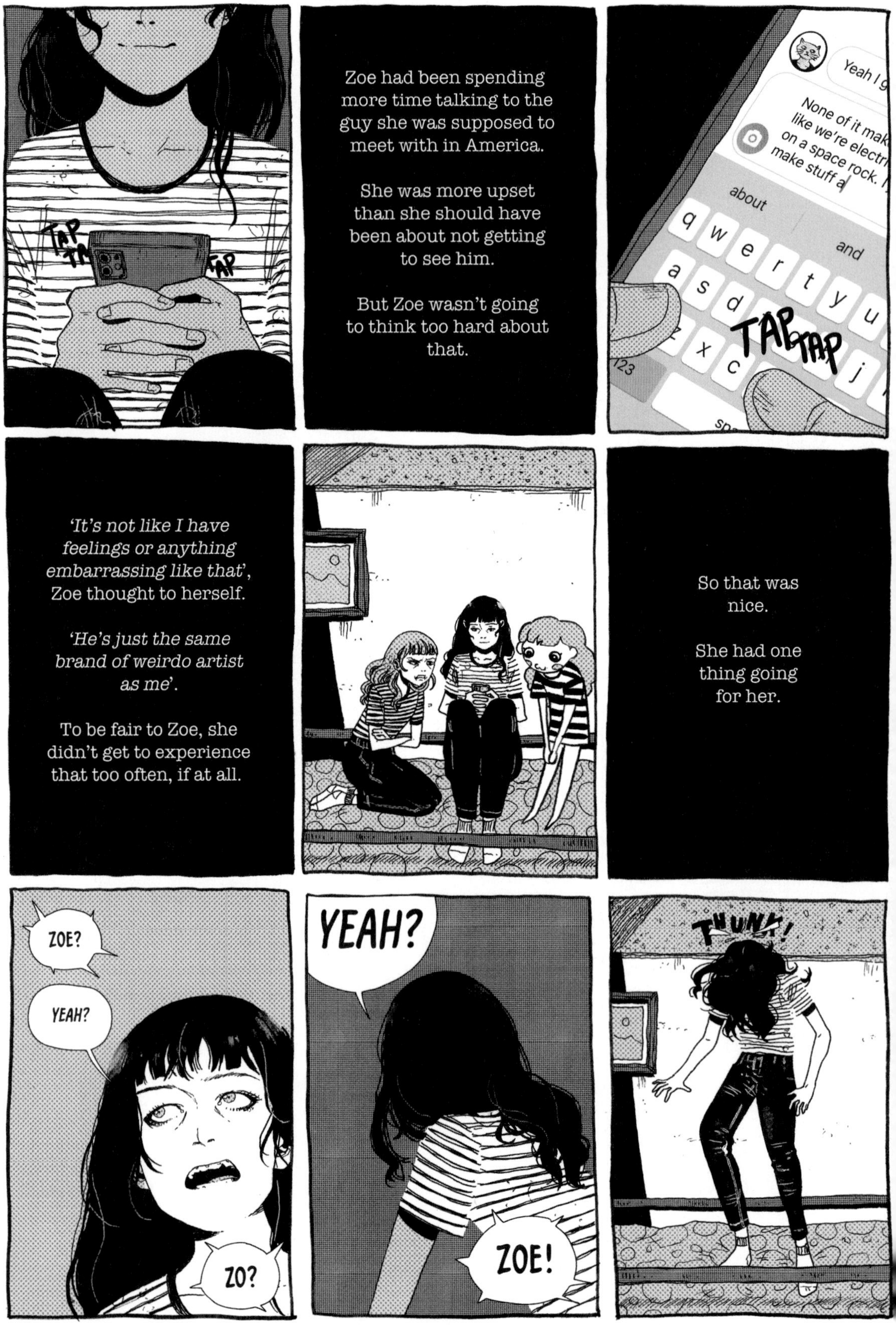
TAP TAP
TAP
Zoe had been spending more time talking to the guy she was supposed to meet with in America.
She was more upset than she should have been about not getting to see him.
But Zoe wasn't going to think too hard about that.
Yeah I g
None of it mak like we're electr on a space rock. I make stuff a
about
and
TAP TAP
'It's not like I have feelings or anything embarrassing like that', Zoe thought to herself.
'He's just the same brand of weirdo artist as me'.
To be fair to Zoe, she didn't get to experience that too often, if at all.
So that was nice.
She had one thing going for her.
ZOE?
YEAH?
ZO?
YEAH?
ZOE!
THUNK!

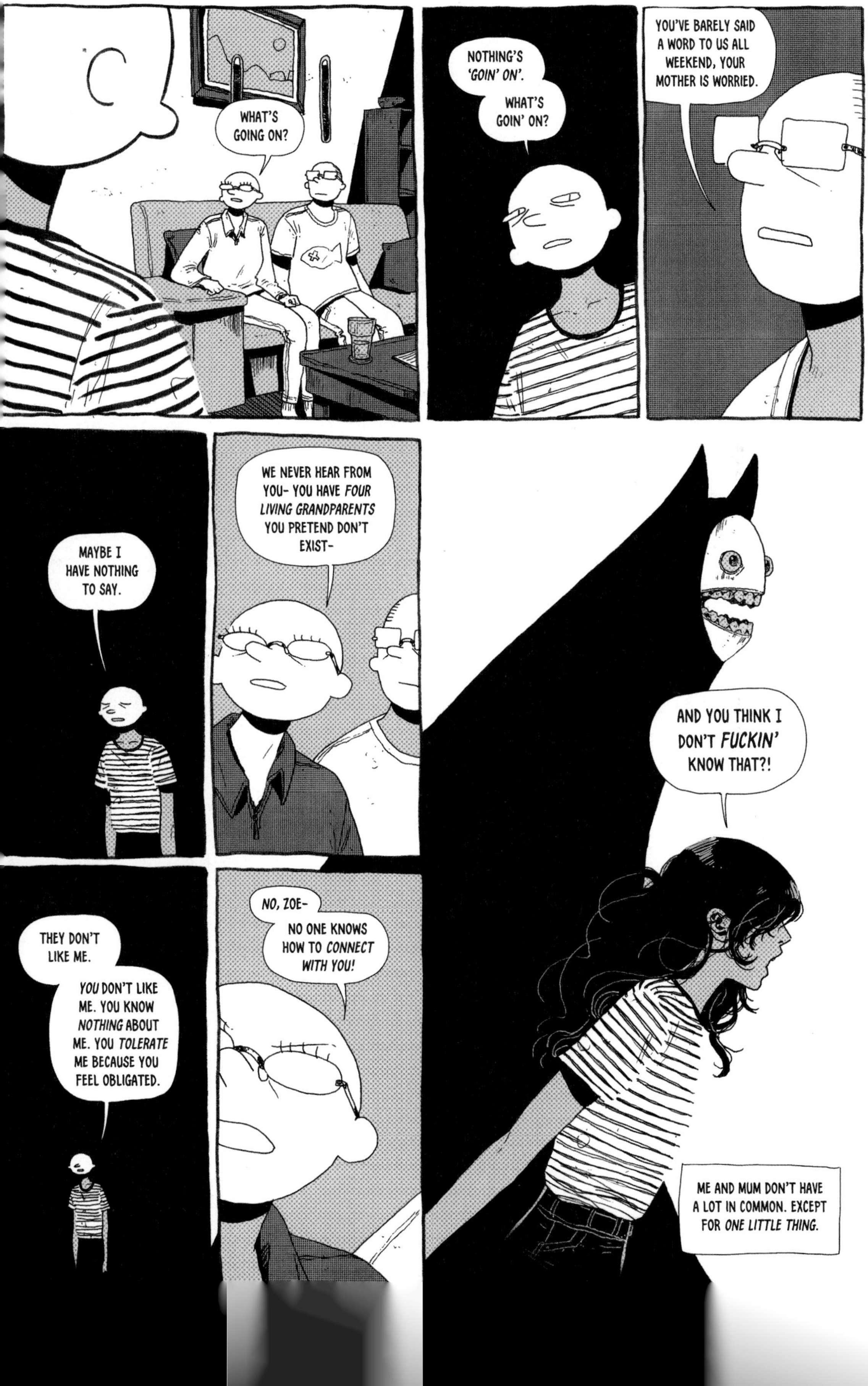
WHAT'S GOING ON?
NOTHING'S 'GOIN' ON'.
WHAT'S GOIN' ON?
YOU'VE BARELY SAID A WORD TO US ALL WEEKEND, YOUR MOTHER IS WORRIED.
MAYBE I HAVE NOTHING TO SAY.
WE NEVER HEAR FROM YOU- YOU HAVE FOUR LIVING GRANDPARENTS YOU PRETEND DON'T EXIST-
THEY DON'T LIKE ME.
YOU DON'T LIKE ME. YOU KNOW NOTHING ABOUT ME. YOU TOLERATE ME BECAUSE YOU FEEL OBLIGATED.
NO, ZOE-
NO ONE KNOWS HOW TO CONNECT WITH YOU!
AND YOU THINK I DON'T FUCKIN' KNOW THAT?!
ME AND MUM DON'T HAVE A LOT IN COMMON. EXCEPT FOR ONE LITTLE THING.

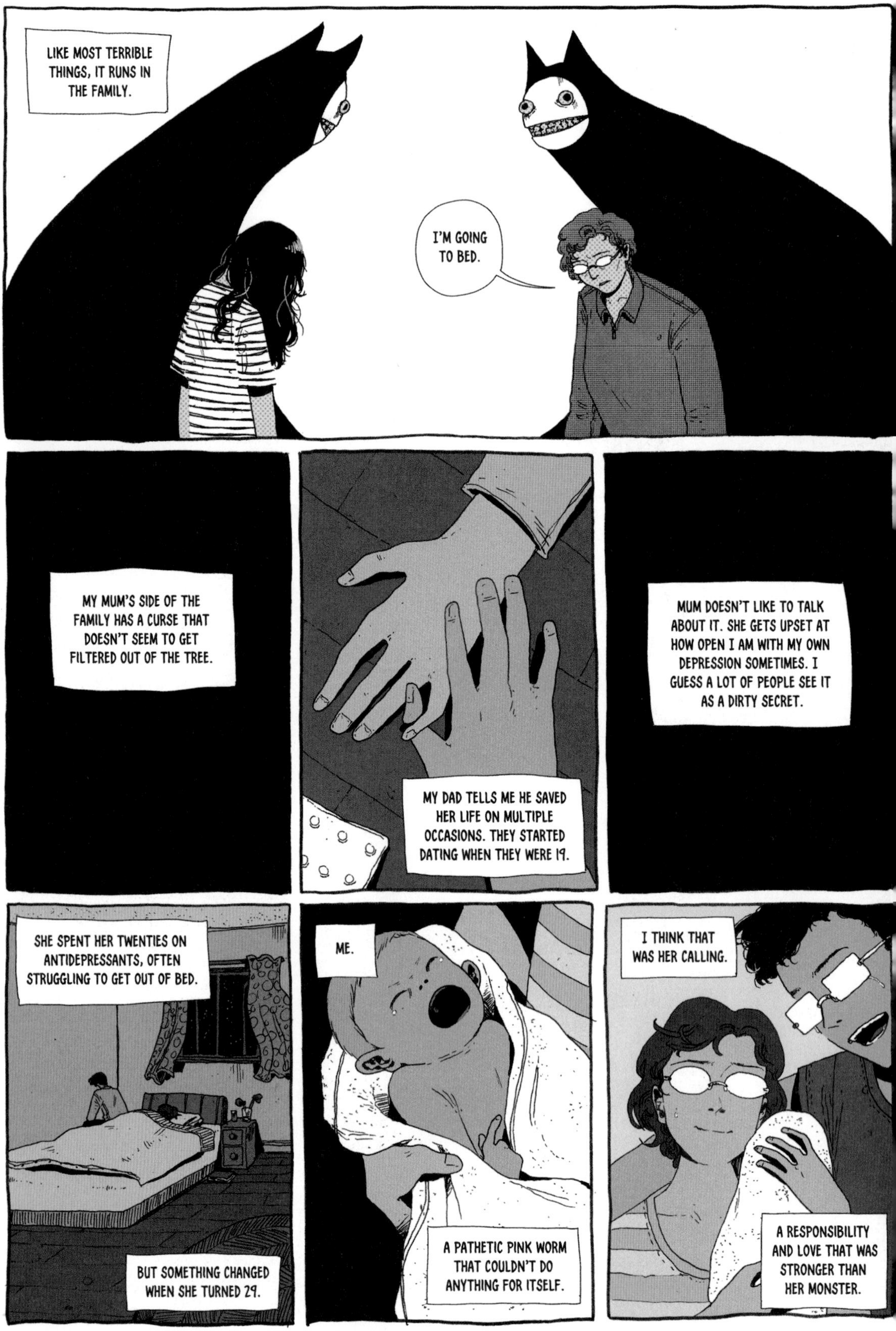
LIKE MOST TERRIBLE THINGS, IT RUNS IN THE FAMILY.
I'M GOING TO BED.
MY MUM'S SIDE OF THE FAMILY HAS A CURSE THAT DOESN'T SEEM TO GET FILTERED OUT OF THE TREE.
MY DAD TELLS ME HE SAVED HER LIFE ON MULTIPLE OCCASIONS. THEY STARTED DATING WHEN THEY WERE 19.
MUM DOESN'T LIKE TO TALK ABOUT IT. SHE GETS UPSET AT HOW OPEN I AM WITH MY OWN DEPRESSION SOMETIMES. I GUESS A LOT OF PEOPLE SEE IT AS A DIRTY SECRET.
SHE SPENT HER TWENTIES ON ANTIDEPRESSANTS, OFTEN STRUGGLING TO GET OUT OF BED.
BUT SOMETHING CHANGED WHEN SHE TURNED 29.
ME.
A PATHETIC PINK WORM THAT COULDN'T DO ANYTHING FOR ITSELF.
I THINK THAT WAS HER CALLING.
A RESPONSIBILITY AND LOVE THAT WAS STRONGER THAN HER MONSTER.

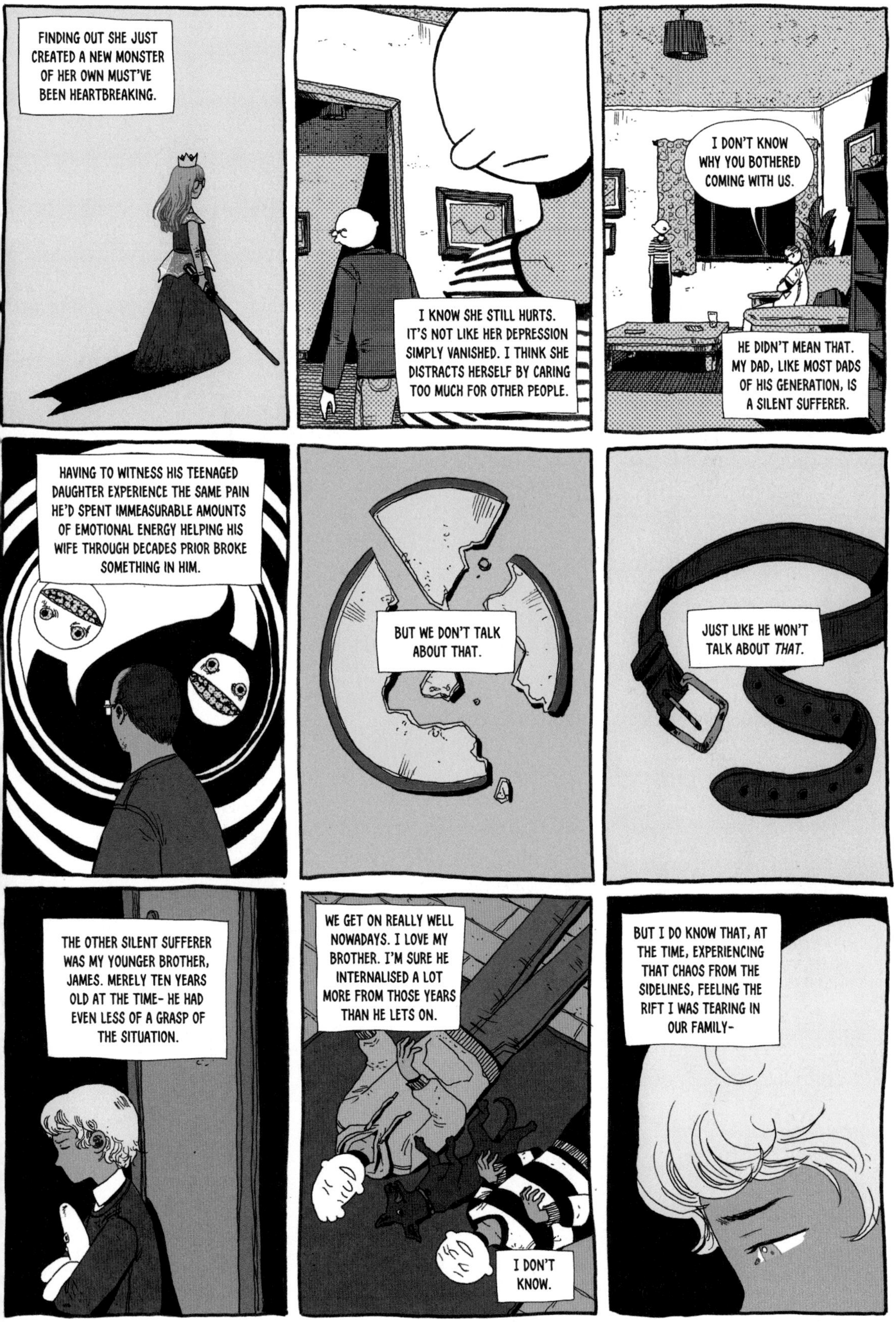

FINDING OUT SHE JUST CREATED A NEW MONSTER OF HER OWN MUST'VE BEEN HEARTBREAKING.
I KNOW SHE STILL HURTS. IT'S NOT LIKE HER DEPRESSION SIMPLY VANISHED. I THINK SHE DISTRACTS HERSELF BY CARING TOO MUCH FOR OTHER PEOPLE.
I DON'T KNOW WHY YOU BOTHERED COMING WITH US.
HE DIDN'T MEAN THAT. MY DAD, LIKE MOST DADS OF HIS GENERATION, IS A SILENT SUFFERER.
HAVING TO WITNESS HIS TEENAGED DAUGHTER EXPERIENCE THE SAME PAIN HE'D SPENT IMMEASURABLE AMOUNTS OF EMOTIONAL ENERGY HELPING HIS WIFE THROUGH DECADES PRIOR BROKE SOMETHING IN HIM.
BUT WE DON'T TALK ABOUT THAT.
JUST LIKE HE WON'T TALK ABOUT *THAT*.
THE OTHER SILENT SUFFERER WAS MY YOUNGER BROTHER, JAMES. MERELY TEN YEARS OLD AT THE TIME- HE HAD EVEN LESS OF A GRASP OF THE SITUATION.
WE GET ON REALLY WELL NOWADAYS. I LOVE MY BROTHER. I'M SURE HE INTERNALISED A LOT MORE FROM THOSE YEARS THAN HE LETS ON.
I DON'T KNOW.
BUT I DO KNOW THAT, AT THE TIME, EXPERIENCING THAT CHAOS FROM THE SIDELINES, FEELING THE RIFT I WAS TEARING IN OUR FAMILY-

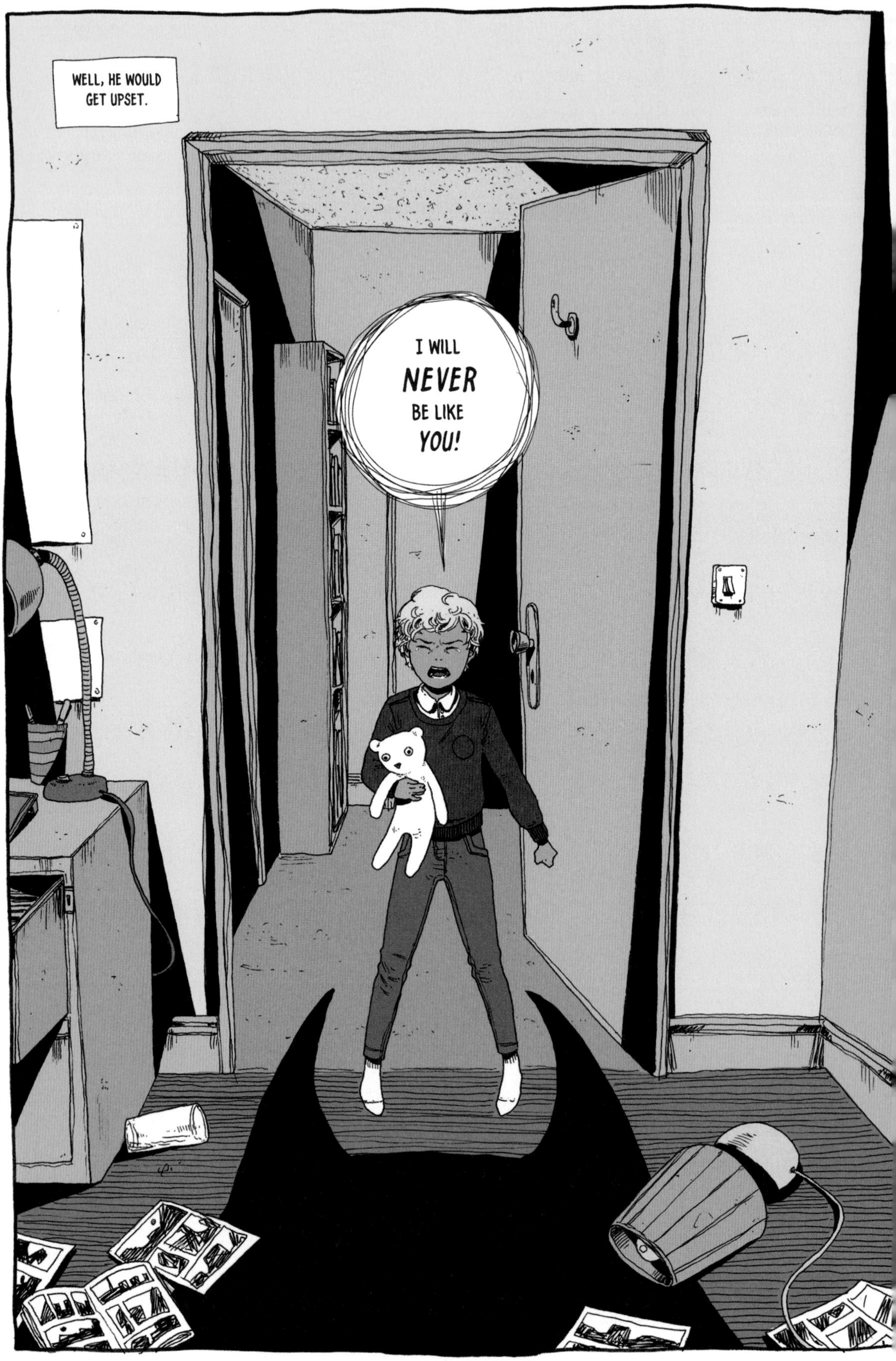
WELL, HE WOULD GET UPSET.
I WILL NEVER BE LIKE YOU!

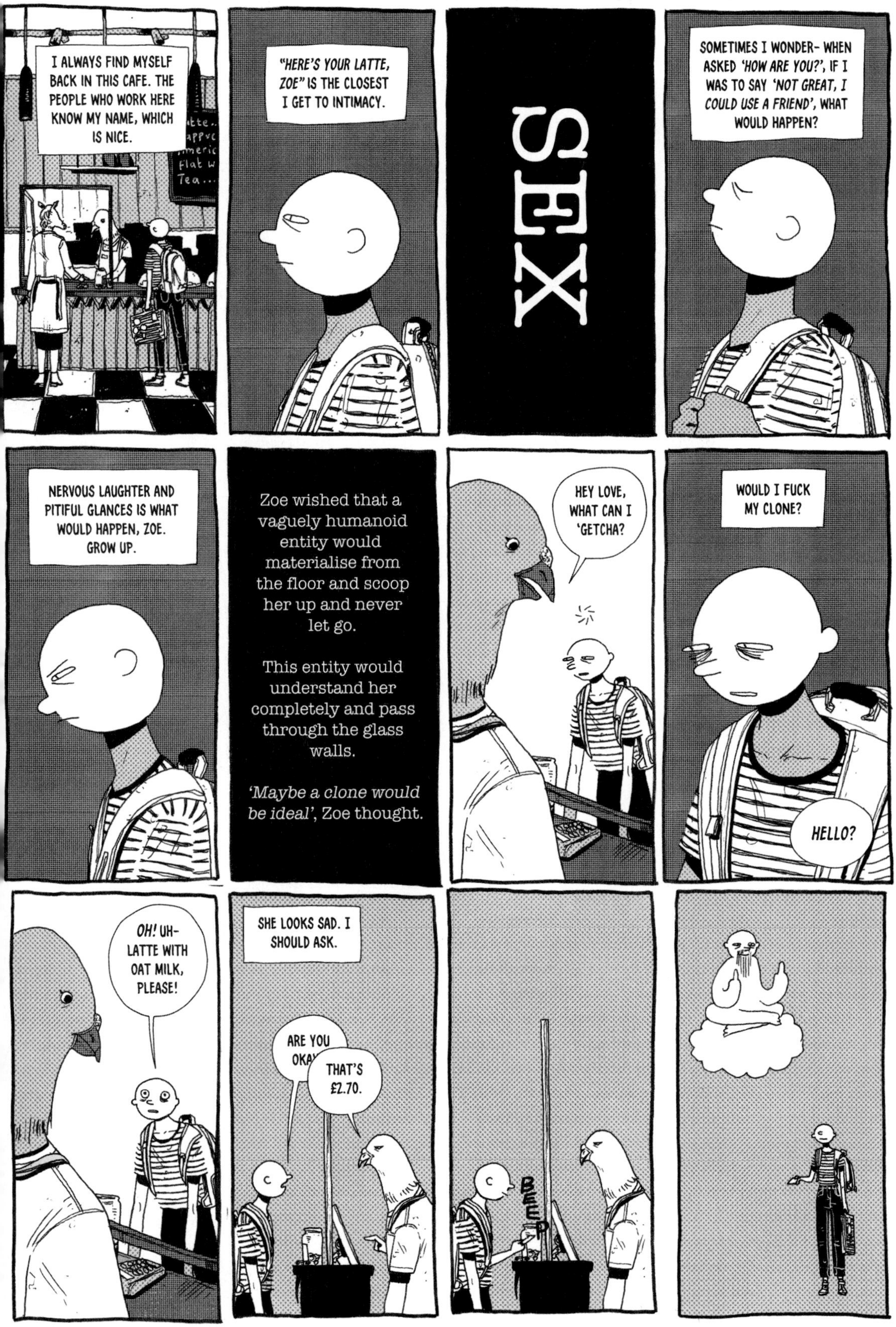

I ALWAYS FIND MYSELF BACK IN THIS CAFE. THE PEOPLE WHO WORK HERE KNOW MY NAME, WHICH IS NICE.
"HERE'S YOUR LATTE, ZOE" IS THE CLOSEST I GET TO INTIMACY.
SEX
SOMETIMES I WONDER- WHEN ASKED 'HOW ARE YOU?', IF I WAS TO SAY 'NOT GREAT, I COULD USE A FRIEND', WHAT WOULD HAPPEN?
NERVOUS LAUGHTER AND PITIFUL GLANCES IS WHAT WOULD HAPPEN, ZOE. GROW UP.
Zoe wished that a vaguely humanoid entity would materialise from the floor and scoop her up and never let go.
This entity would understand her completely and pass through the glass walls.
'Maybe a clone would be ideal', Zoe thought.
HEY LOVE, WHAT CAN I 'GETCHA?
WOULD I FUCK MY CLONE?
HELLO?
OH! UH- LATTE WITH OAT MILK, PLEASE!
SHE LOOKS SAD. I SHOULD ASK.
ARE YOU OKAY
THAT'S £2.70.
BEEP

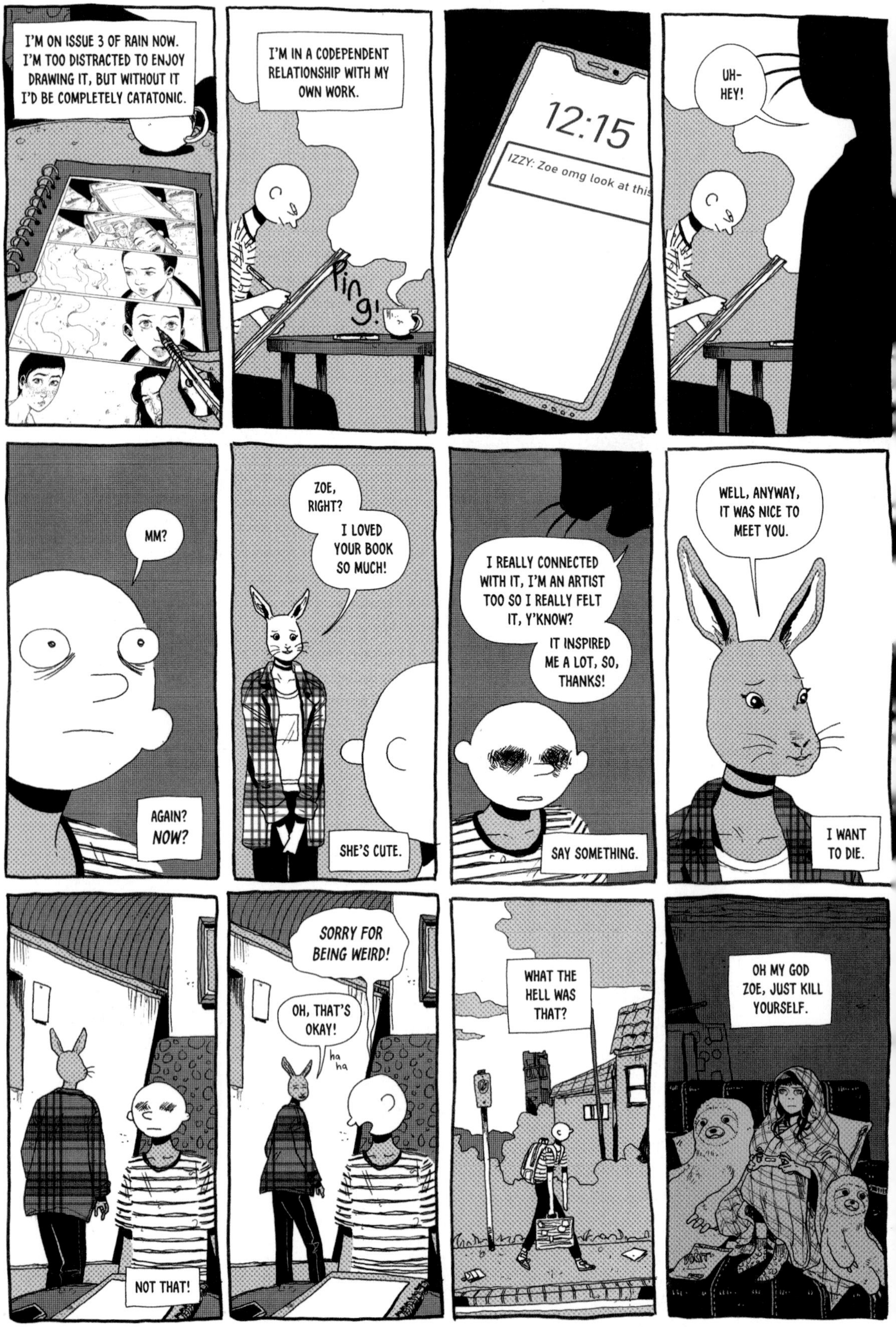
I'M ON ISSUE 3 OF RAIN NOW. I'M TOO DISTRACTED TO ENJOY DRAWING IT, BUT WITHOUT IT I'D BE COMPLETELY CATATONIC.
I'M IN A CODEPENDENT RELATIONSHIP WITH MY OWN WORK.
Ping!
12:15
IZZY: Zoe omg look at this
UH-HEY!
MM?
AGAIN? NOW?
ZOE, RIGHT?
I LOVED YOUR BOOK SO MUCH!
SHE'S CUTE.
I REALLY CONNECTED WITH IT, I'M AN ARTIST TOO SO I REALLY FELT IT, Y'KNOW?
IT INSPIRED ME A LOT, SO, THANKS!
SAY SOMETHING.
WELL, ANYWAY, IT WAS NICE TO MEET YOU.
I WANT TO DIE.
NOT THAT!
SORRY FOR BEING WEIRD!
OH, THAT'S OKAY!
ha ha
WHAT THE HELL WAS THAT?
OH MY GOD ZOE, JUST KILL YOURSELF.

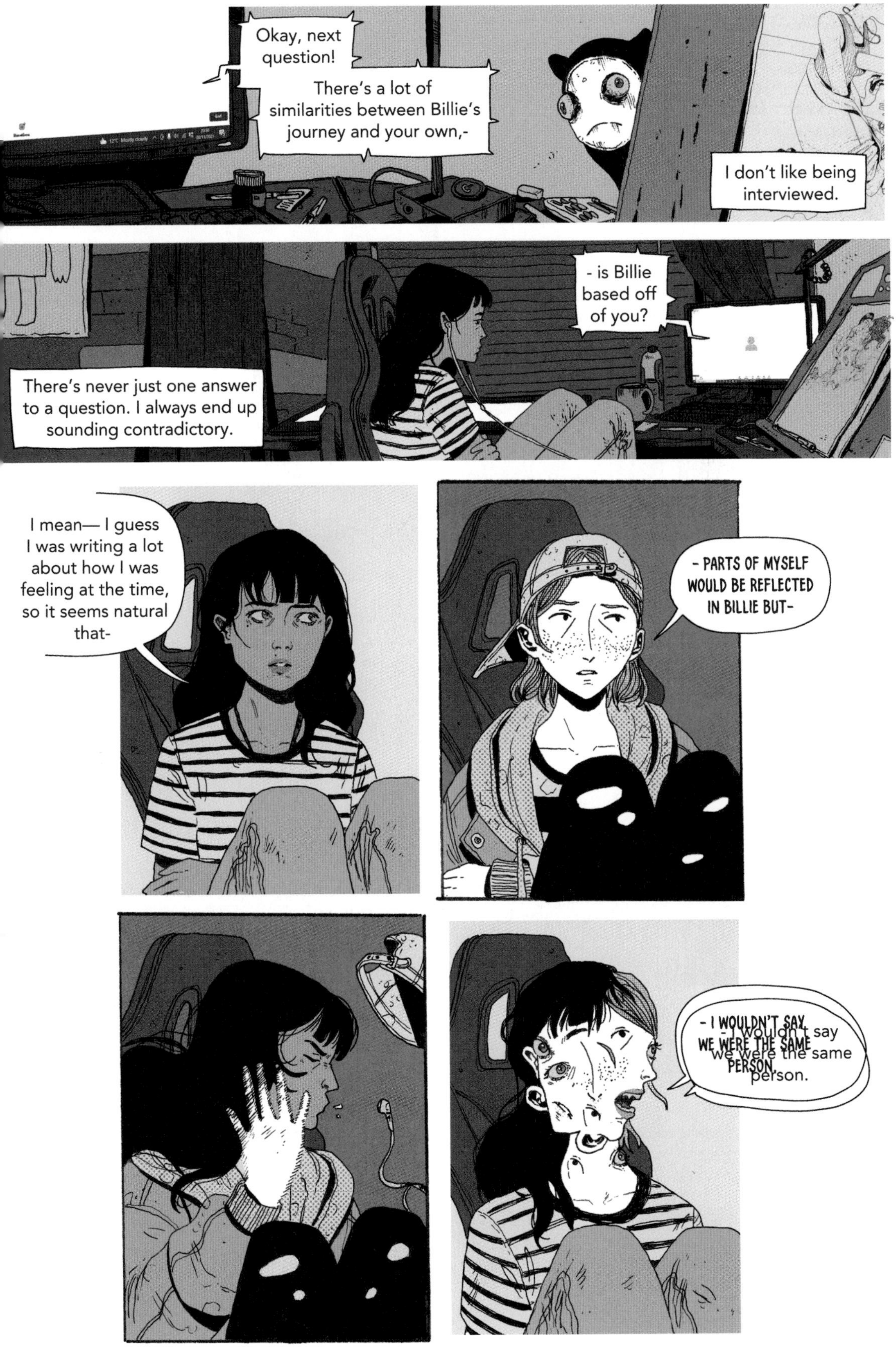
Okay, next question!
There's a lot of similarities between Billie's journey and your own,-
I don't like being interviewed.
- is Billie based off of you?
There's never just one answer to a question. I always end up sounding contradictory.
I mean— I guess I was writing a lot about how I was feeling at the time, so it seems natural that-
- PARTS OF MYSELF WOULD BE REFLECTED IN BILLIE BUT-
- I WOULDN'T SAY WE WERE THE SAME PERSON.
- I wouldn't say we were the same person.

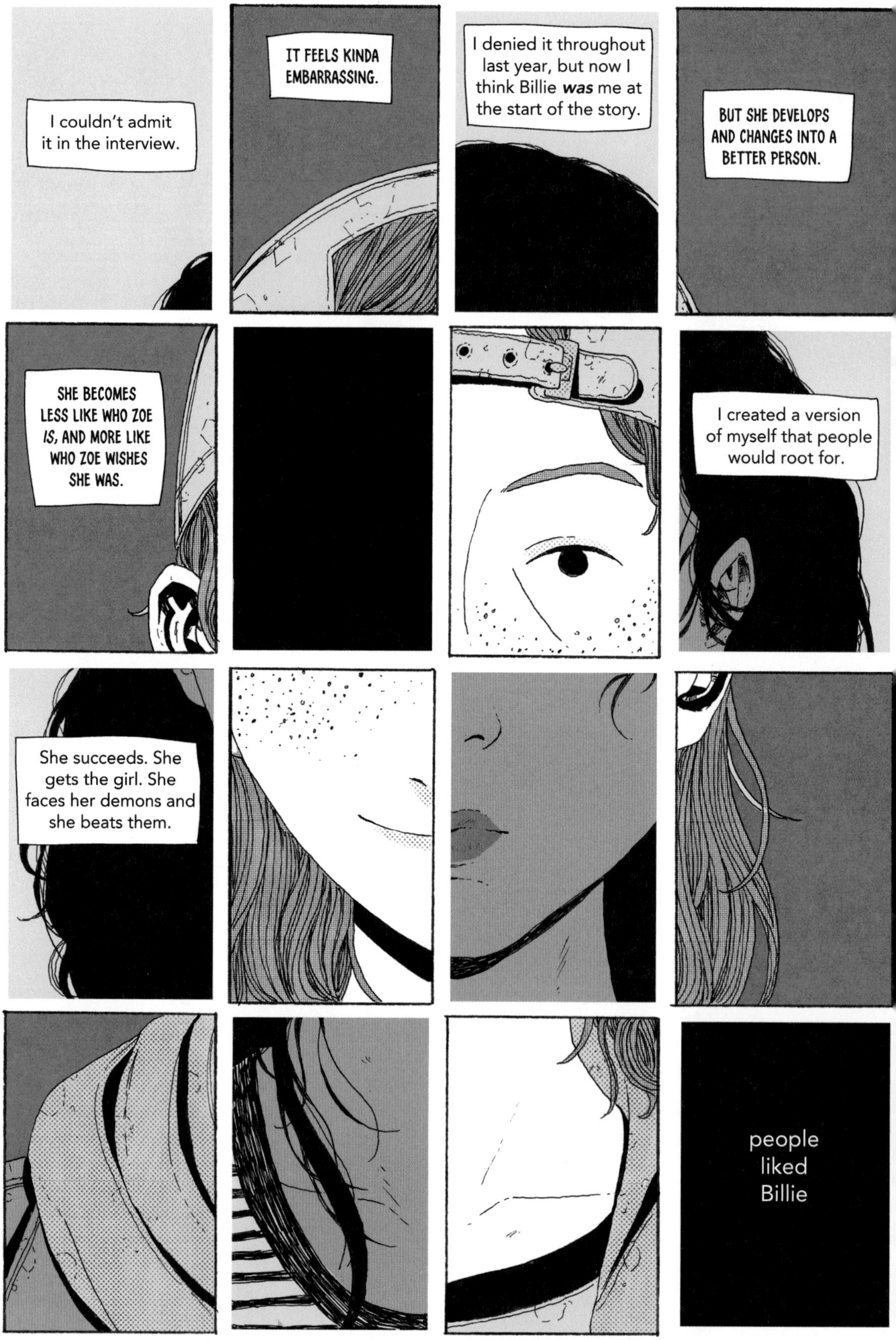
I couldn't admit
it in the interview.
IT FEELS KINDA
EMBARRASSING.
I denied it throughout
last year, but now I
think Billie *was* me at
the start of the story.
BUT SHE DEVELOPS
AND CHANGES INTO A
BETTER PERSON.
SHE BECOMES
LESS LIKE WHO ZOE
IS, AND MORE LIKE
WHO ZOE WISHES
SHE WAS.
I created a version
of myself that people
would root for.
She succeeds. She
gets the girl. She
faces her demons and
she beats them.
people
liked
Billie

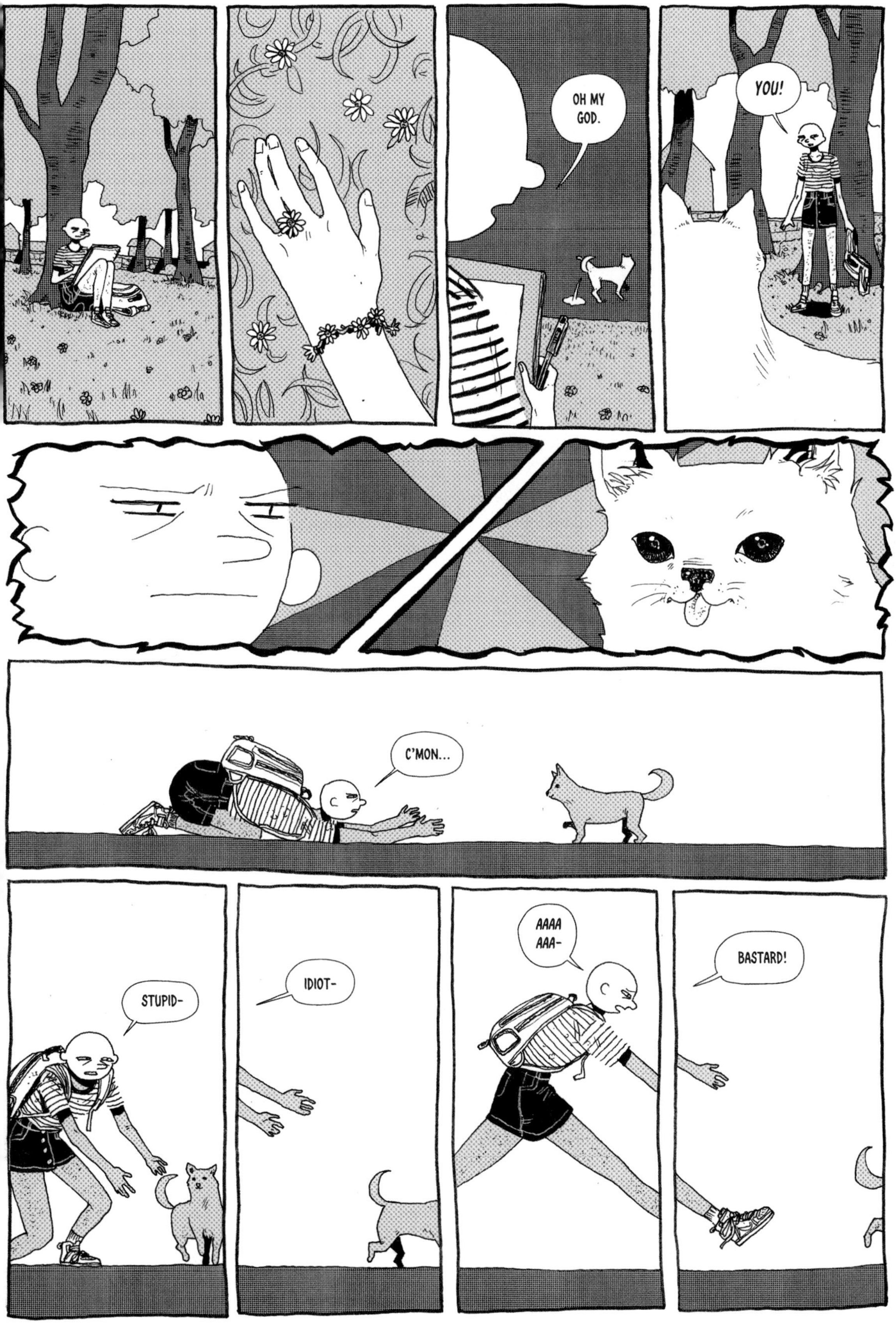
OH MY GOD.
YOU!
C'MON...
STUPID-
IDIOT-
AAAA AAA-
BASTARD!

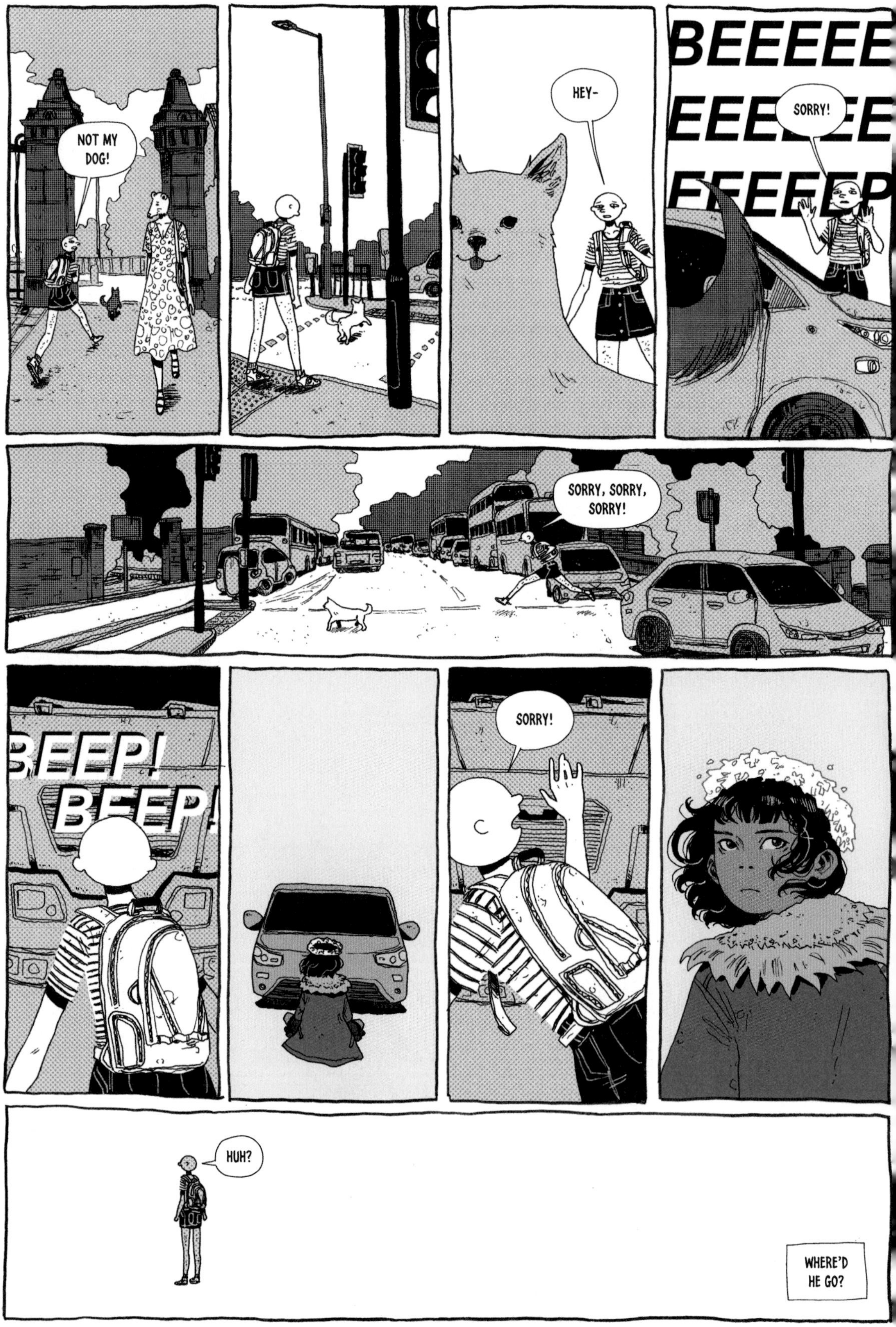
NOT MY DOG!
HEY-
BEEEEEEEEEEEEEEEP
SORRY!
SORRY, SORRY, SORRY!
BEEP! BEEP!
SORRY!
HUH?
WHERE'D HE GO?

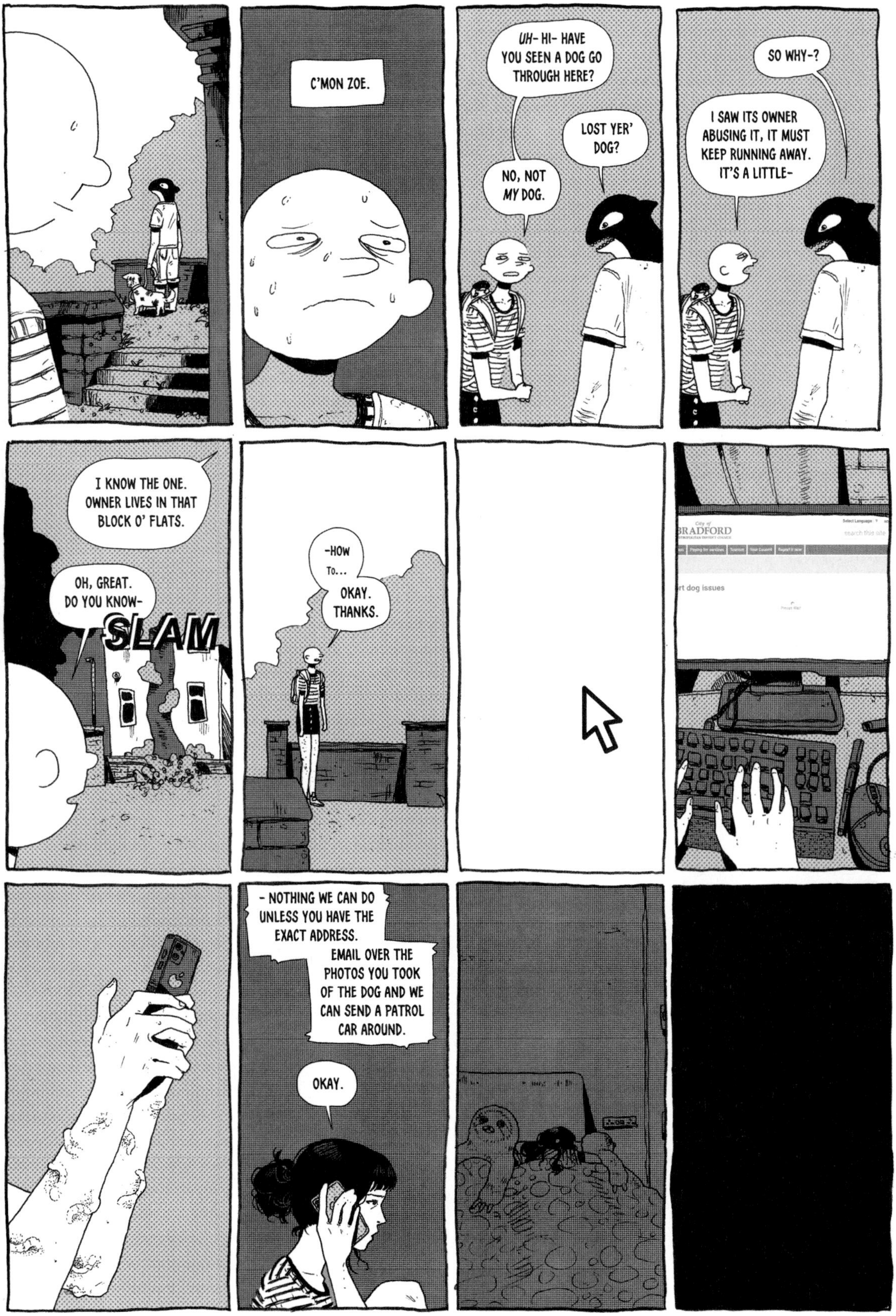
C'MON ZOE.
UH- HI- HAVE YOU SEEN A DOG GO THROUGH HERE?
LOST YER' DOG?
NO, NOT MY DOG.
SO WHY-?
I SAW ITS OWNER ABUSING IT, IT MUST KEEP RUNNING AWAY. IT'S A LITTLE-
I KNOW THE ONE. OWNER LIVES IN THAT BLOCK O' FLATS.
OH, GREAT. DO YOU KNOW-
SLAM
-HOW TO...
OKAY. THANKS.
BRADFORD
rt dog issues
- NOTHING WE CAN DO UNLESS YOU HAVE THE EXACT ADDRESS.
EMAIL OVER THE PHOTOS YOU TOOK OF THE DOG AND WE CAN SEND A PATROL CAR AROUND.
OKAY.

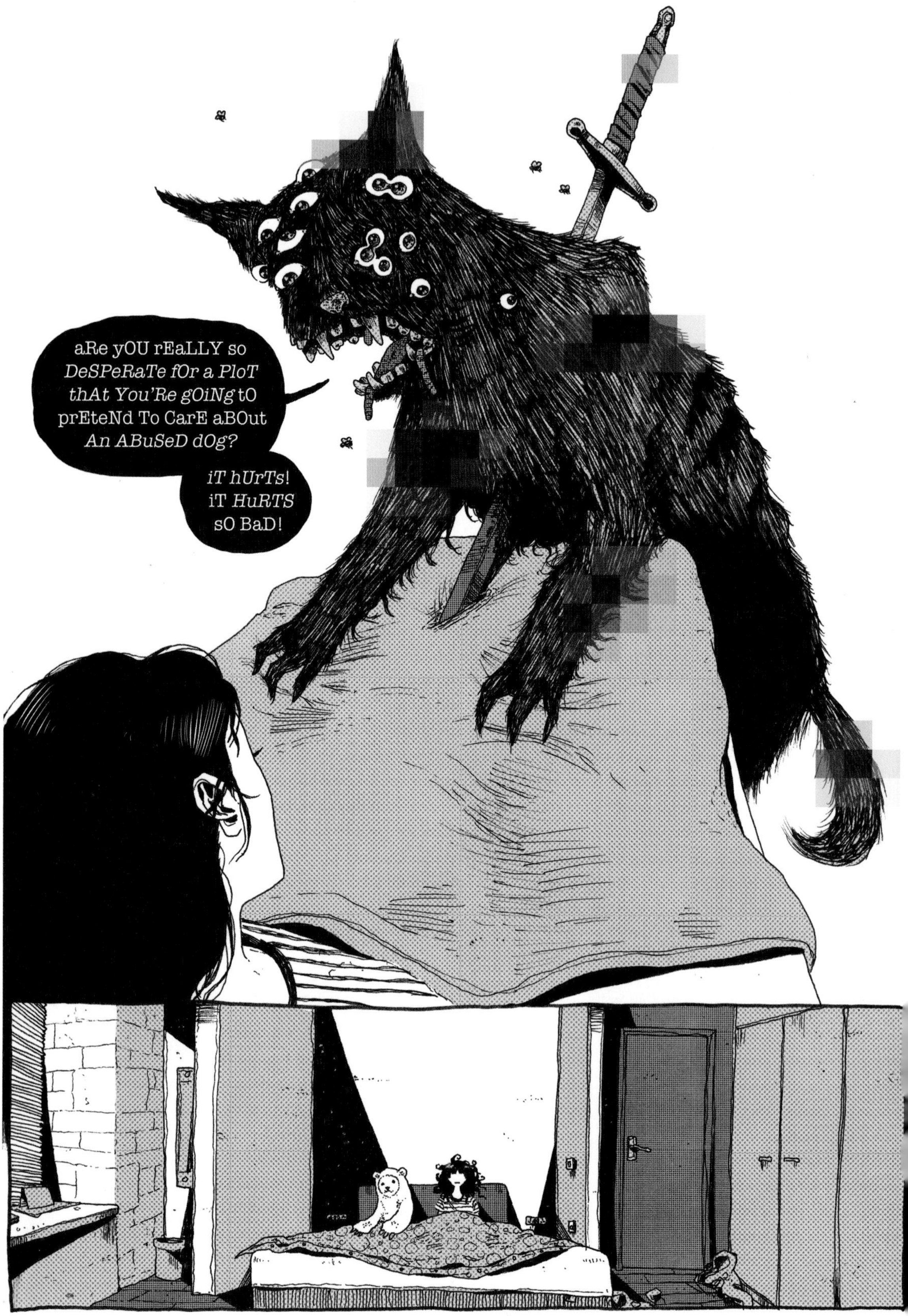
aRe yOU rEaLLY so DeSPeRaTe fOr a PloT thAt You'Re gOiNg tO prEteNd To CarE aBOut An ABuSeD dOg?
iT hUrTs! iT HuRTS sO BaD!

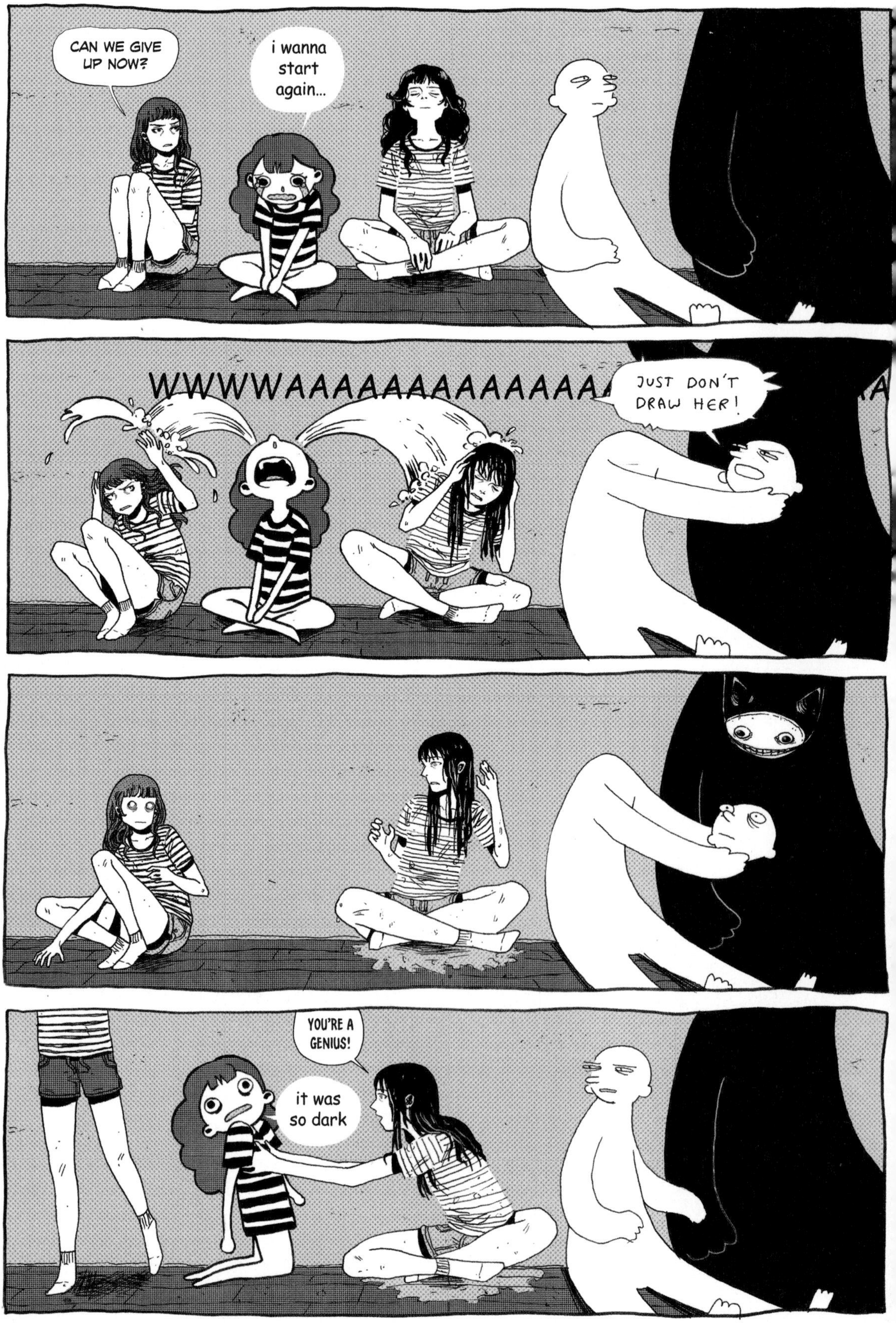
CAN WE GIVE UP NOW?
i wanna start again...
WWWWAAAAAAAAAAAAAA
JUST DON'T DRAW HER!
YOU'RE A GENIUS!
it was so dark

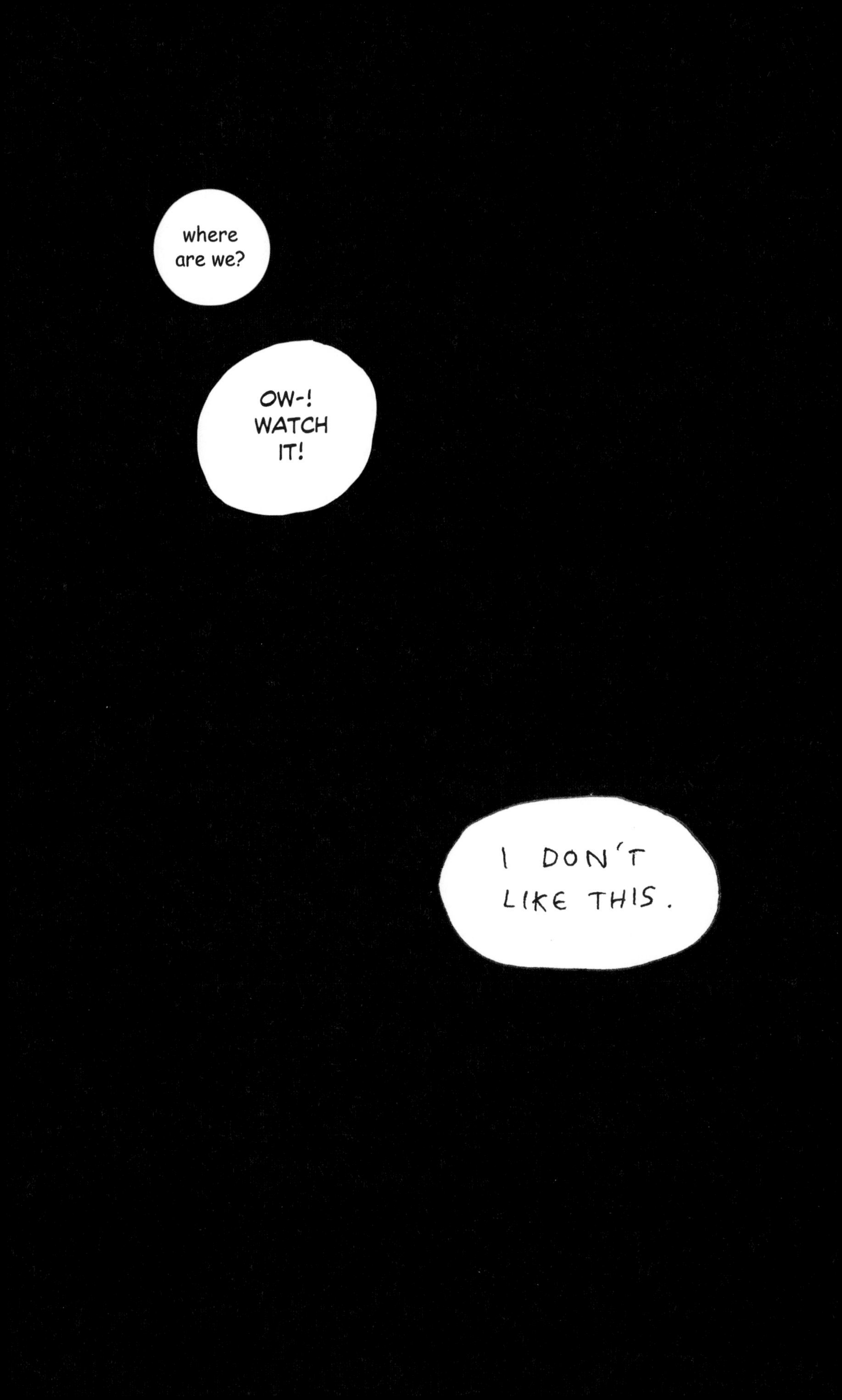
where are we?
OW-! WATCH IT!
I DON'T LIKE THIS.

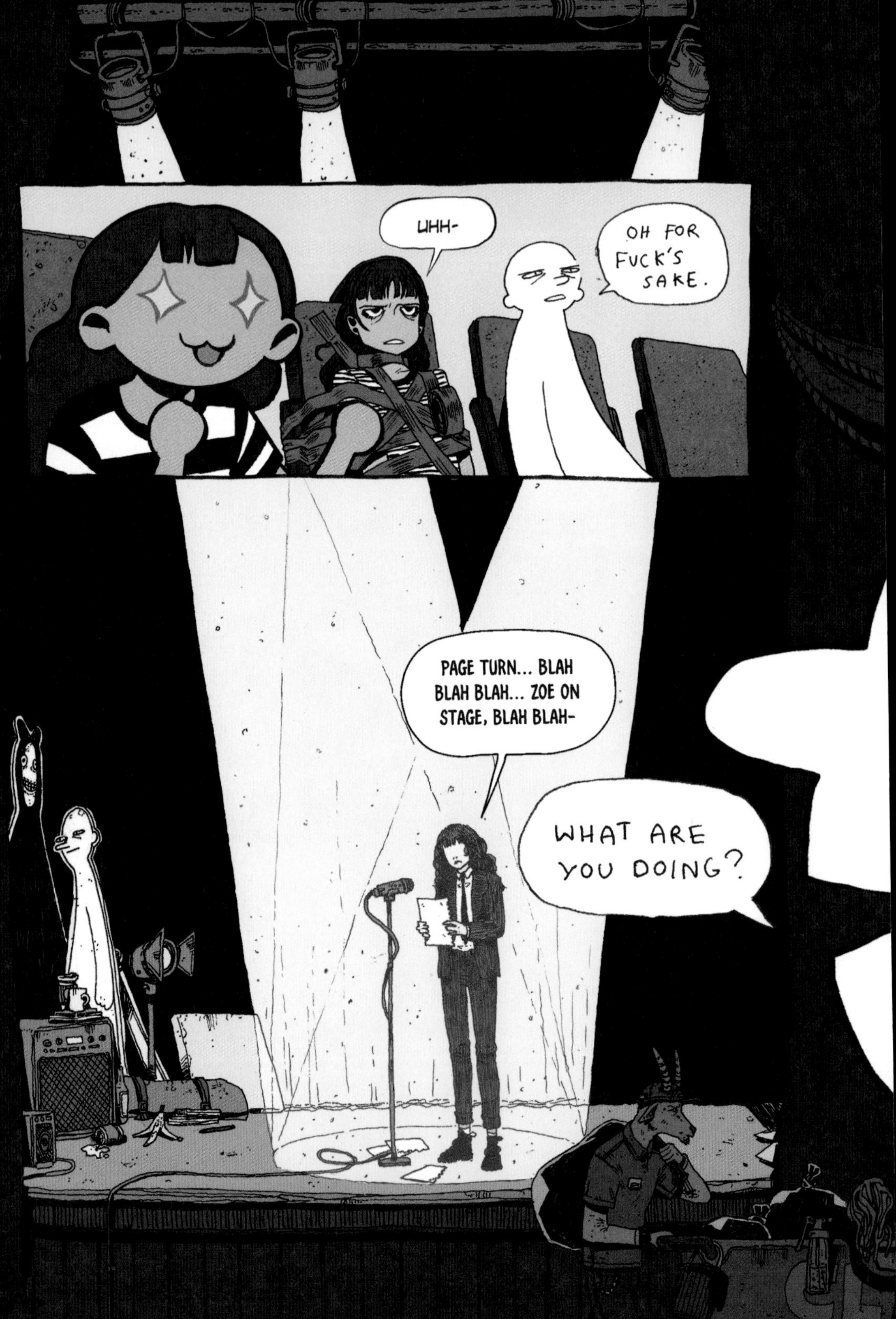

UHH-
OH FOR FUCK'S SAKE.
PAGE TURN... BLAH BLAH BLAH... ZOE ON STAGE, BLAH BLAH-
WHAT ARE YOU DOING?

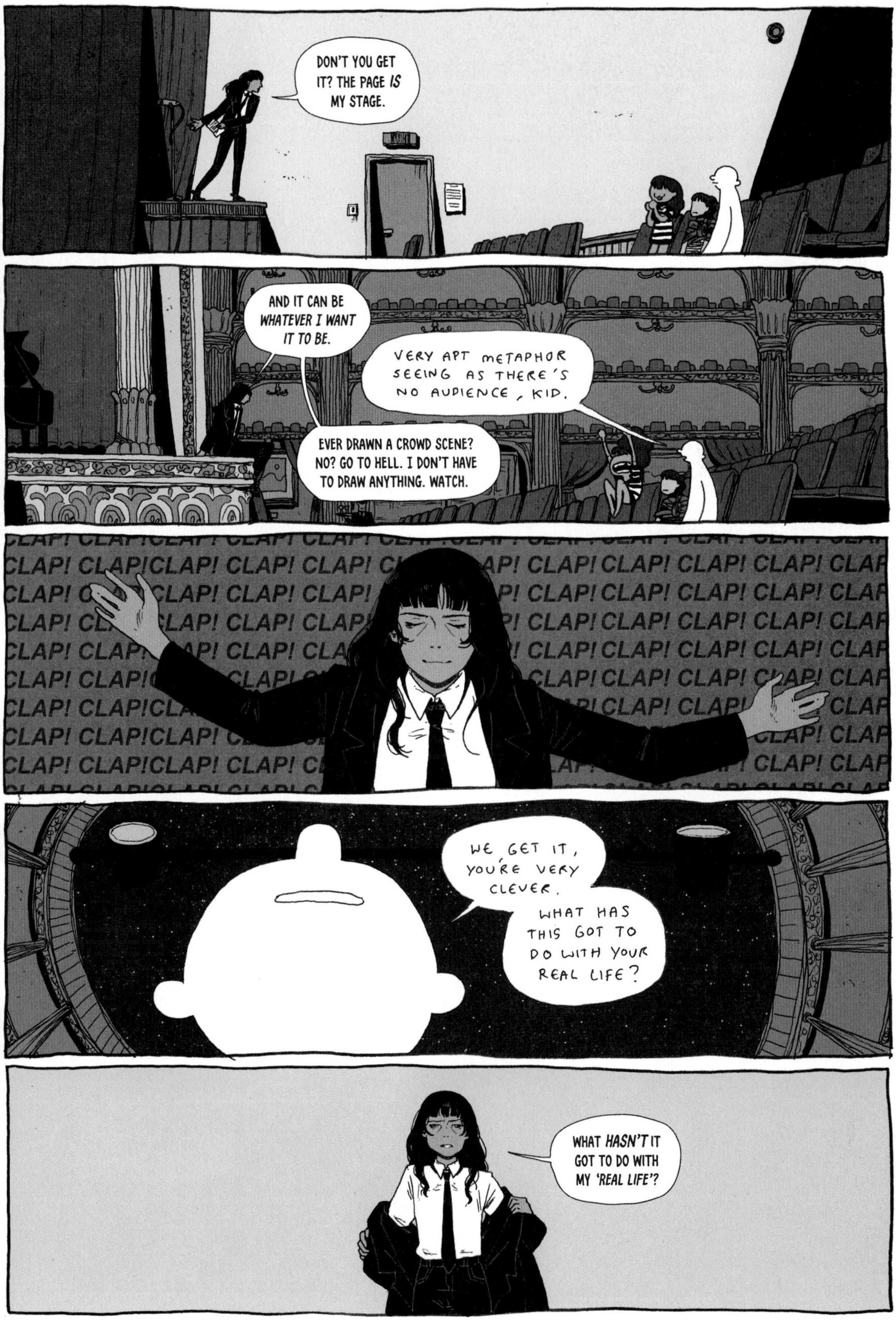
DON'T YOU GET IT? THE PAGE *IS* MY STAGE.
AND IT CAN BE *WHATEVER I WANT IT TO BE.*
VERY APT METAPHOR SEEING AS THERE'S NO AUDIENCE, KID.
EVER DRAWN A CROWD SCENE? NO? GO TO HELL. I DON'T HAVE TO DRAW ANYTHING. WATCH.
CLAP! CLAP! CLAP! CLAP! CLAP! CLAP! CLAP! CLAP!
WE GET IT, YOU'RE VERY CLEVER.
WHAT HAS THIS GOT TO DO WITH YOUR REAL LIFE?
WHAT *HASN'T* IT GOT TO DO WITH MY *'REAL LIFE'*?

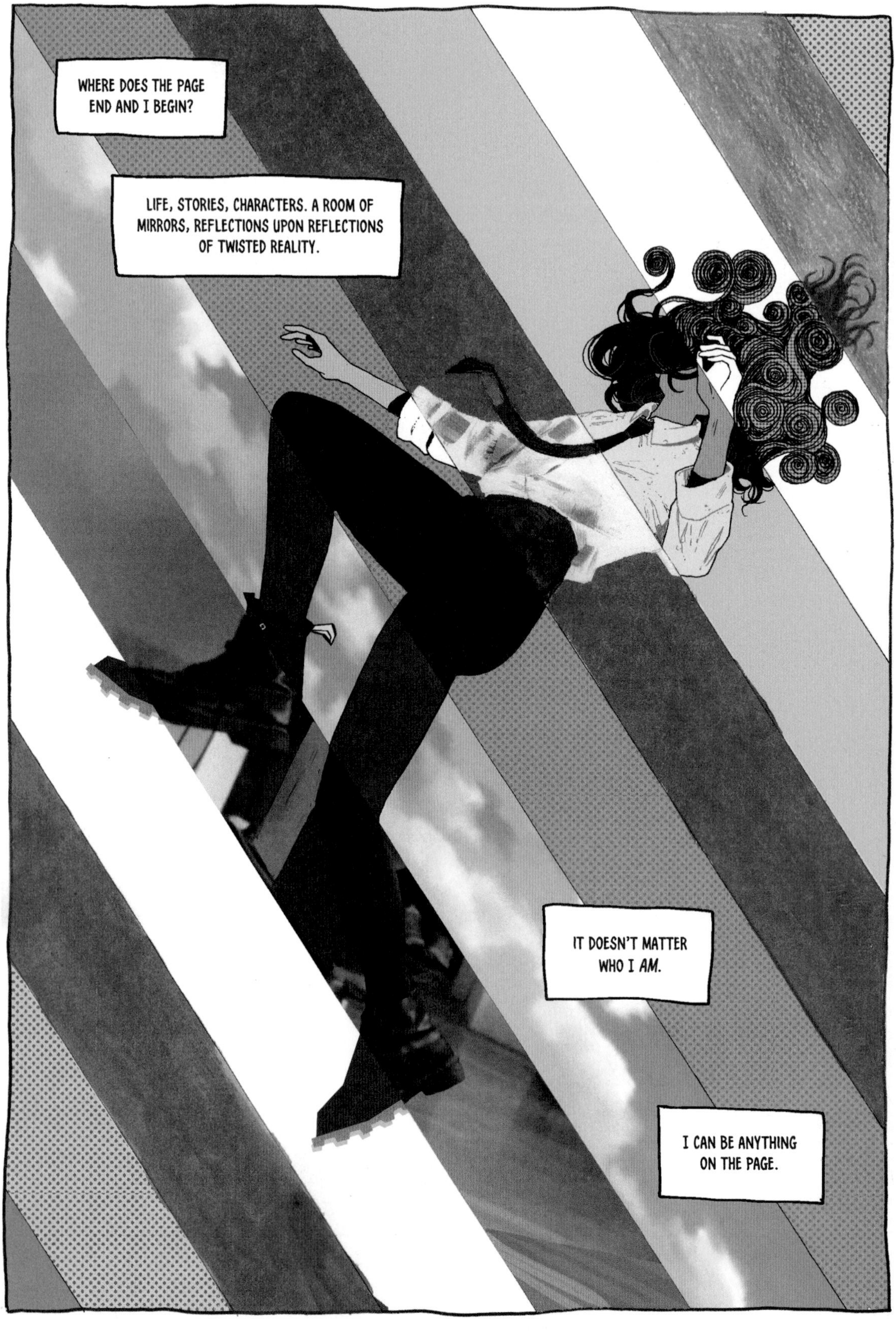
WHERE DOES THE PAGE END AND I BEGIN?
LIFE, STORIES, CHARACTERS. A ROOM OF MIRRORS, REFLECTIONS UPON REFLECTIONS OF TWISTED REALITY.
IT DOESN'T MATTER WHO I *AM*.
I CAN BE ANYTHING ON THE PAGE.

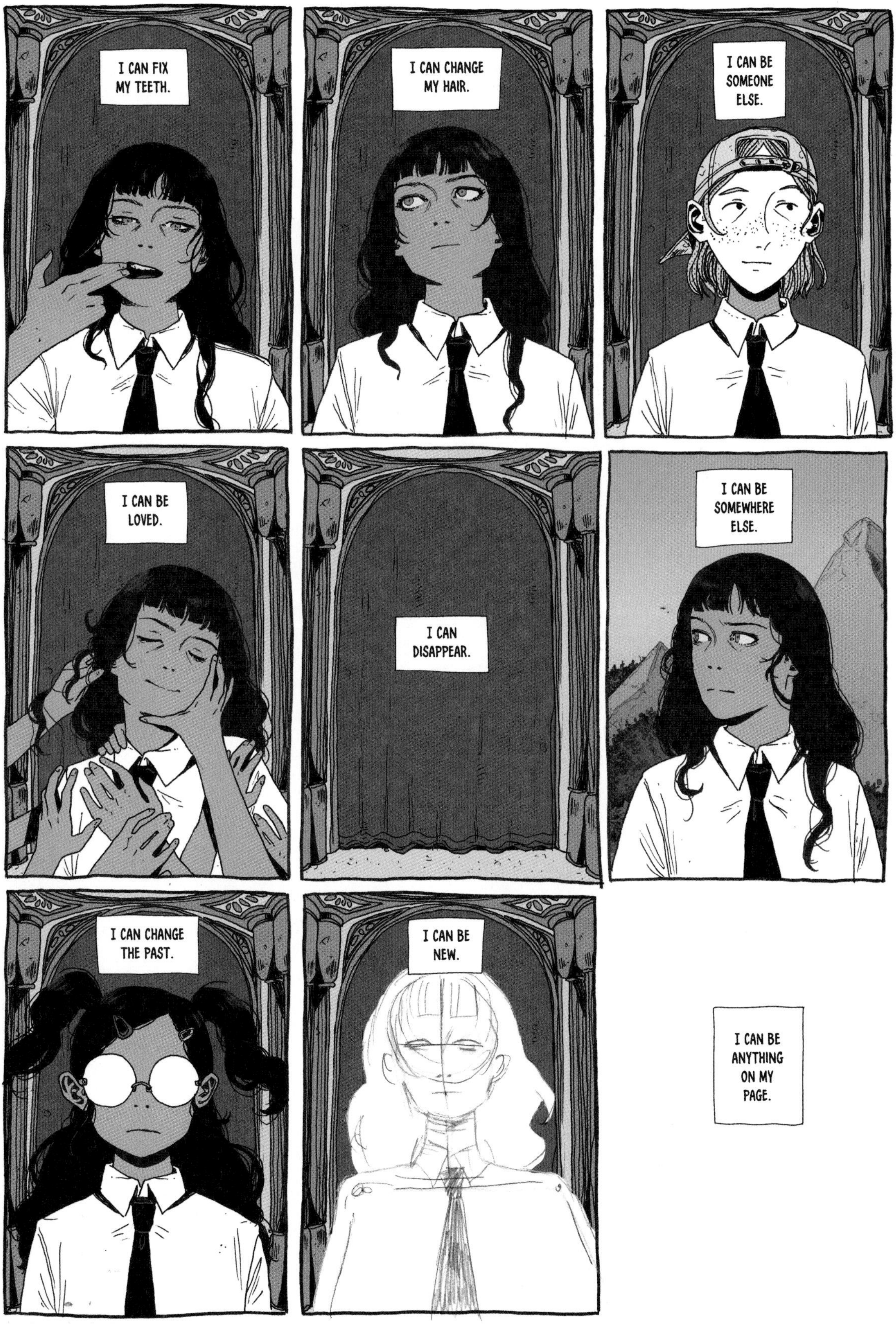

I CAN FIX MY TEETH.
I CAN CHANGE MY HAIR.
I CAN BE SOMEONE ELSE.
I CAN BE LOVED.
I CAN DISAPPEAR.
I CAN BE SOMEWHERE ELSE.
I CAN CHANGE THE PAST.
I CAN BE NEW.
I CAN BE ANYTHING ON MY PAGE.

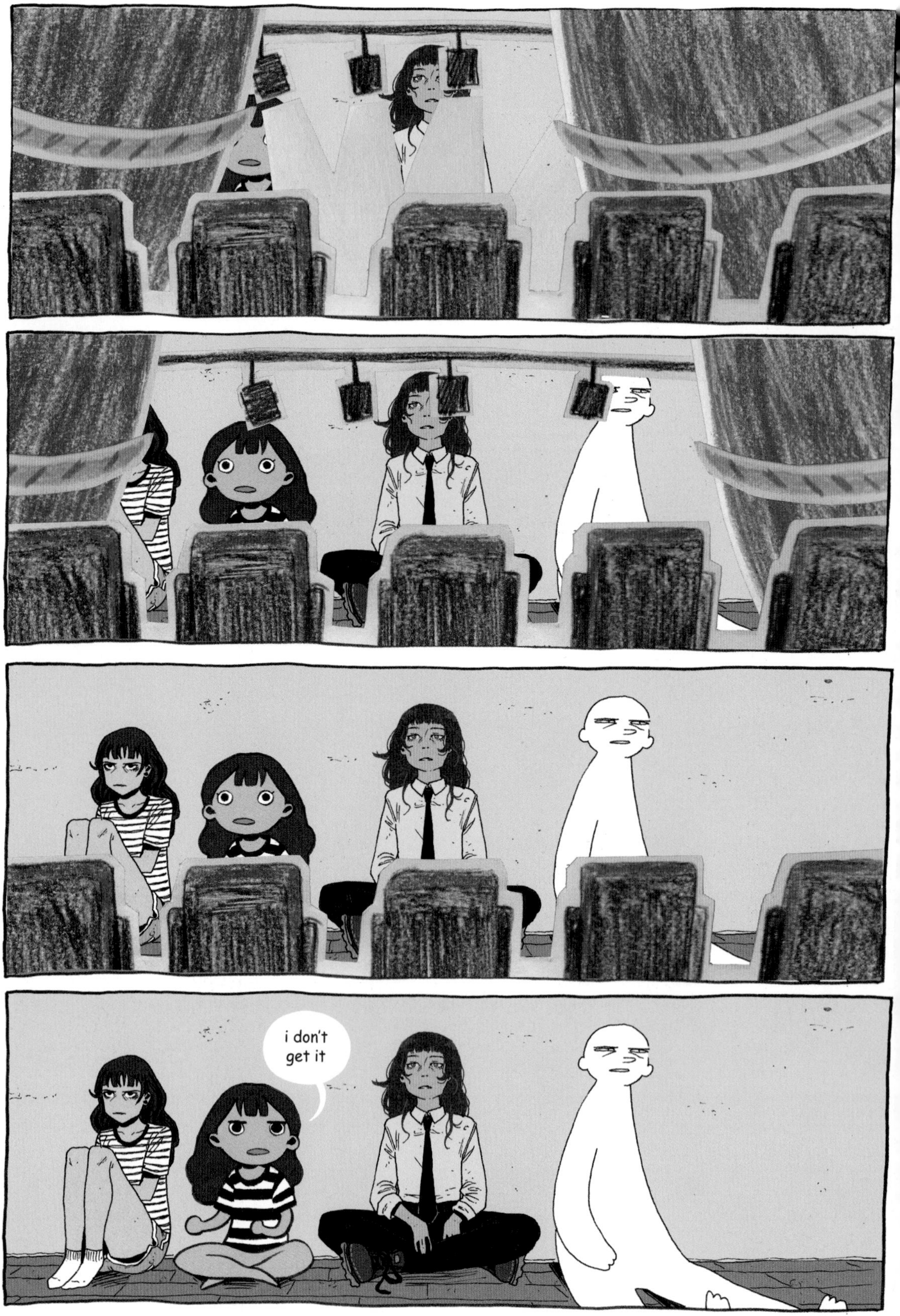
i don't get it

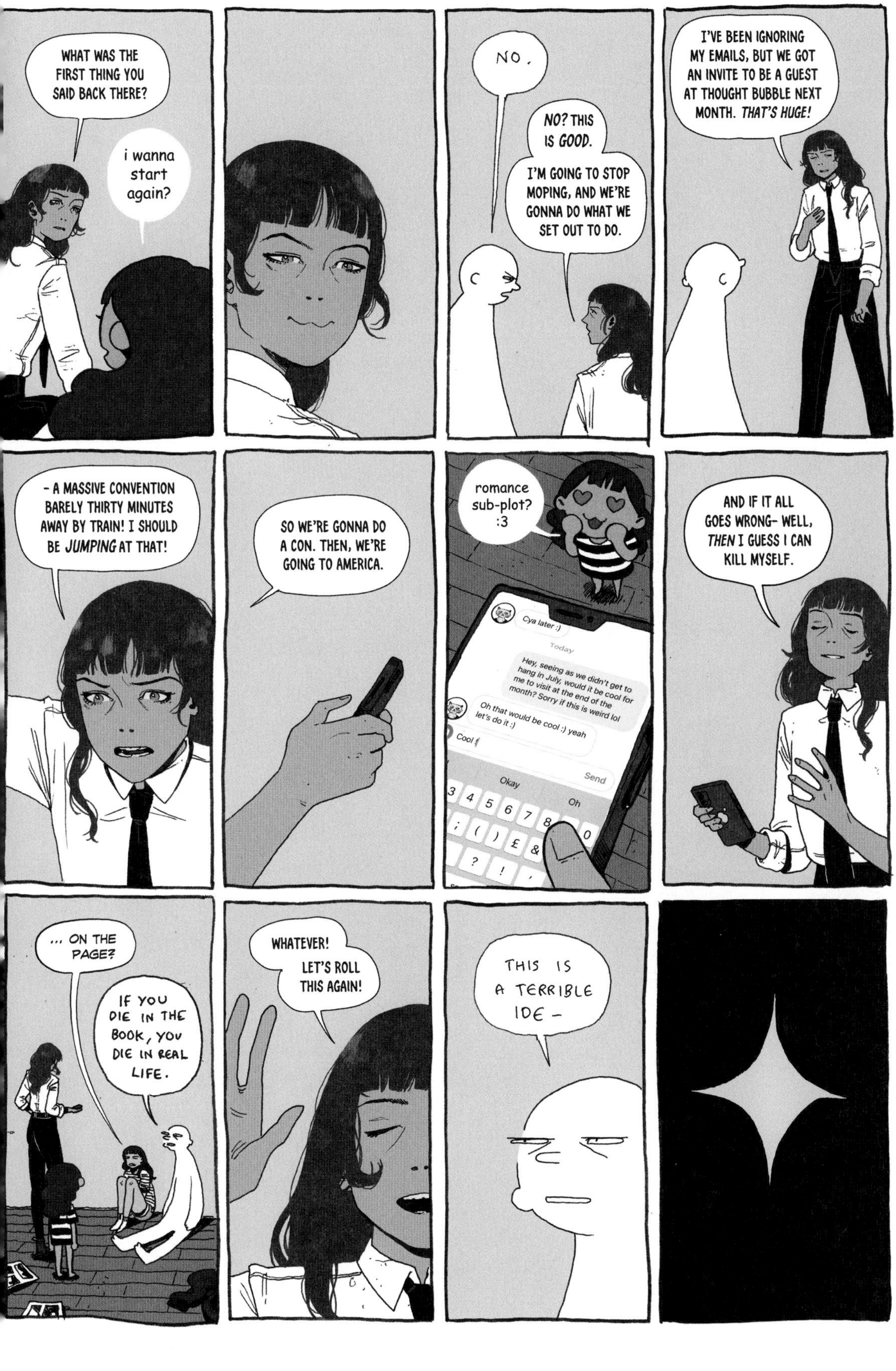
WHAT WAS THE FIRST THING YOU SAID BACK THERE?
i wanna start again?
NO.
NO? THIS IS GOOD.
I'M GOING TO STOP MOPING, AND WE'RE GONNA DO WHAT WE SET OUT TO DO.
I'VE BEEN IGNORING MY EMAILS, BUT WE GOT AN INVITE TO BE A GUEST AT THOUGHT BUBBLE NEXT MONTH. THAT'S HUGE!
- A MASSIVE CONVENTION BARELY THIRTY MINUTES AWAY BY TRAIN! I SHOULD BE JUMPING AT THAT!
SO WE'RE GONNA DO A CON. THEN, WE'RE GOING TO AMERICA.
romance sub-plot? :3
Cya later :)
Today
Hey, seeing as we didn't get to hang in July, would it be cool for me to visit at the end of the month? Sorry if this is weird lol
Oh that would be cool :) yeah let's do it :)
Cool
Send
Okay
Oh
AND IF IT ALL GOES WRONG- WELL, THEN I GUESS I CAN KILL MYSELF.
... ON THE PAGE?
IF YOU DIE IN THE BOOK, YOU DIE IN REAL LIFE.
WHATEVER!
LET'S ROLL THIS AGAIN!
THIS IS A TERRIBLE IDE -

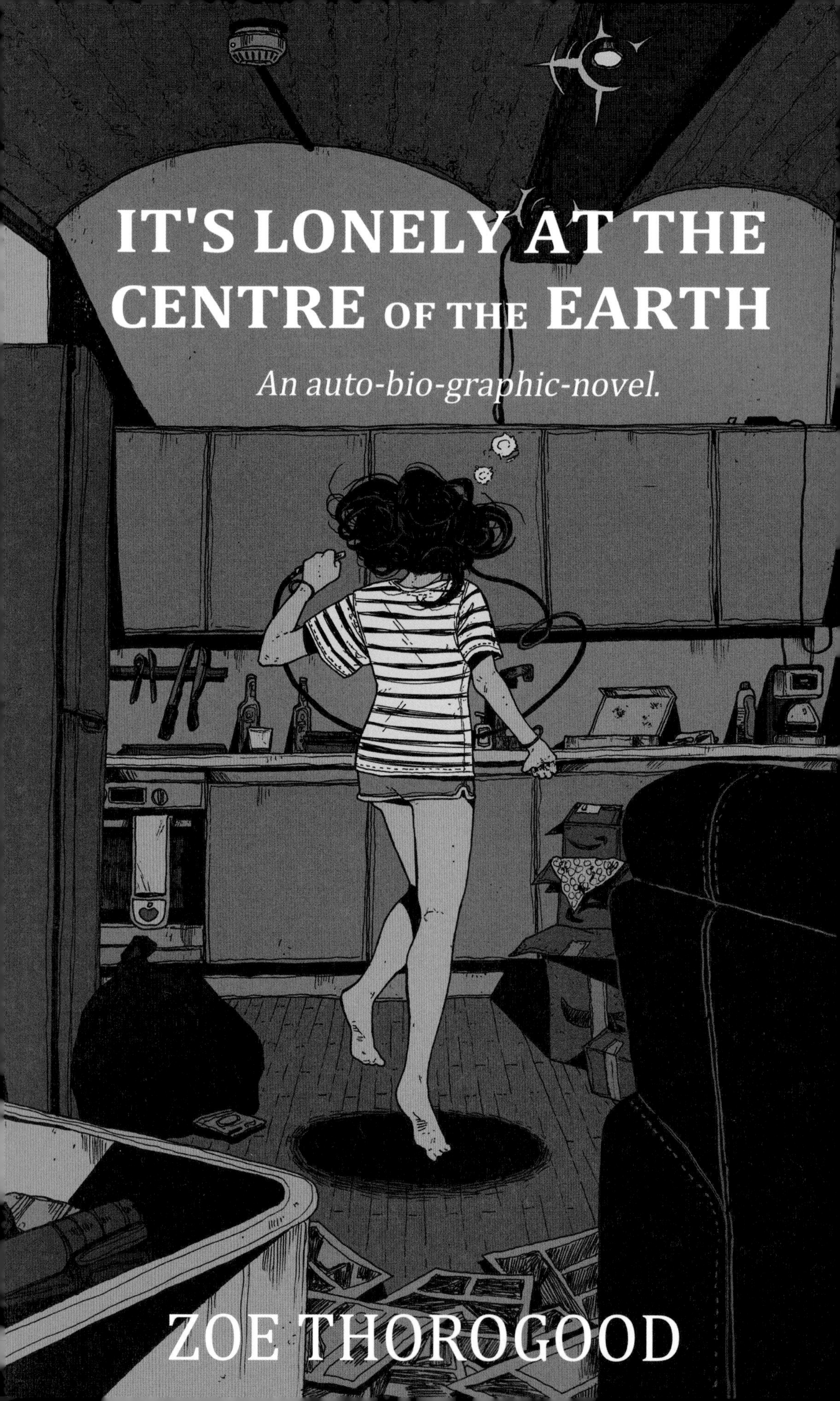
IT'S LONELY AT THE CENTRE OF THE EARTH
An auto-bio-graphic-novel.
ZOE THOROGOOD

IT'S LONELY AT THE CENTRE OF THE EARTH

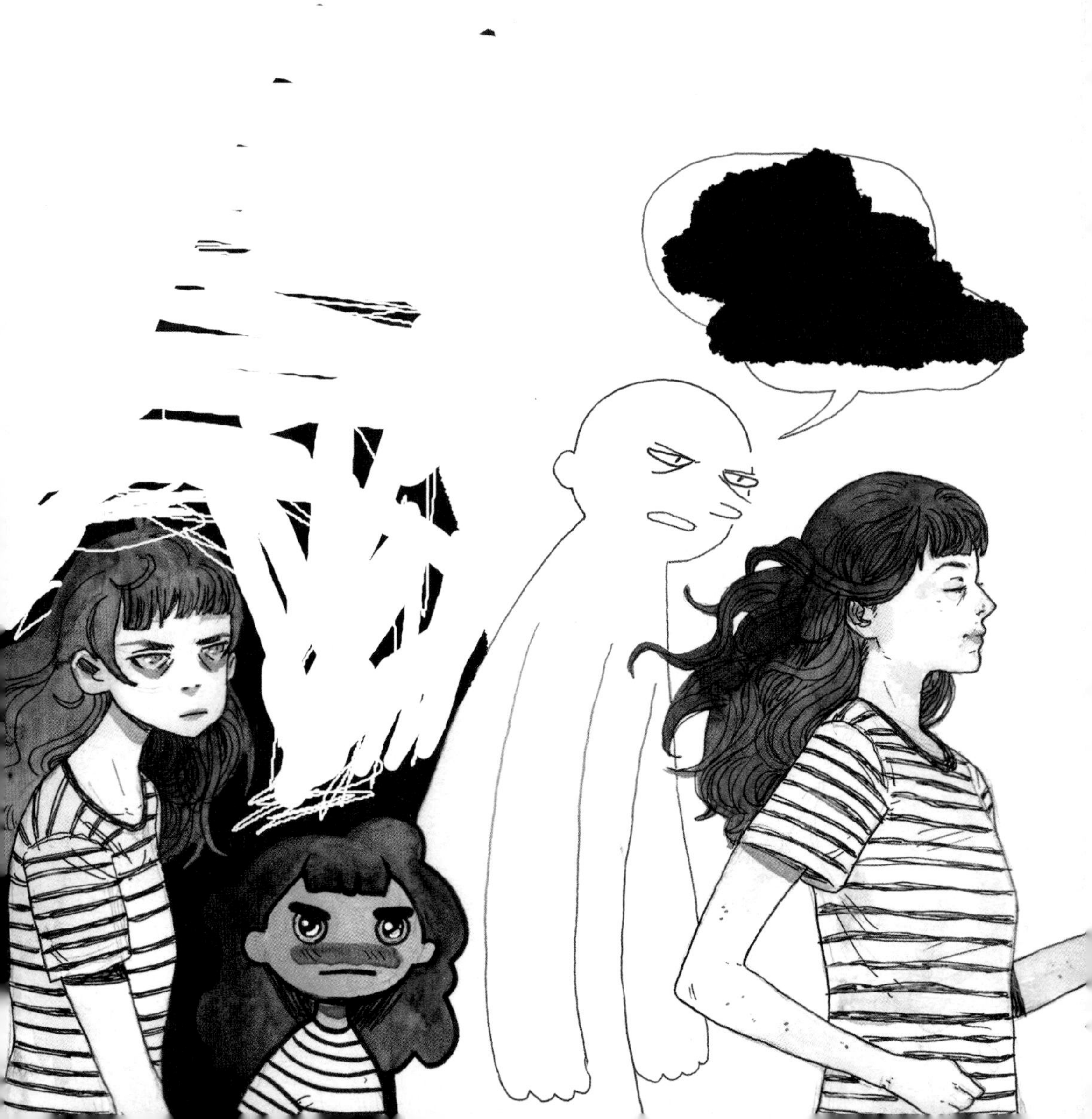

IT'S LONELY AT THE CENTRE OF THE EARTH. Fourth printing. September 2023. Published by Image Comics, Inc. Office of publication: PO BOX 14457, Portland, OR 97293. Copyright © 2023 Zoe Thorogood. All rights reserved. "It's Lonely at the Centre of the Earth," its logos, and the likenesses of all characters herein are trademarks of Zoe Thorogood, unless otherwise noted. "Image" and the Image Comics logos are registered trademarks of Image Comics, Inc. No part of this publication may be reproduced or transmitted, in any form or by any means (except for short excerpts for journalistic or review purposes), without the express written permission of Zoe Thorogood or Image Comics, Inc. Printed in the USA. For international rights, contact: foreignlicensing@imagecomics.com. ISBN: 978-1-5343-2386-5.

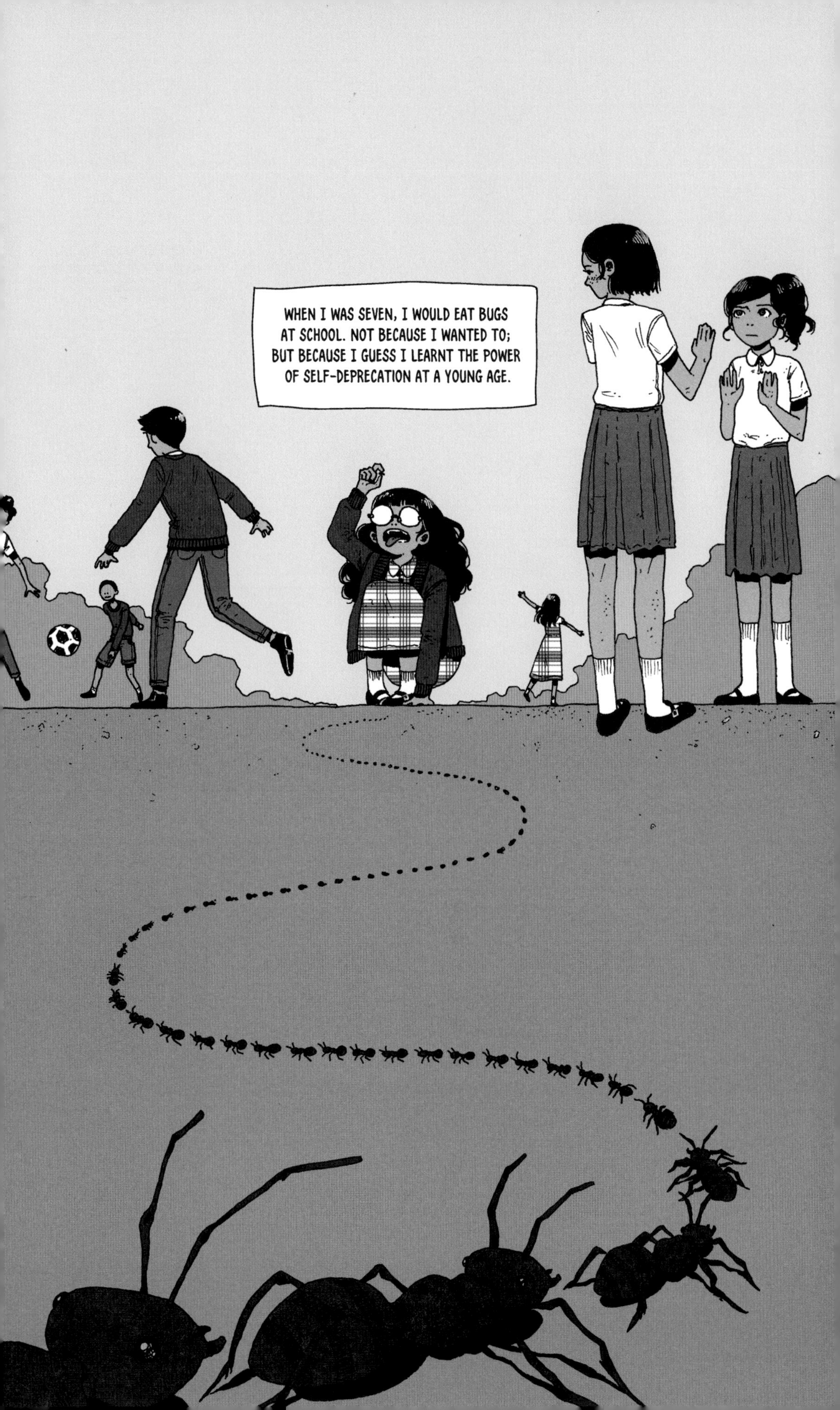
WHEN I WAS SEVEN, I WOULD EAT BUGS AT SCHOOL. NOT BECAUSE I WANTED TO; BUT BECAUSE I GUESS I LEARNT THE POWER OF SELF-DEPRECATION AT A YOUNG AGE.

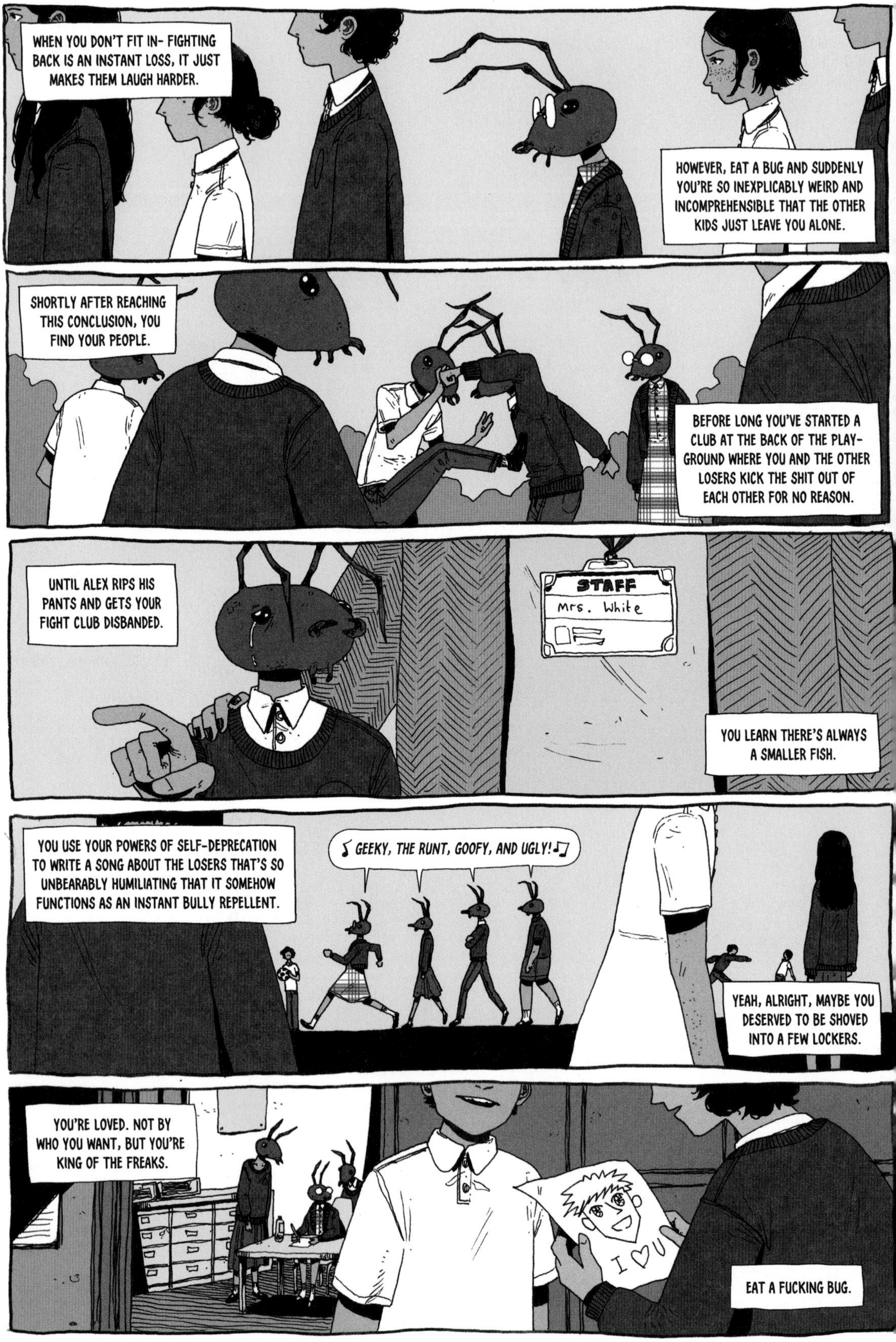
WHEN YOU DON'T FIT IN- FIGHTING BACK IS AN INSTANT LOSS, IT JUST MAKES THEM LAUGH HARDER.
HOWEVER, EAT A BUG AND SUDDENLY YOU'RE SO INEXPLICABLY WEIRD AND INCOMPREHENSIBLE THAT THE OTHER KIDS JUST LEAVE YOU ALONE.
SHORTLY AFTER REACHING THIS CONCLUSION, YOU FIND YOUR PEOPLE.
BEFORE LONG YOU'VE STARTED A CLUB AT THE BACK OF THE PLAY-GROUND WHERE YOU AND THE OTHER LOSERS KICK THE SHIT OUT OF EACH OTHER FOR NO REASON.
UNTIL ALEX RIPS HIS PANTS AND GETS YOUR FIGHT CLUB DISBANDED.
STAFF
Mrs. White
YOU LEARN THERE'S ALWAYS A SMALLER FISH.
YOU USE YOUR POWERS OF SELF-DEPRECATION TO WRITE A SONG ABOUT THE LOSERS THAT'S SO UNBEARABLY HUMILIATING THAT IT SOMEHOW FUNCTIONS AS AN INSTANT BULLY REPELLENT.
GEEKY, THE RUNT, GOOFY, AND UGLY!
YEAH, ALRIGHT, MAYBE YOU DESERVED TO BE SHOVED INTO A FEW LOCKERS.
YOU'RE LOVED. NOT BY WHO YOU WANT, BUT YOU'RE KING OF THE FREAKS.
I ♥ U
EAT A FUCKING BUG.

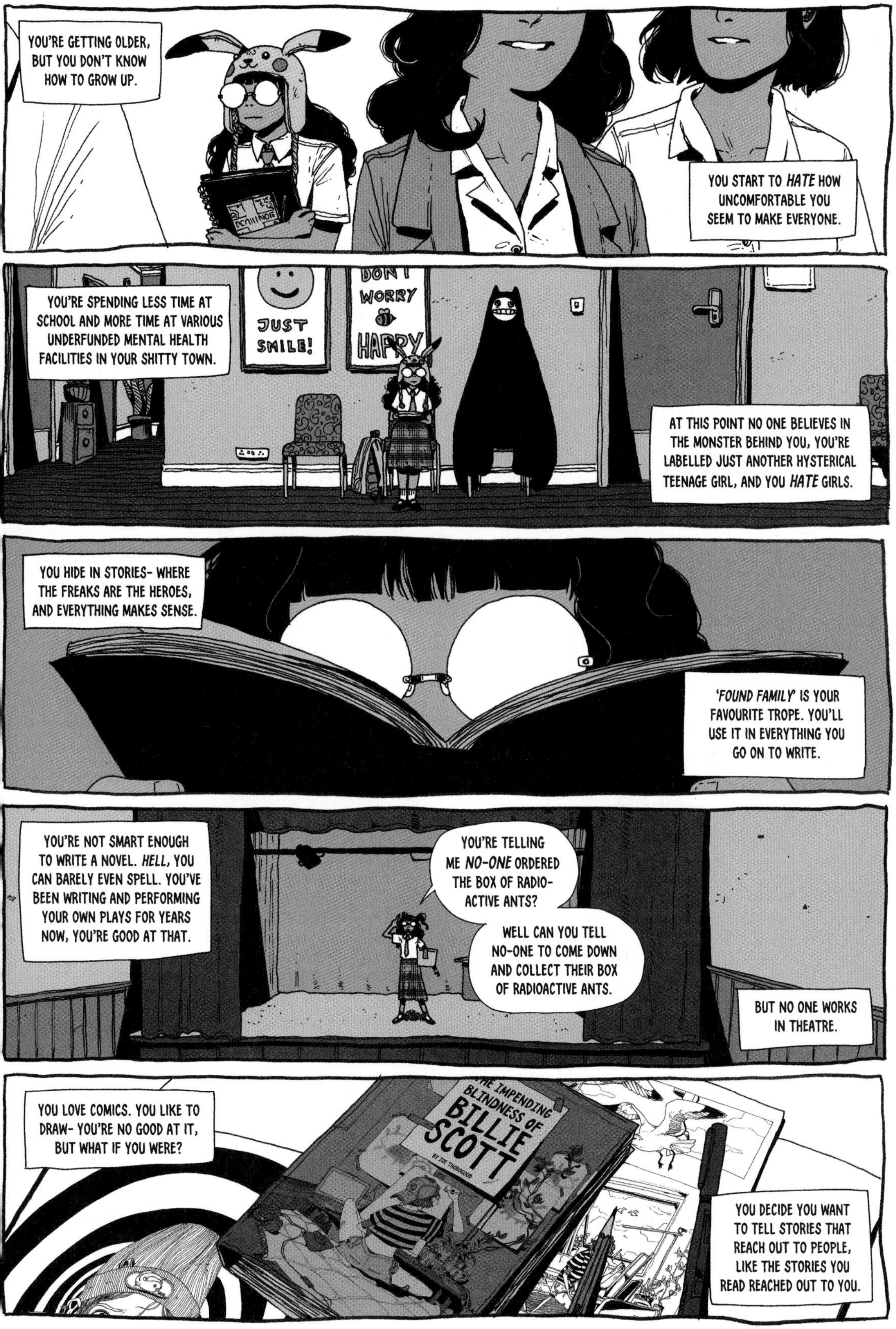

YOU'RE GETTING OLDER, BUT YOU DON'T KNOW HOW TO GROW UP.
YOU START TO *HATE* HOW UNCOMFORTABLE YOU SEEM TO MAKE EVERYONE.
YOU'RE SPENDING LESS TIME AT SCHOOL AND MORE TIME AT VARIOUS UNDERFUNDED MENTAL HEALTH FACILITIES IN YOUR SHITTY TOWN.
JUST SMILE!
DON'T WORRY BE HAPPY
AT THIS POINT NO ONE BELIEVES IN THE MONSTER BEHIND YOU, YOU'RE LABELLED JUST ANOTHER HYSTERICAL TEENAGE GIRL, AND YOU *HATE* GIRLS.
YOU HIDE IN STORIES- WHERE THE FREAKS ARE THE HEROES, AND EVERYTHING MAKES SENSE.
'FOUND FAMILY' IS YOUR FAVOURITE TROPE. YOU'LL USE IT IN EVERYTHING YOU GO ON TO WRITE.
YOU'RE NOT SMART ENOUGH TO WRITE A NOVEL. *HELL*, YOU CAN BARELY EVEN SPELL. YOU'VE BEEN WRITING AND PERFORMING YOUR OWN PLAYS FOR YEARS NOW, YOU'RE GOOD AT THAT.
YOU'RE TELLING ME *NO-ONE* ORDERED THE BOX OF RADIO-ACTIVE ANTS?
WELL CAN YOU TELL NO-ONE TO COME DOWN AND COLLECT THEIR BOX OF RADIOACTIVE ANTS.
BUT NO ONE WORKS IN THEATRE.
YOU LOVE COMICS. YOU LIKE TO DRAW- YOU'RE NO GOOD AT IT, BUT WHAT IF YOU WERE?
THE IMPENDING BLINDNESS OF BILLIE SCOTT
BY ZOE THOROGOOD
YOU DECIDE YOU WANT TO TELL STORIES THAT REACH OUT TO PEOPLE, LIKE THE STORIES YOU READ REACHED OUT TO YOU.

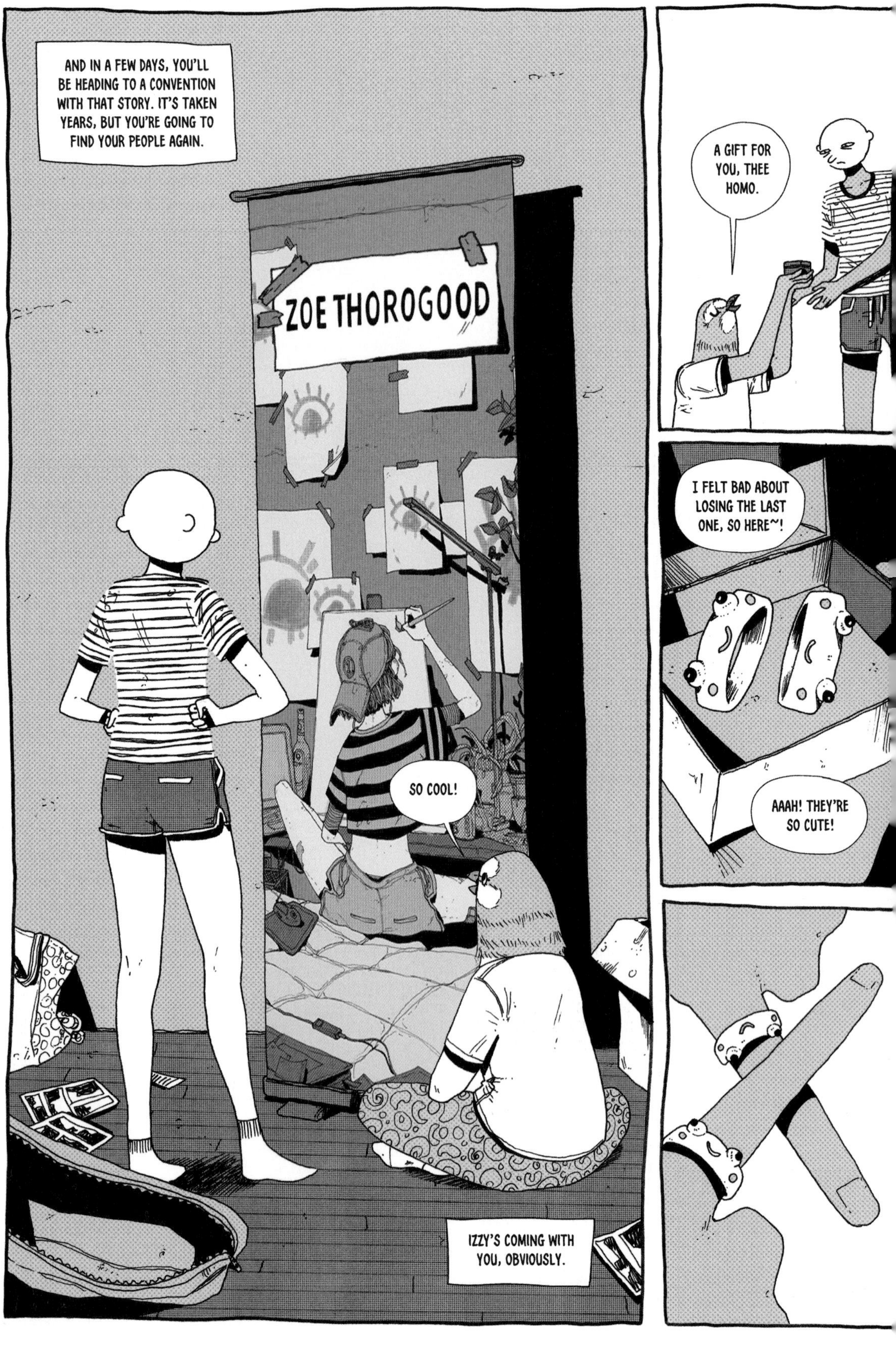
AND IN A FEW DAYS, YOU'LL BE HEADING TO A CONVENTION WITH THAT STORY. IT'S TAKEN YEARS, BUT YOU'RE GOING TO FIND YOUR PEOPLE AGAIN.
ZOE THOROGOOD
SO COOL!
IZZY'S COMING WITH YOU, OBVIOUSLY.
A GIFT FOR YOU, THEE HOMO.
I FELT BAD ABOUT LOSING THE LAST ONE, SO HERE~!
AAAH! THEY'RE SO CUTE!

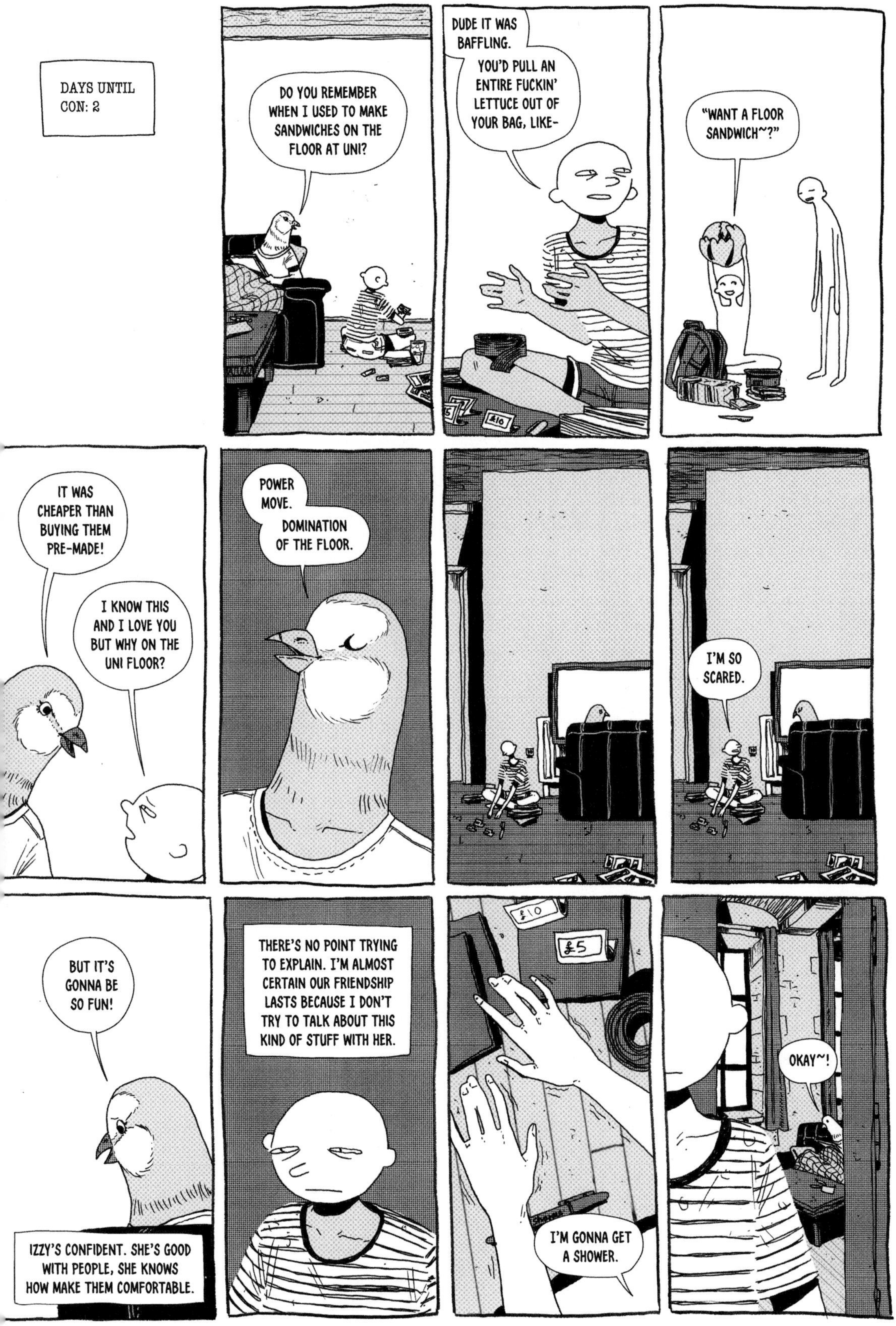

DAYS UNTIL CON: 2
DO YOU REMEMBER WHEN I USED TO MAKE SANDWICHES ON THE FLOOR AT UNI?
DUDE IT WAS BAFFLING.
YOU'D PULL AN ENTIRE FUCKIN' LETTUCE OUT OF YOUR BAG, LIKE-
"WANT A FLOOR SANDWICH~?"
IT WAS CHEAPER THAN BUYING THEM PRE-MADE!
I KNOW THIS AND I LOVE YOU BUT WHY ON THE UNI FLOOR?
POWER MOVE.
DOMINATION OF THE FLOOR.
I'M SO SCARED.
BUT IT'S GONNA BE SO FUN!
IZZY'S CONFIDENT. SHE'S GOOD WITH PEOPLE, SHE KNOWS HOW MAKE THEM COMFORTABLE.
THERE'S NO POINT TRYING TO EXPLAIN. I'M ALMOST CERTAIN OUR FRIENDSHIP LASTS BECAUSE I DON'T TRY TO TALK ABOUT THIS KIND OF STUFF WITH HER.
£10
£5
I'M GONNA GET A SHOWER.
OKAY~!

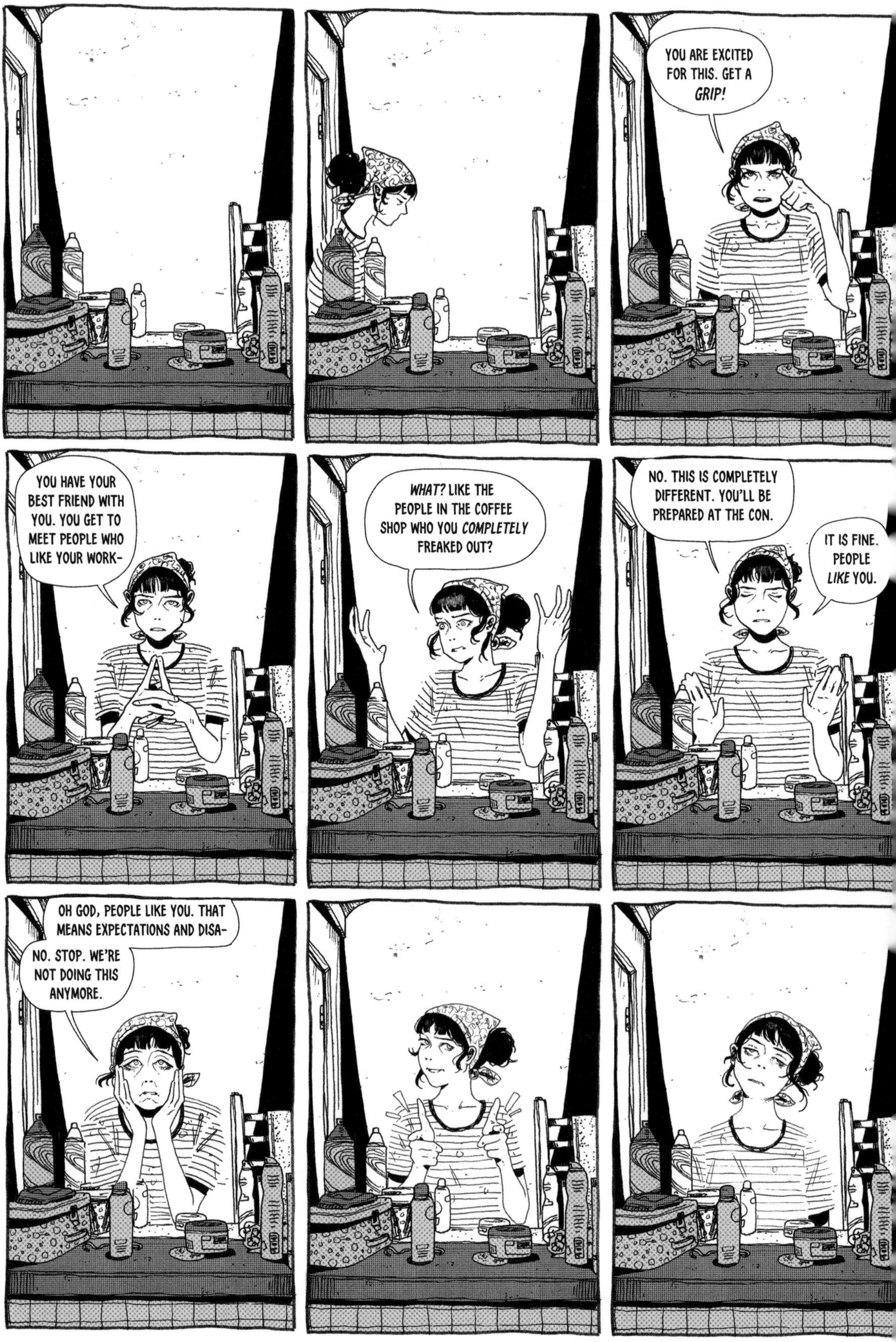
YOU ARE EXCITED FOR THIS. GET A GRIP!
YOU HAVE YOUR BEST FRIEND WITH YOU. YOU GET TO MEET PEOPLE WHO LIKE YOUR WORK-
WHAT? LIKE THE PEOPLE IN THE COFFEE SHOP WHO YOU COMPLETELY FREAKED OUT?
NO. THIS IS COMPLETELY DIFFERENT. YOU'LL BE PREPARED AT THE CON.
IT IS FINE. PEOPLE LIKE YOU.
OH GOD, PEOPLE LIKE YOU. THAT MEANS EXPECTATIONS AND DISA-
NO. STOP. WE'RE NOT DOING THIS ANYMORE.

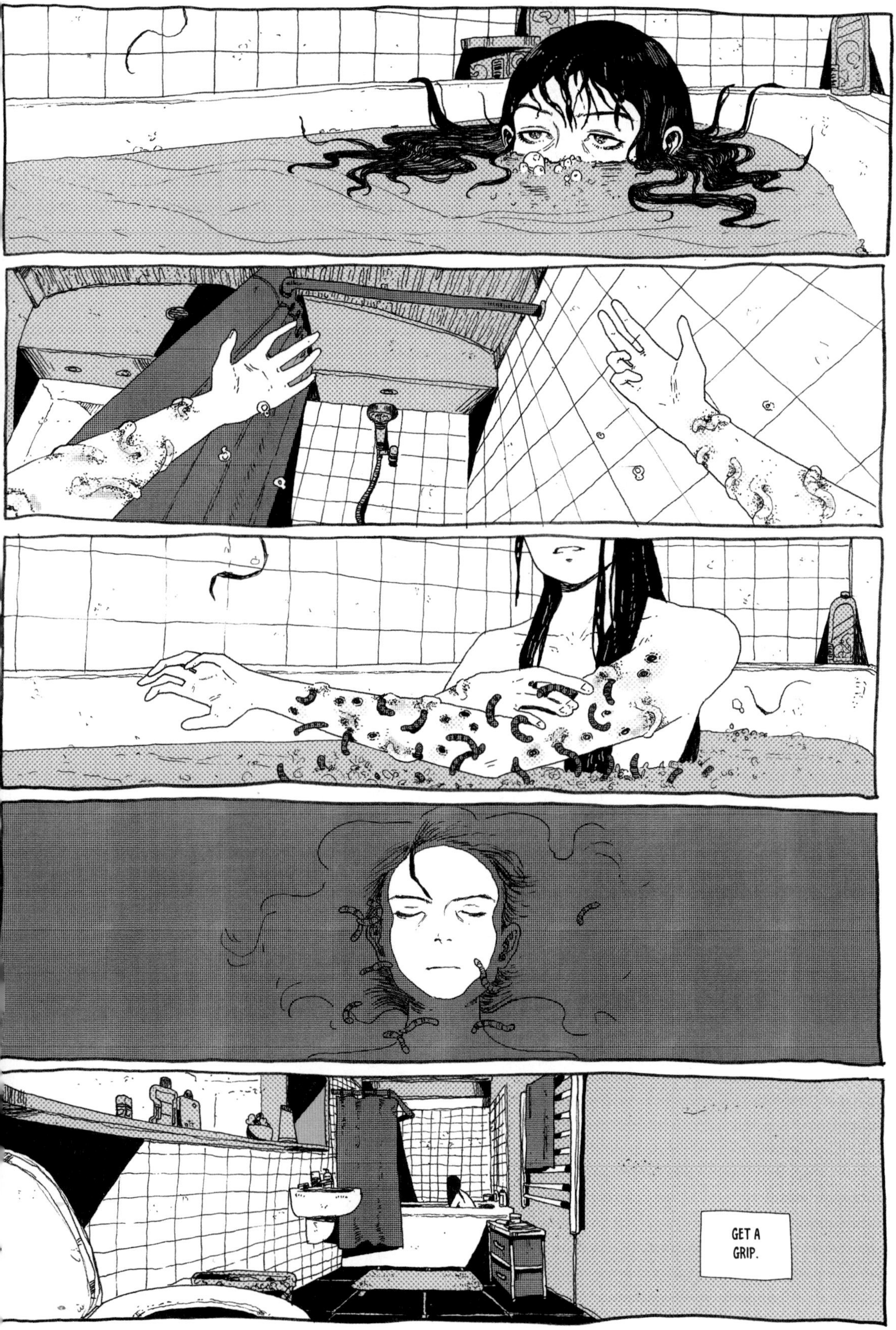
GET A
GRIP.

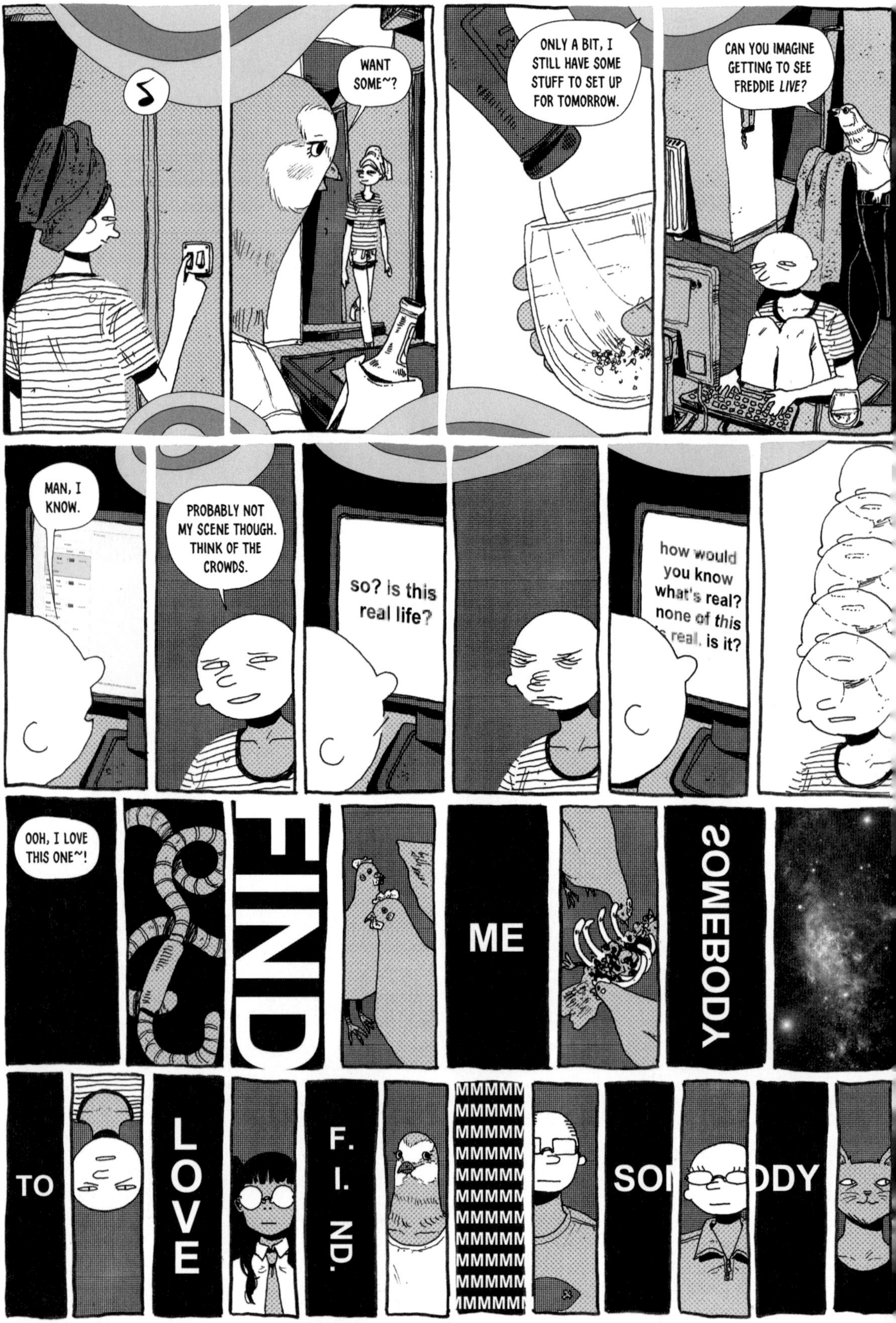
WANT SOME~?
ONLY A BIT, I STILL HAVE SOME STUFF TO SET UP FOR TOMORROW.
CAN YOU IMAGINE GETTING TO SEE FREDDIE *LIVE?*
MAN, I KNOW.
PROBABLY NOT MY SCENE THOUGH. THINK OF THE CROWDS.
so? is this real life?
how would you know what's real? none of *this* is real, is it?
OOH, I LOVE THIS ONE~!
FIND
ME
SOMEBODY
TO
LOVE
F. I. ND.
MMMMM
SOMEBODY

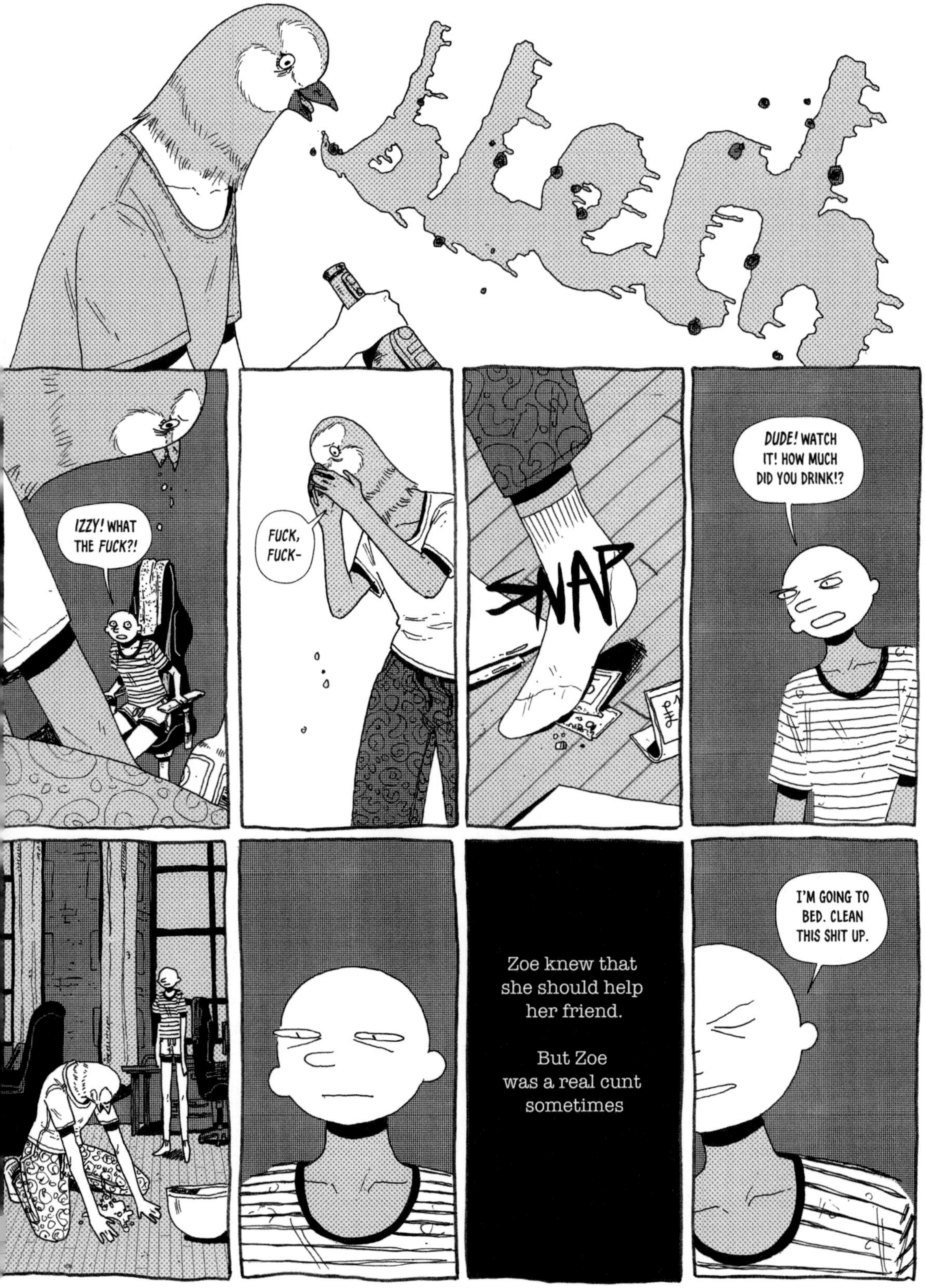
IZZY! WHAT THE FUCK?!
FUCK, FUCK-
SNAP
DUDE! WATCH IT! HOW MUCH DID YOU DRINK!?
Zoe knew that she should help her friend.
But Zoe was a real cunt sometimes
I'M GOING TO BED. CLEAN THIS SHIT UP.

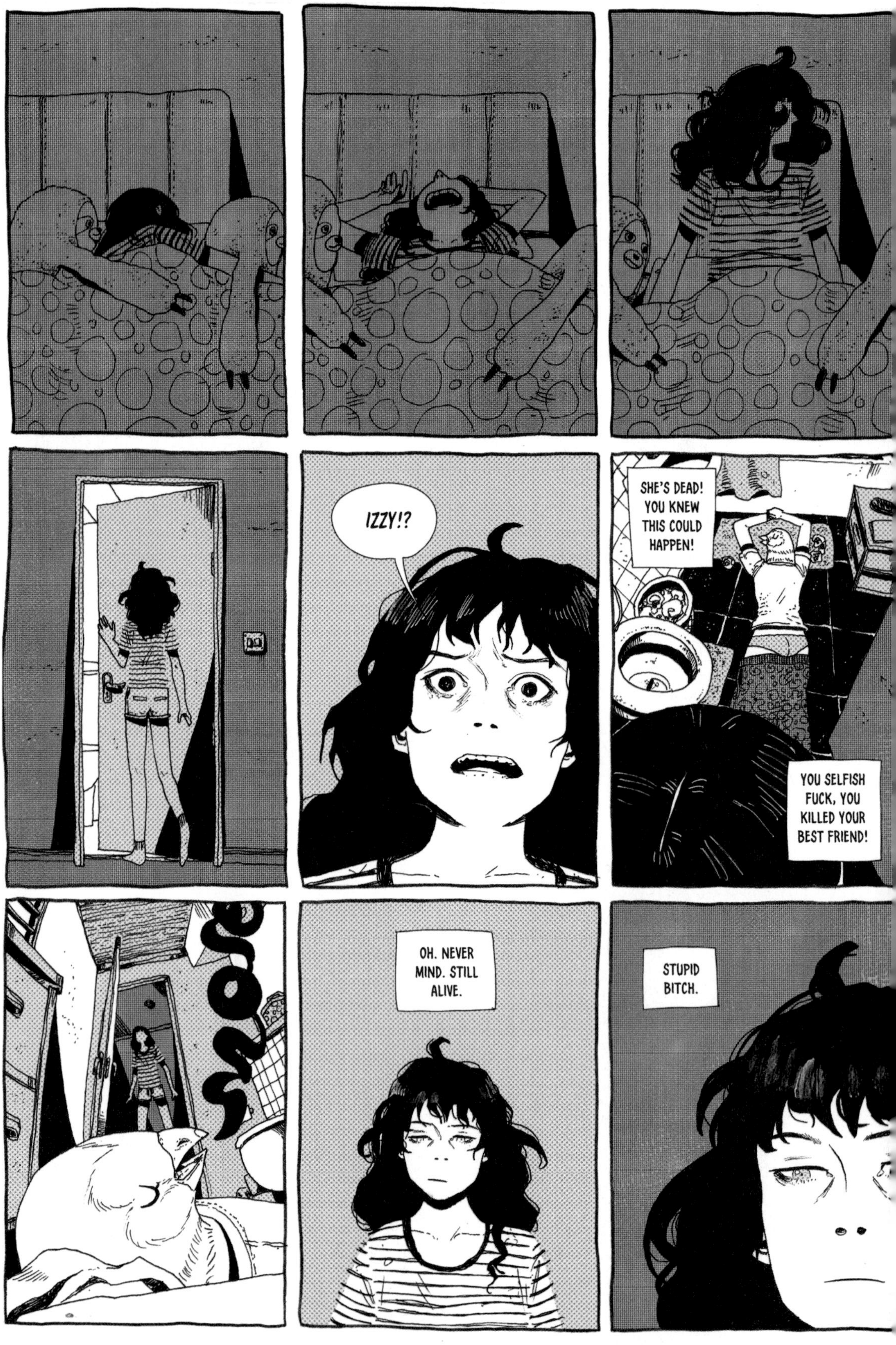
IZZY!?
SHE'S DEAD! YOU KNEW THIS COULD HAPPEN!
YOU SELFISH FUCK, YOU KILLED YOUR BEST FRIEND!
OH. NEVER MIND. STILL ALIVE.
STUPID BITCH.

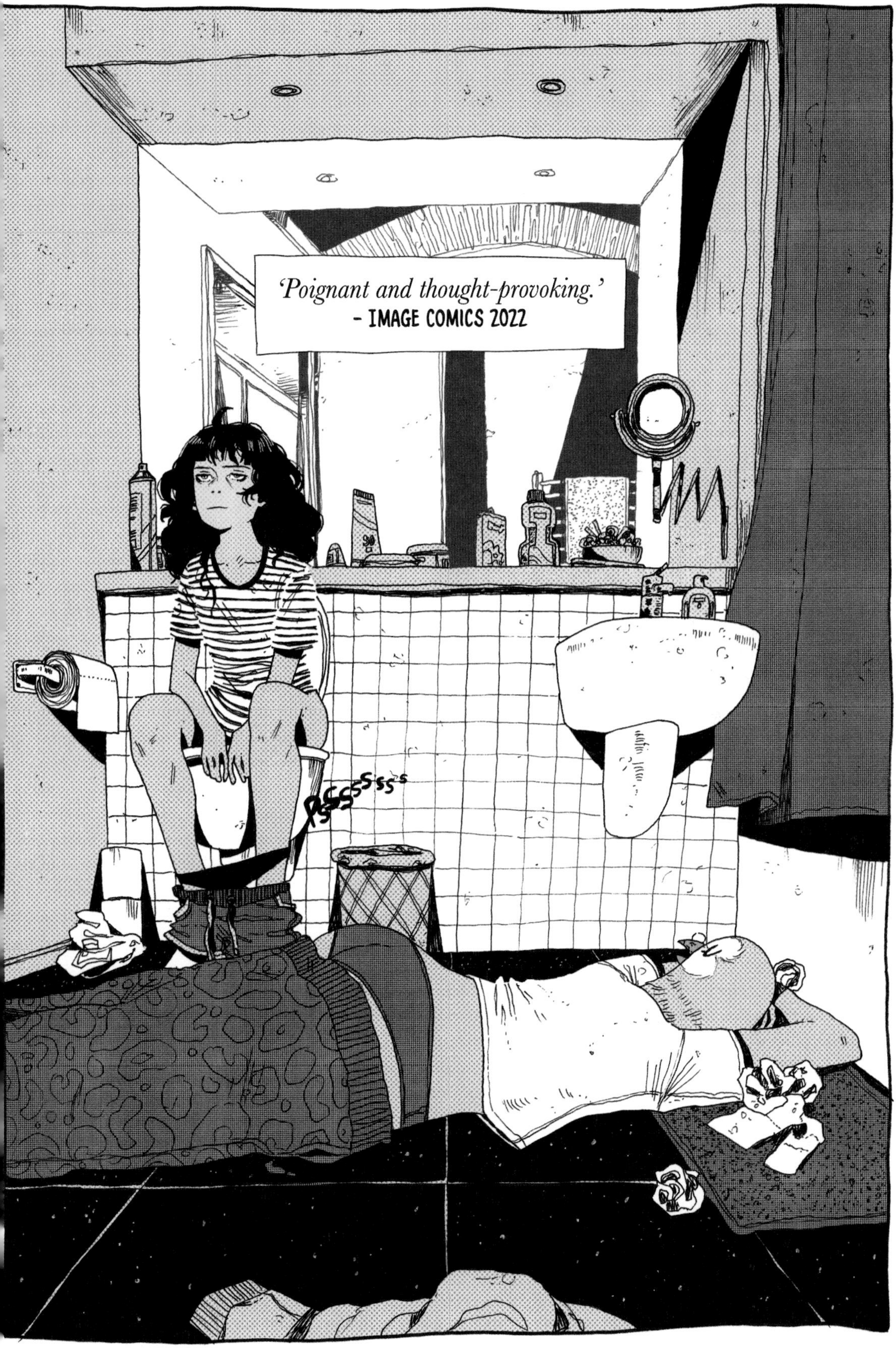
'Poignant and thought-provoking.'
- IMAGE COMICS 2022
PSSSSSSSSS

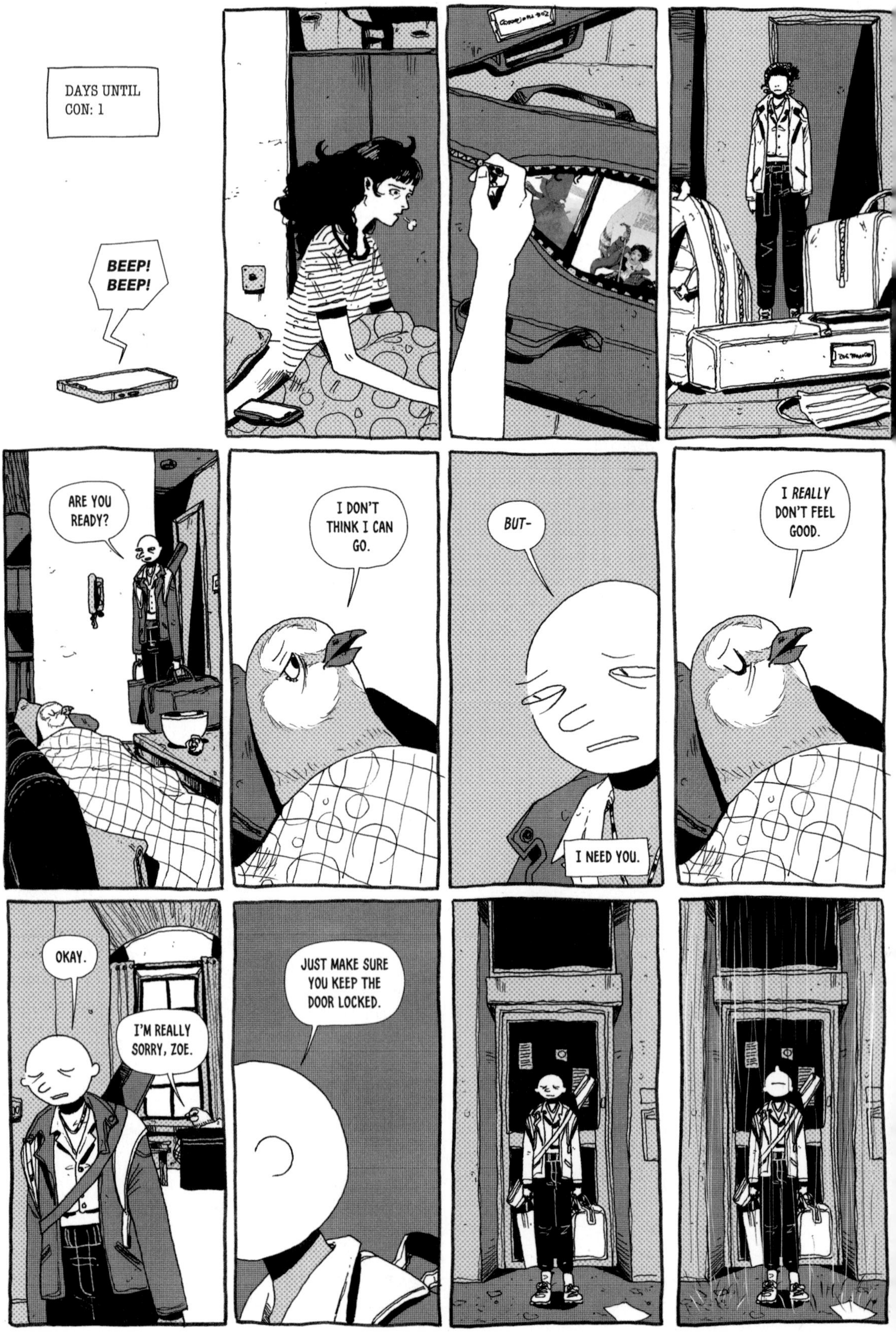
DAYS UNTIL CON: 1
BEEP! BEEP!
ARE YOU READY?
I DON'T THINK I CAN GO.
BUT-
I NEED YOU.
I *REALLY* DON'T FEEL GOOD.
OKAY.
I'M REALLY SORRY, ZOE.
JUST MAKE SURE YOU KEEP THE DOOR LOCKED.

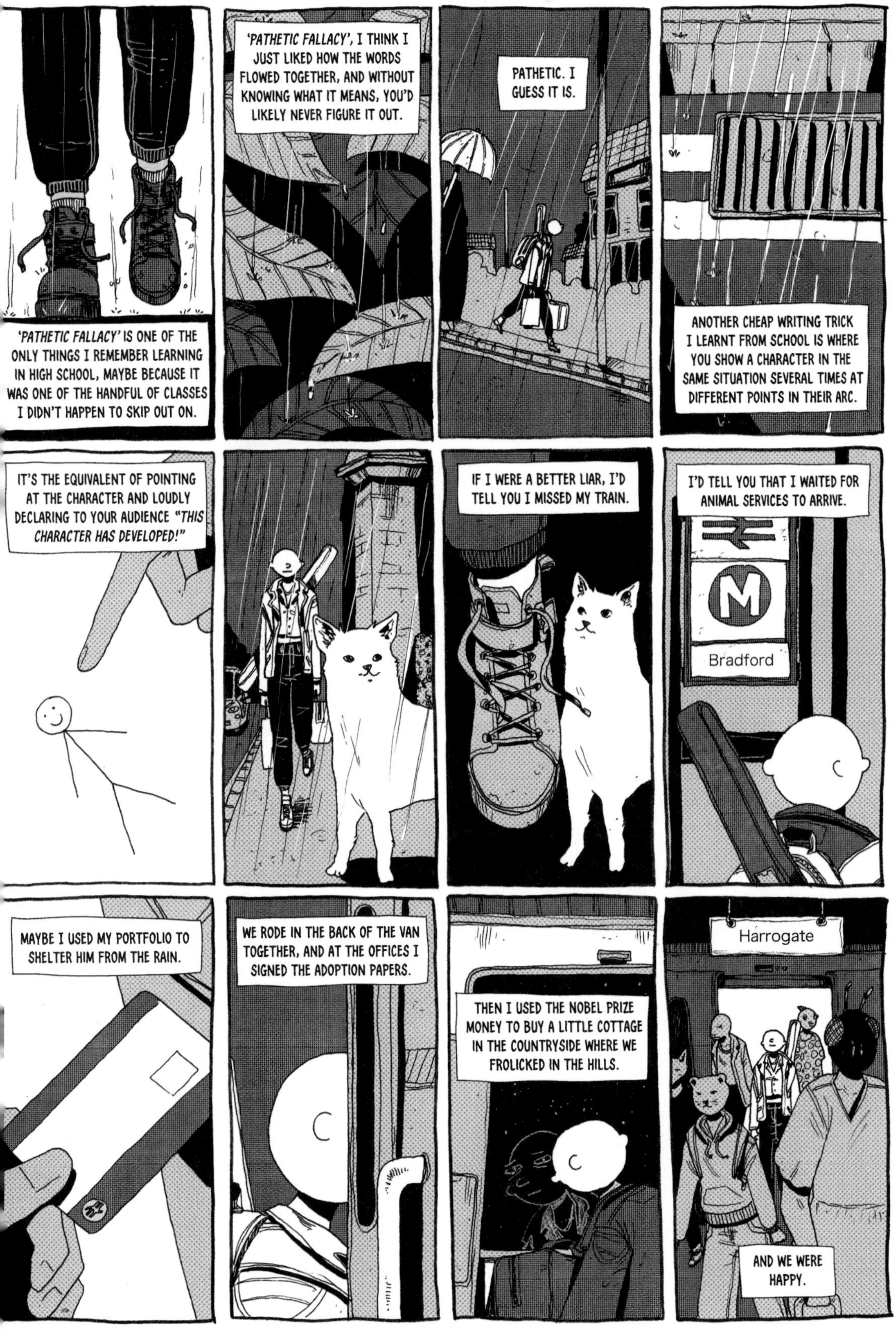
'PATHETIC FALLACY' IS ONE OF THE ONLY THINGS I REMEMBER LEARNING IN HIGH SCHOOL, MAYBE BECAUSE IT WAS ONE OF THE HANDFUL OF CLASSES I DIDN'T HAPPEN TO SKIP OUT ON.
'PATHETIC FALLACY', I THINK I JUST LIKED HOW THE WORDS FLOWED TOGETHER, AND WITHOUT KNOWING WHAT IT MEANS, YOU'D LIKELY NEVER FIGURE IT OUT.
PATHETIC. I GUESS IT IS.
ANOTHER CHEAP WRITING TRICK I LEARNT FROM SCHOOL IS WHERE YOU SHOW A CHARACTER IN THE SAME SITUATION SEVERAL TIMES AT DIFFERENT POINTS IN THEIR ARC.
IT'S THE EQUIVALENT OF POINTING AT THE CHARACTER AND LOUDLY DECLARING TO YOUR AUDIENCE "THIS CHARACTER HAS DEVELOPED!"
IF I WERE A BETTER LIAR, I'D TELL YOU I MISSED MY TRAIN.
I'D TELL YOU THAT I WAITED FOR ANIMAL SERVICES TO ARRIVE.
M
Bradford
MAYBE I USED MY PORTFOLIO TO SHELTER HIM FROM THE RAIN.
WE RODE IN THE BACK OF THE VAN TOGETHER, AND AT THE OFFICES I SIGNED THE ADOPTION PAPERS.
THEN I USED THE NOBEL PRIZE MONEY TO BUY A LITTLE COTTAGE IN THE COUNTRYSIDE WHERE WE FROLICKED IN THE HILLS.
Harrogate
AND WE WERE HAPPY.

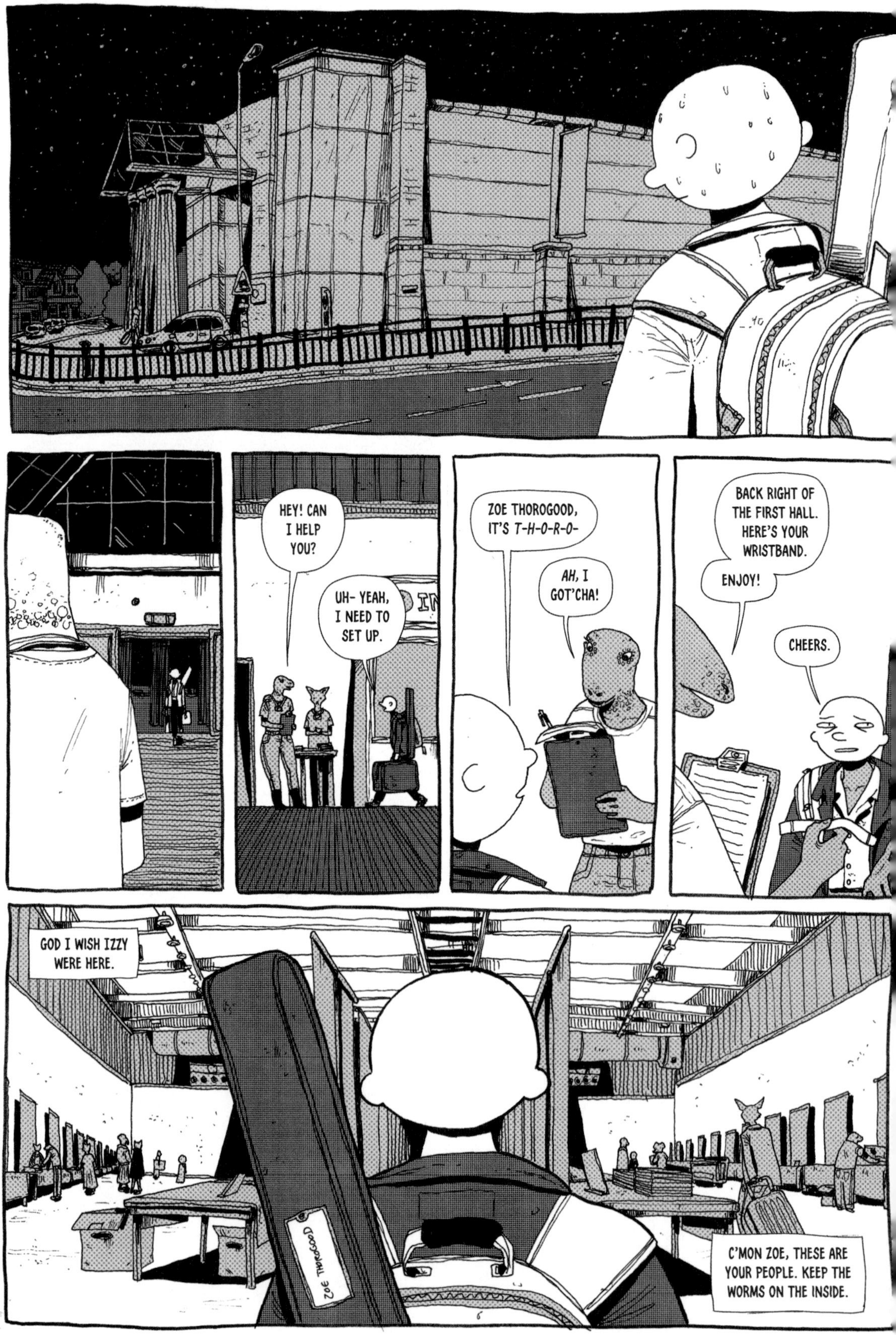
HEY! CAN I HELP YOU?
UH- YEAH, I NEED TO SET UP.
ZOE THOROGOOD, IT'S *T-H-O-R-O-*
AH, I GOT'CHA!
BACK RIGHT OF THE FIRST HALL. HERE'S YOUR WRISTBAND.
ENJOY!
CHEERS.
GOD I WISH IZZY WERE HERE.
ZOE THOROGOOD
C'MON ZOE, THESE ARE YOUR PEOPLE. KEEP THE WORMS ON THE INSIDE.

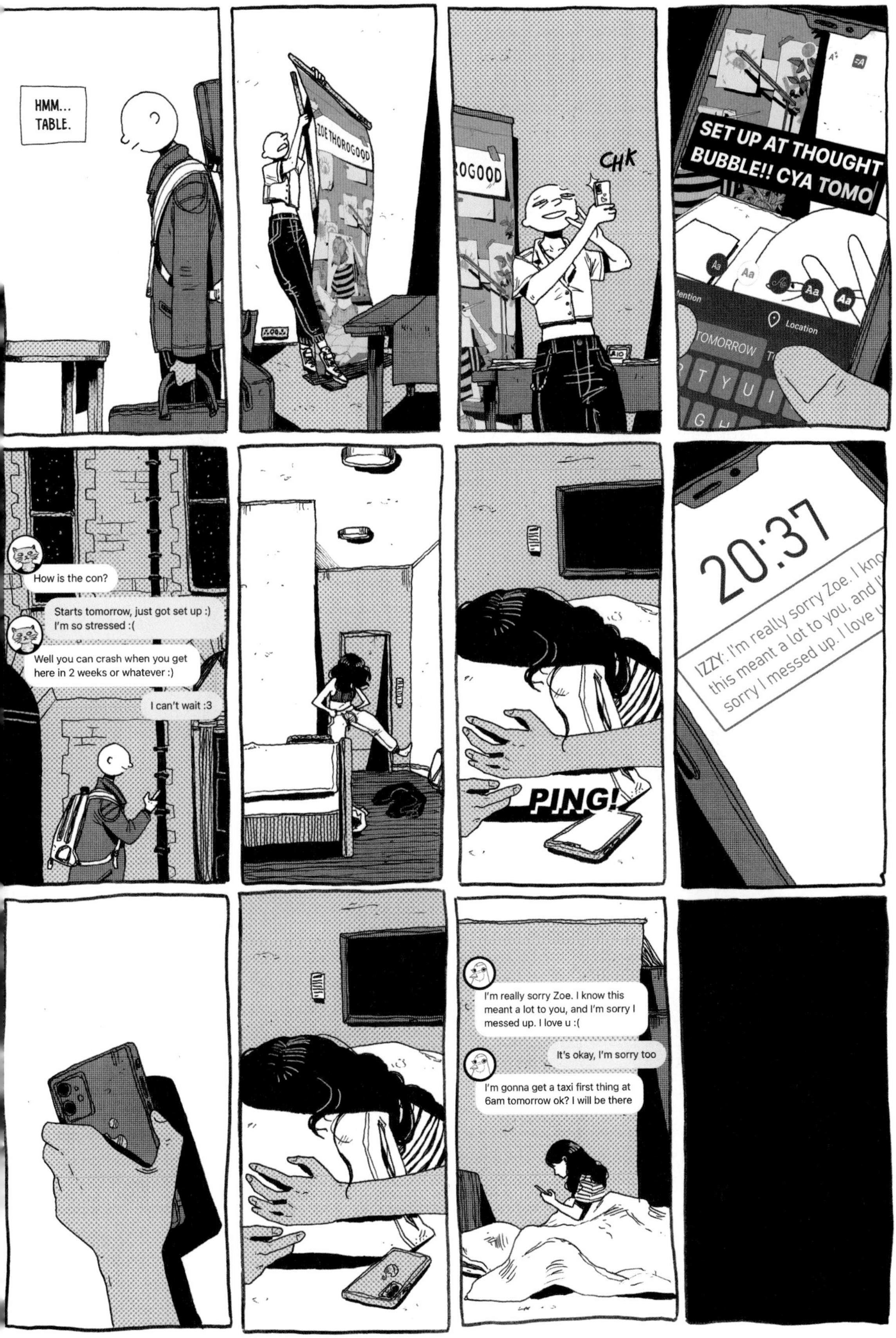
HMM... TABLE.
ZOE THOROGOOD
CHK
SET UP AT THOUGHT BUBBLE!! CYA TOMO
Location
TOMORROW
How is the con?
Starts tomorrow, just got set up :) I'm so stressed :(
Well you can crash when you get here in 2 weeks or whatever :)
I can't wait :3
PING!
20:37
IZZY: I'm really sorry Zoe. I know this meant a lot to you, and I'm sorry I messed up. I love u
I'm really sorry Zoe. I know this meant a lot to you, and I'm sorry I messed up. I love u :(
It's okay, I'm sorry too
I'm gonna get a taxi first thing at 6am tomorrow ok? I will be there

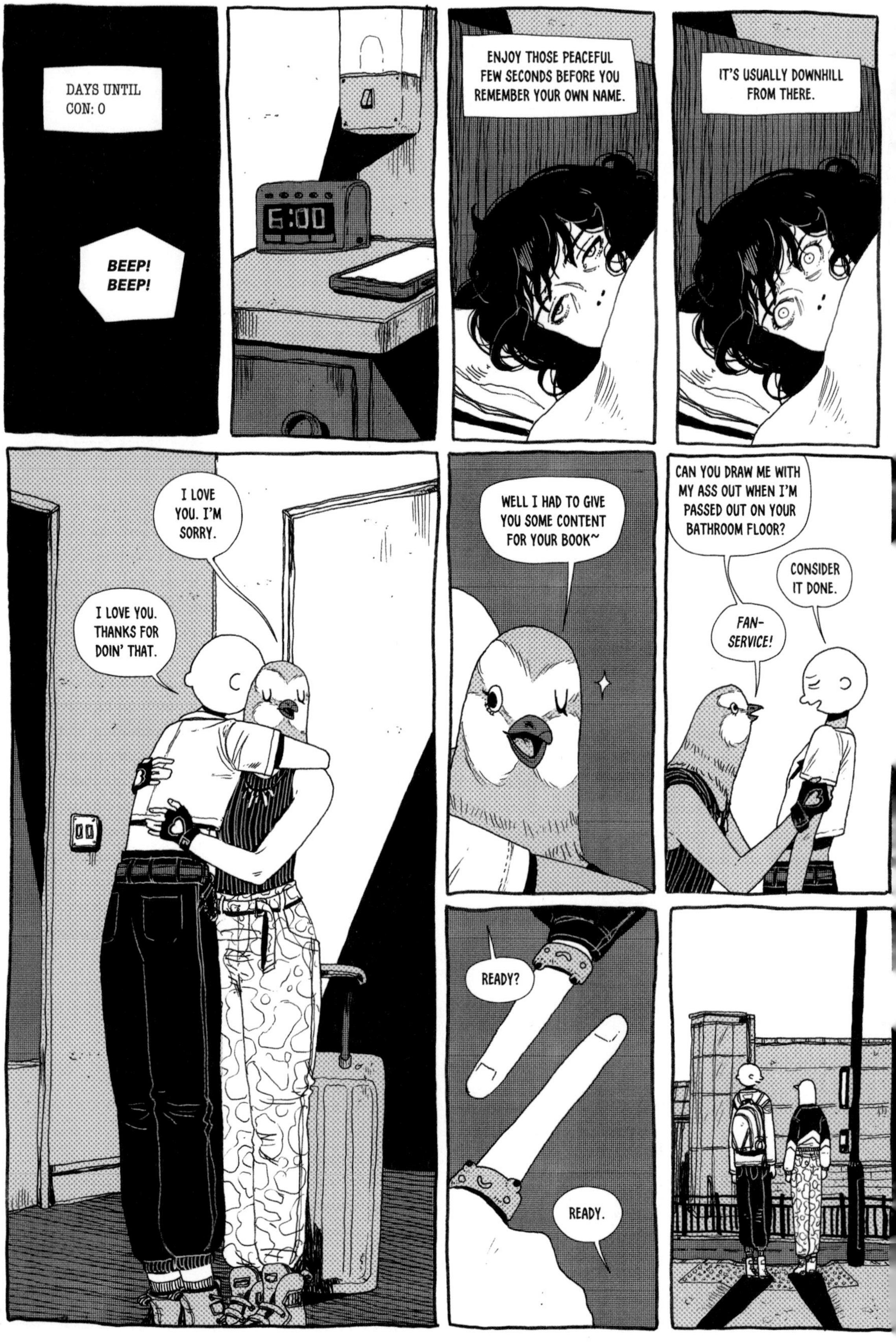
DAYS UNTIL CON: 0
BEEP! BEEP!
6:00
ENJOY THOSE PEACEFUL FEW SECONDS BEFORE YOU REMEMBER YOUR OWN NAME.
IT'S USUALLY DOWNHILL FROM THERE.
I LOVE YOU. THANKS FOR DOIN' THAT.
I LOVE YOU. I'M SORRY.
WELL I HAD TO GIVE YOU SOME CONTENT FOR YOUR BOOK~
CAN YOU DRAW ME WITH MY ASS OUT WHEN I'M PASSED OUT ON YOUR BATHROOM FLOOR?
FAN-SERVICE!
CONSIDER IT DONE.
READY?
READY.

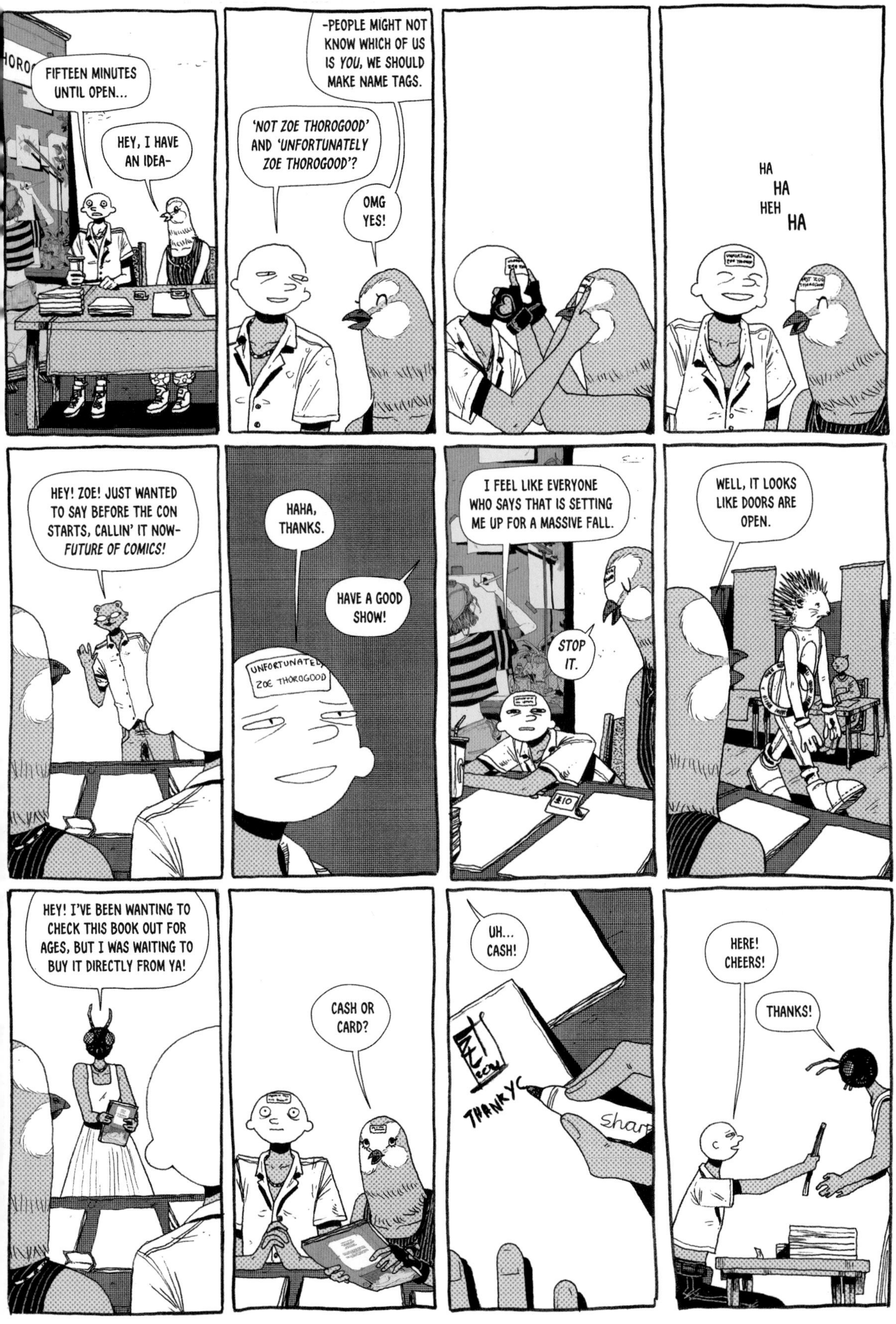

FIFTEEN MINUTES UNTIL OPEN...
HEY, I HAVE AN IDEA-
-PEOPLE MIGHT NOT KNOW WHICH OF US IS *YOU*, WE SHOULD MAKE NAME TAGS.
'NOT ZOE THOROGOOD' AND 'UNFORTUNATELY ZOE THOROGOOD'?
OMG YES!
HA
HA
HEH
HA
HEY! ZOE! JUST WANTED TO SAY BEFORE THE CON STARTS, CALLIN' IT NOW- *FUTURE OF COMICS!*
HAHA, THANKS.
HAVE A GOOD SHOW!
UNFORTUNATELY ZOE THOROGOOD
I FEEL LIKE EVERYONE WHO SAYS THAT IS SETTING ME UP FOR A MASSIVE FALL.
STOP IT.
£10
WELL, IT LOOKS LIKE DOORS ARE OPEN.
HEY! I'VE BEEN WANTING TO CHECK THIS BOOK OUT FOR AGES, BUT I WAS WAITING TO BUY IT DIRECTLY FROM YA!
CASH OR CARD?
UH... CASH!
THANKYO
HERE! CHEERS!
THANKS!

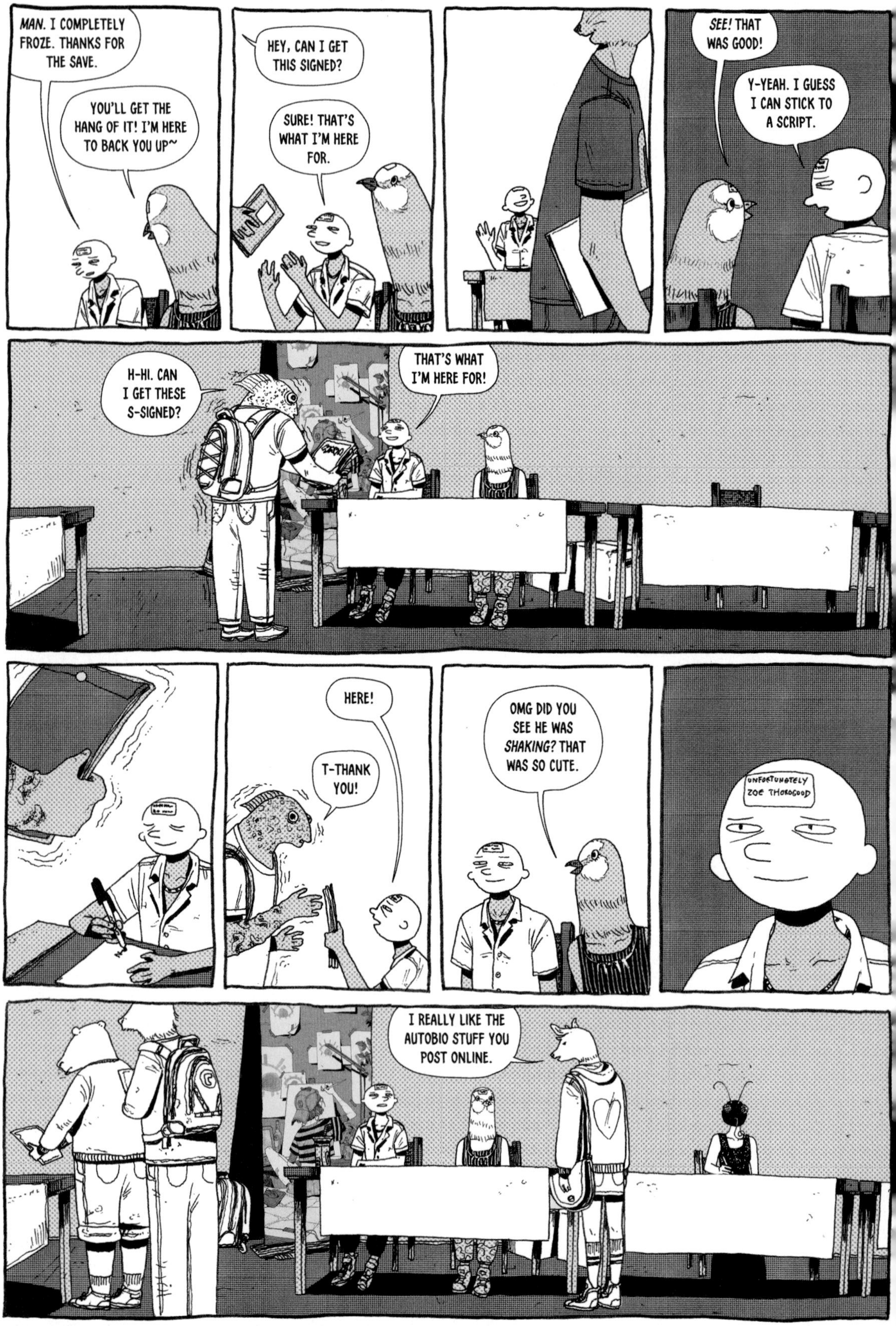
MAN. I COMPLETELY FROZE. THANKS FOR THE SAVE.
YOU'LL GET THE HANG OF IT! I'M HERE TO BACK YOU UP~
HEY, CAN I GET THIS SIGNED?
SURE! THAT'S WHAT I'M HERE FOR.
SEE! THAT WAS GOOD!
Y-YEAH. I GUESS I CAN STICK TO A SCRIPT.
H-HI. CAN I GET THESE S-SIGNED?
THAT'S WHAT I'M HERE FOR!
HERE!
T-THANK YOU!
OMG DID YOU SEE HE WAS SHAKING? THAT WAS SO CUTE.
UNFORTUNATELY ZOE THOROGOOD
I REALLY LIKE THE AUTOBIO STUFF YOU POST ONLINE.

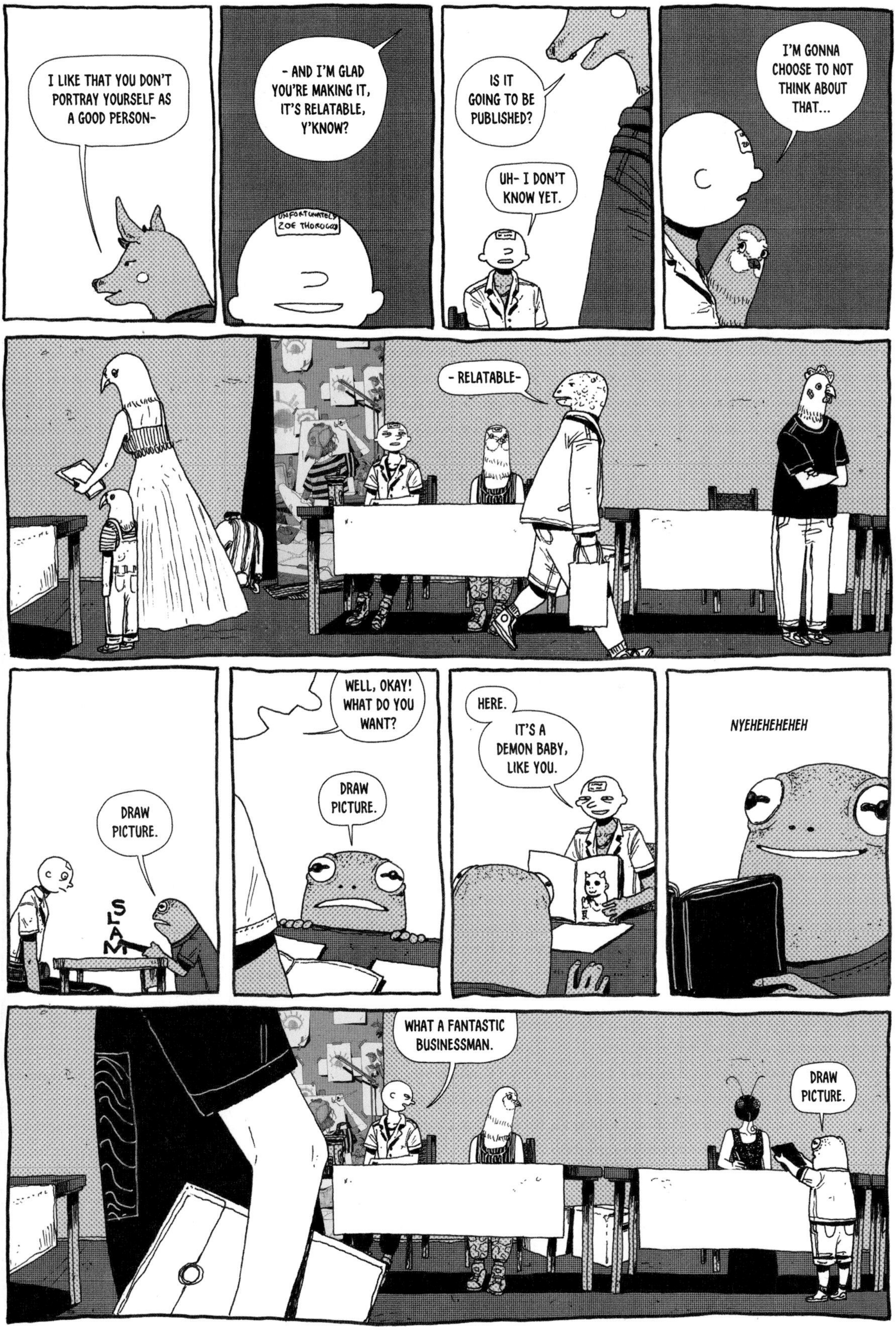
I LIKE THAT YOU DON'T PORTRAY YOURSELF AS A GOOD PERSON-
- AND I'M GLAD YOU'RE MAKING IT, IT'S RELATABLE, Y'KNOW?
UNFORTUNATELY ZOE THOROGOOD
IS IT GOING TO BE PUBLISHED?
UH- I DON'T KNOW YET.
I'M GONNA CHOOSE TO NOT THINK ABOUT THAT...
- RELATABLE-
DRAW PICTURE.
SLAM
WELL, OKAY! WHAT DO YOU WANT?
DRAW PICTURE.
HERE.
IT'S A DEMON BABY, LIKE YOU.
NYEHEHEHEHEH
WHAT A FANTASTIC BUSINESSMAN.
DRAW PICTURE.

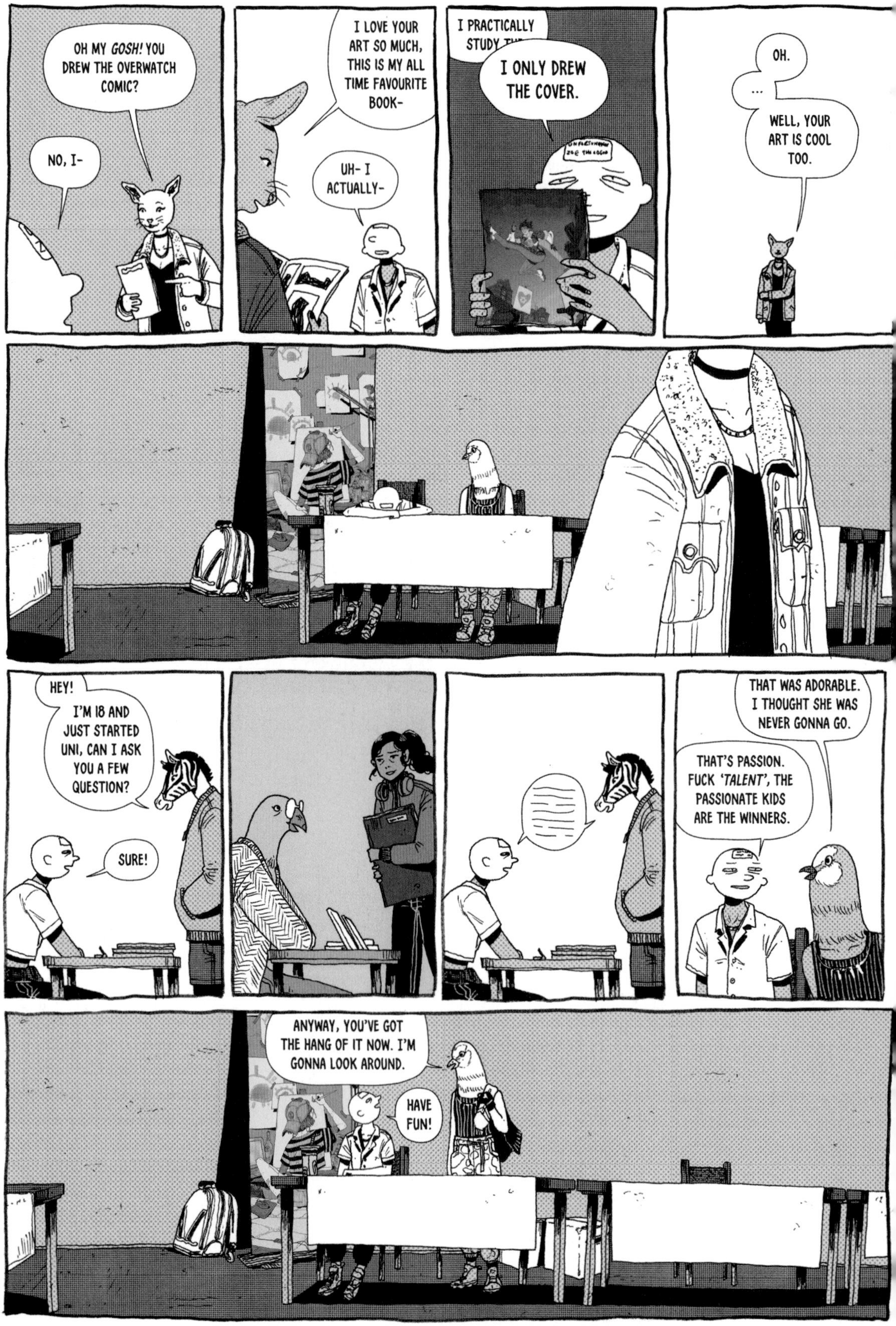
OH MY *GOSH!* YOU DREW THE OVERWATCH COMIC?
NO, I-
I LOVE YOUR ART SO MUCH, THIS IS MY ALL TIME FAVOURITE BOOK-
UH- I ACTUALLY-
I PRACTICALLY STUDY
I ONLY DREW THE COVER.
OH.
...
WELL, YOUR ART IS COOL TOO.
HEY!
I'M 18 AND JUST STARTED UNI, CAN I ASK YOU A FEW QUESTION?
SURE!
THAT WAS ADORABLE. I THOUGHT SHE WAS NEVER GONNA GO.
THAT'S PASSION. FUCK '*TALENT*', THE PASSIONATE KIDS ARE THE WINNERS.
ANYWAY, YOU'VE GOT THE HANG OF IT NOW. I'M GONNA LOOK AROUND.
HAVE FUN!

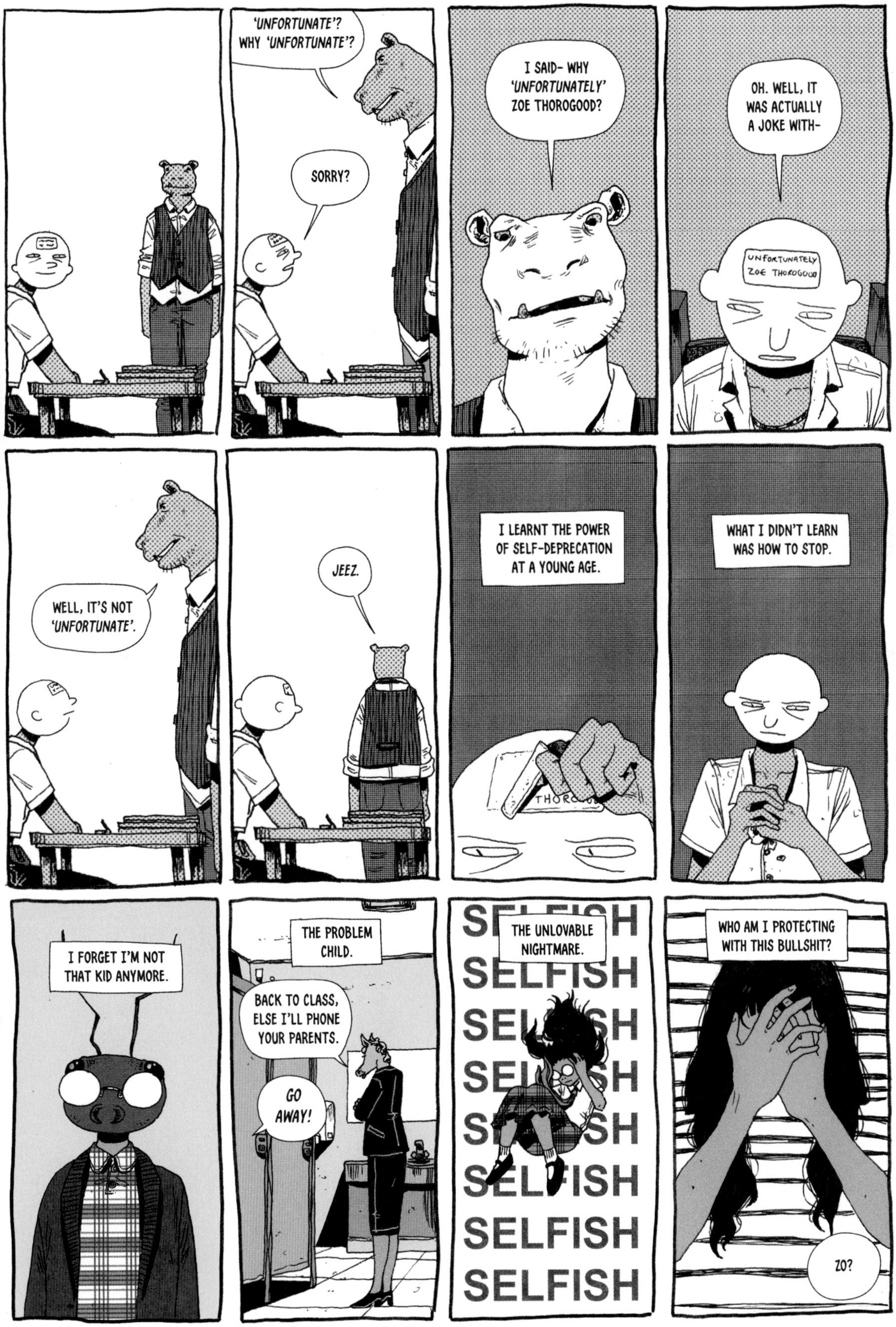

'UNFORTUNATE'? WHY 'UNFORTUNATE'?
SORRY?
I SAID- WHY 'UNFORTUNATELY' ZOE THOROGOOD?
OH. WELL, IT WAS ACTUALLY A JOKE WITH-
UNFORTUNATELY ZOE THOROGOOD
WELL, IT'S NOT 'UNFORTUNATE'.
JEEZ.
I LEARNT THE POWER OF SELF-DEPRECATION AT A YOUNG AGE.
WHAT I DIDN'T LEARN WAS HOW TO STOP.
I FORGET I'M NOT THAT KID ANYMORE.
THE PROBLEM CHILD.
BACK TO CLASS, ELSE I'LL PHONE YOUR PARENTS.
GO AWAY!
THE UNLOVABLE NIGHTMARE.
SELFISH
SELFISH
SELFISH
SELFISH
WHO AM I PROTECTING WITH THIS BULLSHIT?
ZO?

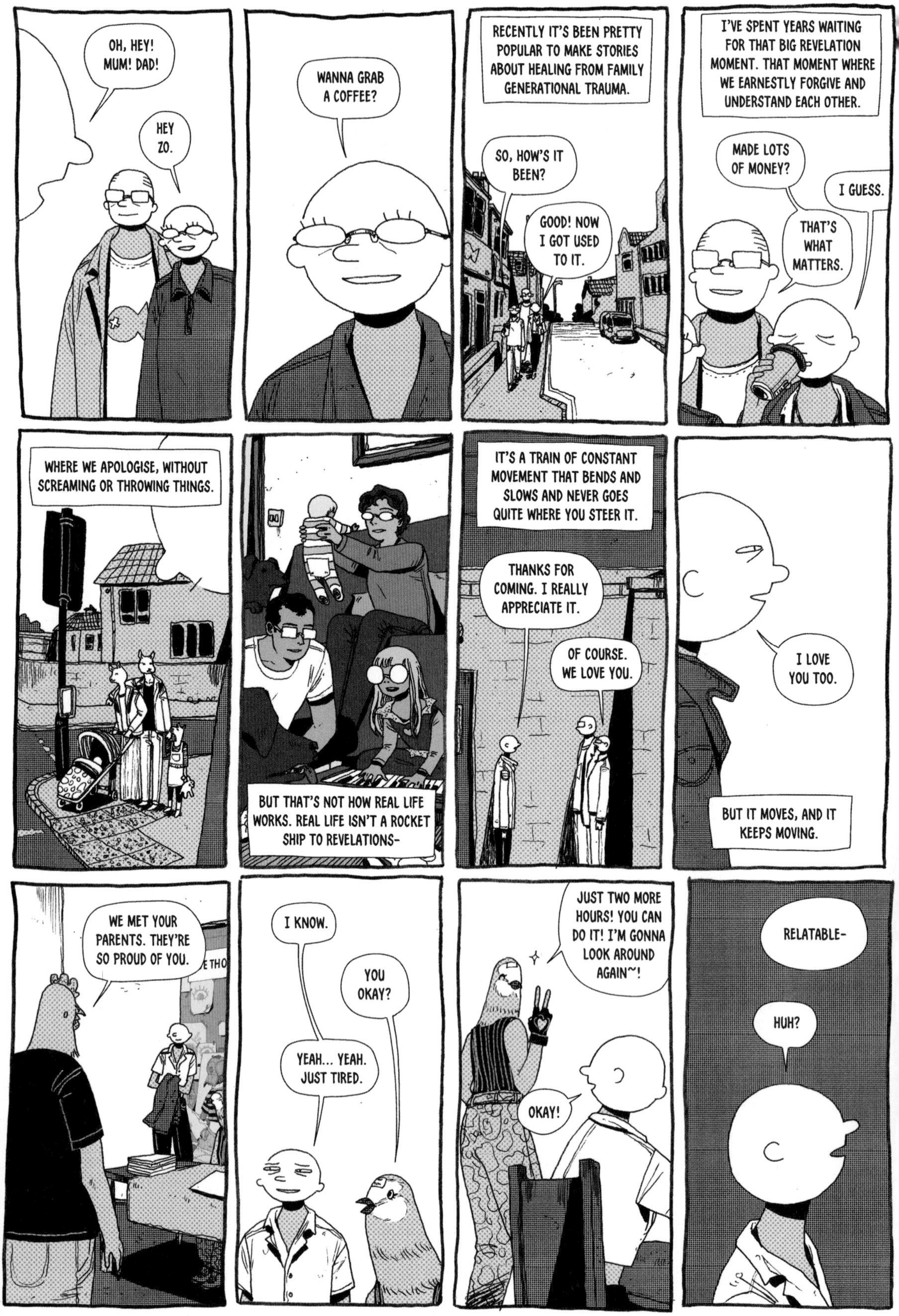
OH, HEY! MUM! DAD!
HEY ZO.
WANNA GRAB A COFFEE?
RECENTLY IT'S BEEN PRETTY POPULAR TO MAKE STORIES ABOUT HEALING FROM FAMILY GENERATIONAL TRAUMA.
SO, HOW'S IT BEEN?
GOOD! NOW I GOT USED TO IT.
I'VE SPENT YEARS WAITING FOR THAT BIG REVELATION MOMENT. THAT MOMENT WHERE WE EARNESTLY FORGIVE AND UNDERSTAND EACH OTHER.
MADE LOTS OF MONEY?
I GUESS.
THAT'S WHAT MATTERS.
WHERE WE APOLOGISE, WITHOUT SCREAMING OR THROWING THINGS.
BUT THAT'S NOT HOW REAL LIFE WORKS. REAL LIFE ISN'T A ROCKET SHIP TO REVELATIONS-
IT'S A TRAIN OF CONSTANT MOVEMENT THAT BENDS AND SLOWS AND NEVER GOES QUITE WHERE YOU STEER IT.
THANKS FOR COMING. I REALLY APPRECIATE IT.
OF COURSE. WE LOVE YOU.
I LOVE YOU TOO.
BUT IT MOVES, AND IT KEEPS MOVING.
WE MET YOUR PARENTS. THEY'RE SO PROUD OF YOU.
I KNOW.
YOU OKAY?
YEAH... YEAH. JUST TIRED.
JUST TWO MORE HOURS! YOU CAN DO IT! I'M GONNA LOOK AROUND AGAIN~!
OKAY!
RELATABLE-
HUH?

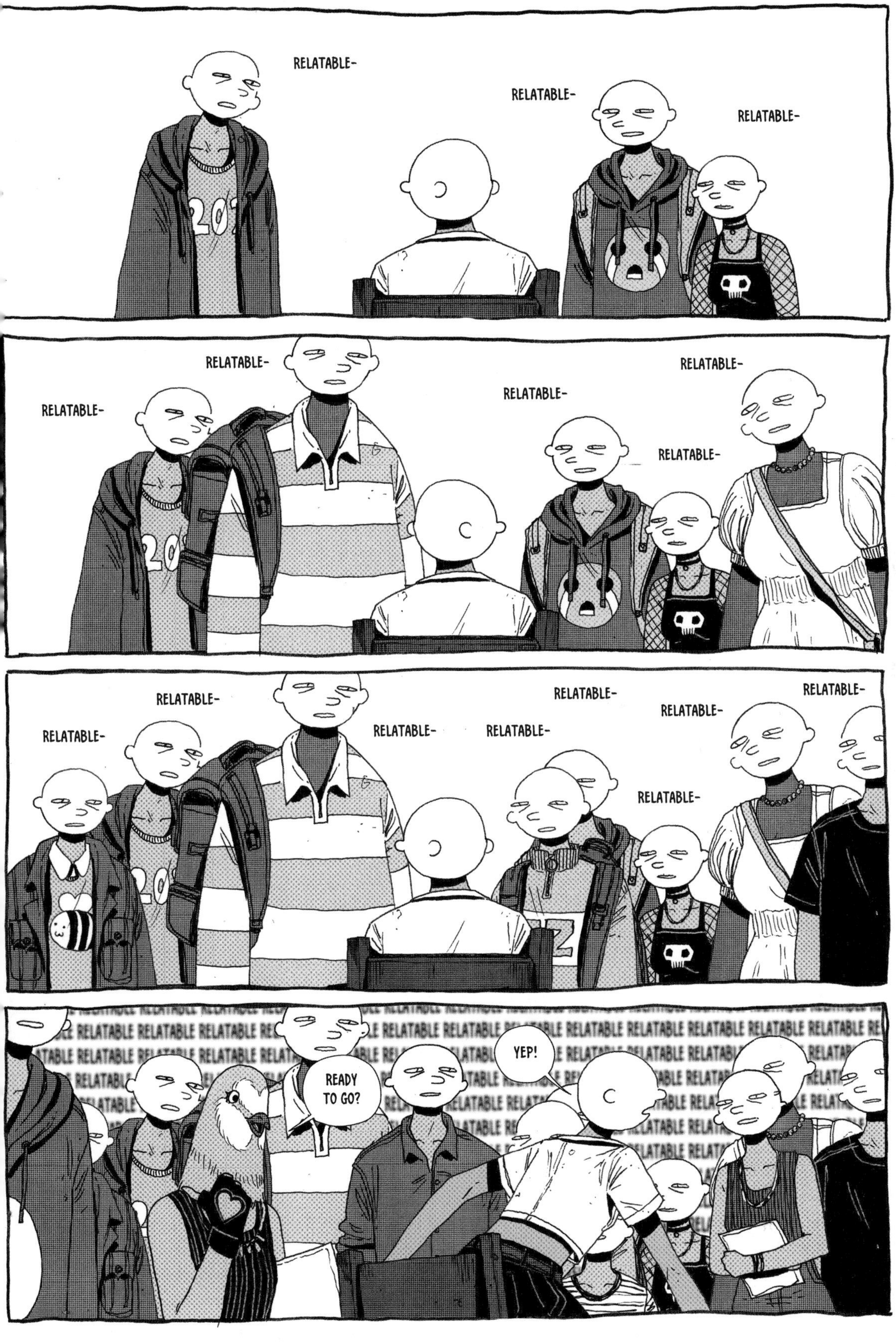
RELATABLE-
RELATABLE-
RELATABLE-
RELATABLE-
RELATABLE-
RELATABLE-
RELATABLE-
RELATABLE-
RELATABLE-
RELATABLE-
RELATABLE-
RELATABLE-
RELATABLE-
RELATABLE-
RELATABLE-
RELATABLE-
READY TO GO?
YEP!

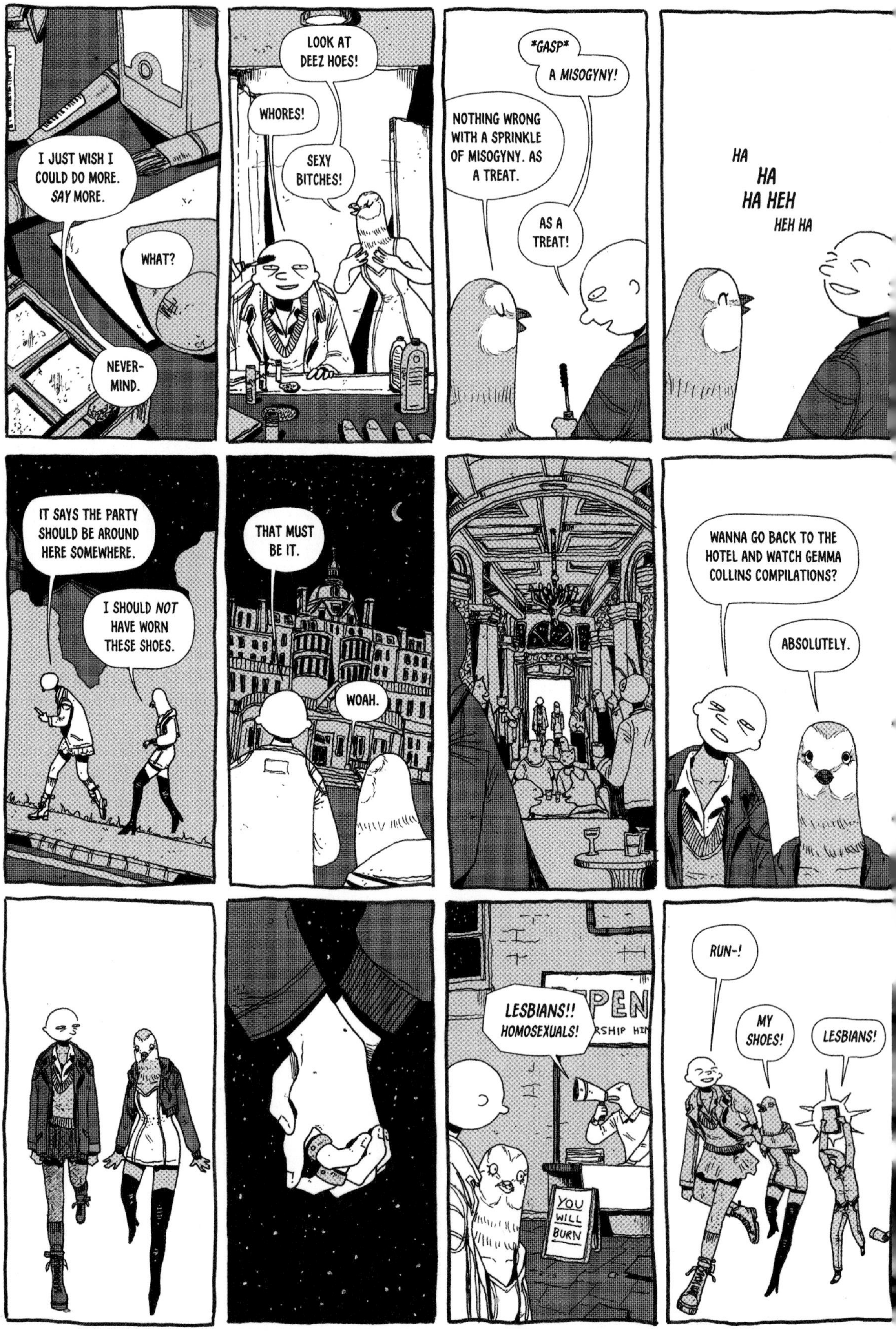
I JUST WISH I COULD DO MORE. *SAY* MORE.
WHAT?
NEVER-MIND.
LOOK AT DEEZ HOES!
WHORES!
SEXY BITCHES!
GASP
A MISOGYNY!
NOTHING WRONG WITH A SPRINKLE OF MISOGYNY. AS A TREAT.
AS A TREAT!
HA HA HA HEH HEH HA
IT SAYS THE PARTY SHOULD BE AROUND HERE SOMEWHERE.
I SHOULD *NOT* HAVE WORN THESE SHOES.
THAT MUST BE IT.
WOAH.
WANNA GO BACK TO THE HOTEL AND WATCH GEMMA COLLINS COMPILATIONS?
ABSOLUTELY.
LESBIANS!! HOMOSEXUALS!
YOU WILL BURN
RUN-!
MY SHOES!
LESBIANS!

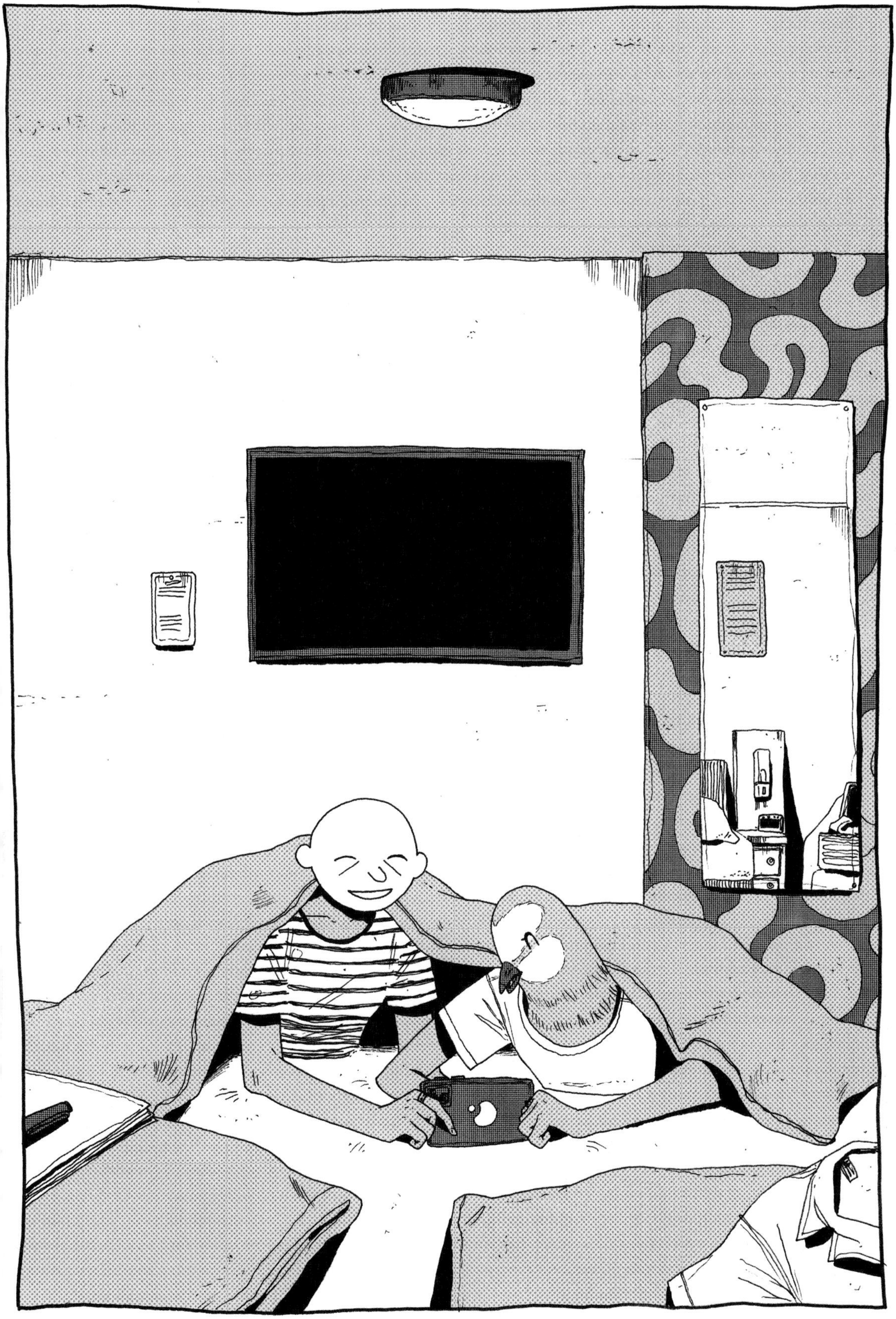

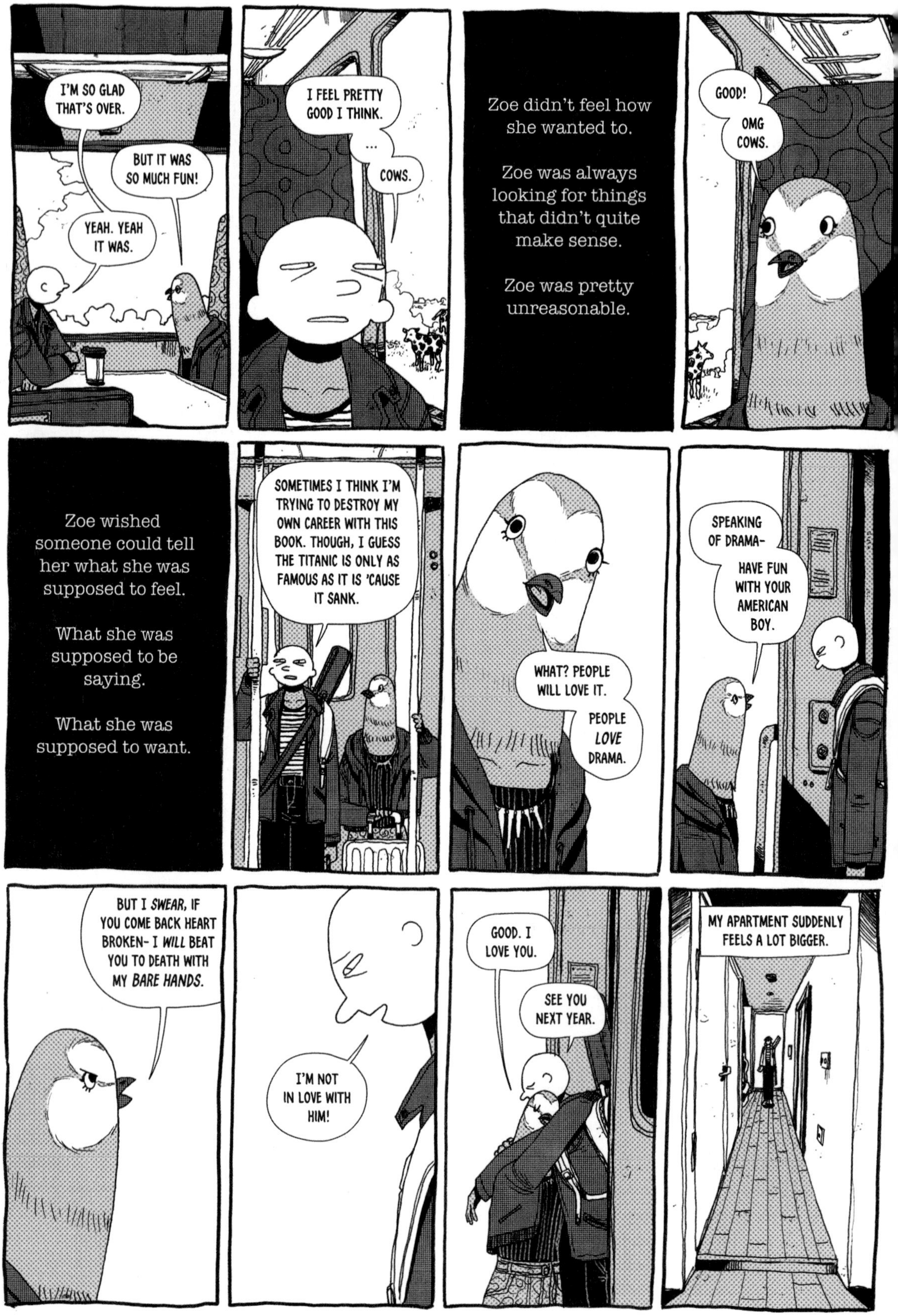
I'M SO GLAD THAT'S OVER.
BUT IT WAS SO MUCH FUN!
YEAH. YEAH IT WAS.
I FEEL PRETTY GOOD I THINK.
...
COWS.
Zoe didn't feel how she wanted to.
Zoe was always looking for things that didn't quite make sense.
Zoe was pretty unreasonable.
GOOD!
OMG COWS.
Zoe wished someone could tell her what she was supposed to feel.
What she was supposed to be saying.
What she was supposed to want.
SOMETIMES I THINK I'M TRYING TO DESTROY MY OWN CAREER WITH THIS BOOK. THOUGH, I GUESS THE TITANIC IS ONLY AS FAMOUS AS IT IS 'CAUSE IT SANK.
WHAT? PEOPLE WILL LOVE IT.
PEOPLE *LOVE* DRAMA.
SPEAKING OF DRAMA-
HAVE FUN WITH YOUR AMERICAN BOY.
BUT I *SWEAR*, IF YOU COME BACK HEART BROKEN- I *WILL* BEAT YOU TO DEATH WITH MY *BARE HANDS*.
I'M NOT IN LOVE WITH HIM!
GOOD. I LOVE YOU.
SEE YOU NEXT YEAR.
MY APARTMENT SUDDENLY FEELS A LOT BIGGER.

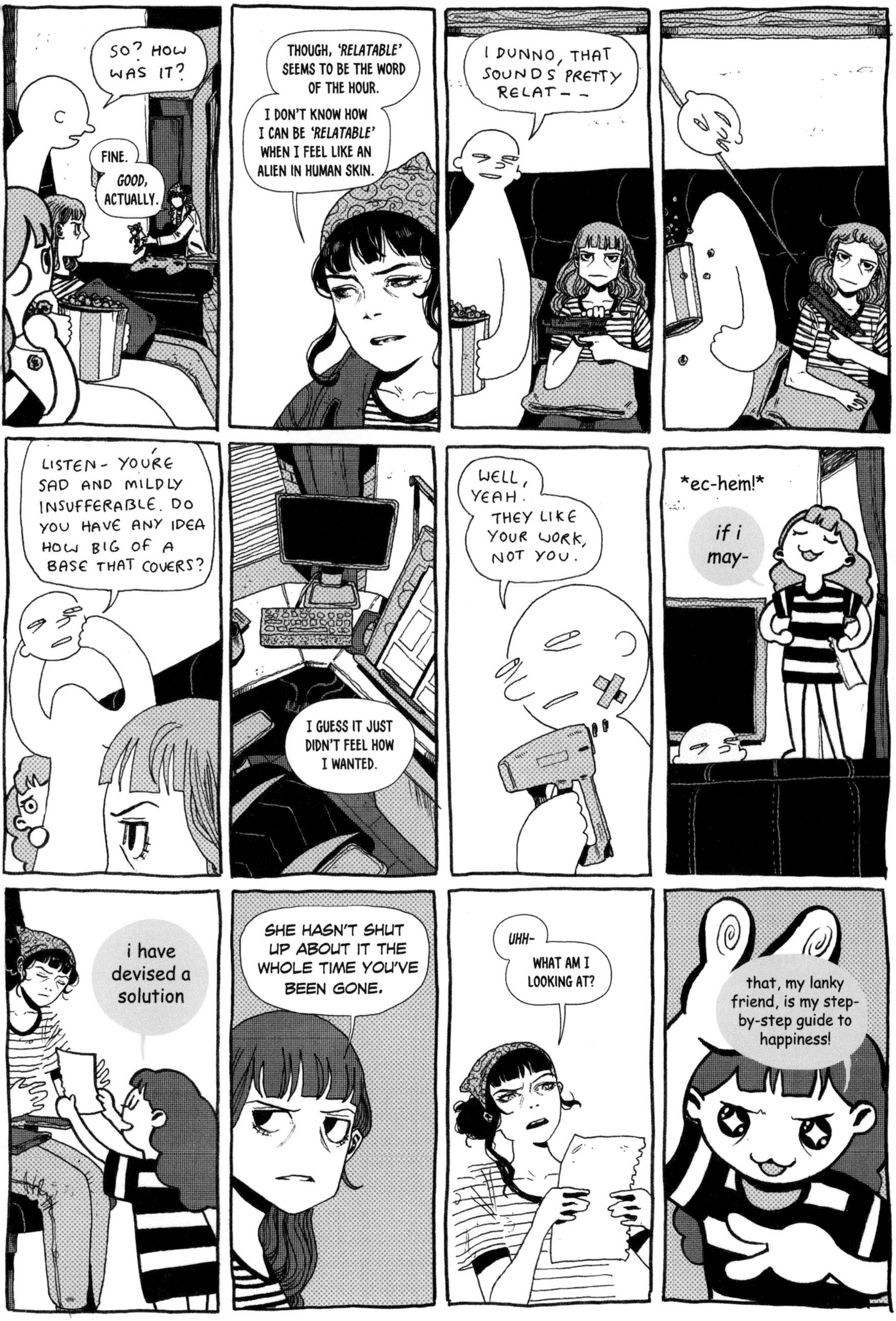
SO? HOW WAS IT?
FINE.
GOOD, ACTUALLY.
THOUGH, 'RELATABLE' SEEMS TO BE THE WORD OF THE HOUR.
I DON'T KNOW HOW I CAN BE 'RELATABLE' WHEN I FEEL LIKE AN ALIEN IN HUMAN SKIN.
I DUNNO, THAT SOUNDS PRETTY RELAT--
LISTEN- YOU'RE SAD AND MILDLY INSUFFERABLE. DO YOU HAVE ANY IDEA HOW BIG OF A BASE THAT COVERS?
I GUESS IT JUST DIDN'T FEEL HOW I WANTED.
WELL, YEAH.
THEY LIKE YOUR WORK, NOT YOU.
ec-hem!
if i may-
i have devised a solution
SHE HASN'T SHUT UP ABOUT IT THE WHOLE TIME YOU'VE BEEN GONE.
UHH-
WHAT AM I LOOKING AT?
that, my lanky friend, is my step-by-step guide to happiness!

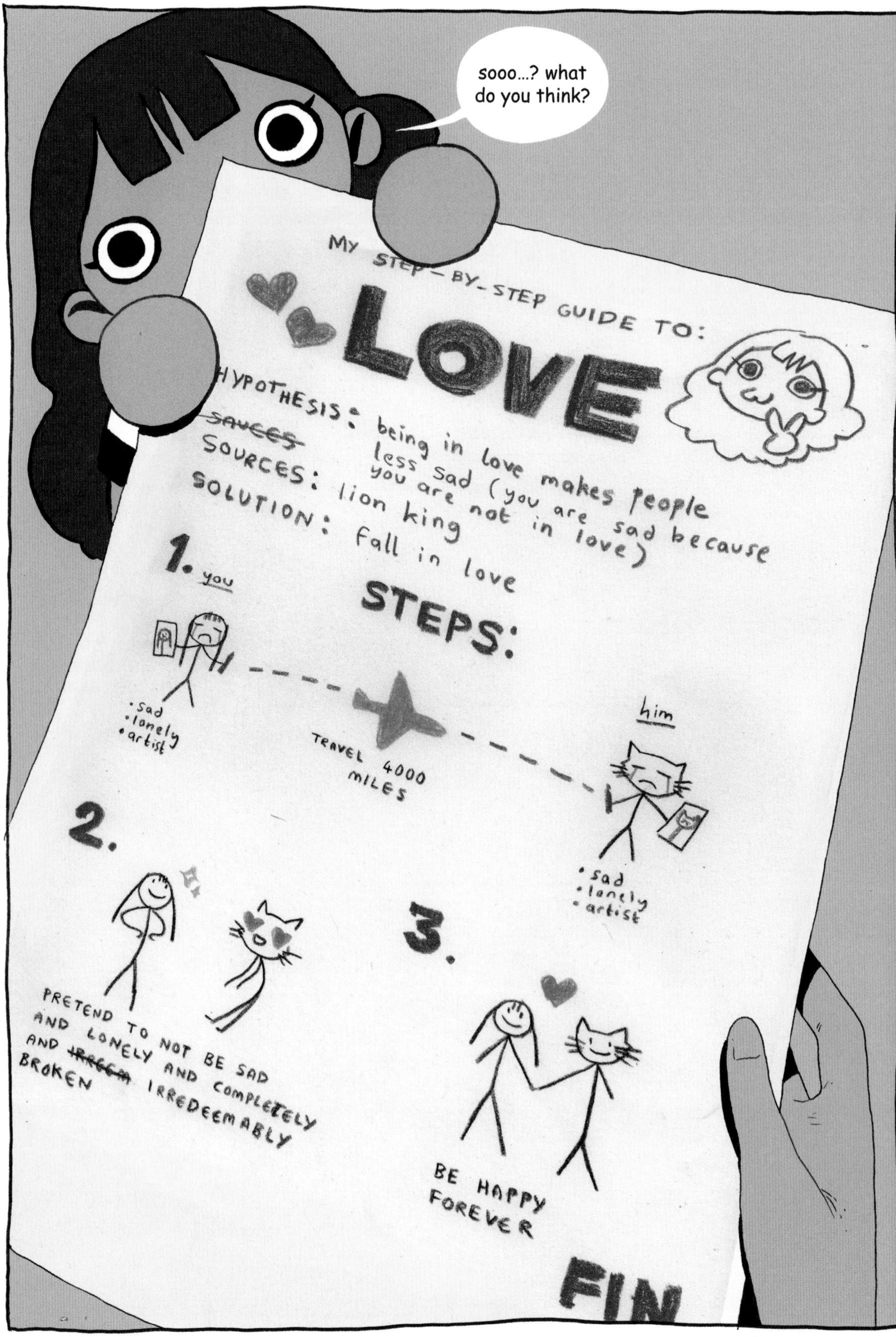
sooo...? what do you think?
MY STEP-BY-STEP GUIDE TO:
LOVE
HYPOTHESIS: being in love makes people less sad (you are sad because you are not in love)
~~SAUCES~~
SOURCES: lion king
SOLUTION: fall in love
STEPS:
1. you
• sad
• lonely
• artist
TRAVEL 4000 MILES
him
• sad
• lonely
• artist
2.
PRETEND TO NOT BE SAD AND LONELY AND COMPLETELY AND ~~IRREEM~~ IRREDEEMABLY BROKEN
3.
BE HAPPY FOREVER
FIN

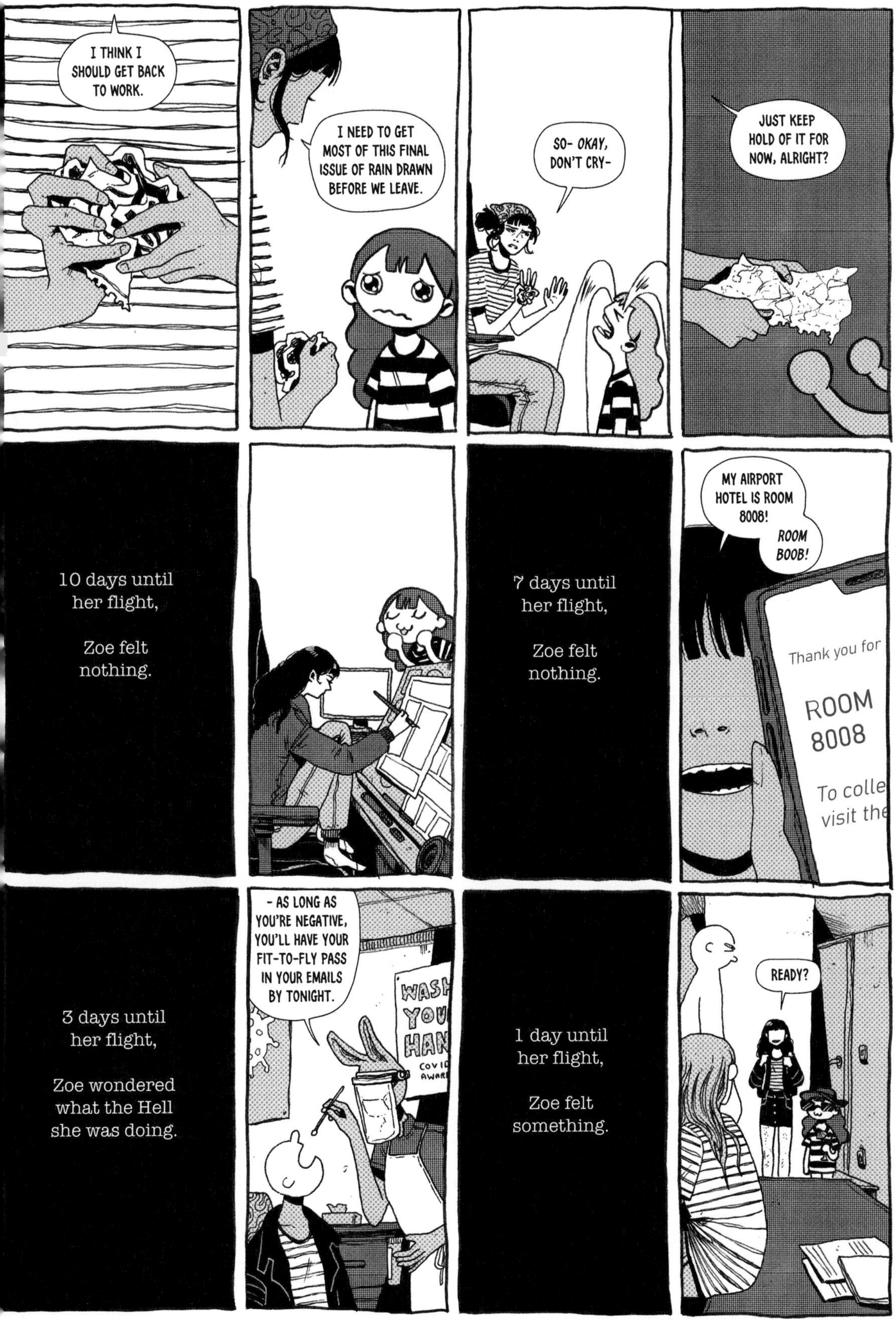
I THINK I SHOULD GET BACK TO WORK.
I NEED TO GET MOST OF THIS FINAL ISSUE OF RAIN DRAWN BEFORE WE LEAVE.
SO- OKAY, DON'T CRY-
JUST KEEP HOLD OF IT FOR NOW, ALRIGHT?
10 days until her flight,
Zoe felt nothing.
7 days until her flight,
Zoe felt nothing.
MY AIRPORT HOTEL IS ROOM 8008!
ROOM BOOB!
Thank you for
ROOM 8008
To colle
visit the
3 days until her flight,
Zoe wondered what the Hell she was doing.
- AS LONG AS YOU'RE NEGATIVE, YOU'LL HAVE YOUR FIT-TO-FLY PASS IN YOUR EMAILS BY TONIGHT.
WASH YOU HAN
COVID AWAR
1 day until her flight,
Zoe felt something.
READY?

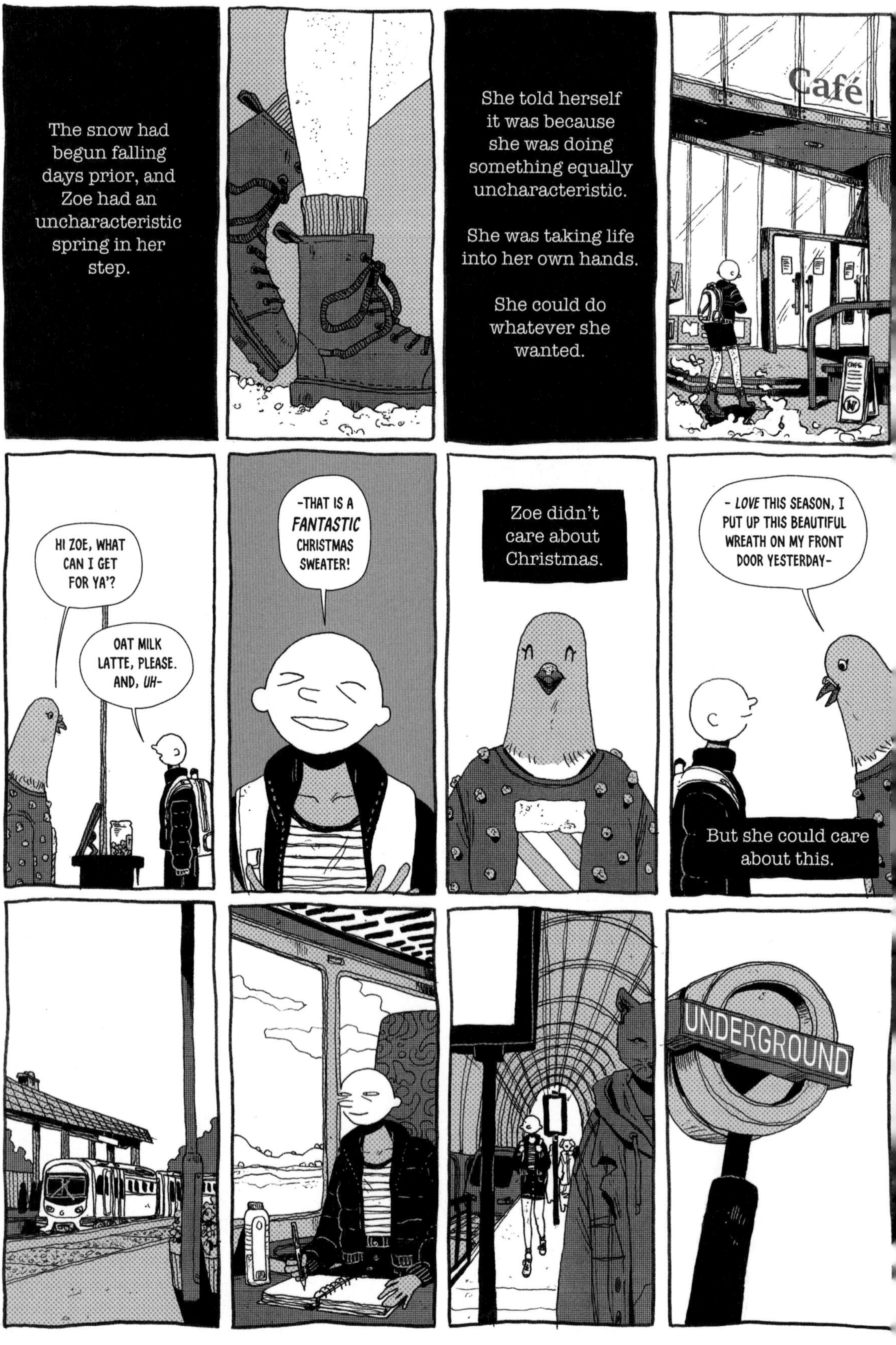

The snow had begun falling days prior, and Zoe had an uncharacteristic spring in her step.
She told herself it was because she was doing something equally uncharacteristic.
She was taking life into her own hands.
She could do whatever she wanted.
Café
HI ZOE, WHAT CAN I GET FOR YA'?
OAT MILK LATTE, PLEASE. AND, UH-
-THAT IS A FANTASTIC CHRISTMAS SWEATER!
Zoe didn't care about Christmas.
- LOVE THIS SEASON, I PUT UP THIS BEAUTIFUL WREATH ON MY FRONT DOOR YESTERDAY-
But she could care about this.
UNDERGROUND

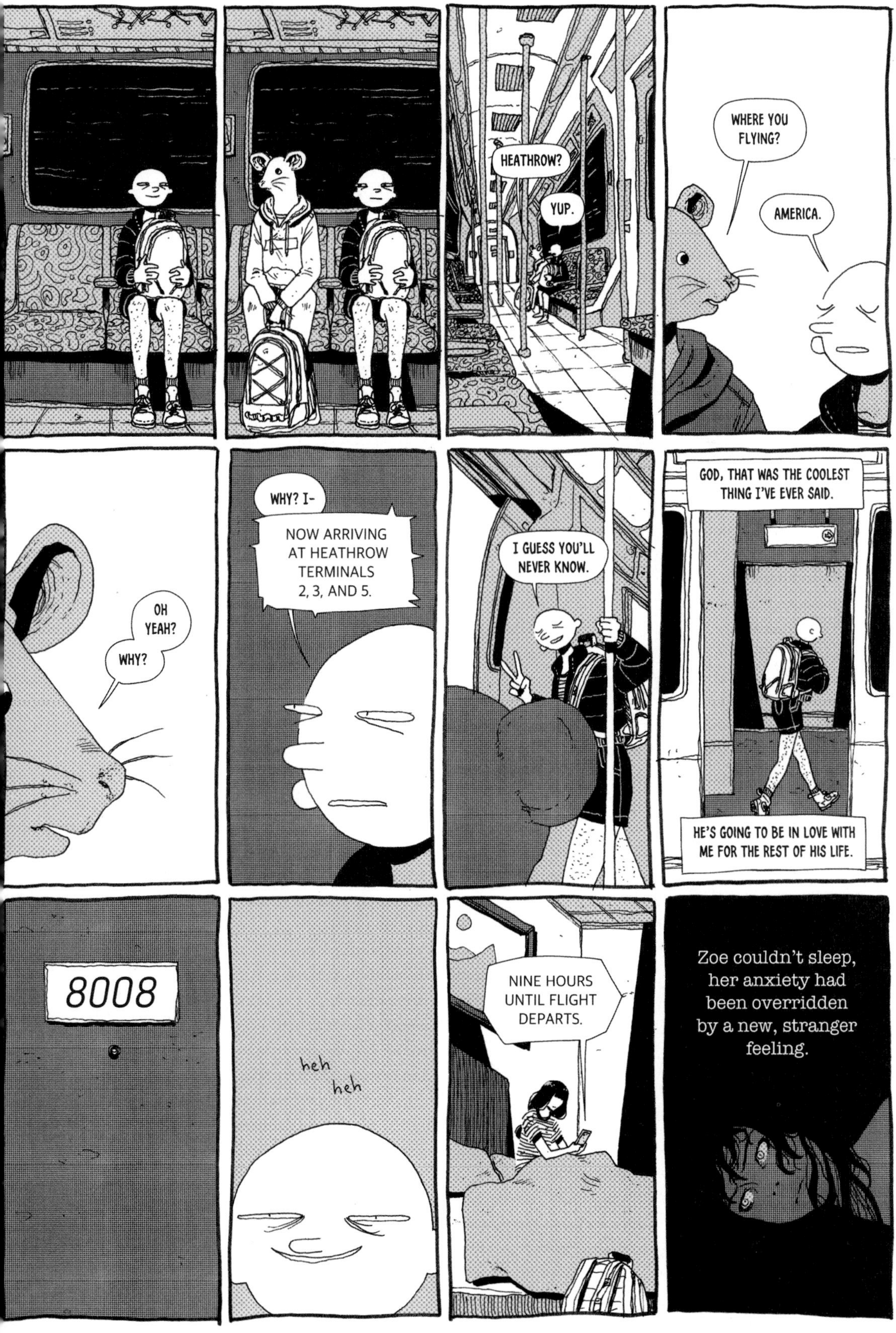
HEATHROW?
YUP.
WHERE YOU FLYING?
AMERICA.
OH YEAH?
WHY?
WHY? I-
NOW ARRIVING AT HEATHROW TERMINALS 2, 3, AND 5.
I GUESS YOU'LL NEVER KNOW.
GOD, THAT WAS THE COOLEST THING I'VE EVER SAID.
HE'S GOING TO BE IN LOVE WITH ME FOR THE REST OF HIS LIFE.
8008
heh heh
NINE HOURS UNTIL FLIGHT DEPARTS.
Zoe couldn't sleep, her anxiety had been overridden by a new, stranger feeling.

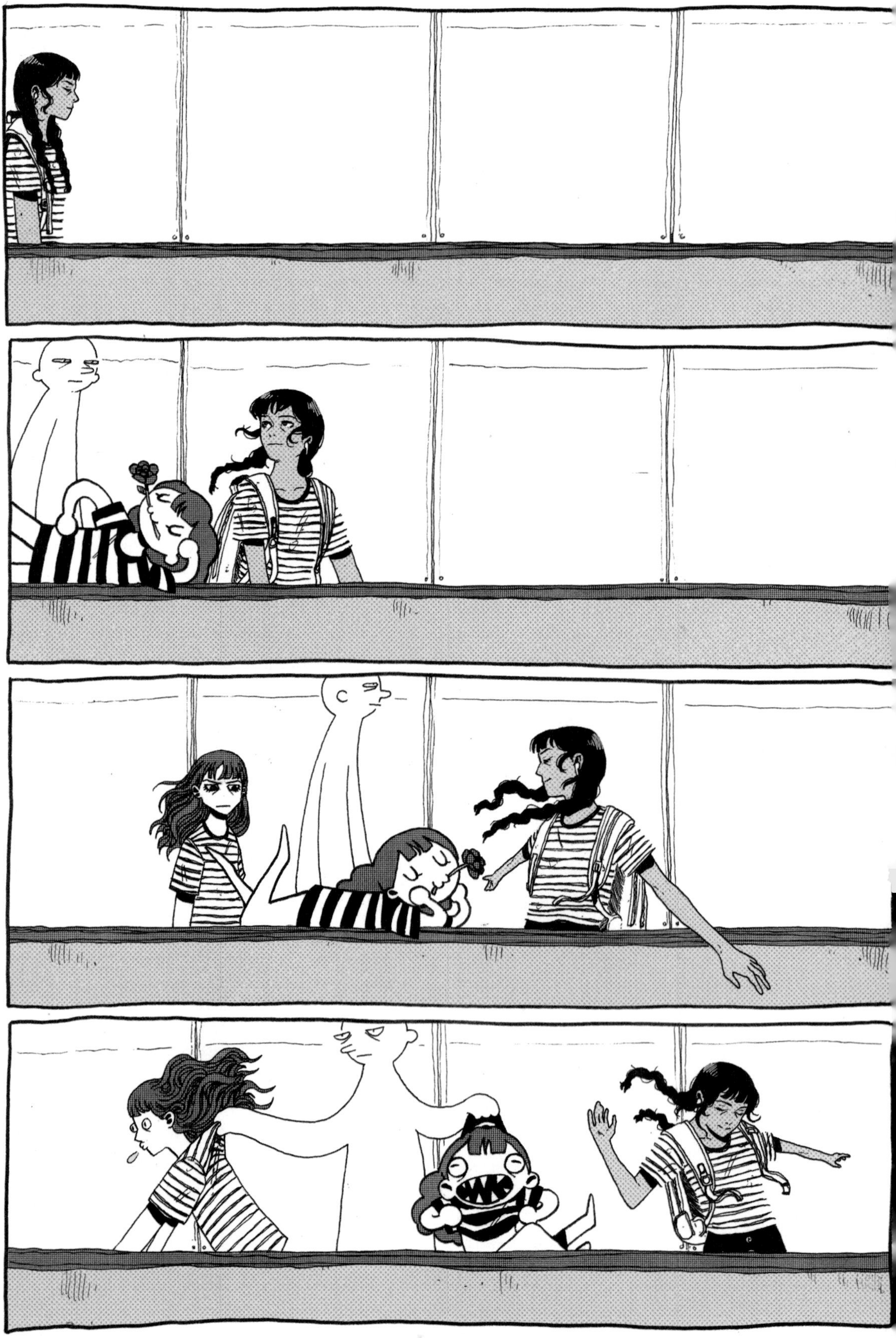

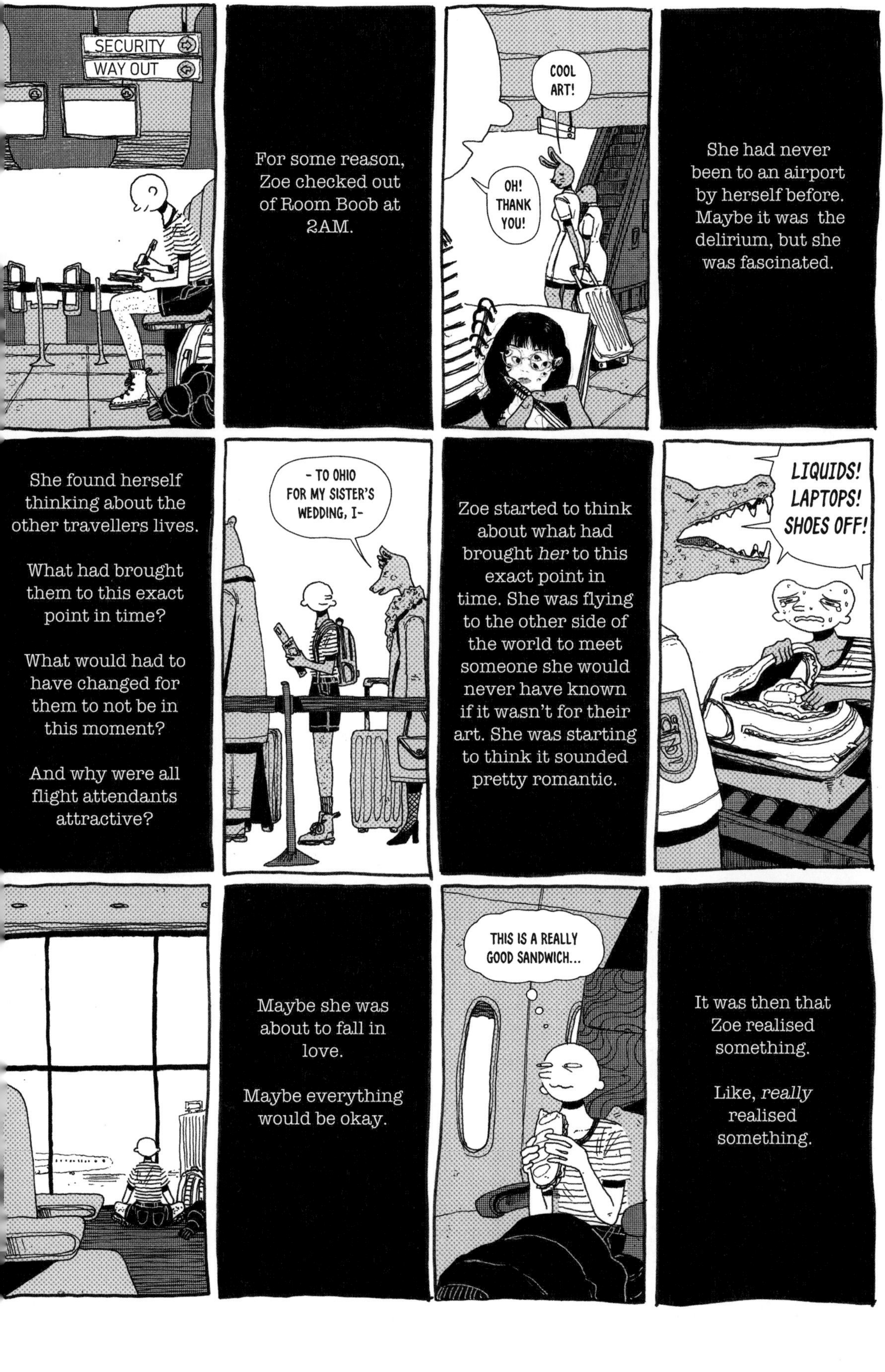
SECURITY
WAY OUT
For some reason, Zoe checked out of Room Boob at 2AM.
COOL ART!
OH! THANK YOU!
She had never been to an airport by herself before. Maybe it was the delirium, but she was fascinated.
She found herself thinking about the other travellers lives.
What had brought them to this exact point in time?
What would had to have changed for them to not be in this moment?
And why were all flight attendants attractive?
- TO OHIO FOR MY SISTER'S WEDDING, I-
Zoe started to think about what had brought *her* to this exact point in time. She was flying to the other side of the world to meet someone she would never have known if it wasn't for their art. She was starting to think it sounded pretty romantic.
LIQUIDS! LAPTOPS! SHOES OFF!
Maybe she was about to fall in love.
Maybe everything would be okay.
THIS IS A REALLY GOOD SANDWICH...
It was then that Zoe realised something.
Like, *really* realised something.

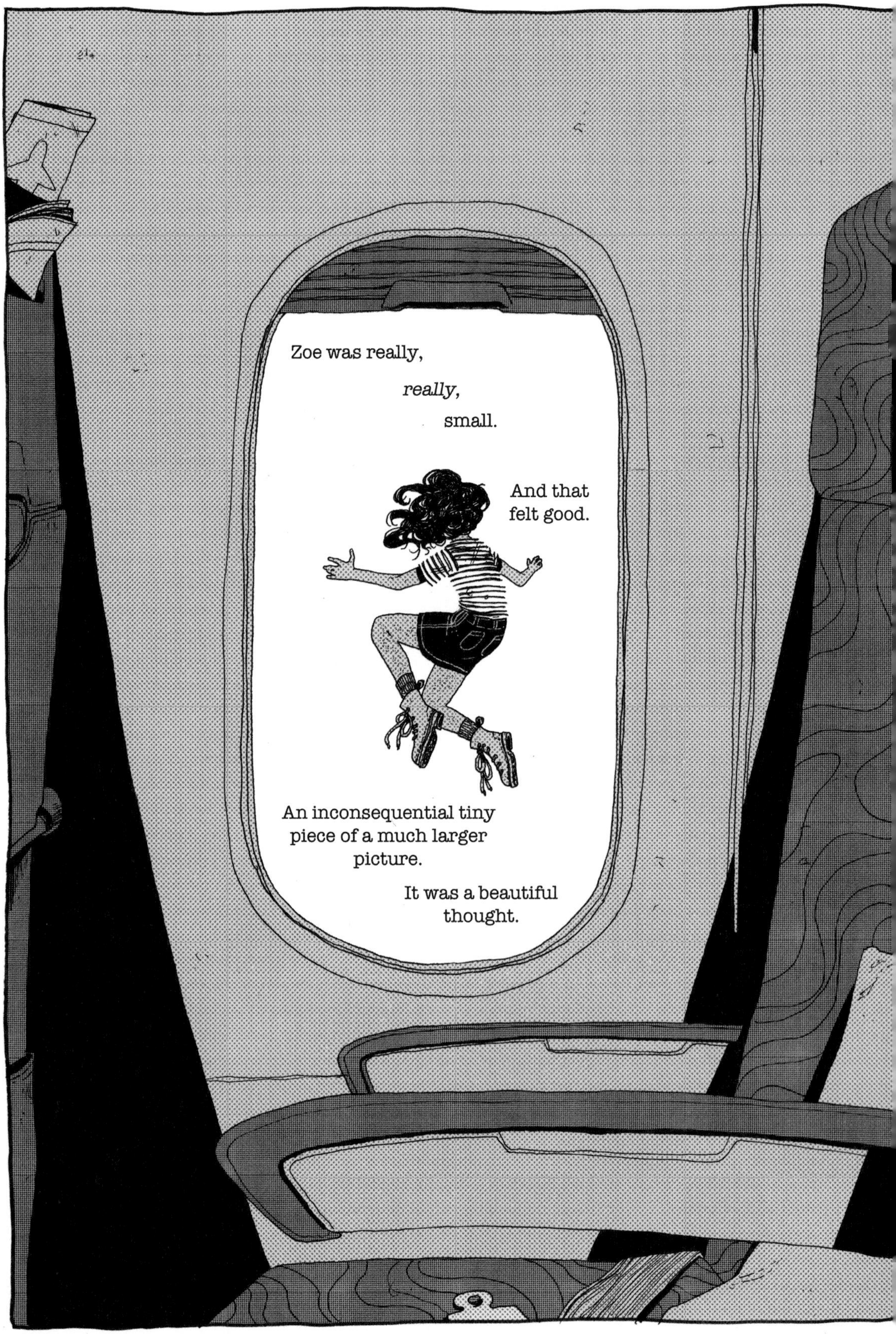

Zoe was really,
really,
small.
And that felt good.
An inconsequential tiny piece of a much larger picture.
It was a beautiful thought.

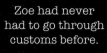
AND WHAT IS IT YOU DO?

UH- COMICS. APPARENTLY.

Zoe had never had to go through customs before.

She found it strangely enjoyable.

MAN. THEM'S SOME SERIOUS BANGS.

WELL, WELCOME TO THE STATES, COMIC GIRL.

Zoe Thorogood

She had a changeover flight, which meant she had several stationary hours to think.

She felt calm.

She was all alone, and so far from home. But it felt right.

It felt good.

That was until she discovered something truly terrible had happened.

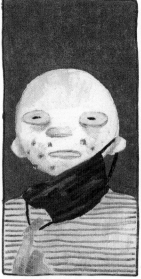

Zoe decided she would simply have to hide her face for the week.

Yeah.

Zoe decided she was going to fall in love.

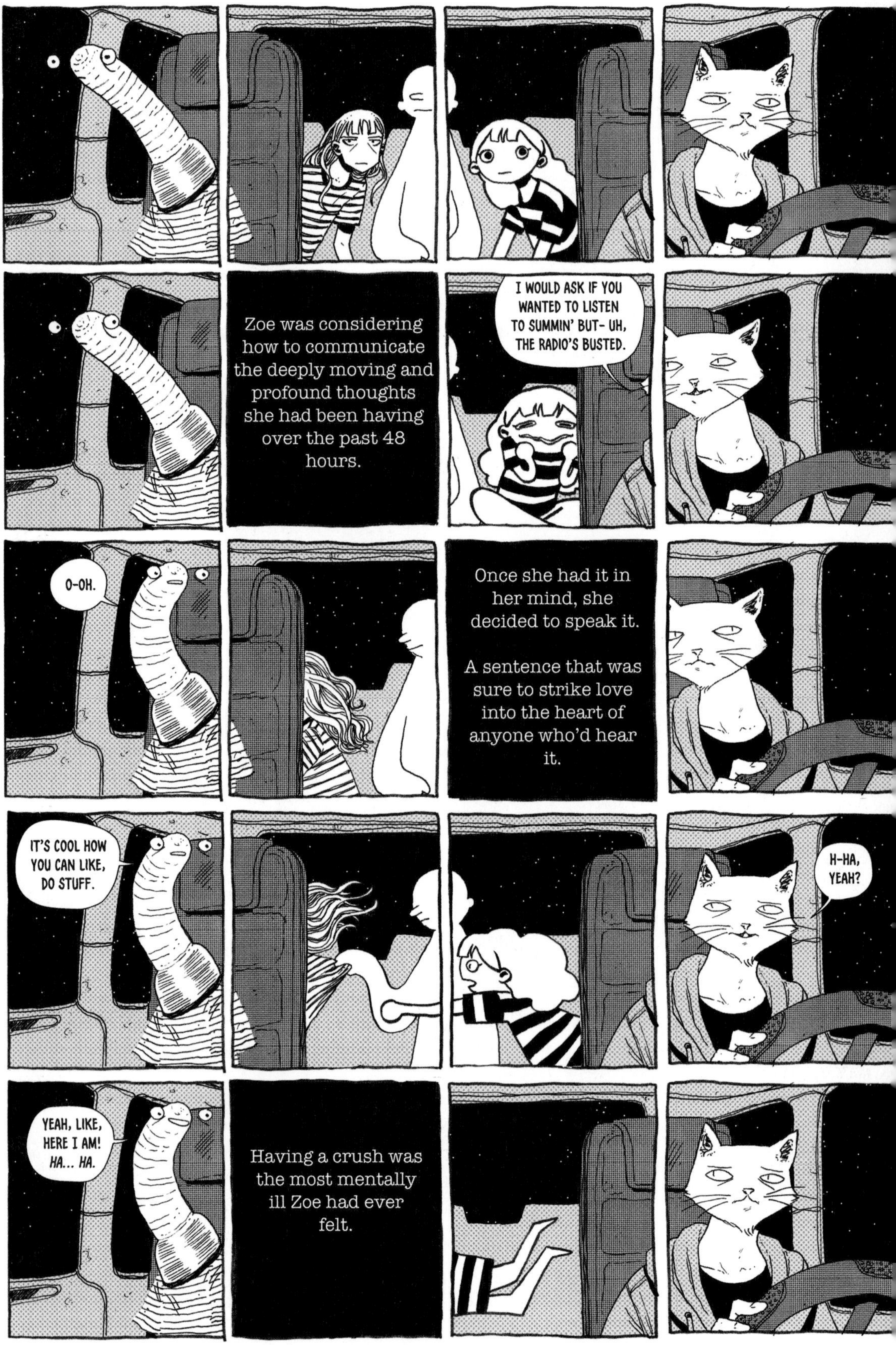
Zoe was considering how to communicate the deeply moving and profound thoughts she had been having over the past 48 hours.
I WOULD ASK IF YOU WANTED TO LISTEN TO SUMMIN' BUT- UH, THE RADIO'S BUSTED.
O-OH.
Once she had it in her mind, she decided to speak it.
A sentence that was sure to strike love into the heart of anyone who'd hear it.
IT'S COOL HOW YOU CAN LIKE, DO STUFF.
H-HA, YEAH?
YEAH, LIKE, HERE I AM! HA... HA.
Having a crush was the most mentally ill Zoe had ever felt.

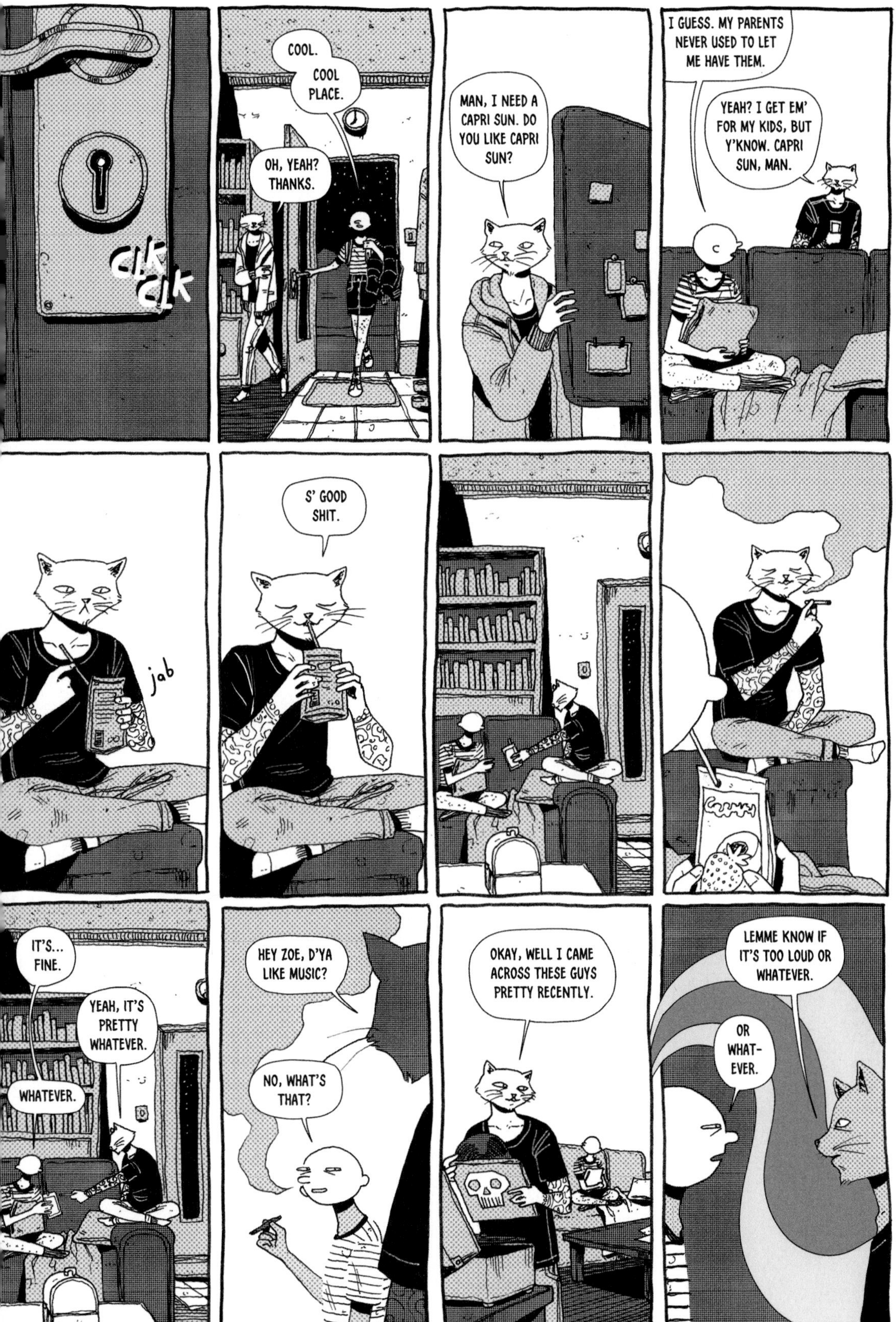
CLK CLK
COOL.
COOL PLACE.
OH, YEAH? THANKS.
MAN, I NEED A CAPRI SUN. DO YOU LIKE CAPRI SUN?
I GUESS. MY PARENTS NEVER USED TO LET ME HAVE THEM.
YEAH? I GET EM' FOR MY KIDS, BUT Y'KNOW. CAPRI SUN, MAN.
jab
S' GOOD SHIT.
IT'S... FINE.
YEAH, IT'S PRETTY WHATEVER.
WHATEVER.
HEY ZOE, D'YA LIKE MUSIC?
NO, WHAT'S THAT?
OKAY, WELL I CAME ACROSS THESE GUYS PRETTY RECENTLY.
LEMME KNOW IF IT'S TOO LOUD OR WHATEVER.
OR WHAT-EVER.

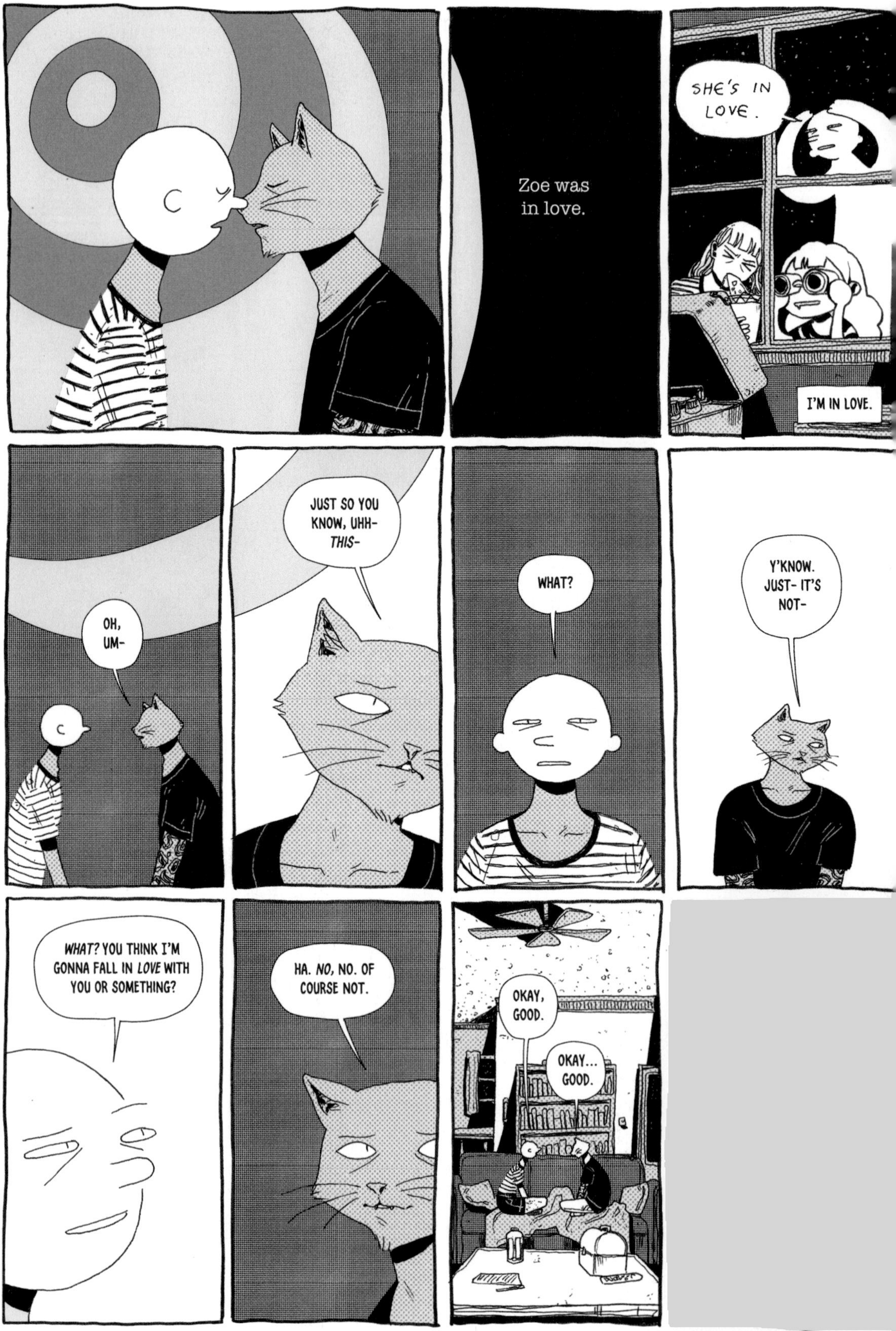
Zoe was in love.
SHE'S IN LOVE.
I'M IN LOVE.
OH, UM-
JUST SO YOU KNOW, UHH- THIS-
WHAT?
Y'KNOW. JUST- IT'S NOT-
WHAT? YOU THINK I'M GONNA FALL IN LOVE WITH YOU OR SOMETHING?
HA. NO, NO. OF COURSE NOT.
OKAY, GOOD.
OKAY... GOOD.

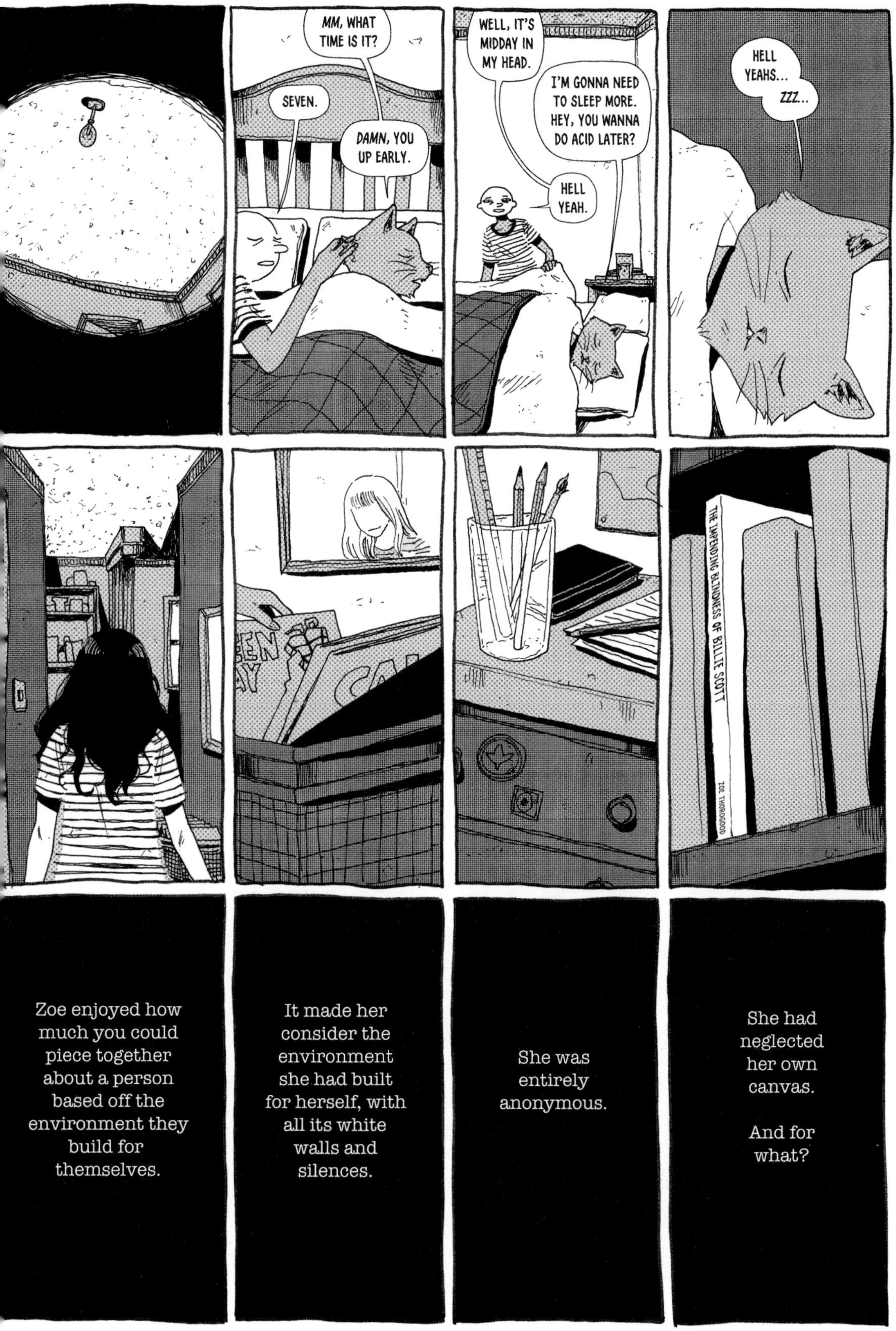
MM, WHAT TIME IS IT?
SEVEN.
DAMN, YOU UP EARLY.
WELL, IT'S MIDDAY IN MY HEAD.
I'M GONNA NEED TO SLEEP MORE. HEY, YOU WANNA DO ACID LATER?
HELL YEAH.
HELL YEAHS...
ZZZ...
THE IMPENDING BLINDNESS OF BILLIE SCOTT
ZOE THOROGOOD
Zoe enjoyed how much you could piece together about a person based off the environment they build for themselves.
It made her consider the environment she had built for herself, with all its white walls and silences.
She was entirely anonymous.
She had neglected her own canvas.
And for what?

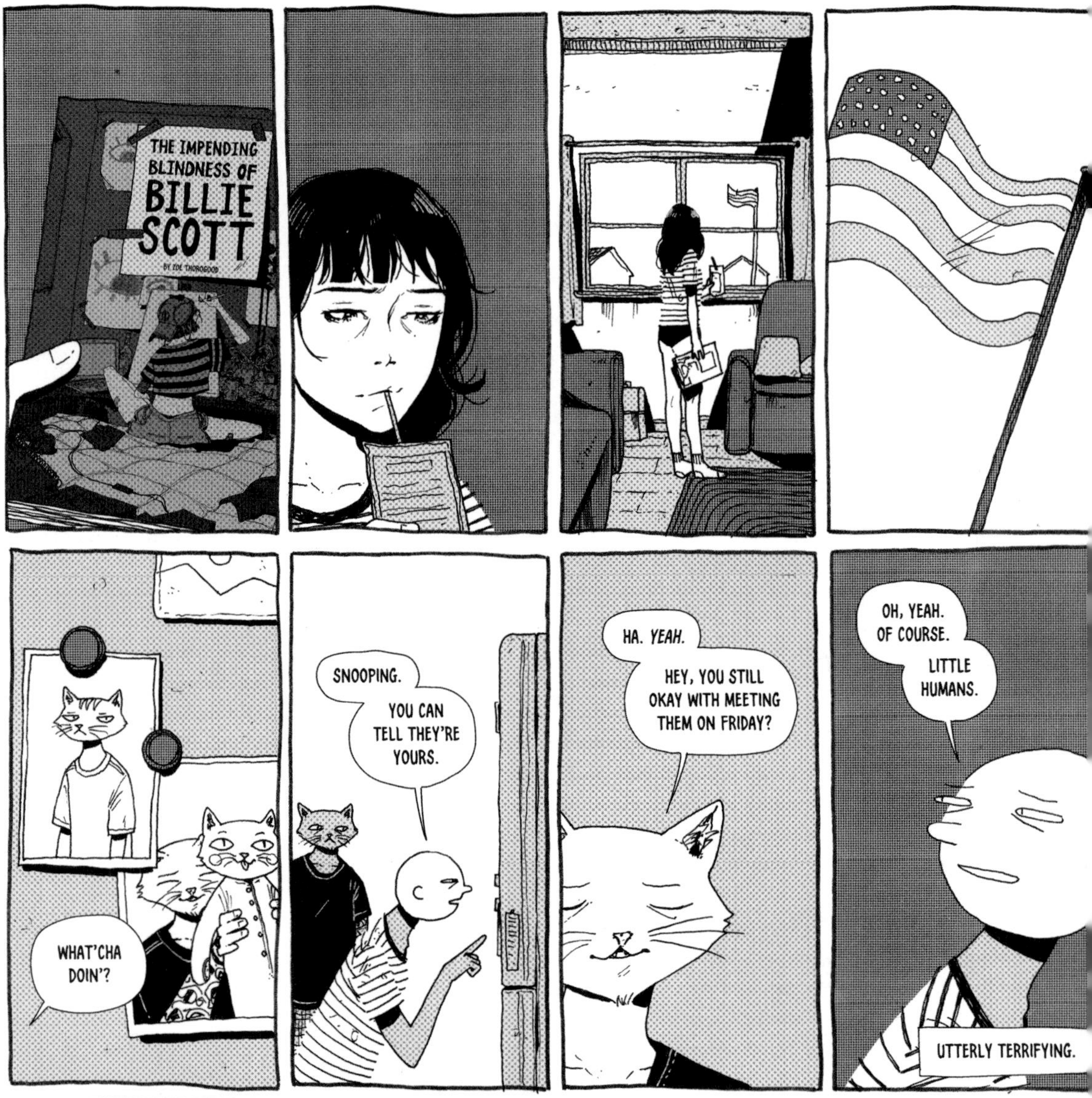
THE IMPENDING BLINDNESS OF BILLIE SCOTT
BY ZOE THOROGOOD
WHAT'CHA DOIN'?
SNOOPING.
YOU CAN TELL THEY'RE YOURS.
HA. *YEAH.*
HEY, YOU STILL OKAY WITH MEETING THEM ON FRIDAY?
OH, YEAH. OF COURSE.
LITTLE HUMANS.
UTTERLY TERRIFYING.

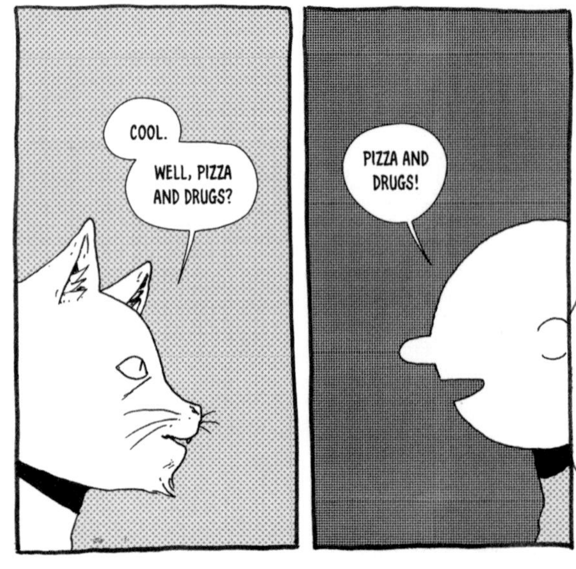
COOL.
WELL, PIZZA AND DRUGS?
PIZZA AND DRUGS!

ZOE SAYS:

<u>Don't do drugs!</u>

(But if you're reading a 23 year old's comic book in search of a moralistic role model then, what the hell, do drugs.)

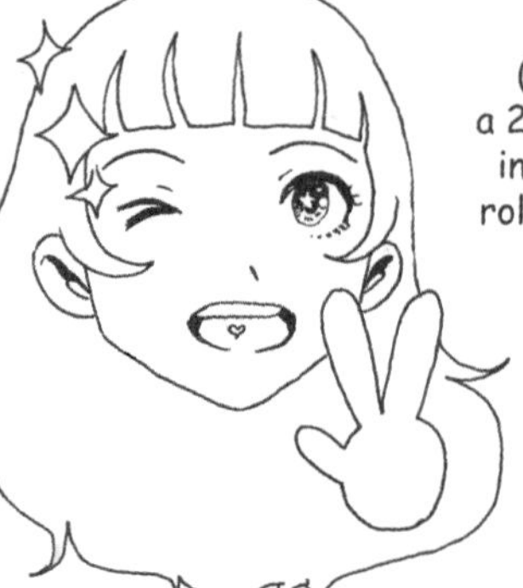

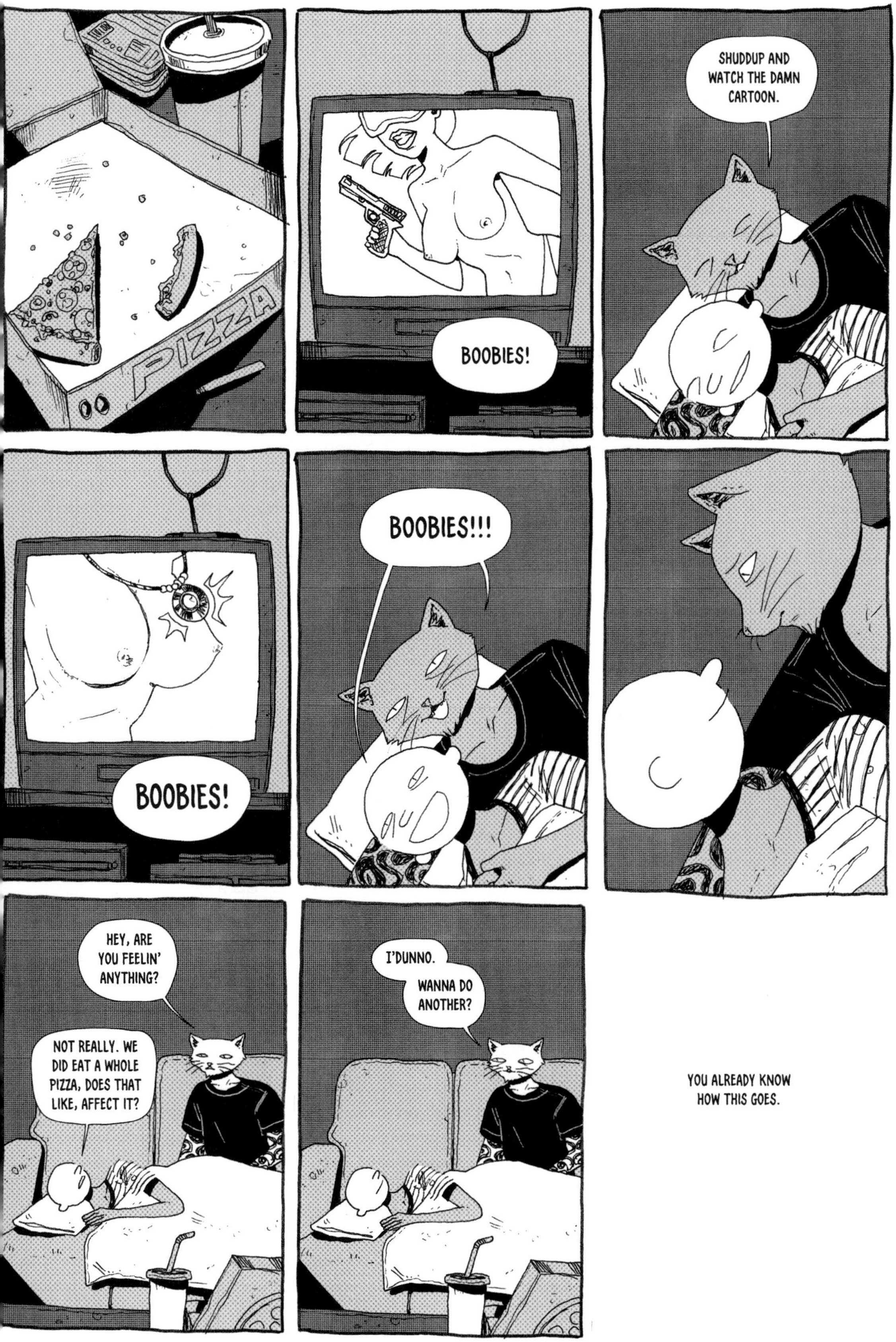
PIZZA
BOOBIES!
SHUDDUP AND WATCH THE DAMN CARTOON.
BOOBIES!
BOOBIES!!!
HEY, ARE YOU FEELIN' ANYTHING?
NOT REALLY. WE DID EAT A WHOLE PIZZA, DOES THAT LIKE, AFFECT IT?
I'DUNNO.
WANNA DO ANOTHER?
YOU ALREADY KNOW HOW THIS GOES.

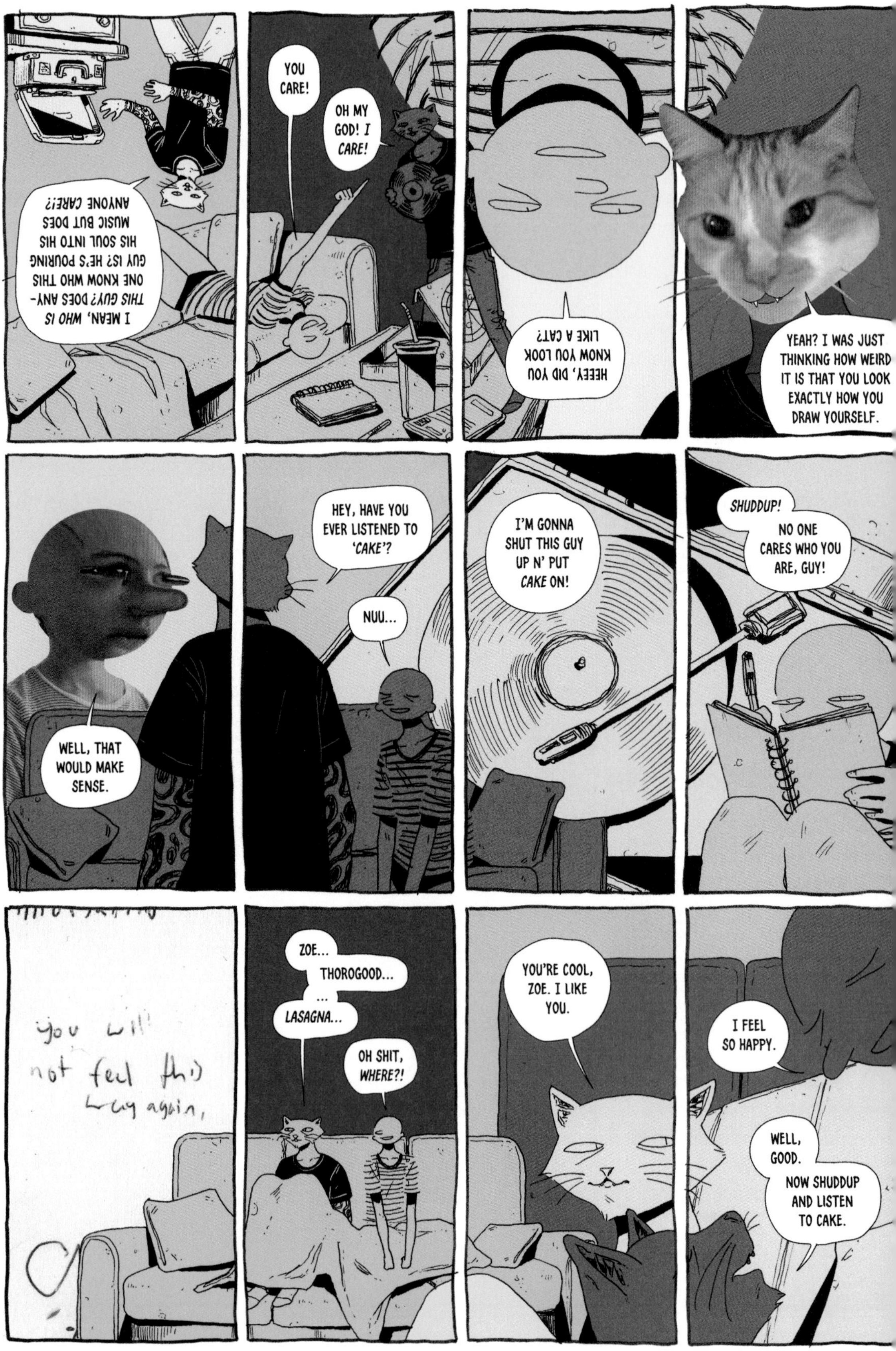
I MEAN, WHO IS THIS GUY? DOES ANY-ONE KNOW WHO THIS GUY IS? HE'S POURING HIS SOUL INTO HIS MUSIC BUT DOES ANYONE CARE!?
YOU CARE!
OH MY GOD! I CARE!
HEEEY, DID YOU KNOW YOU LOOK LIKE A CAT?
YEAH? I WAS JUST THINKING HOW WEIRD IT IS THAT YOU LOOK EXACTLY HOW YOU DRAW YOURSELF.
WELL, THAT WOULD MAKE SENSE.
HEY, HAVE YOU EVER LISTENED TO 'CAKE'?
NUU...
I'M GONNA SHUT THIS GUY UP N' PUT CAKE ON!
SHUDDUP!
NO ONE CARES WHO YOU ARE, GUY!
you will not feel this way again,
ZOE...
THOROGOOD...
...
LASAGNA...
OH SHIT, WHERE?!
YOU'RE COOL, ZOE. I LIKE YOU.
I FEEL SO HAPPY.
WELL, GOOD.
NOW SHUDDUP AND LISTEN TO CAKE.

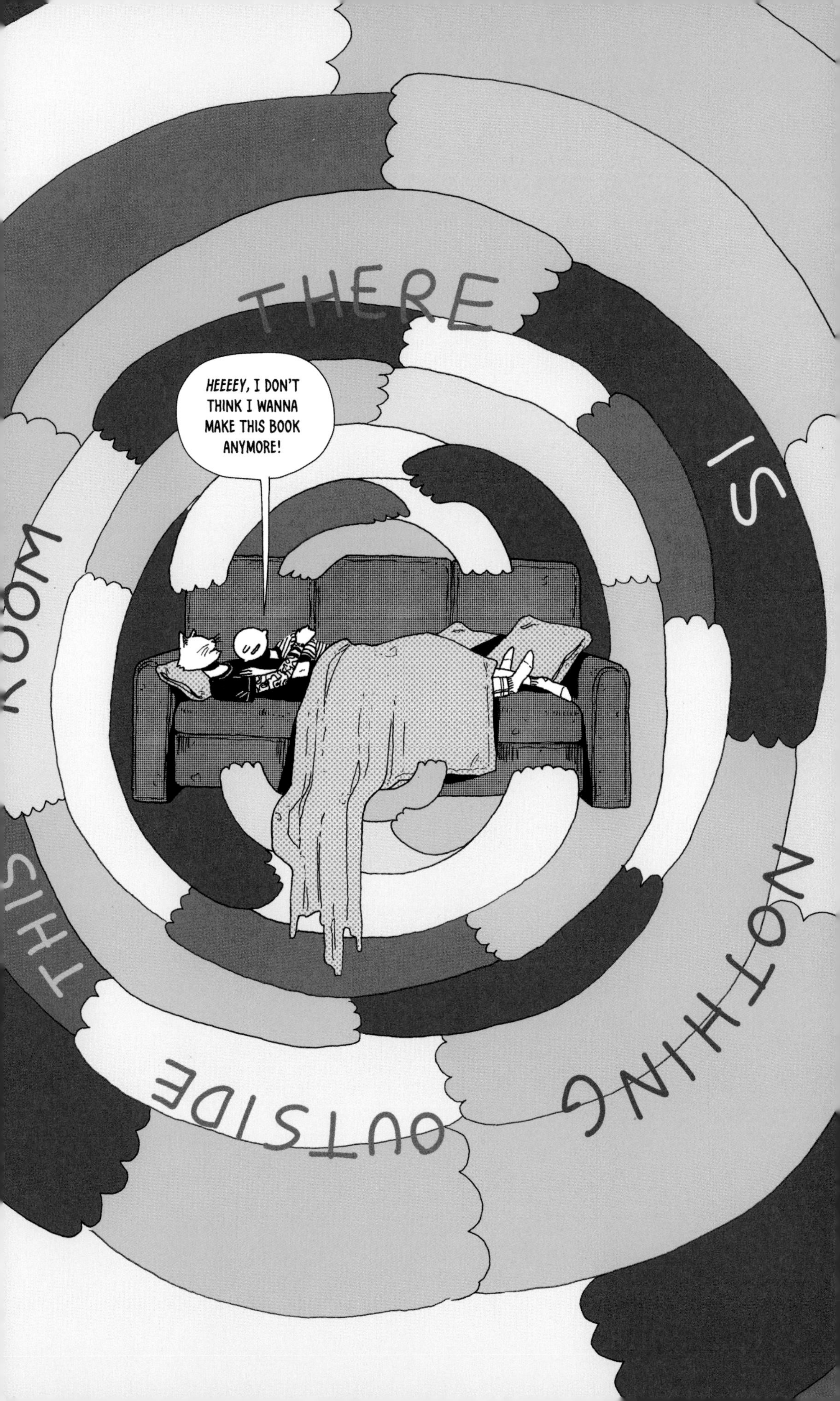
HEEEEY, I DON'T THINK I WANNA MAKE THIS BOOK ANYMORE!
THERE IS NOTHING OUTSIDE THIS ROOM

Open Book
CAKE

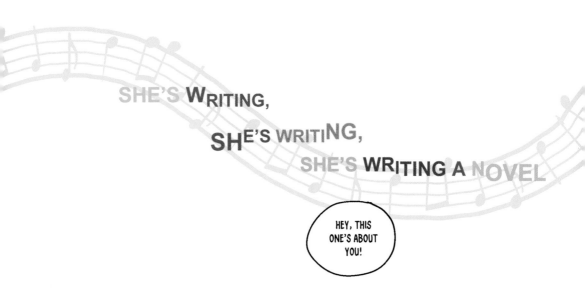

SHE'S WRITING,
SHE'S WRITING,
SHE'S WRITING A NOVEL

HEY, THIS ONE'S ABOUT YOU!

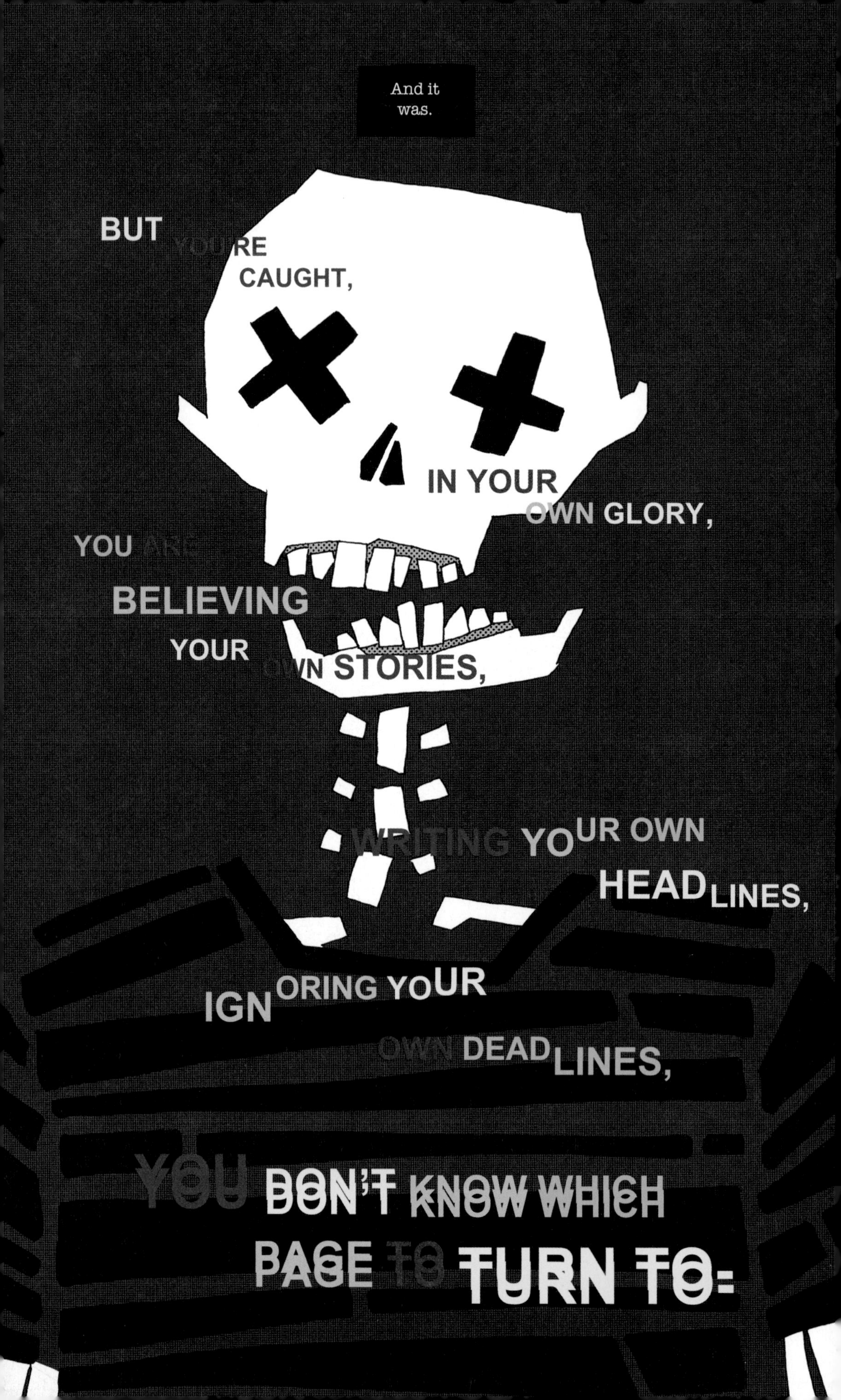
And it was.
BUT YOU'RE CAUGHT,
IN YOUR OWN GLORY,
YOU ARE BELIEVING YOUR OWN STORIES,
WRITING YOUR OWN HEADLINES,
IGNORING YOUR OWN DEADLINES,
YOU DON'T KNOW WHICH PAGE TO TURN TO:

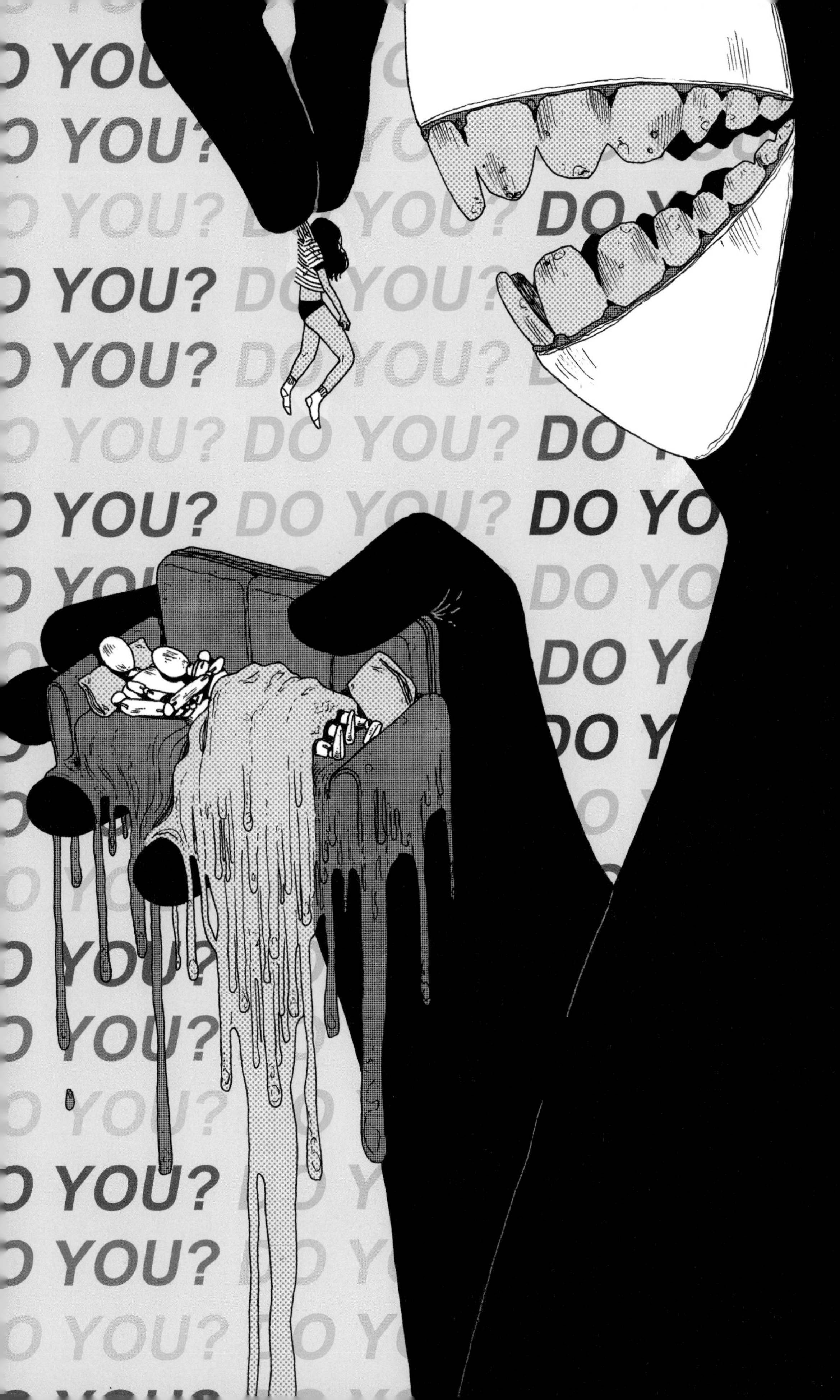
DO YOU?

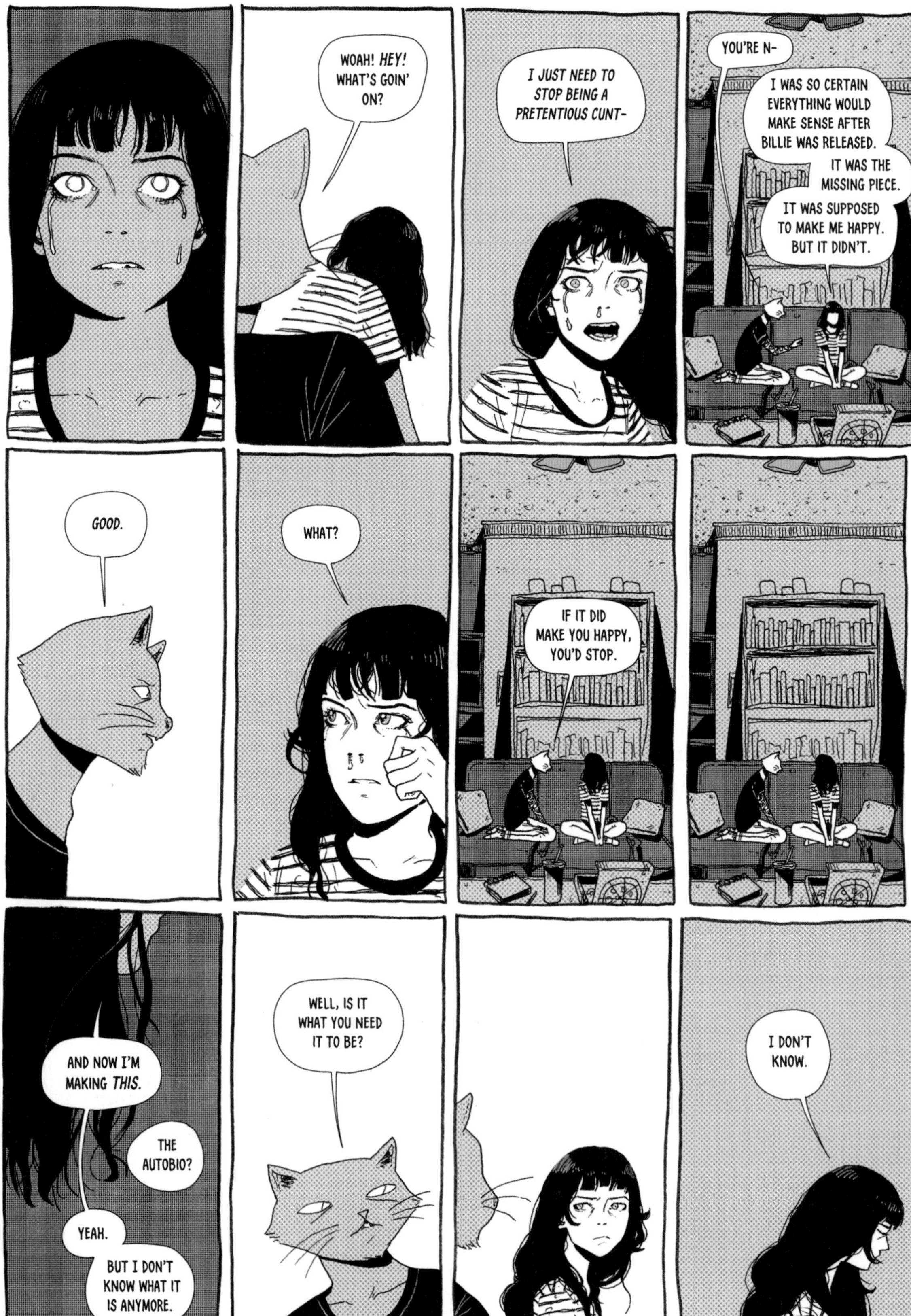

WOAH! HEY! WHAT'S GOIN' ON?
I JUST NEED TO STOP BEING A PRETENTIOUS CUNT-
YOU'RE N-
I WAS SO CERTAIN EVERYTHING WOULD MAKE SENSE AFTER BILLIE WAS RELEASED.
IT WAS THE MISSING PIECE.
IT WAS SUPPOSED TO MAKE ME HAPPY. BUT IT DIDN'T.
GOOD.
WHAT?
IF IT DID MAKE YOU HAPPY, YOU'D STOP.
AND NOW I'M MAKING THIS.
THE AUTOBIO?
YEAH.
BUT I DON'T KNOW WHAT IT IS ANYMORE.
WELL, IS IT WHAT YOU NEED IT TO BE?
I DON'T KNOW.

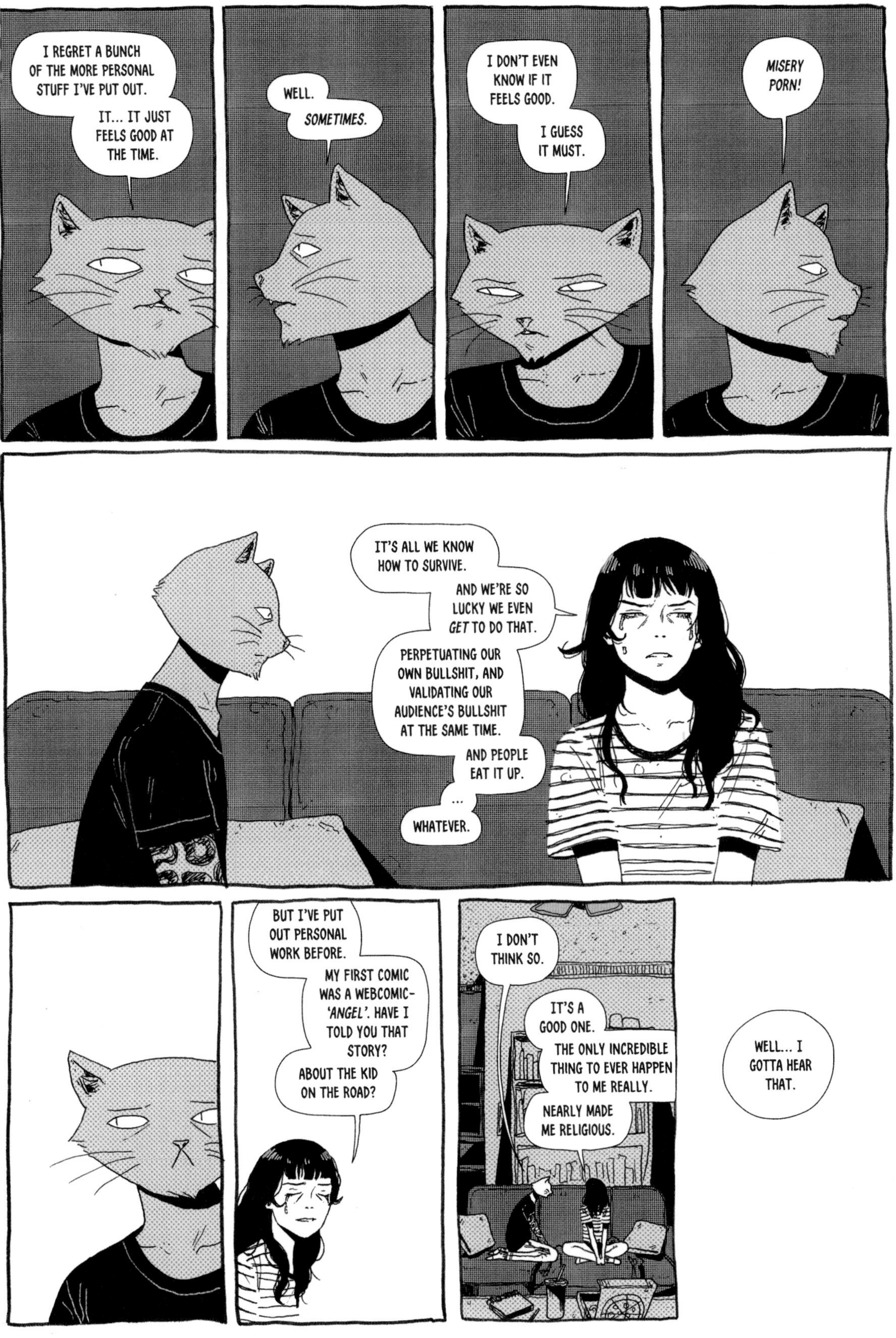
I REGRET A BUNCH OF THE MORE PERSONAL STUFF I'VE PUT OUT.
IT... IT JUST FEELS GOOD AT THE TIME.
WELL.
SOMETIMES.
I DON'T EVEN KNOW IF IT FEELS GOOD.
I GUESS IT MUST.
MISERY PORN!
IT'S ALL WE KNOW HOW TO SURVIVE.
AND WE'RE SO LUCKY WE EVEN *GET* TO DO THAT.
PERPETUATING OUR OWN BULLSHIT, AND VALIDATING OUR AUDIENCE'S BULLSHIT AT THE SAME TIME.
AND PEOPLE EAT IT UP.
...
WHATEVER.
BUT I'VE PUT OUT PERSONAL WORK BEFORE.
MY FIRST COMIC WAS A WEBCOMIC- *'ANGEL'*. HAVE I TOLD YOU THAT STORY?
ABOUT THE KID ON THE ROAD?
I DON'T THINK SO.
IT'S A GOOD ONE.
THE ONLY INCREDIBLE THING TO EVER HAPPEN TO ME REALLY.
NEARLY MADE ME RELIGIOUS.
WELL... I GOTTA HEAR THAT.

SO, WHEN I WAS FIFTEEN, I TRIED TO KILL MYSELF.

...ng this you're probably wondering ... did this, I'm only 15 after all. I'm useless, I really am. I can't live up to your expectations and I don't want to disapoint you, and I have no real talent or ambition (... sort of draw but as Mrs. Milne it's only manga)

WELL— I DON'T KNOW IF I WAS GONNA GO THROUGH WITH IT, BUT FOR THE SAKE OF STORYTELLING, I WAS.

I HAD BEEN LOOKIN' UP AT THIS NOOSE FOR A WHILE, LISTENING TO QUEEN—

HAHA, QUEEN? REALLY?

I WAS A THEATRE KID.

ANYWAY— SO I'M ABOUT TO KILL MYSELF, I THINK, WHEN I HEAR THIS WOMAN SCREAMING IN THE DISTANCE.

INSTINCT KICKS IN AND I RUN TOWARDS THE NOISE—

—OR MAYBE I'M JUST THANKFUL FOR THE EXCUSE TO NOT GO THROUGH WITH IT. I DON'T KNOW.

THE SCREAMS WERE COMING FROM MY NEIGHBOUR, OLD LADY, SHE'S STOOD BY THE SIDE OF THE ROAD LIKE—

OH THANK GOODNESS! YOU'RE YOUNG, MAYBE YOU CAN HELP.

SHE INDICATES TOWARDS THE FRONT OF THE CAR PARKED IN THE ROAD, AND I SEE THIS KID JUST SITTING THERE, BLOCKIN' THE CAR.

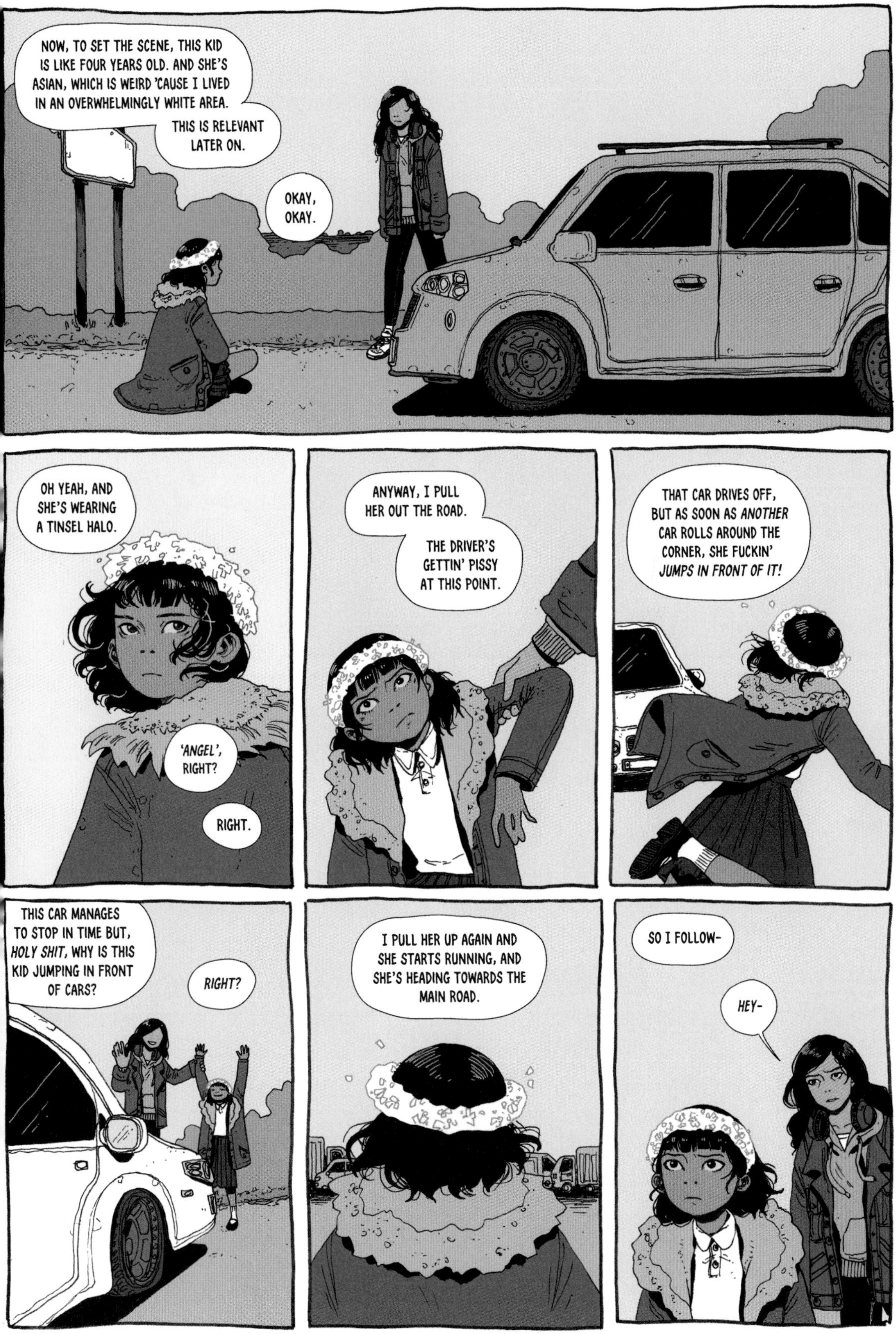

NOW, TO SET THE SCENE, THIS KID IS LIKE FOUR YEARS OLD. AND SHE'S ASIAN, WHICH IS WEIRD 'CAUSE I LIVED IN AN OVERWHELMINGLY WHITE AREA.
THIS IS RELEVANT LATER ON.
OKAY, OKAY.
OH YEAH, AND SHE'S WEARING A TINSEL HALO.
'ANGEL', RIGHT?
RIGHT.
ANYWAY, I PULL HER OUT THE ROAD.
THE DRIVER'S GETTIN' PISSY AT THIS POINT.
THAT CAR DRIVES OFF, BUT AS SOON AS *ANOTHER* CAR ROLLS AROUND THE CORNER, SHE FUCKIN' *JUMPS IN FRONT OF IT!*
THIS CAR MANAGES TO STOP IN TIME BUT, *HOLY SHIT*, WHY IS THIS KID JUMPING IN FRONT OF CARS?
RIGHT?
I PULL HER UP AGAIN AND SHE STARTS RUNNING, AND SHE'S HEADING TOWARDS THE MAIN ROAD.
SO I FOLLOW-
HEY-

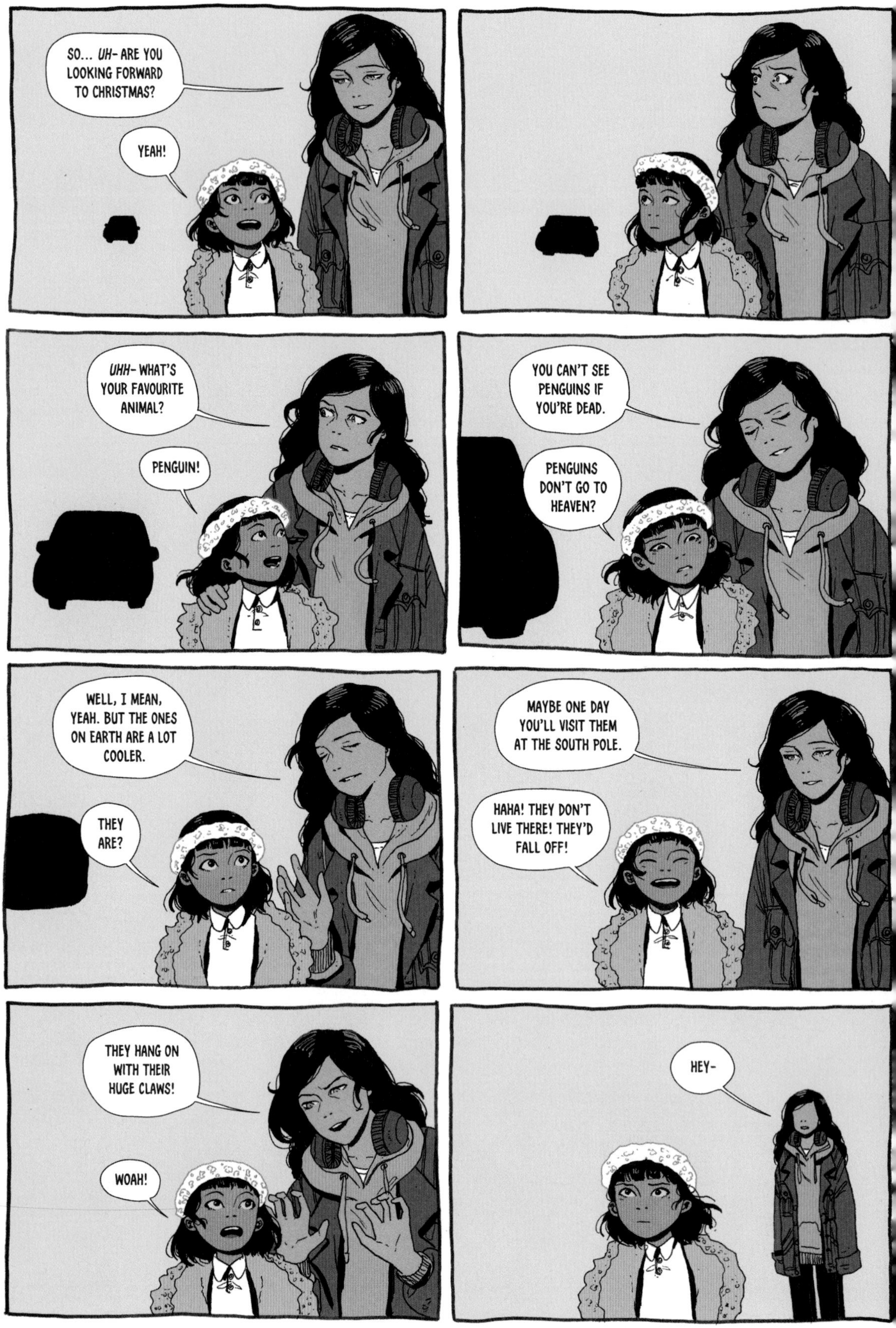
SO... UH- ARE YOU LOOKING FORWARD TO CHRISTMAS?
YEAH!
UHH- WHAT'S YOUR FAVOURITE ANIMAL?
PENGUIN!
YOU CAN'T SEE PENGUINS IF YOU'RE DEAD.
PENGUINS DON'T GO TO HEAVEN?
WELL, I MEAN, YEAH. BUT THE ONES ON EARTH ARE A LOT COOLER.
THEY ARE?
MAYBE ONE DAY YOU'LL VISIT THEM AT THE SOUTH POLE.
HAHA! THEY DON'T LIVE THERE! THEY'D FALL OFF!
THEY HANG ON WITH THEIR HUGE CLAWS!
WOAH!
HEY-

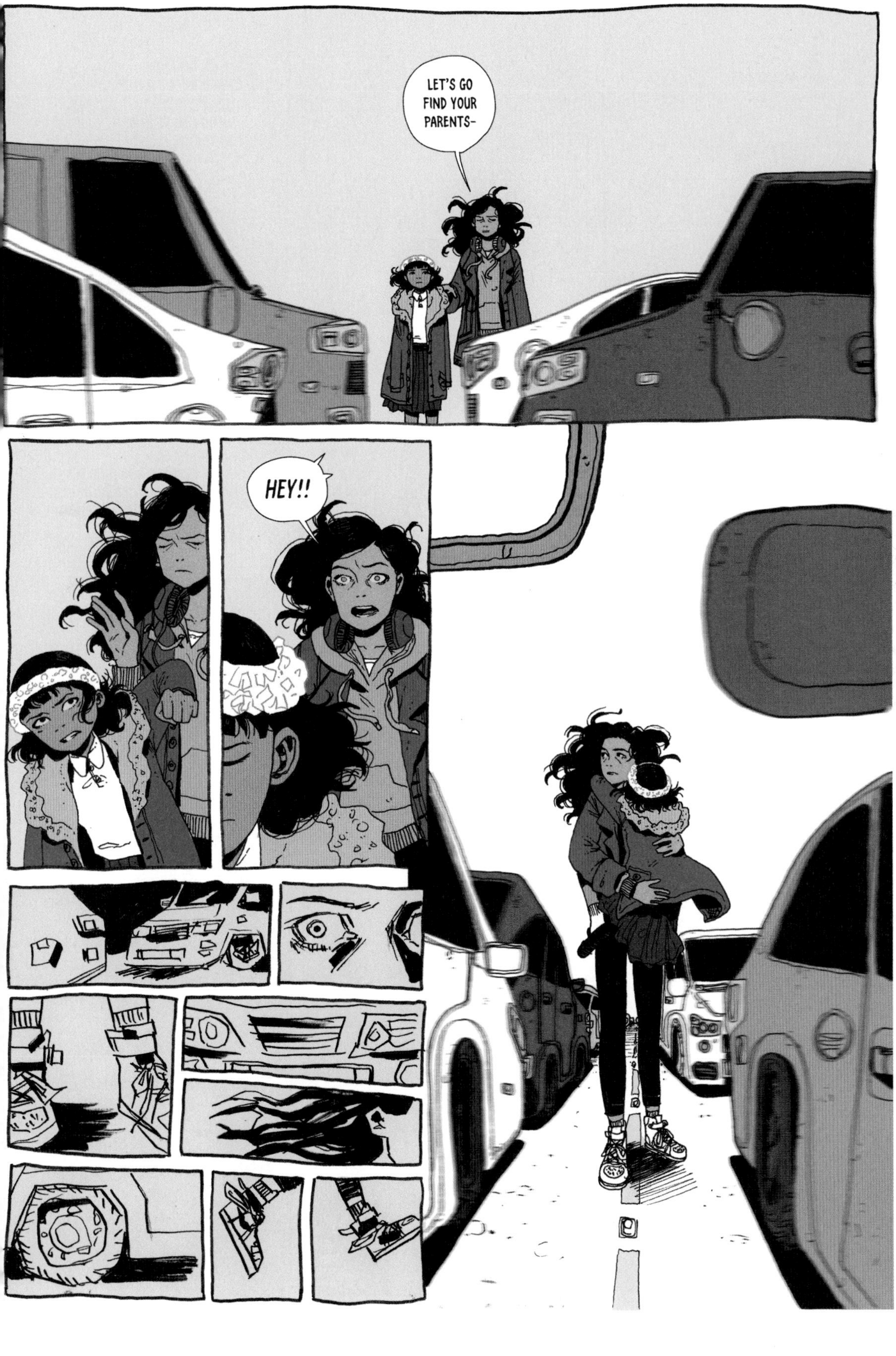
LET'S GO FIND YOUR PARENTS-
HEY!!

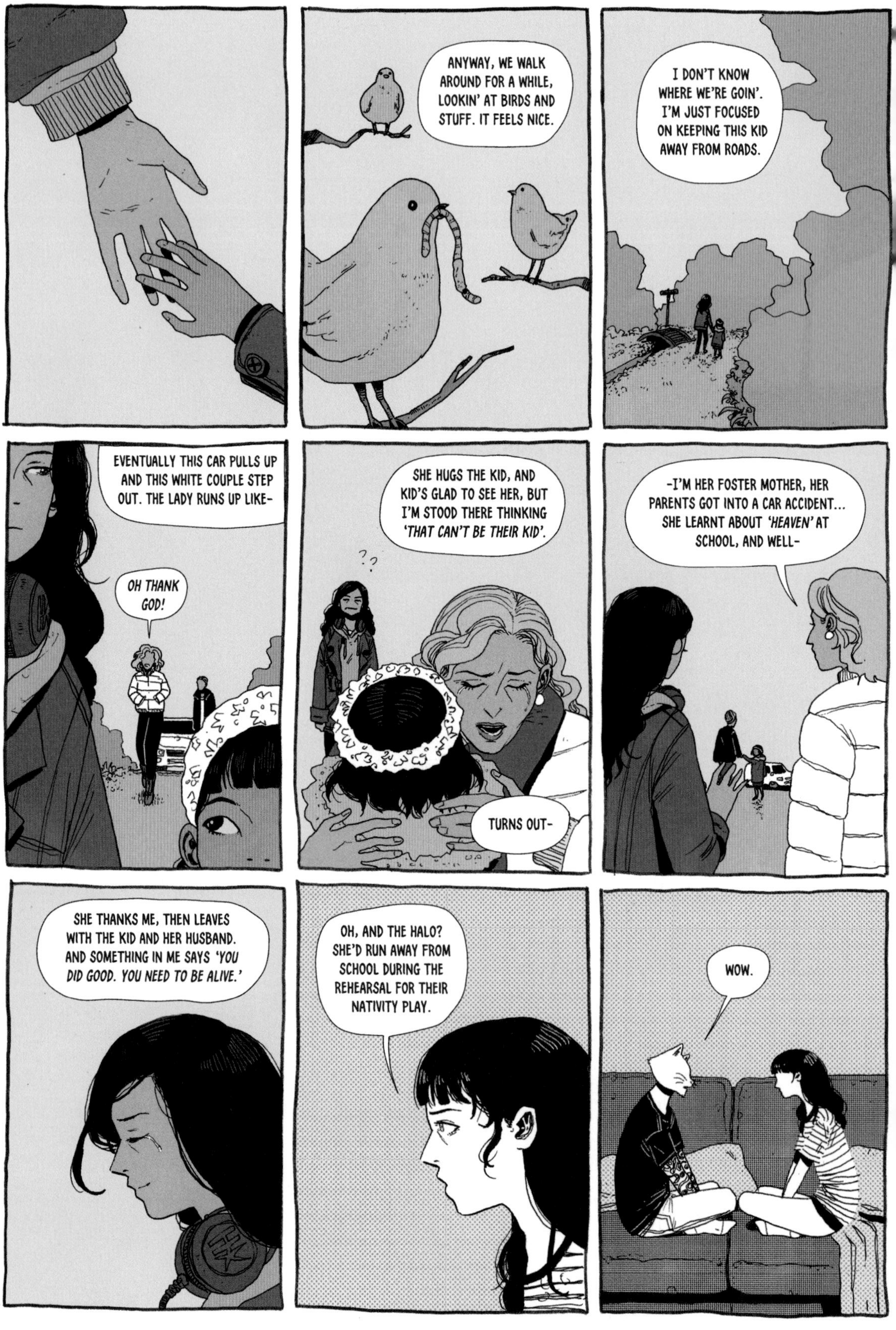
ANYWAY, WE WALK AROUND FOR A WHILE, LOOKIN' AT BIRDS AND STUFF. IT FEELS NICE.
I DON'T KNOW WHERE WE'RE GOIN'. I'M JUST FOCUSED ON KEEPING THIS KID AWAY FROM ROADS.
EVENTUALLY THIS CAR PULLS UP AND THIS WHITE COUPLE STEP OUT. THE LADY RUNS UP LIKE-
OH THANK GOD!
SHE HUGS THE KID, AND KID'S GLAD TO SEE HER, BUT I'M STOOD THERE THINKING 'THAT CAN'T BE THEIR KID'.
TURNS OUT-
-I'M HER FOSTER MOTHER, HER PARENTS GOT INTO A CAR ACCIDENT... SHE LEARNT ABOUT 'HEAVEN' AT SCHOOL, AND WELL-
SHE THANKS ME, THEN LEAVES WITH THE KID AND HER HUSBAND. AND SOMETHING IN ME SAYS 'YOU DID GOOD. YOU NEED TO BE ALIVE.'
OH, AND THE HALO? SHE'D RUN AWAY FROM SCHOOL DURING THE REHEARSAL FOR THEIR NATIVITY PLAY.
WOW.

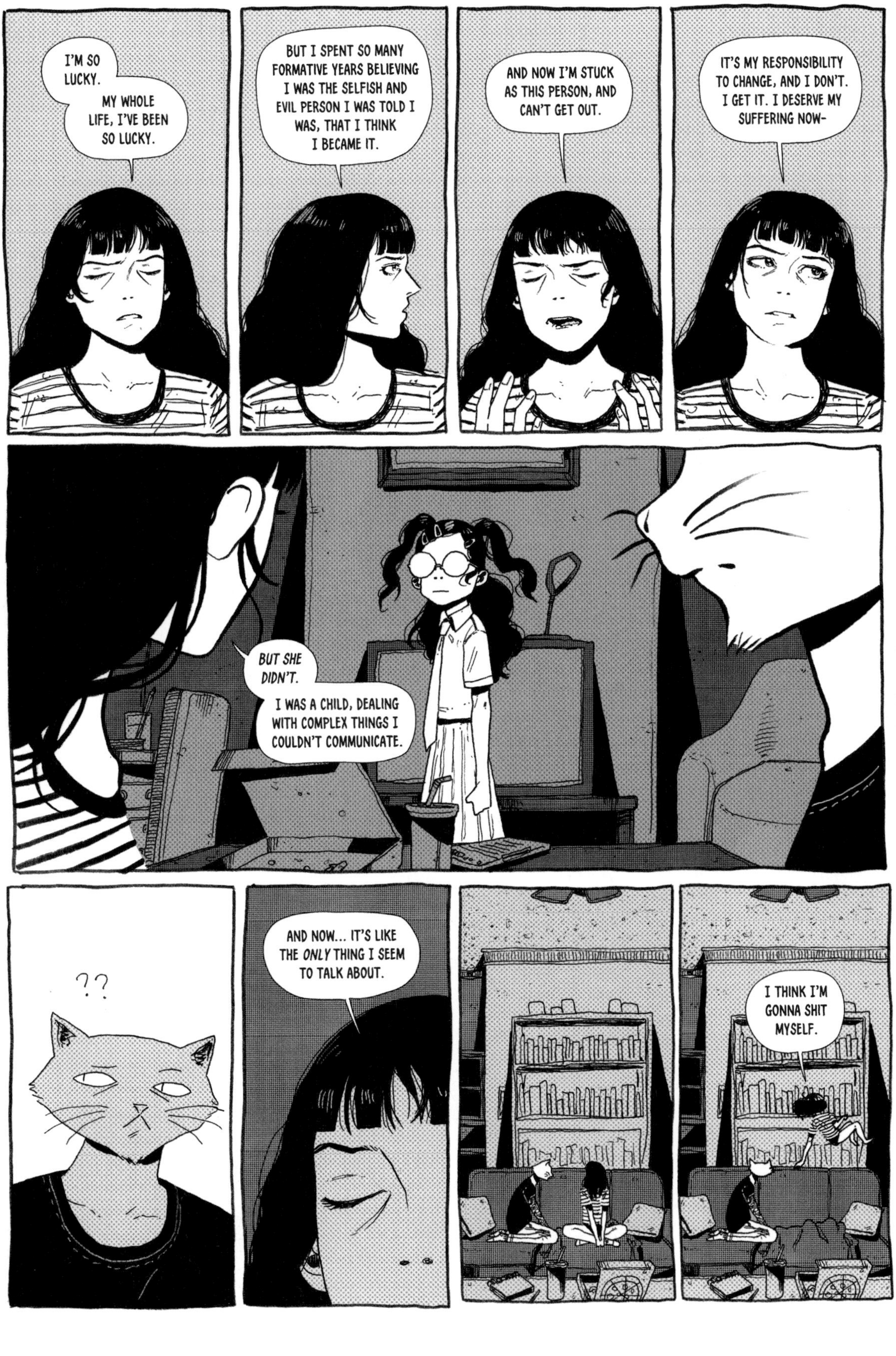
I'M SO LUCKY.
MY WHOLE LIFE, I'VE BEEN SO LUCKY.
BUT I SPENT SO MANY FORMATIVE YEARS BELIEVING I WAS THE SELFISH AND EVIL PERSON I WAS TOLD I WAS, THAT I THINK I BECAME IT.
AND NOW I'M STUCK AS THIS PERSON, AND CAN'T GET OUT.
IT'S MY RESPONSIBILITY TO CHANGE, AND I DON'T. I GET IT. I DESERVE MY SUFFERING NOW-
BUT SHE DIDN'T.
I WAS A CHILD, DEALING WITH COMPLEX THINGS I COULDN'T COMMUNICATE.
??
AND NOW... IT'S LIKE THE *ONLY* THING I SEEM TO TALK ABOUT.
I THINK I'M GONNA SHIT MYSELF.

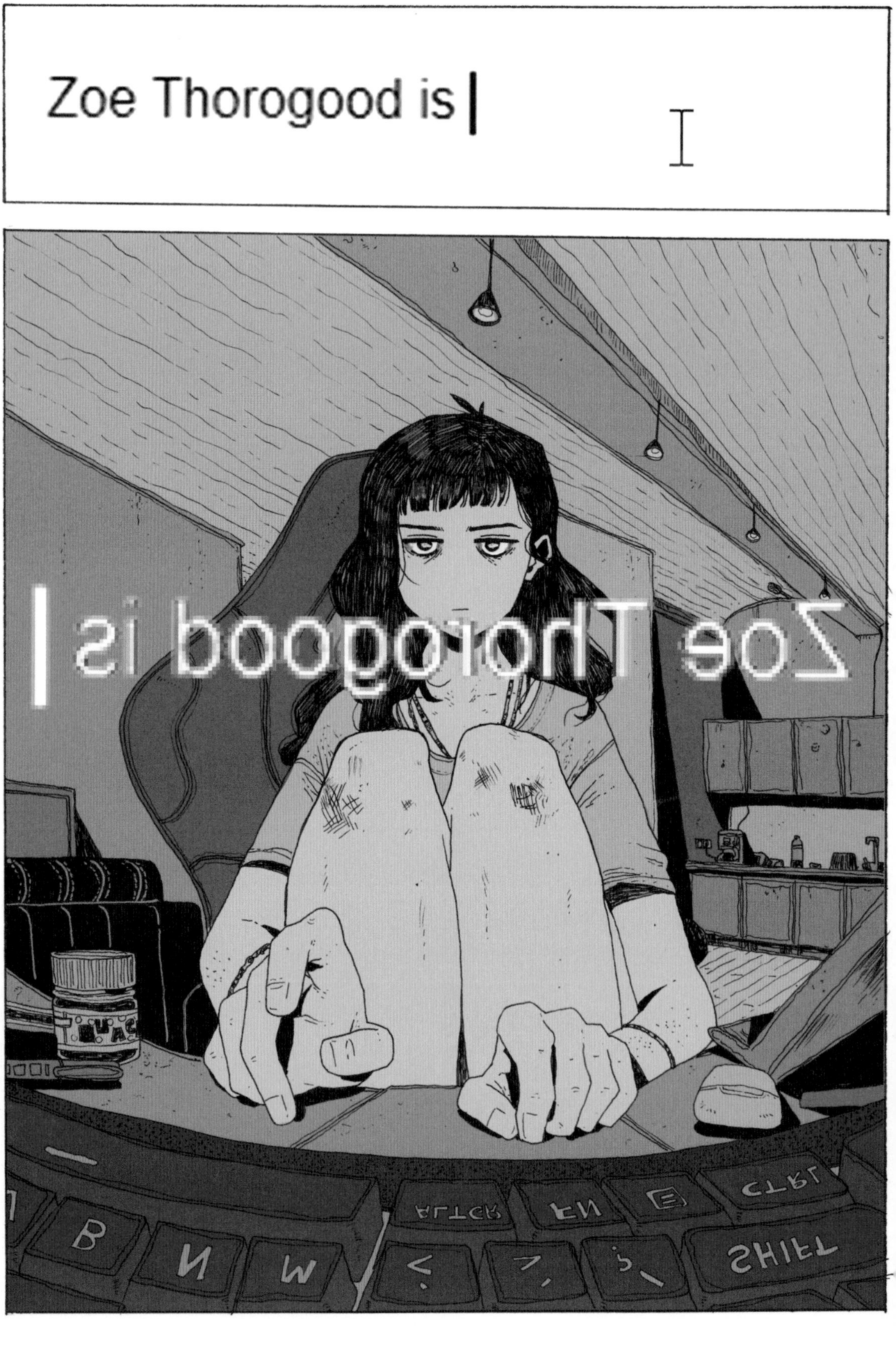
Zoe Thorogood is

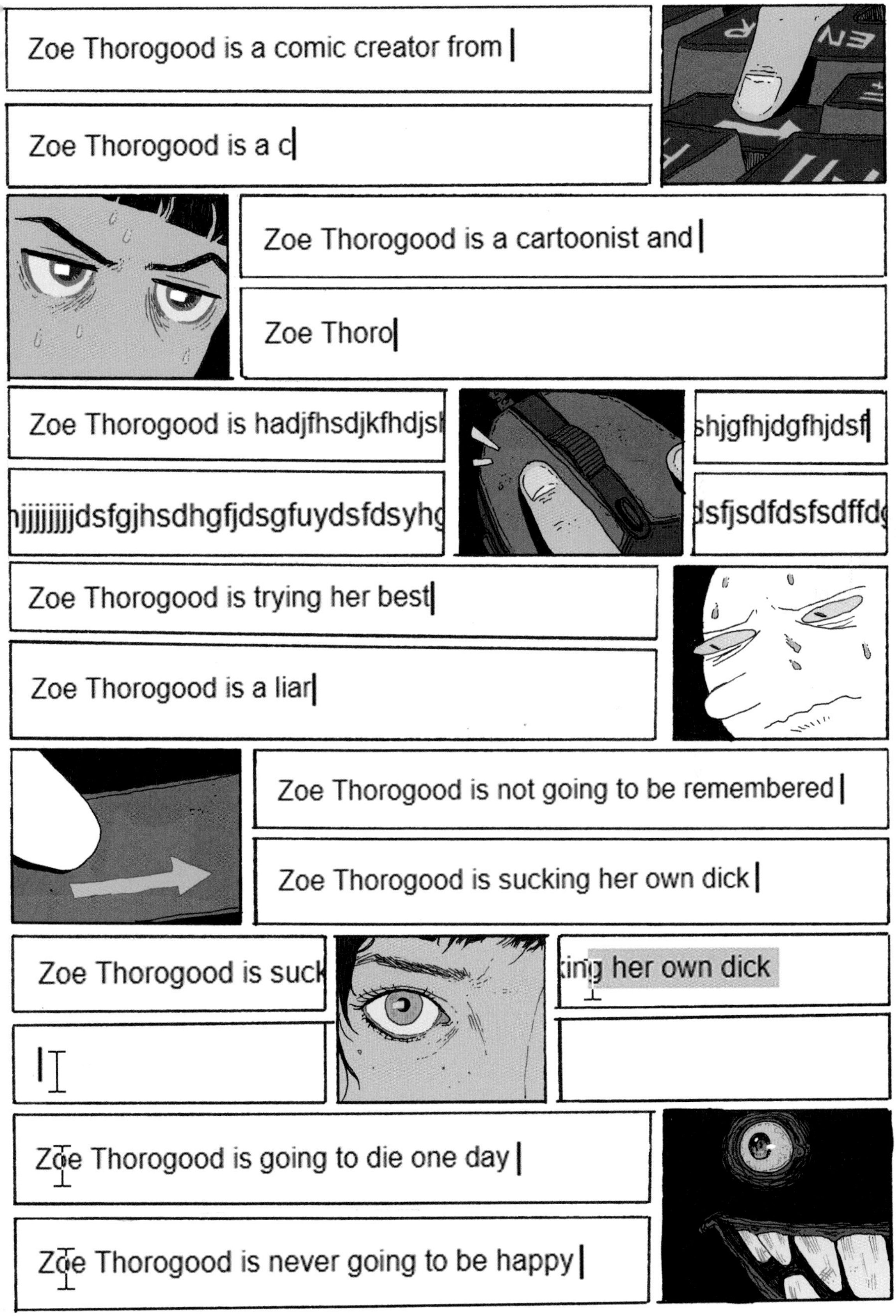

Zoe Thorogood is a comic creator from
Zoe Thorogood is a c
Zoe Thorogood is a cartoonist and
Zoe Thoro
Zoe Thorogood is hadjfhsdjkfhdjs
shjgfhjdgfhjdsf
hjjjjjjjdsfgjhsdhgfjdsgfuydsfdsyhg
dsfjsdfdsfsdffdg
Zoe Thorogood is trying her best
Zoe Thorogood is a liar
Zoe Thorogood is not going to be remembered
Zoe Thorogood is sucking her own dick
Zoe Thorogood is suck
king her own dick
Zoe Thorogood is going to die one day
Zoe Thorogood is never going to be happy

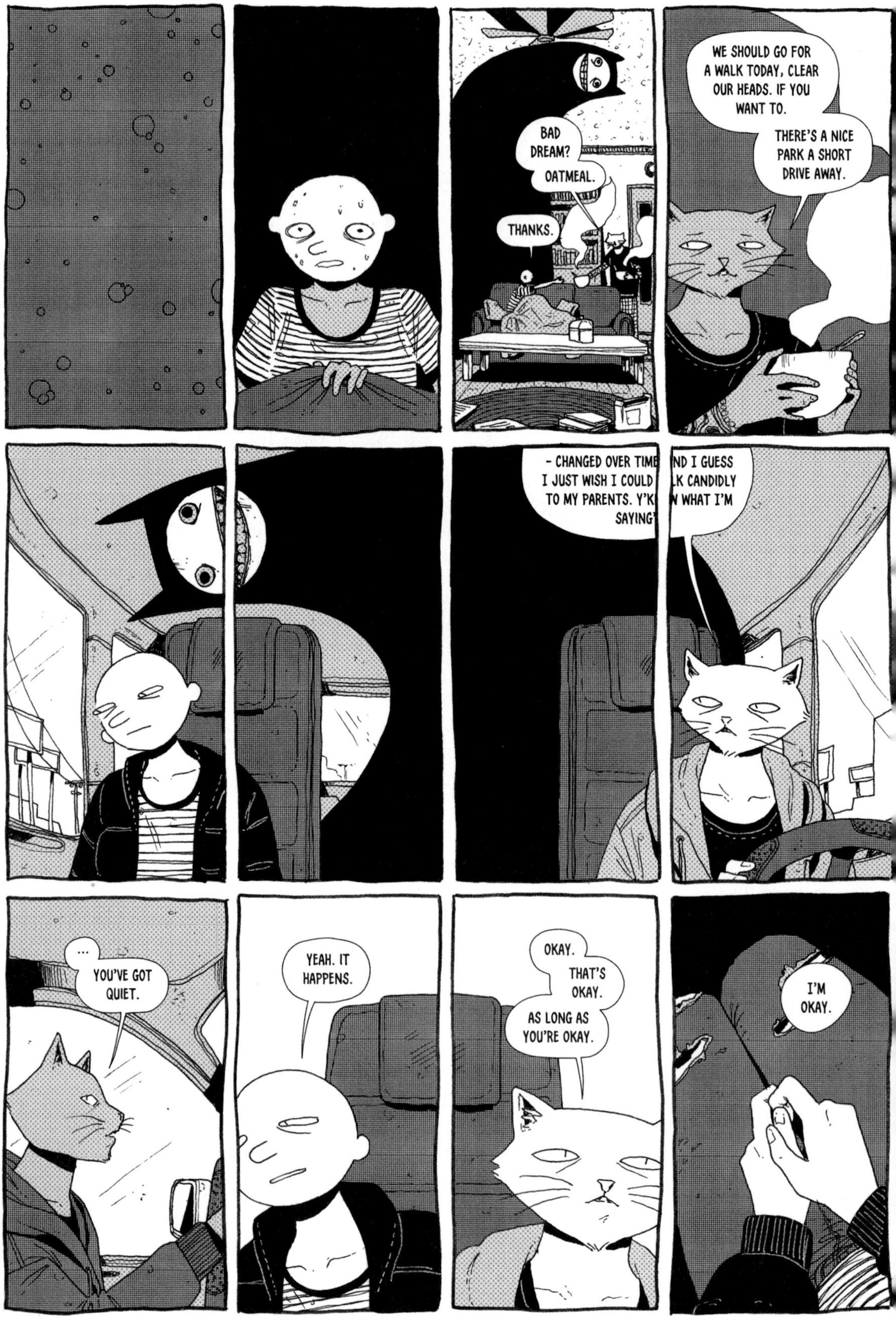

BAD DREAM?
OATMEAL.
THANKS.
WE SHOULD GO FOR A WALK TODAY, CLEAR OUR HEADS. IF YOU WANT TO.
THERE'S A NICE PARK A SHORT DRIVE AWAY.
- CHANGED OVER TIME AND I GUESS I JUST WISH I COULD TALK CANDIDLY TO MY PARENTS. Y'KNOW WHAT I'M SAYING?
...
YOU'VE GOT QUIET.
YEAH. IT HAPPENS.
OKAY.
THAT'S OKAY.
AS LONG AS YOU'RE OKAY.
I'M OKAY.

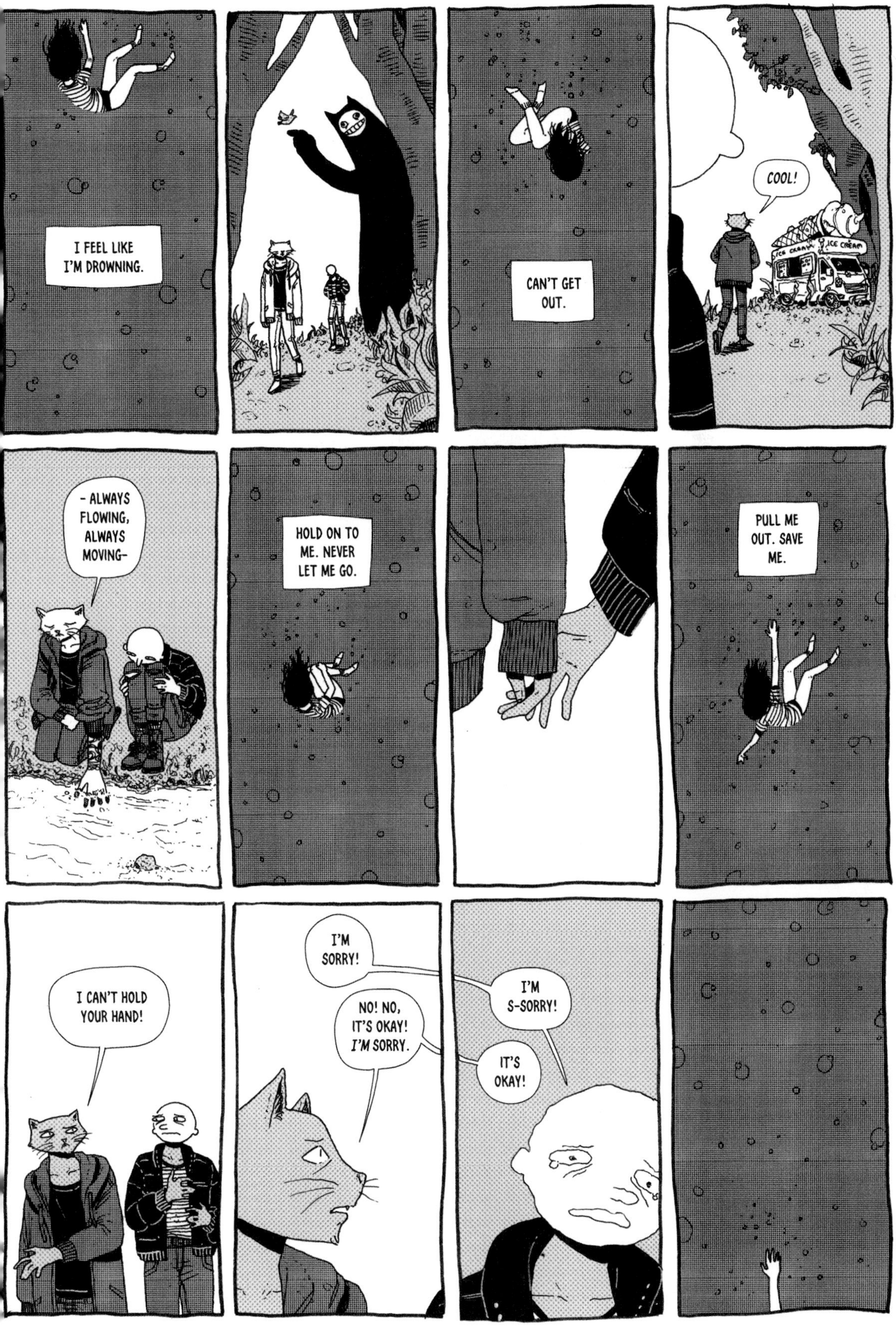
I FEEL LIKE I'M DROWNING.
CAN'T GET OUT.
COOL!
- ALWAYS FLOWING, ALWAYS MOVING-
HOLD ON TO ME. NEVER LET ME GO.
PULL ME OUT. SAVE ME.
I CAN'T HOLD YOUR HAND!
I'M SORRY!
NO! NO, IT'S OKAY! *I'M* SORRY.
I'M S-SORRY!
IT'S OKAY!

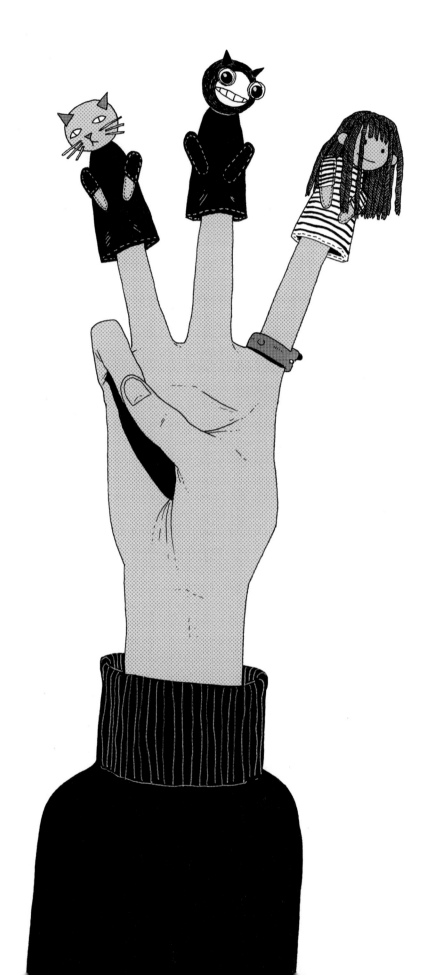

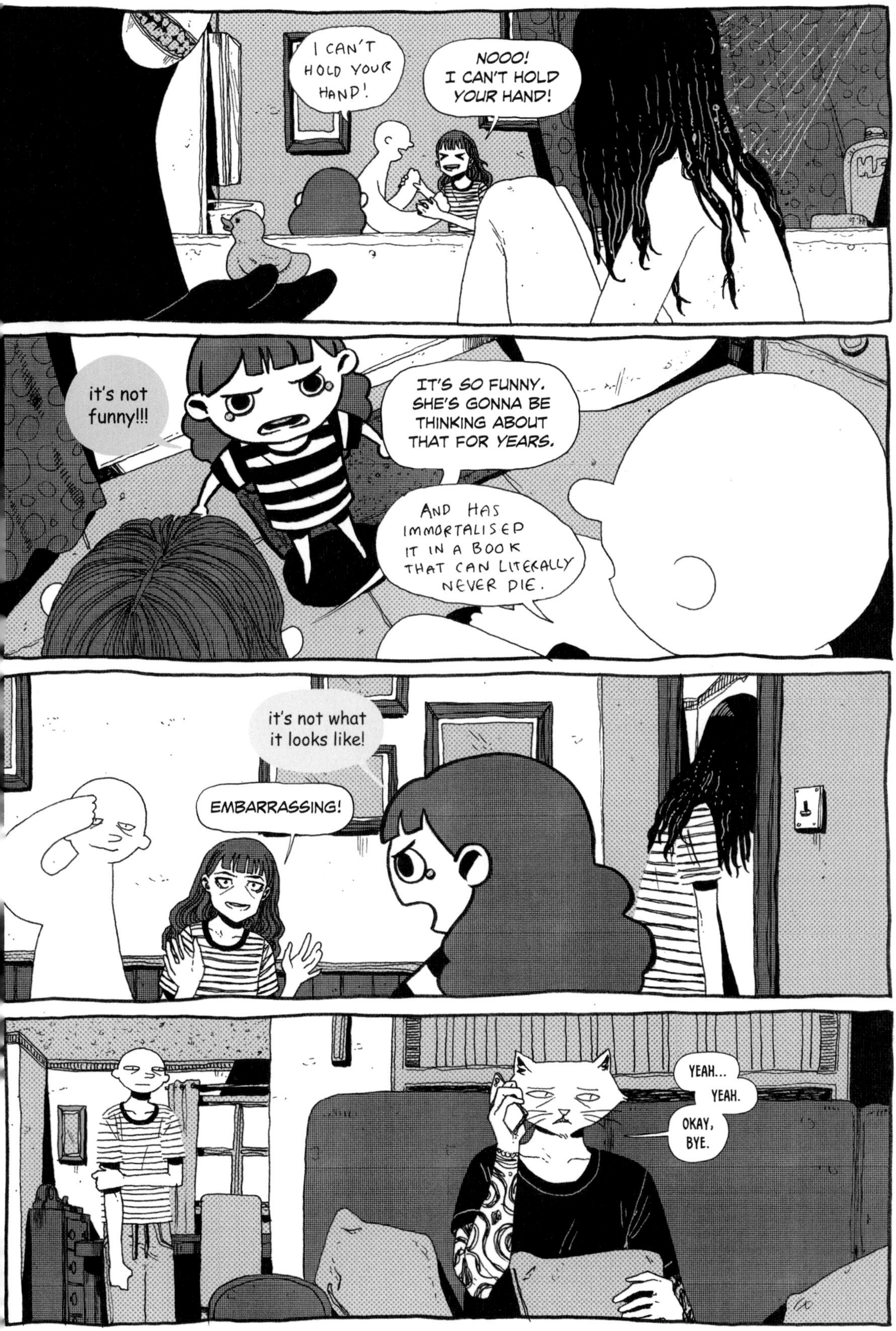
I CAN'T HOLD YOUR HAND!
NOOO! I CAN'T HOLD YOUR HAND!
it's not funny!!!
IT'S SO FUNNY. SHE'S GONNA BE THINKING ABOUT THAT FOR YEARS.
AND HAS IMMORTALISED IT IN A BOOK THAT CAN LITERALLY NEVER DIE.
it's not what it looks like!
EMBARRASSING!
YEAH... YEAH.
OKAY, BYE.

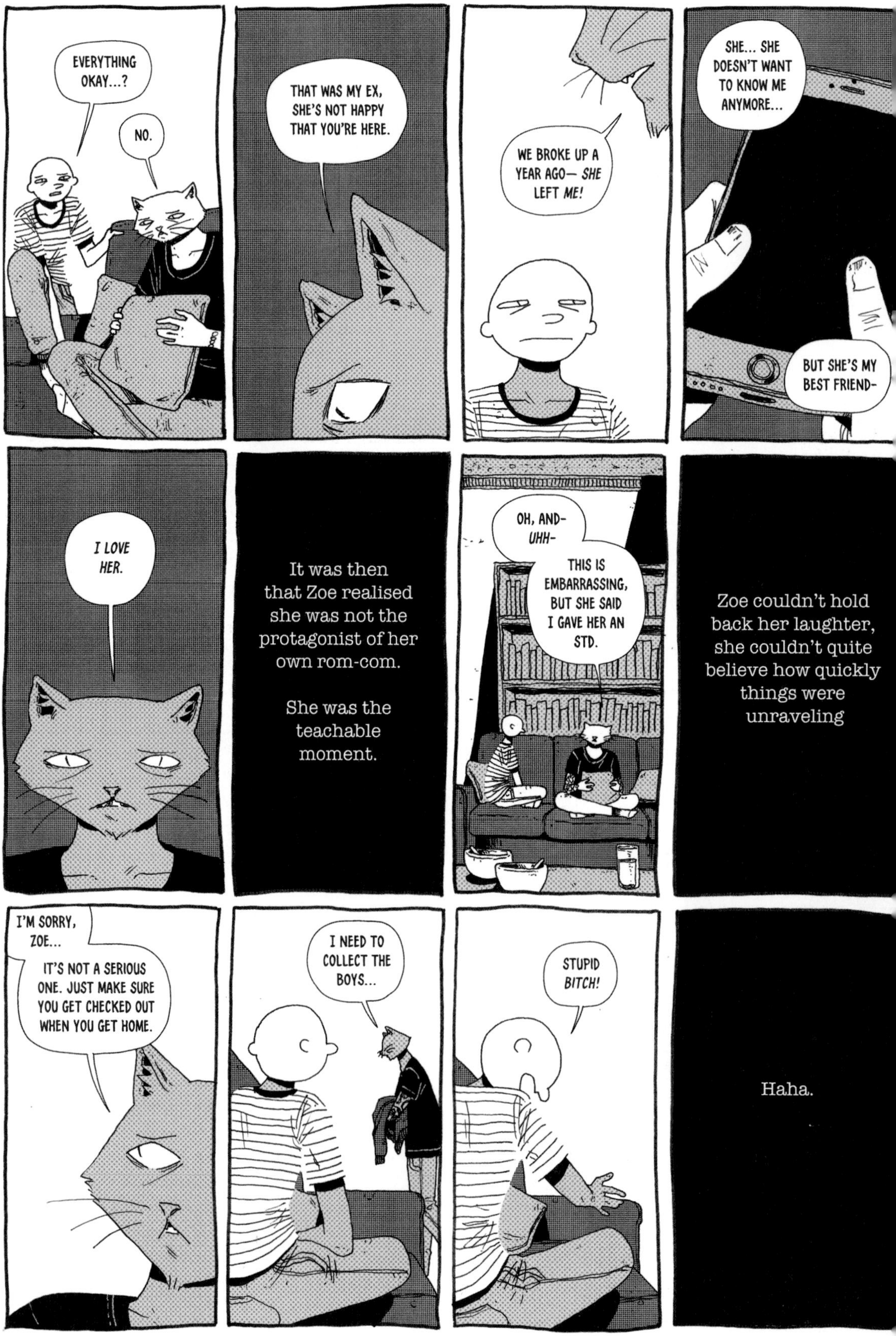
EVERYTHING OKAY...?
NO.
THAT WAS MY EX, SHE'S NOT HAPPY THAT YOU'RE HERE.
WE BROKE UP A YEAR AGO— SHE LEFT ME!
SHE... SHE DOESN'T WANT TO KNOW ME ANYMORE...
BUT SHE'S MY BEST FRIEND-
I LOVE HER.
It was then that Zoe realised she was not the protagonist of her own rom-com.
She was the teachable moment.
OH, AND- UHH-
THIS IS EMBARRASSING, BUT SHE SAID I GAVE HER AN STD.
Zoe couldn't hold back her laughter, she couldn't quite believe how quickly things were unraveling
I'M SORRY, ZOE...
IT'S NOT A SERIOUS ONE. JUST MAKE SURE YOU GET CHECKED OUT WHEN YOU GET HOME.
I NEED TO COLLECT THE BOYS...
STUPID BITCH!
Haha.

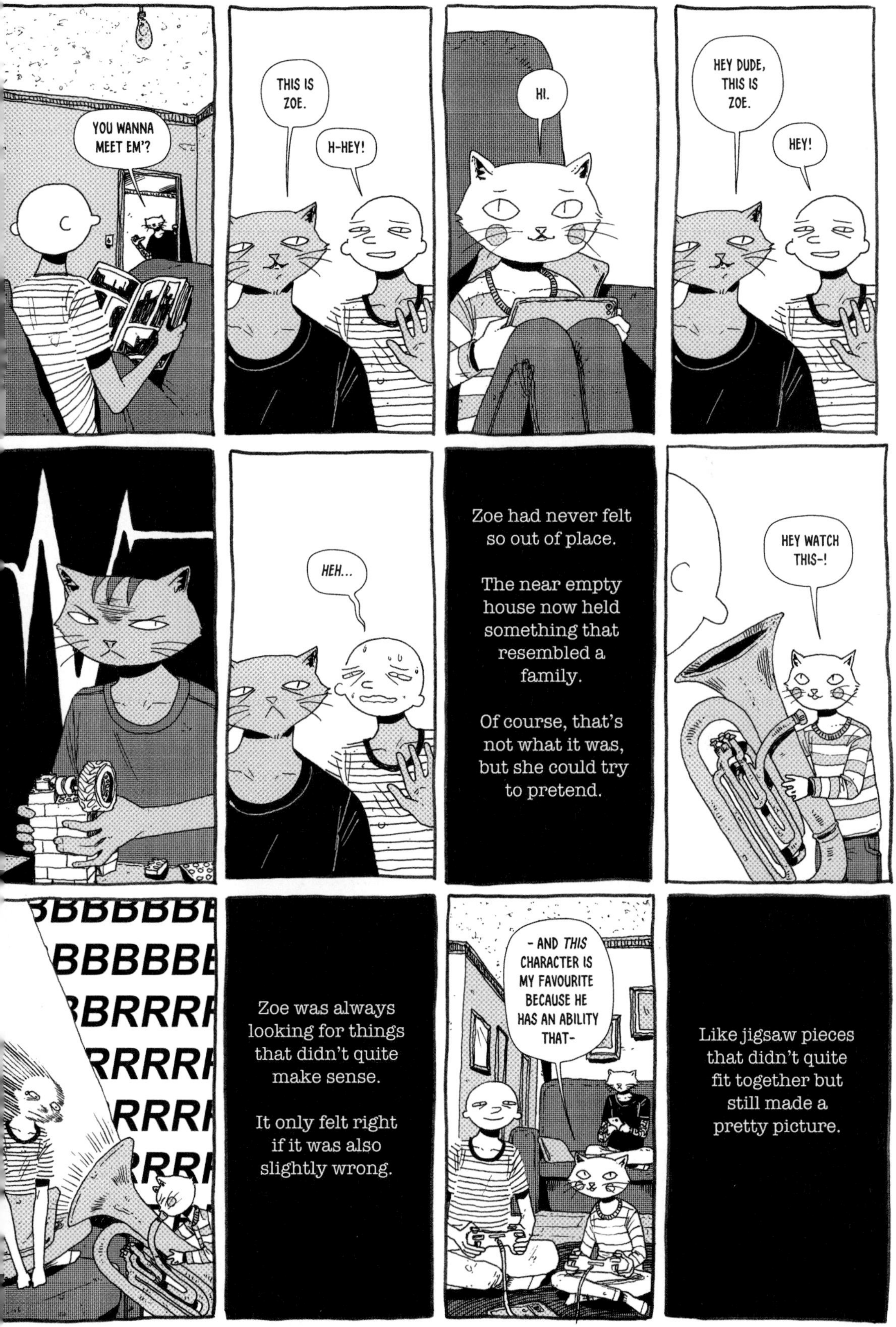

YOU WANNA MEET EM'?
THIS IS ZOE.
H-HEY!
HI.
HEY DUDE, THIS IS ZOE.
HEY!
HEH...
Zoe had never felt so out of place.
The near empty house now held something that resembled a family.
Of course, that's not what it was, but she could try to pretend.
HEY WATCH THIS-!
BBBBBBBBBBBBBBRRRRRRRRRRRRRRRRRRR
Zoe was always looking for things that didn't quite make sense.
It only felt right if it was also slightly wrong.
- AND *THIS* CHARACTER IS MY FAVOURITE BECAUSE HE HAS AN ABILITY THAT-
Like jigsaw pieces that didn't quite fit together but still made a pretty picture.

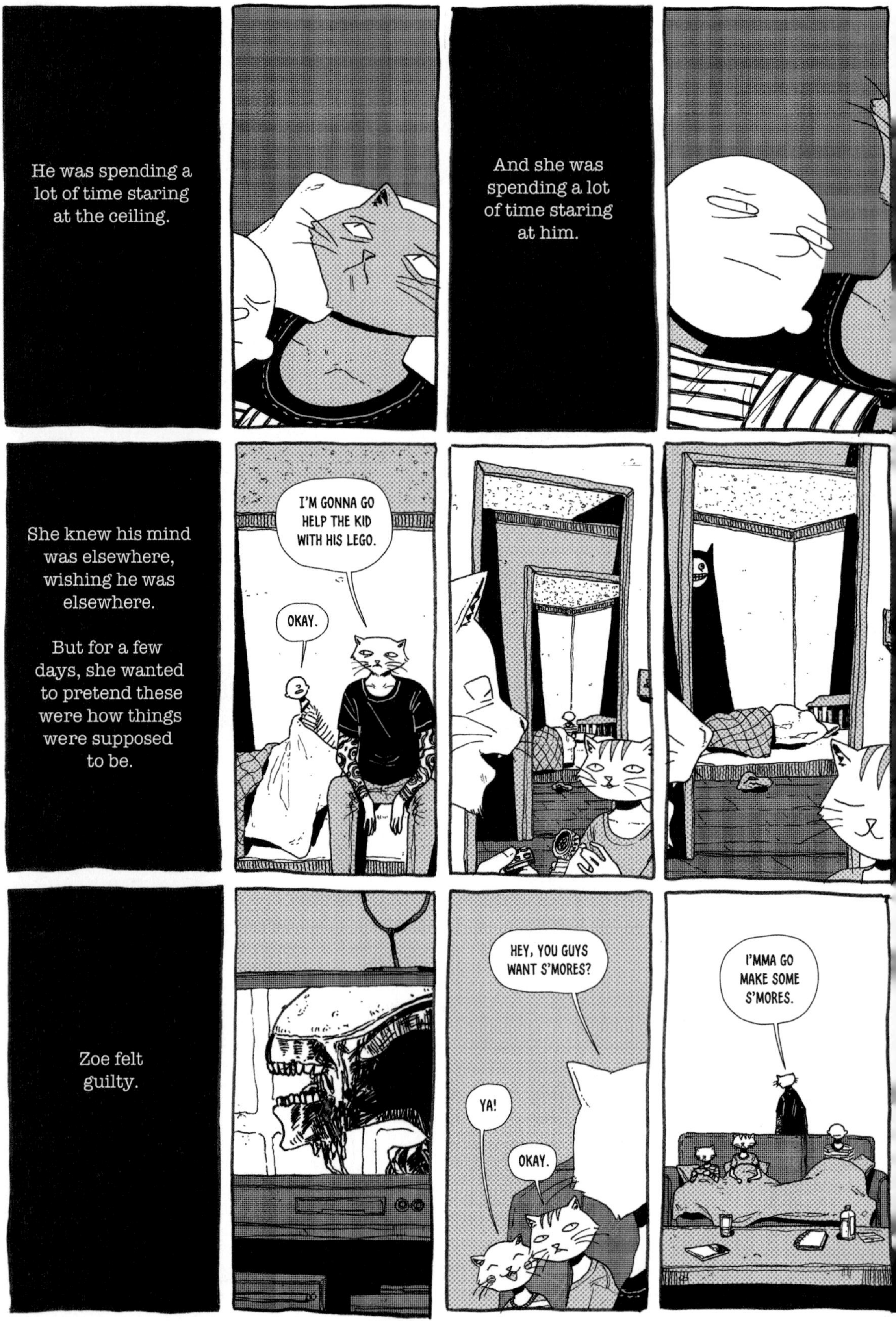
He was spending a lot of time staring at the ceiling.
And she was spending a lot of time staring at him.
She knew his mind was elsewhere, wishing he was elsewhere.
But for a few days, she wanted to pretend these were how things were supposed to be.
I'M GONNA GO HELP THE KID WITH HIS LEGO.
OKAY.
Zoe felt guilty.
HEY, YOU GUYS WANT S'MORES?
YA!
OKAY.
I'MMA GO MAKE SOME S'MORES.

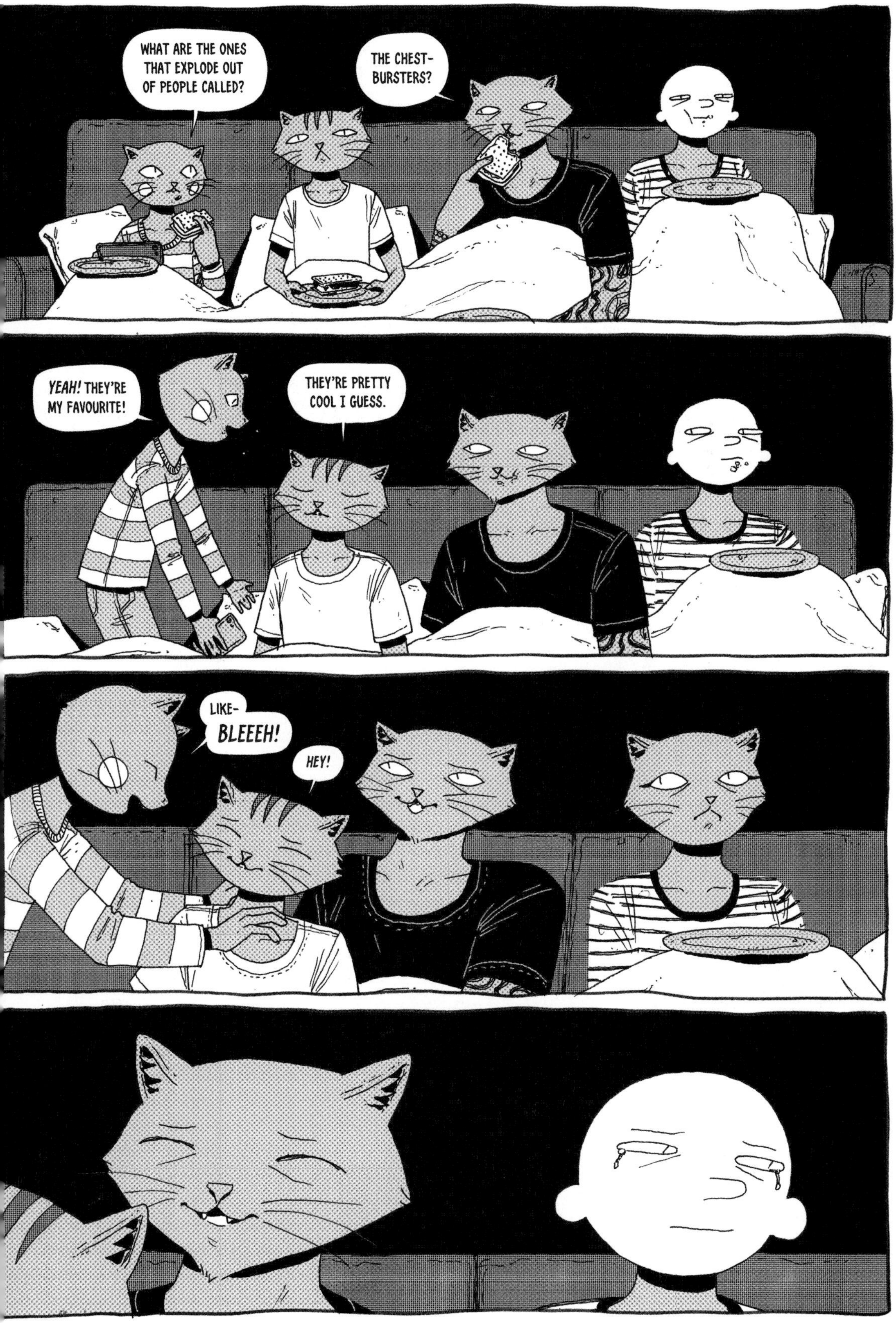
WHAT ARE THE ONES THAT EXPLODE OUT OF PEOPLE CALLED?
THE CHEST-BURSTERS?
YEAH! THEY'RE MY FAVOURITE!
THEY'RE PRETTY COOL I GUESS.
LIKE- BLEEEH!
HEY!

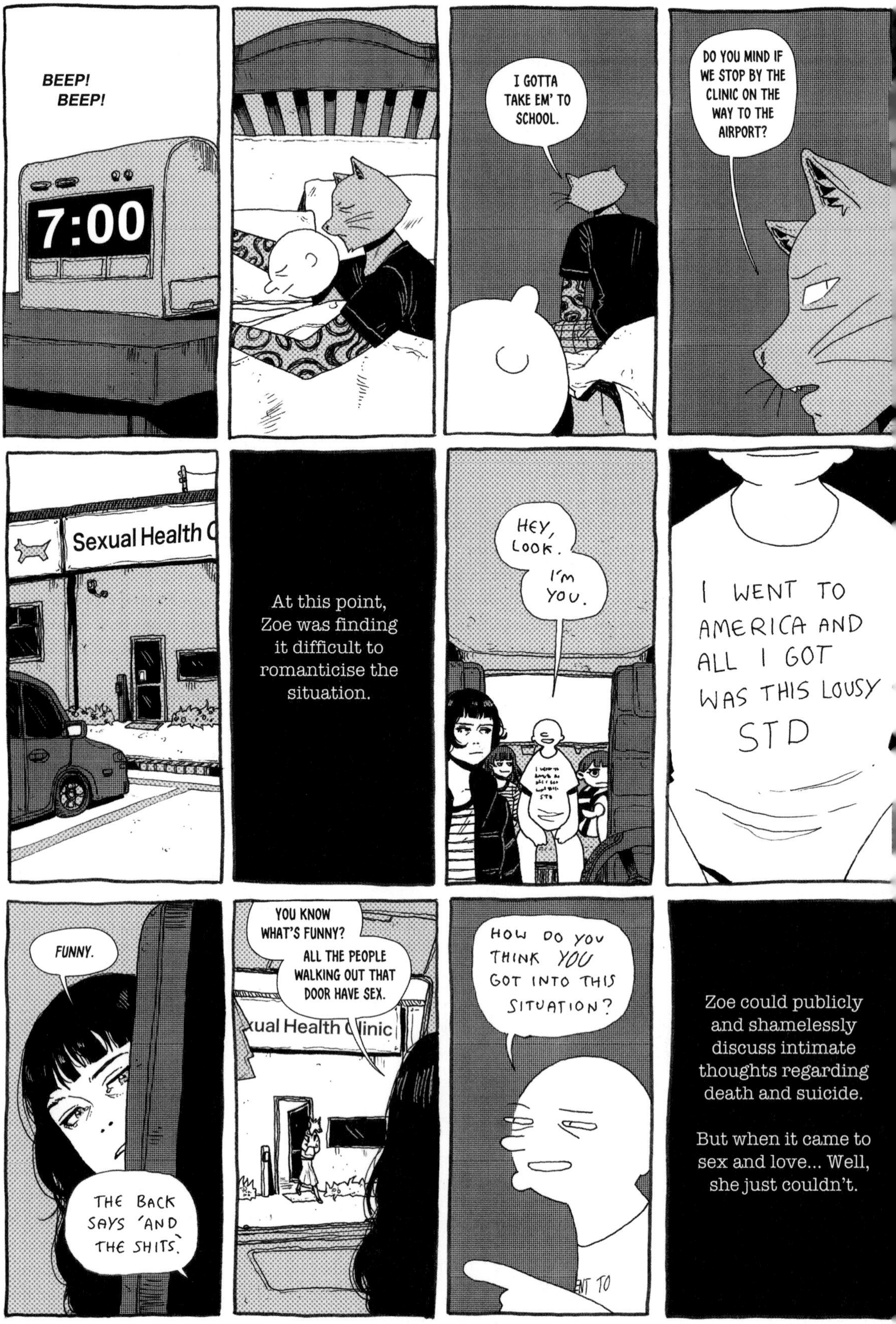

BEEP! BEEP!
7:00
I GOTTA TAKE EM' TO SCHOOL.
DO YOU MIND IF WE STOP BY THE CLINIC ON THE WAY TO THE AIRPORT?
Sexual Health C
At this point, Zoe was finding it difficult to romanticise the situation.
HEY, LOOK.
I'M YOU.
I WENT TO AMERICA AND ALL I GOT WAS THIS LOUSY STD
FUNNY.
THE BACK SAYS 'AND THE SHITS.'
YOU KNOW WHAT'S FUNNY?
ALL THE PEOPLE WALKING OUT THAT DOOR HAVE SEX.
xual Health Clinic
HOW DO YOU THINK YOU GOT INTO THIS SITUATION?
Zoe could publicly and shamelessly discuss intimate thoughts regarding death and suicide.
But when it came to sex and love... Well, she just couldn't.

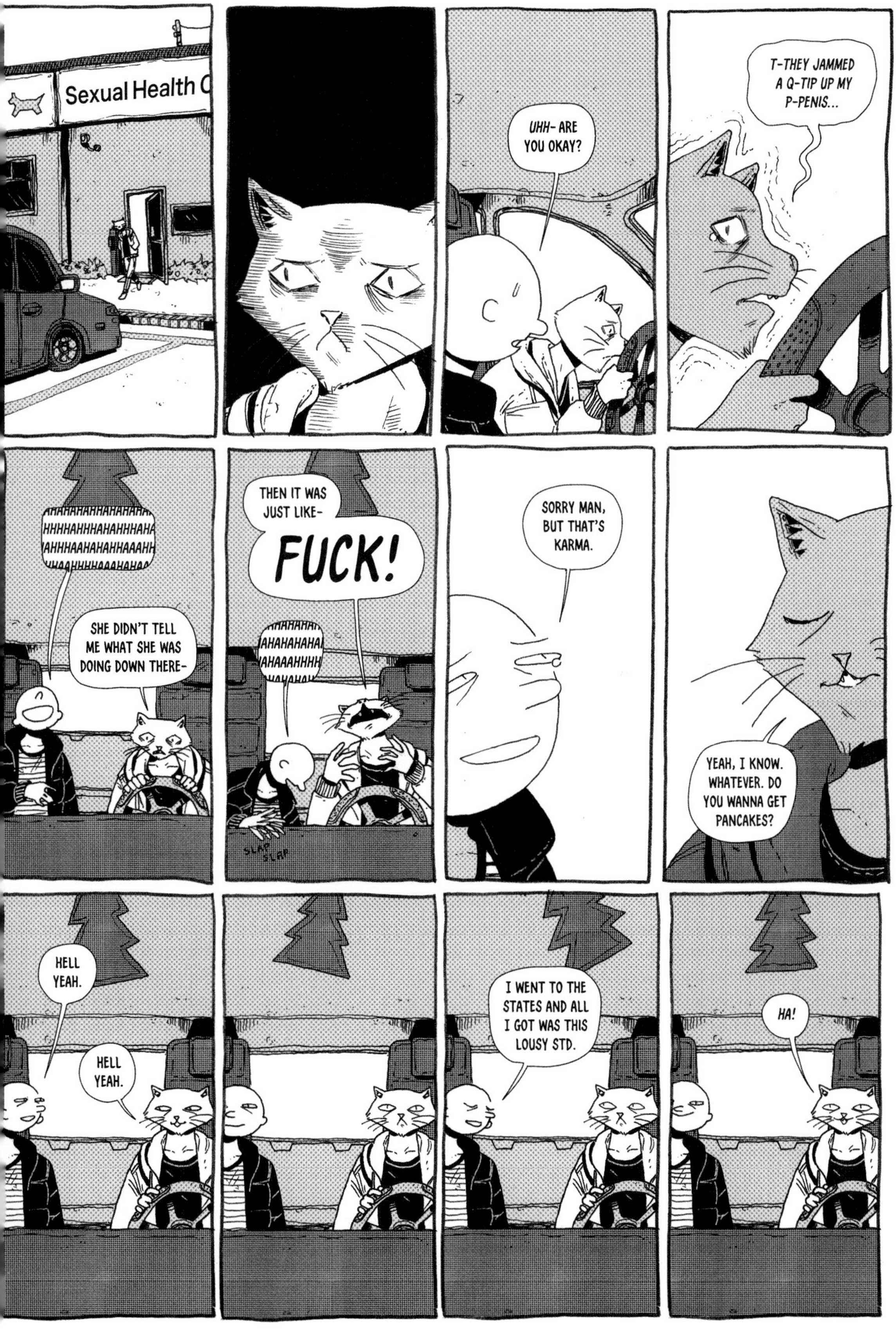
Sexual Health C
UHH- ARE YOU OKAY?
T-THEY JAMMED A Q-TIP UP MY P-PENIS...
SHE DIDN'T TELL ME WHAT SHE WAS DOING DOWN THERE-
THEN IT WAS JUST LIKE-
FUCK!
SLAP SLAP
SORRY MAN, BUT THAT'S KARMA.
YEAH, I KNOW. WHATEVER. DO YOU WANNA GET PANCAKES?
HELL YEAH.
HELL YEAH.
I WENT TO THE STATES AND ALL I GOT WAS THIS LOUSY STD.
HA!

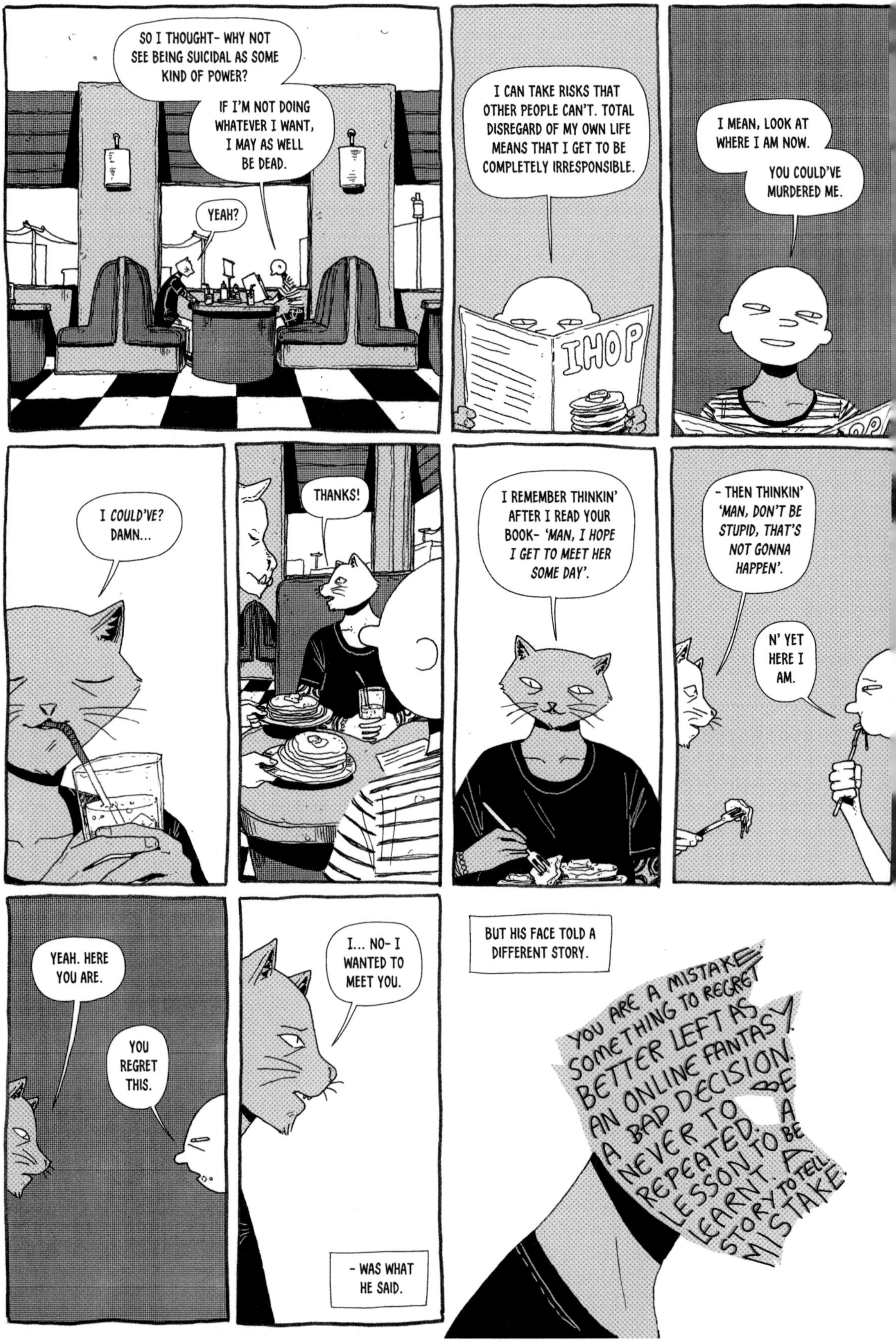
SO I THOUGHT- WHY NOT SEE BEING SUICIDAL AS SOME KIND OF POWER?
IF I'M NOT DOING WHATEVER I WANT, I MAY AS WELL BE DEAD.
YEAH?
I CAN TAKE RISKS THAT OTHER PEOPLE CAN'T. TOTAL DISREGARD OF MY OWN LIFE MEANS THAT I GET TO BE COMPLETELY IRRESPONSIBLE.
IHOP
I MEAN, LOOK AT WHERE I AM NOW.
YOU COULD'VE MURDERED ME.
I *COULD'VE?* DAMN...
THANKS!
I REMEMBER THINKIN' AFTER I READ YOUR BOOK- *'MAN, I HOPE I GET TO MEET HER SOME DAY'.*
- THEN THINKIN' *'MAN, DON'T BE STUPID, THAT'S NOT GONNA HAPPEN'.*
N' YET HERE I AM.
YEAH. HERE YOU ARE.
YOU REGRET THIS.
I... NO- I WANTED TO MEET YOU.
- WAS WHAT HE SAID.
BUT HIS FACE TOLD A DIFFERENT STORY.
YOU ARE A MISTAKE. SOMETHING TO REGRET BETTER LEFT AS AN ONLINE FANTASY. A BAD DECISION. NEVER TO BE REPEATED. A LESSON TO BE LEARNT. A STORY TO TELL. MISTAKE.

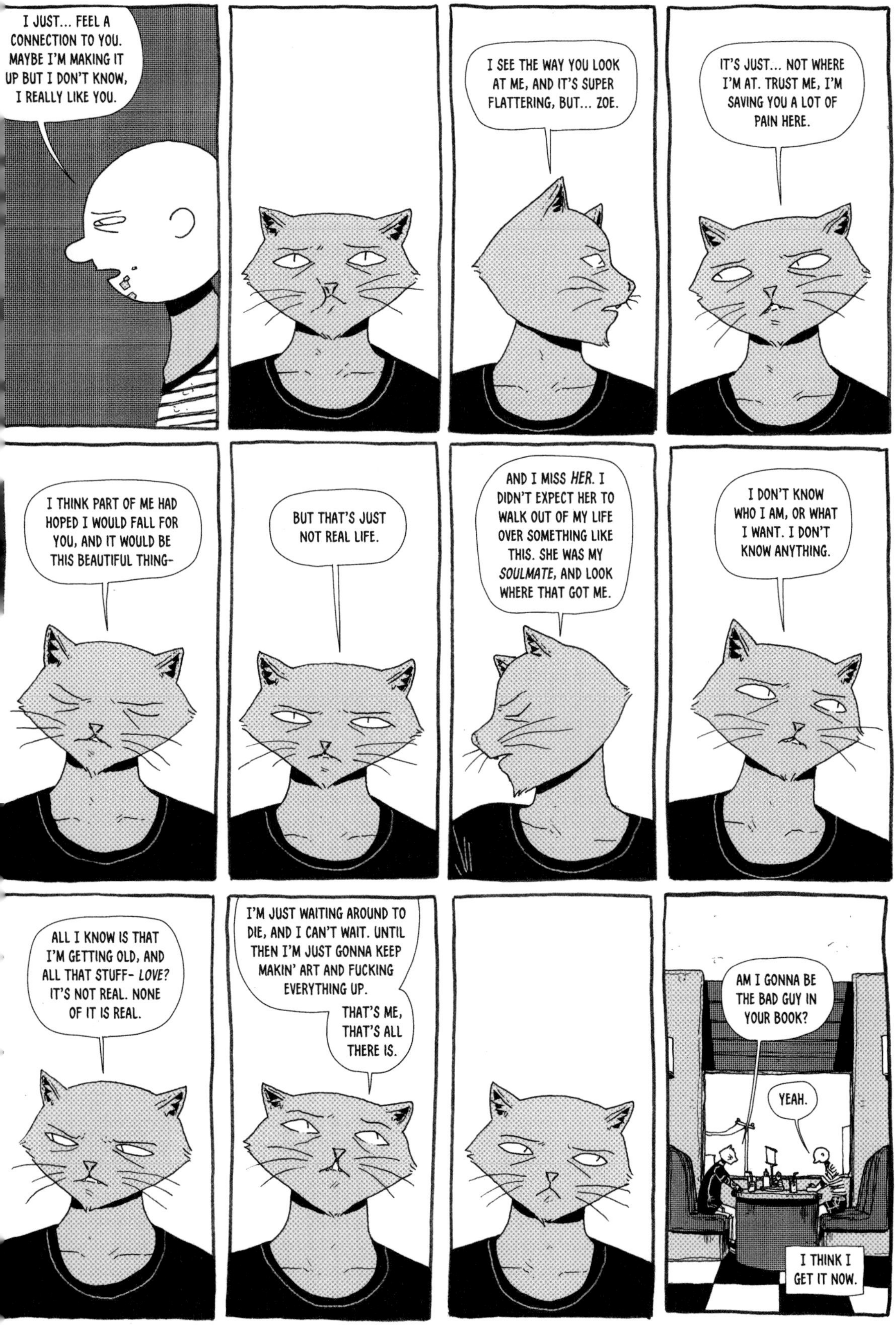

I JUST... FEEL A CONNECTION TO YOU. MAYBE I'M MAKING IT UP BUT I DON'T KNOW, I REALLY LIKE YOU.
I SEE THE WAY YOU LOOK AT ME, AND IT'S SUPER FLATTERING, BUT... ZOE.
IT'S JUST... NOT WHERE I'M AT. TRUST ME, I'M SAVING YOU A LOT OF PAIN HERE.
I THINK PART OF ME HAD HOPED I WOULD FALL FOR YOU, AND IT WOULD BE THIS BEAUTIFUL THING-
BUT THAT'S JUST NOT REAL LIFE.
AND I MISS *HER*. I DIDN'T EXPECT HER TO WALK OUT OF MY LIFE OVER SOMETHING LIKE THIS. SHE WAS MY *SOULMATE*, AND LOOK WHERE THAT GOT ME.
I DON'T KNOW WHO I AM, OR WHAT I WANT. I DON'T KNOW ANYTHING.
ALL I KNOW IS THAT I'M GETTING OLD, AND ALL THAT STUFF- *LOVE?* IT'S NOT REAL. NONE OF IT IS REAL.
I'M JUST WAITING AROUND TO DIE, AND I CAN'T WAIT. UNTIL THEN I'M JUST GONNA KEEP MAKIN' ART AND FUCKING EVERYTHING UP.
THAT'S ME, THAT'S ALL THERE IS.
AM I GONNA BE THE BAD GUY IN YOUR BOOK?
YEAH.
I THINK I GET IT NOW.

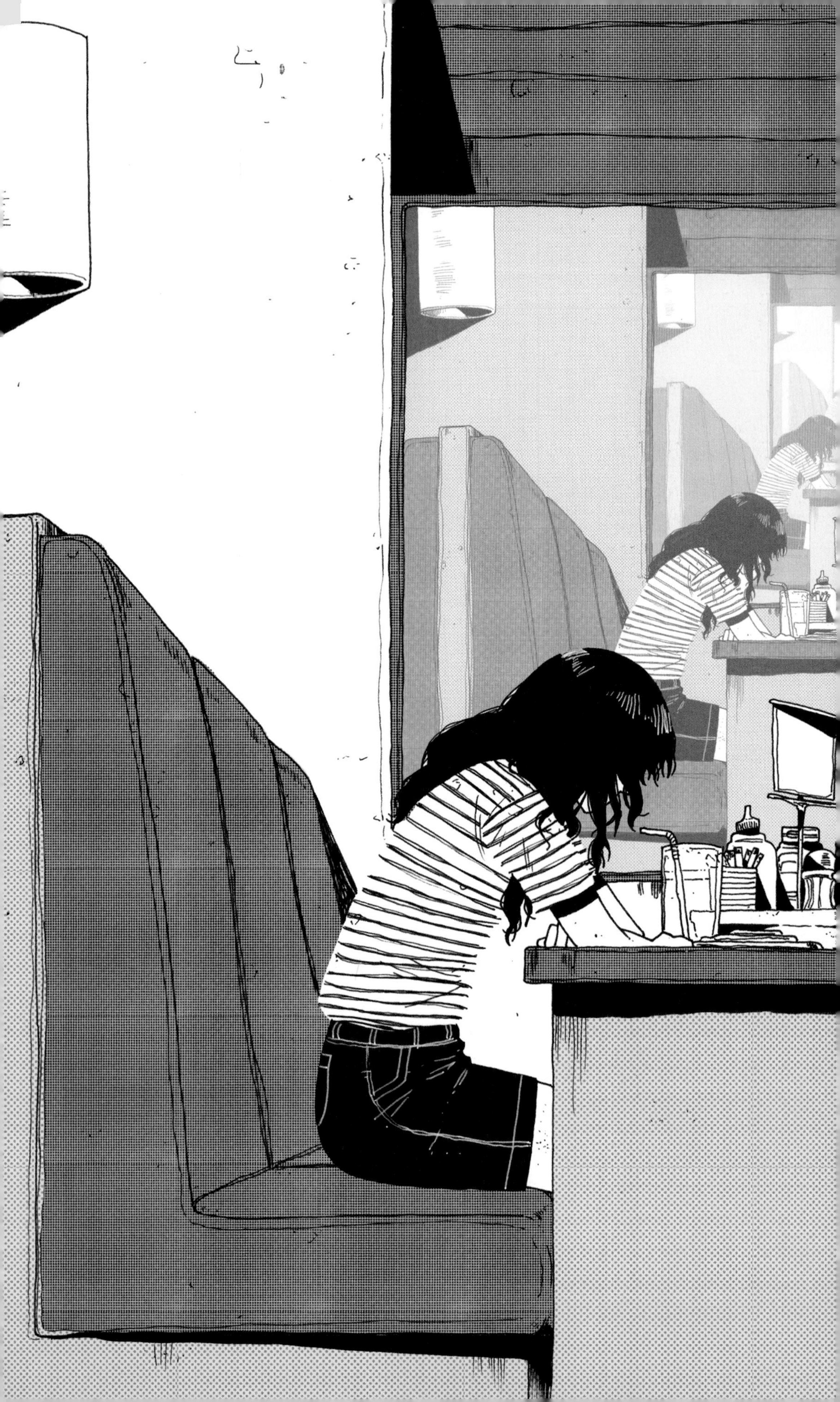

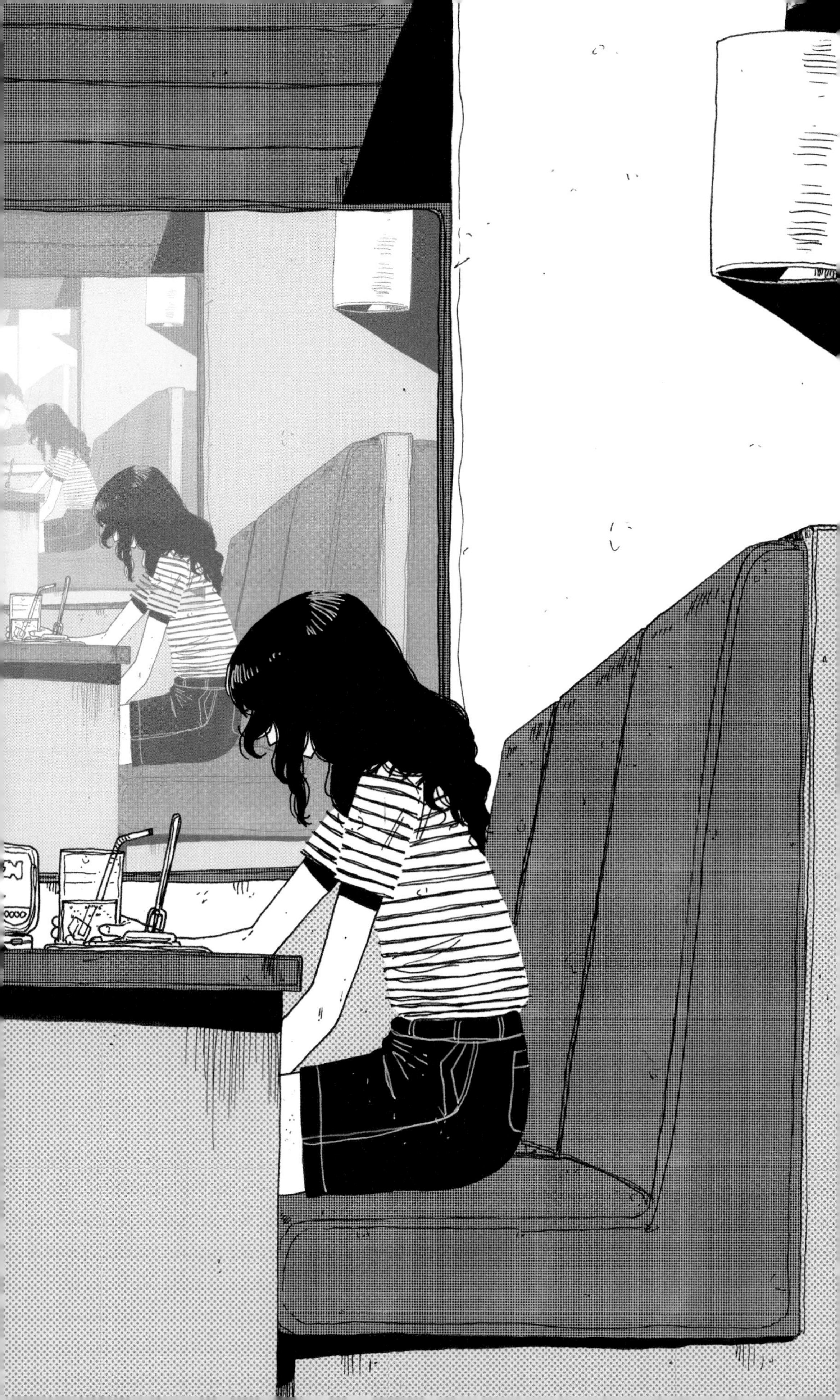

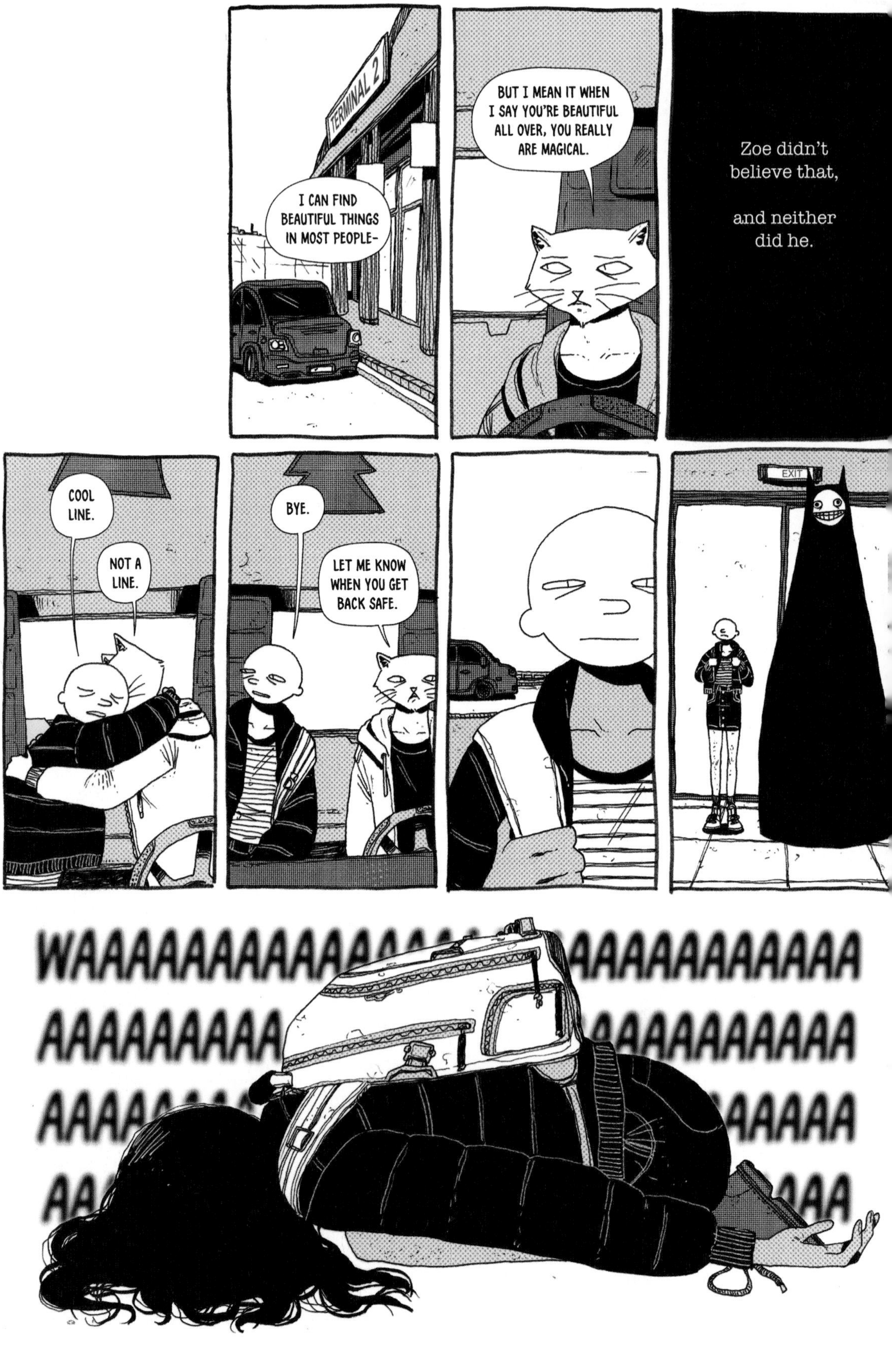
TERMINAL 2
I CAN FIND BEAUTIFUL THINGS IN MOST PEOPLE-
BUT I MEAN IT WHEN I SAY YOU'RE BEAUTIFUL ALL OVER, YOU REALLY ARE MAGICAL.
Zoe didn't believe that,
and neither did he.
COOL LINE.
NOT A LINE.
BYE.
LET ME KNOW WHEN YOU GET BACK SAFE.
EXIT
WAAAAAAAAAAAAAAAAAAAAAAAAAAAAAAAAAAAAAAAAAAAAAAAAAAAAAAAAAAAAAAAA

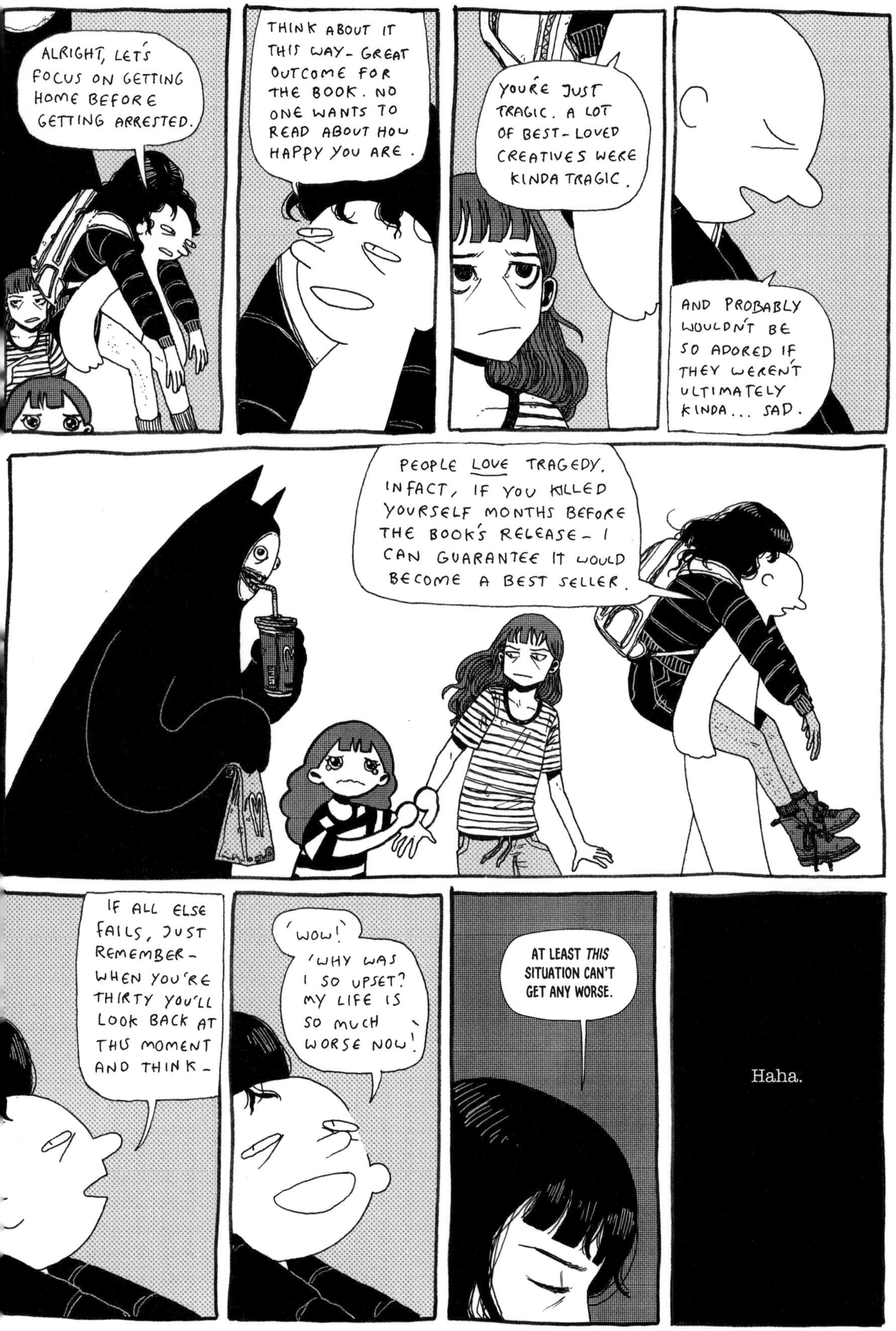
ALRIGHT, LET'S FOCUS ON GETTING HOME BEFORE GETTING ARRESTED.
THINK ABOUT IT THIS WAY- GREAT OUTCOME FOR THE BOOK. NO ONE WANTS TO READ ABOUT HOW HAPPY YOU ARE.
YOU'RE JUST TRAGIC. A LOT OF BEST-LOVED CREATIVES WERE KINDA TRAGIC.
AND PROBABLY WOULDN'T BE SO ADORED IF THEY WEREN'T ULTIMATELY KINDA... SAD.
PEOPLE LOVE TRAGEDY. INFACT, IF YOU KILLED YOURSELF MONTHS BEFORE THE BOOK'S RELEASE- I CAN GUARANTEE IT WOULD BECOME A BEST SELLER.
IF ALL ELSE FAILS, JUST REMEMBER- WHEN YOU'RE THIRTY YOU'LL LOOK BACK AT THIS MOMENT AND THINK-
'WOW!' 'WHY WAS I SO UPSET? MY LIFE IS SO MUCH WORSE NOW!'
AT LEAST THIS SITUATION CAN'T GET ANY WORSE.
Haha.

Autobios can be placed into one of two categories-

Masturbation, or menstruation.

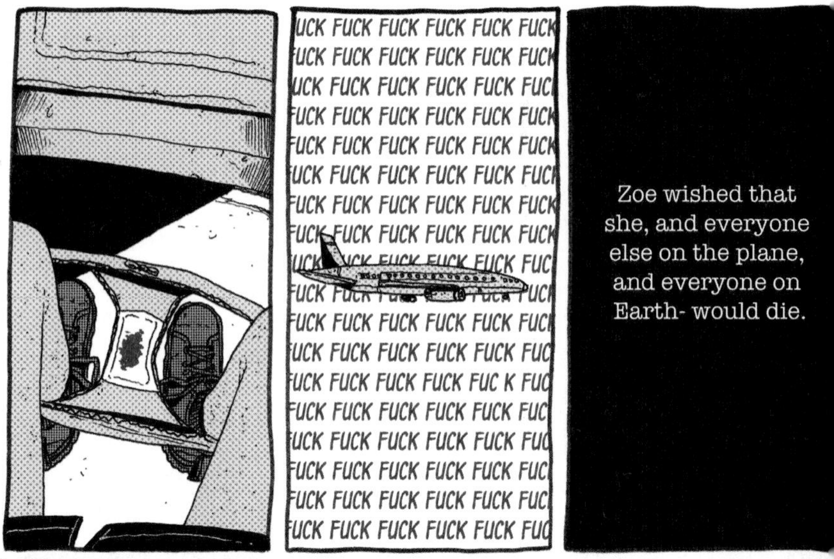
UCK FUCK FUCK FUCK FUCK FUCK
UCK FUCK FUCK FUCK FUCK FUCK
UCK FUCK FUCK FUCK FUCK FUC
UCK FUCK FUCK FUCK FUCK FUCK
UCK FUCK FUCK FUCK FUCK FUCK
UCK FUCK FUCK FUCK FUCK FUCK
UCK FUCK FUCK FUCK FUCK FUCK
UCK FUCK FUCK FUCK FUCK FUCK
UCK FUCK FUCK FUCK FUCK FUC
UCK FUCK FUCK FUCK FUCK FUC
UCK FUCK FUCK FUCK FUC K FUC
UCK FUCK FUCK FUCK FUCK FUC
UCK FUCK FUCK FUCK FUCK FU
UCK FUCK FUCK FUCK FUCK FUC
UCK FUCK FUCK FUCK FUCK FUC
UCK FUCK FUCK FUCK FUCK FU
Zoe wished that she, and everyone else on the plane, and everyone on Earth- would die.

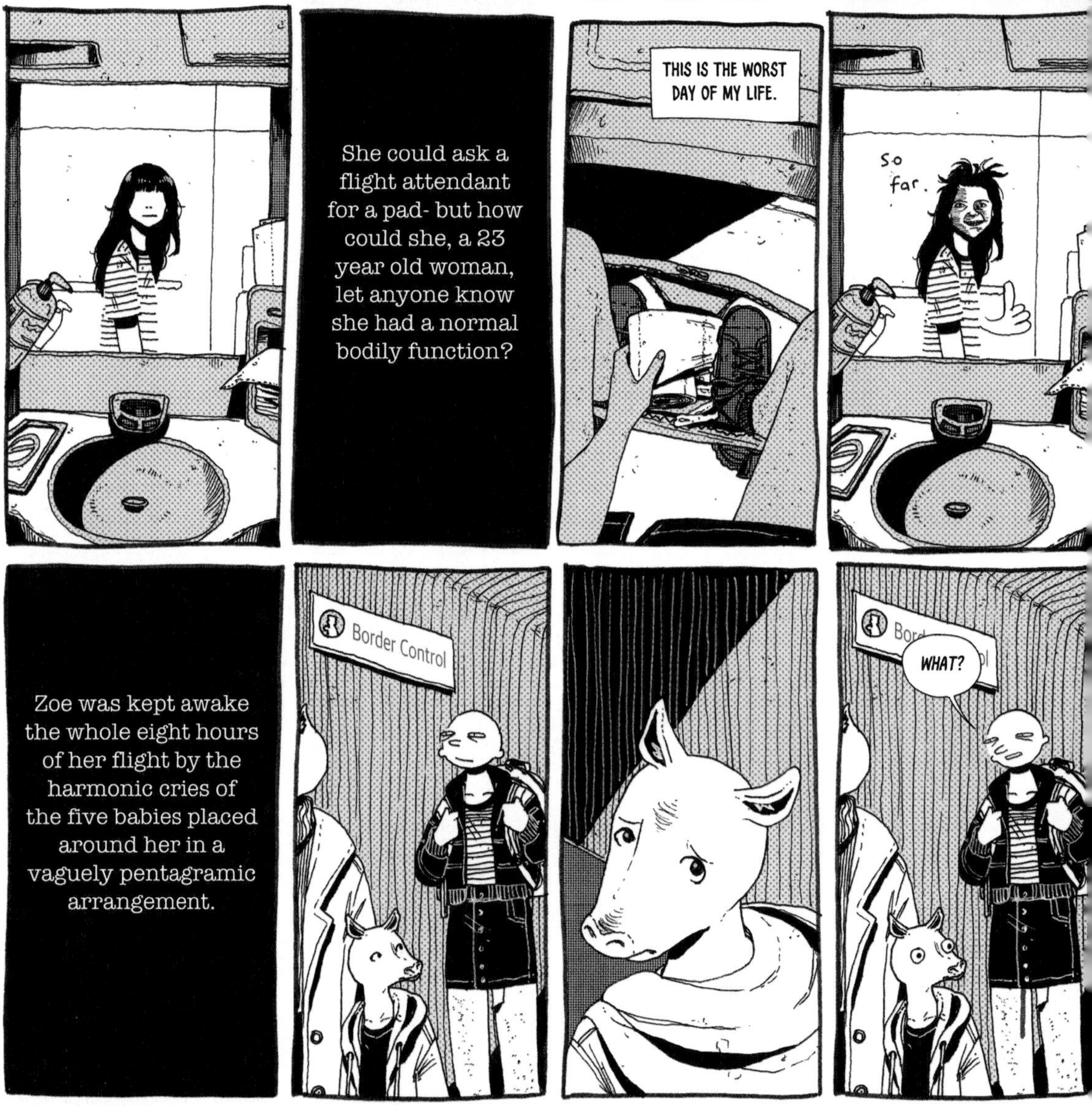
She could ask a flight attendant for a pad- but how could she, a 23 year old woman, let anyone know she had a normal bodily function?
THIS IS THE WORST DAY OF MY LIFE.
So far.
Zoe was kept awake the whole eight hours of her flight by the harmonic cries of the five babies placed around her in a vaguely pentagramic arrangement.
Border Control
WHAT?

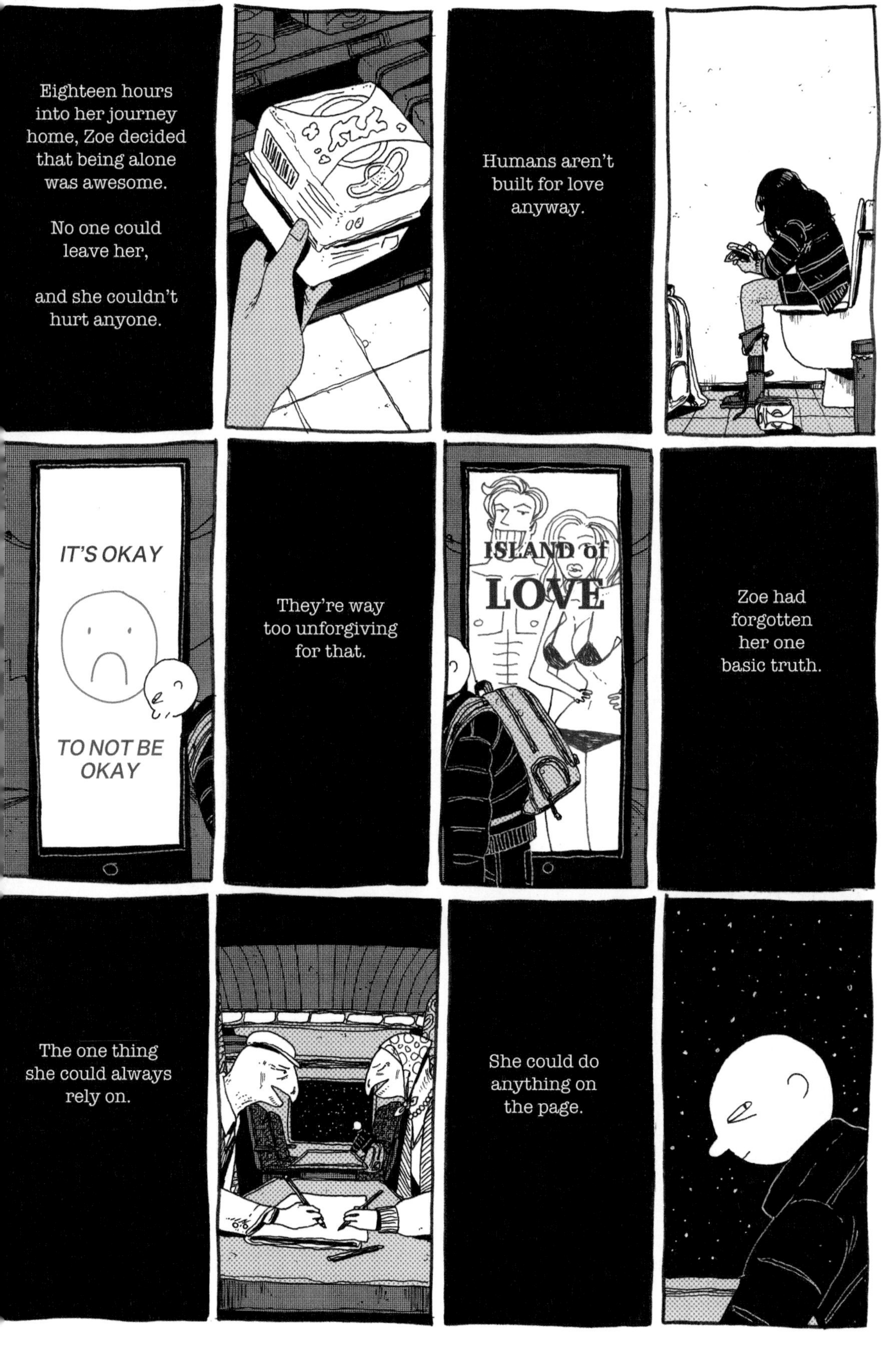

Eighteen hours into her journey home, Zoe decided that being alone was awesome.
No one could leave her,
and she couldn't hurt anyone.
Humans aren't built for love anyway.
IT'S OKAY
TO NOT BE OKAY
They're way too unforgiving for that.
ISLAND of LOVE
Zoe had forgotten her one basic truth.
The one thing she could always rely on.
She could do anything on the page.

ZOE OPENED HER EYES, SHE LOOKED
AROUND, NOTICING SHE WAS BACK IN
HER APARTMENT. AFTER A SHORT
MOMENT OF CONFUSION SHE HAD A
SUDDEN REALISATION.

A REALISATION THAT, WHEN CONSIDERED,
MADE EVERYTHING MAKE A LOT MORE SENSE.

ZOE NODDED TO HERSELF. "Of course.",
SHE MUTTERED, A GRATEFUL SMILE
APPEARING ON HER FACE.

"It was all just a dream."

THE END

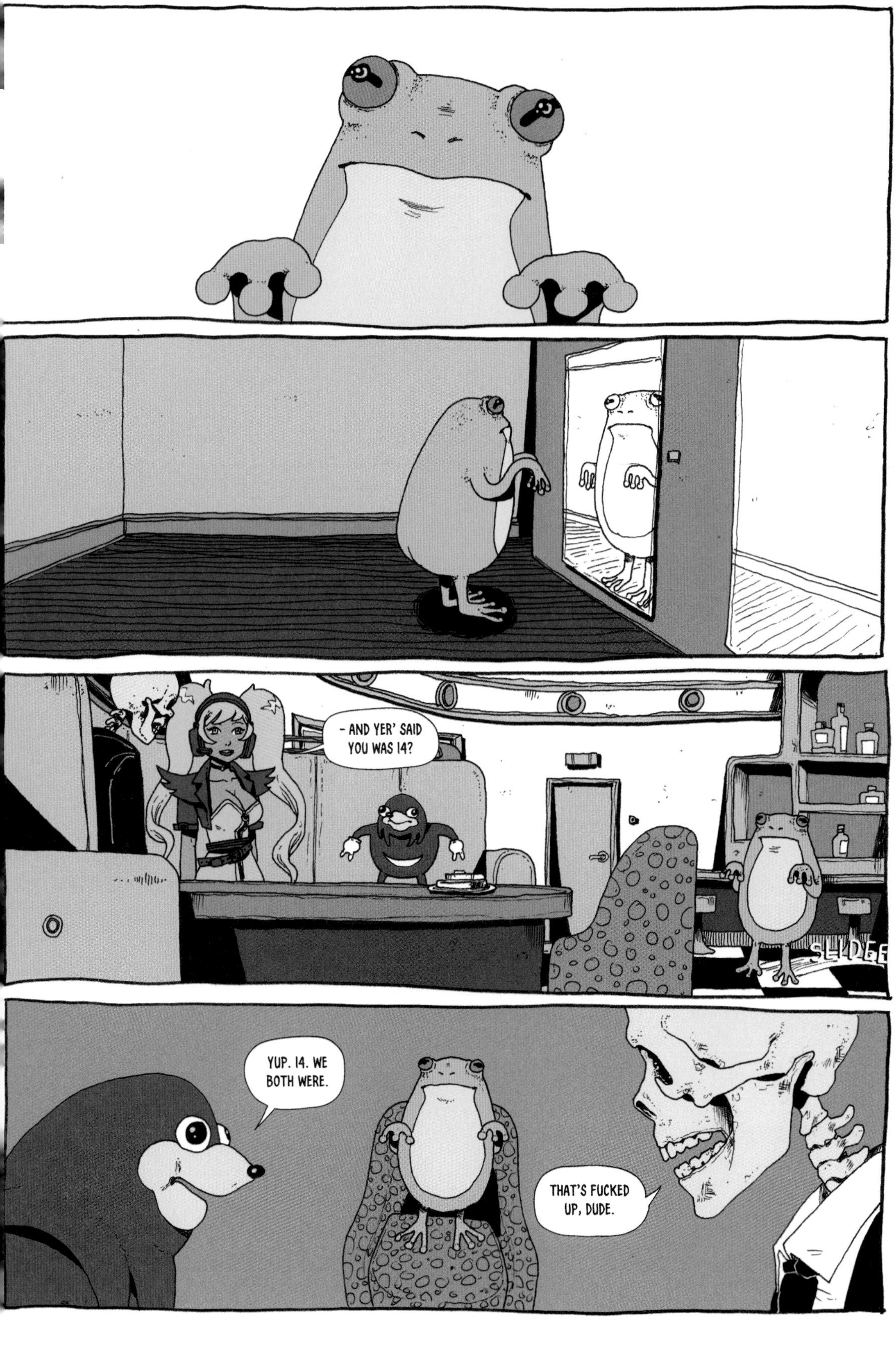
- AND YER' SAID YOU WAS 14?
SLIDGE
YUP. 14. WE BOTH WERE.
THAT'S FUCKED UP, DUDE.

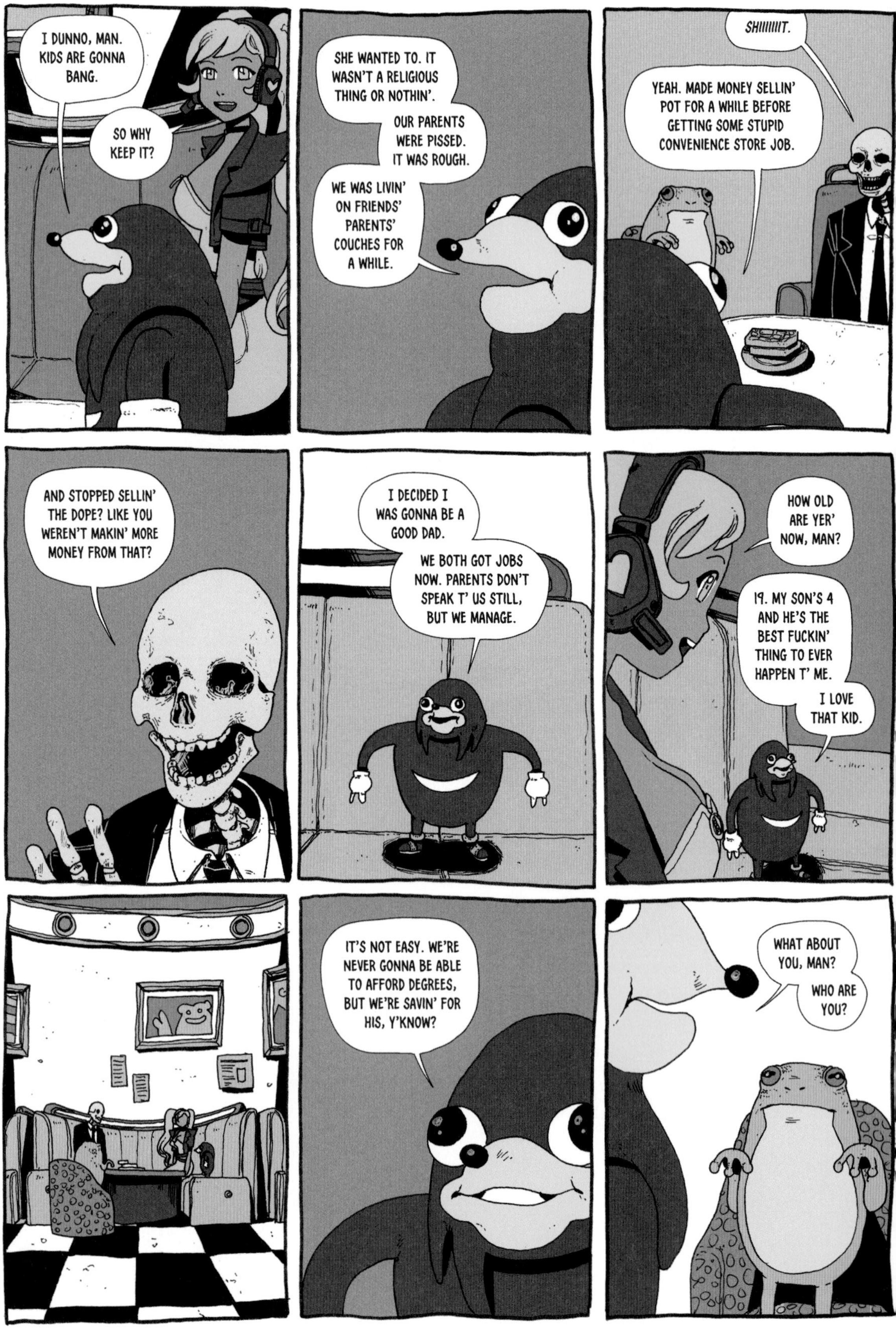
I DUNNO, MAN. KIDS ARE GONNA BANG.
SO WHY KEEP IT?
SHE WANTED TO. IT WASN'T A RELIGIOUS THING OR NOTHIN'.
OUR PARENTS WERE PISSED. IT WAS ROUGH.
WE WAS LIVIN' ON FRIENDS' PARENTS' COUCHES FOR A WHILE.
SHIIIIIIIT.
YEAH. MADE MONEY SELLIN' POT FOR A WHILE BEFORE GETTING SOME STUPID CONVENIENCE STORE JOB.
AND STOPPED SELLIN' THE DOPE? LIKE YOU WEREN'T MAKIN' MORE MONEY FROM THAT?
I DECIDED I WAS GONNA BE A GOOD DAD.
WE BOTH GOT JOBS NOW. PARENTS DON'T SPEAK T' US STILL, BUT WE MANAGE.
HOW OLD ARE YER' NOW, MAN?
19. MY SON'S 4 AND HE'S THE BEST FUCKIN' THING TO EVER HAPPEN T' ME.
I LOVE THAT KID.
IT'S NOT EASY. WE'RE NEVER GONNA BE ABLE TO AFFORD DEGREES, BUT WE'RE SAVIN' FOR HIS, Y'KNOW?
WHAT ABOUT YOU, MAN?
WHO ARE YOU?

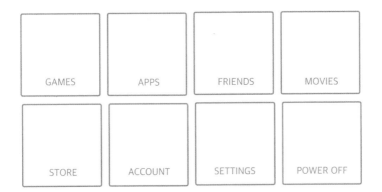

GAMES	APPS	FRIENDS	MOVIES
STORE	ACCOUNT	SETTINGS	POWER OFF

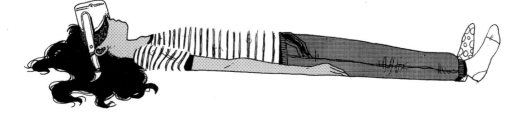

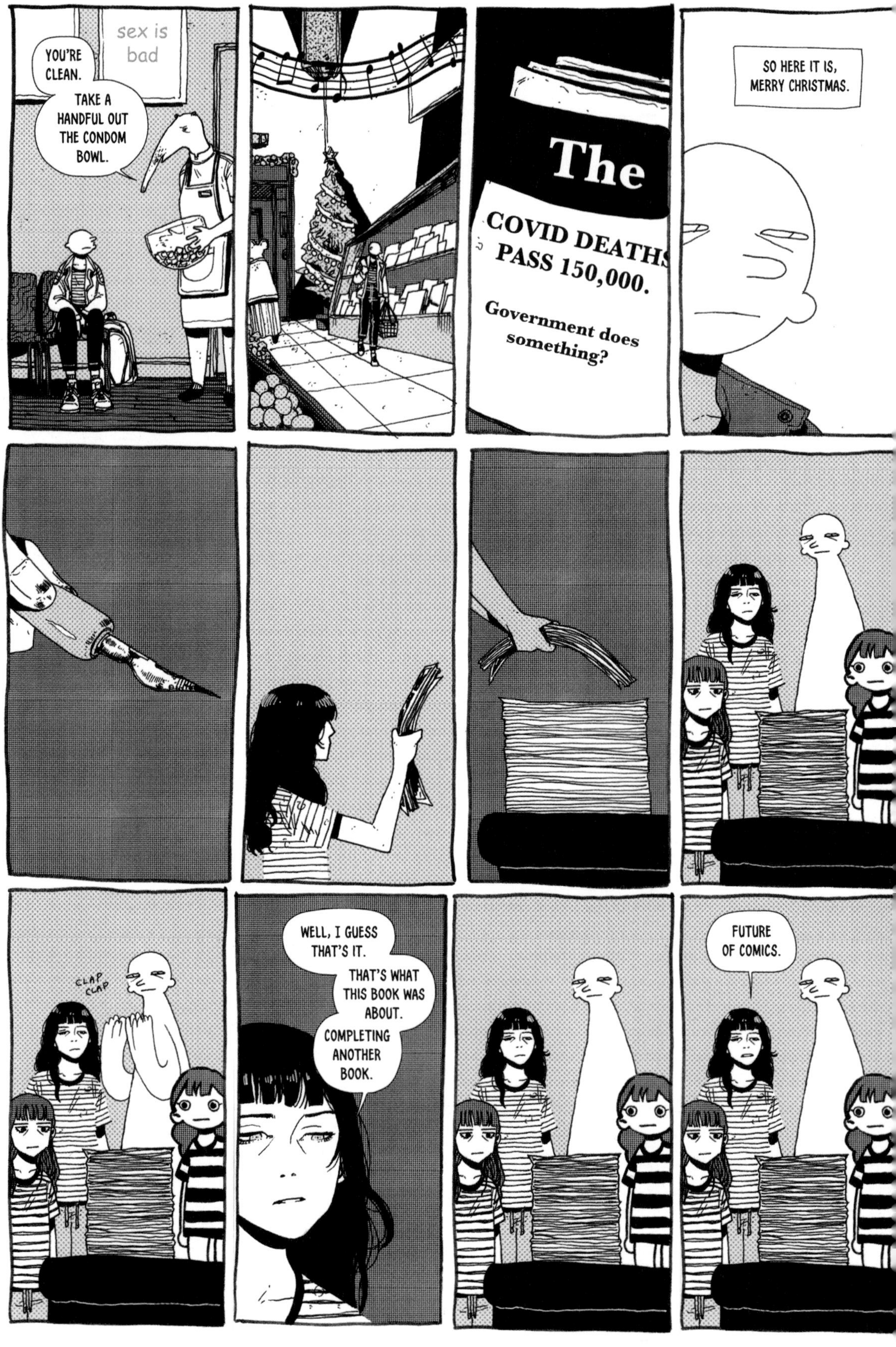
sex is bad
YOU'RE CLEAN.
TAKE A HANDFUL OUT THE CONDOM BOWL.
The
COVID DEATHS PASS 150,000.
Government does something?
SO HERE IT IS, MERRY CHRISTMAS.
CLAP CLAP
WELL, I GUESS THAT'S IT.
THAT'S WHAT THIS BOOK WAS ABOUT.
COMPLETING ANOTHER BOOK.
FUTURE OF COMICS.

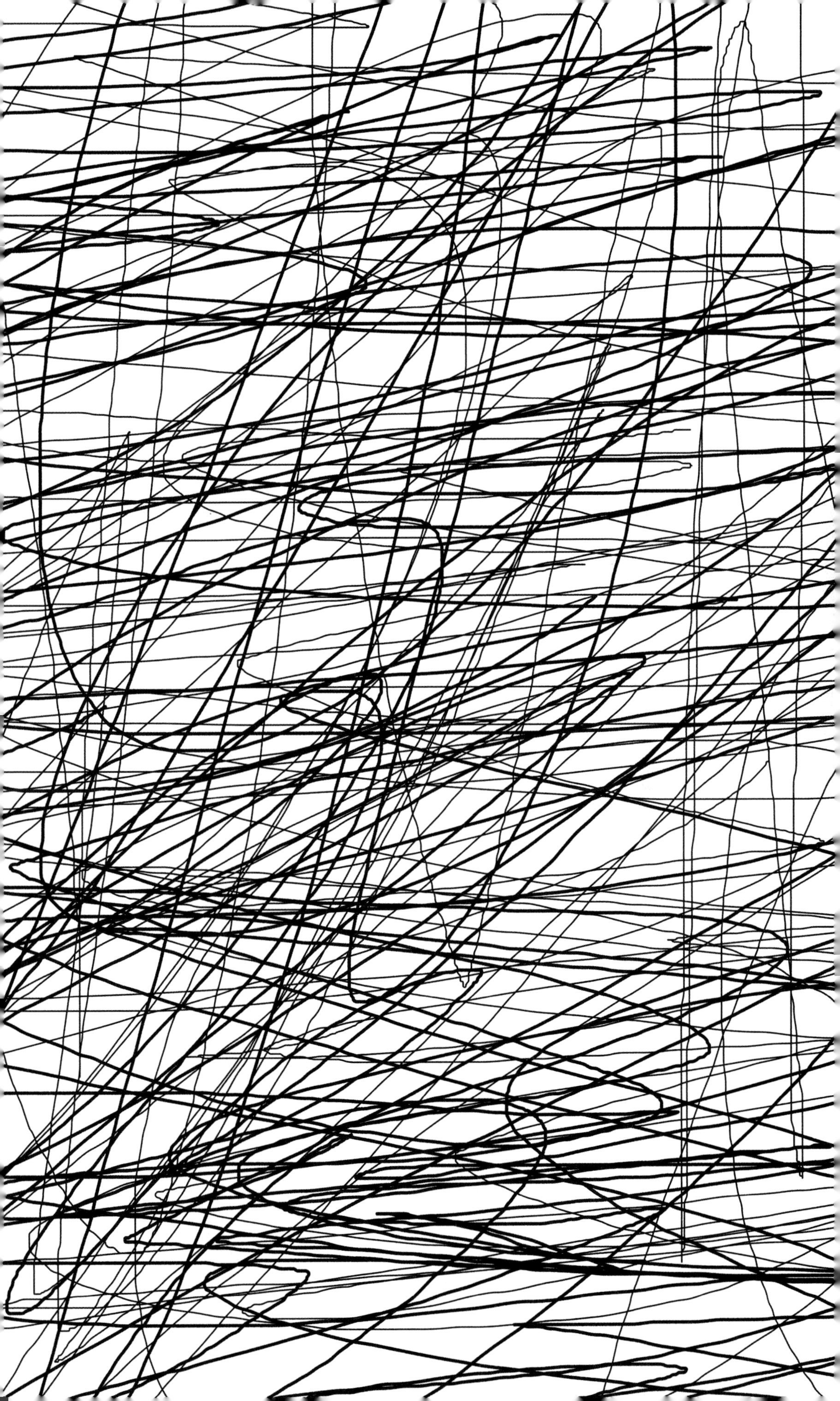

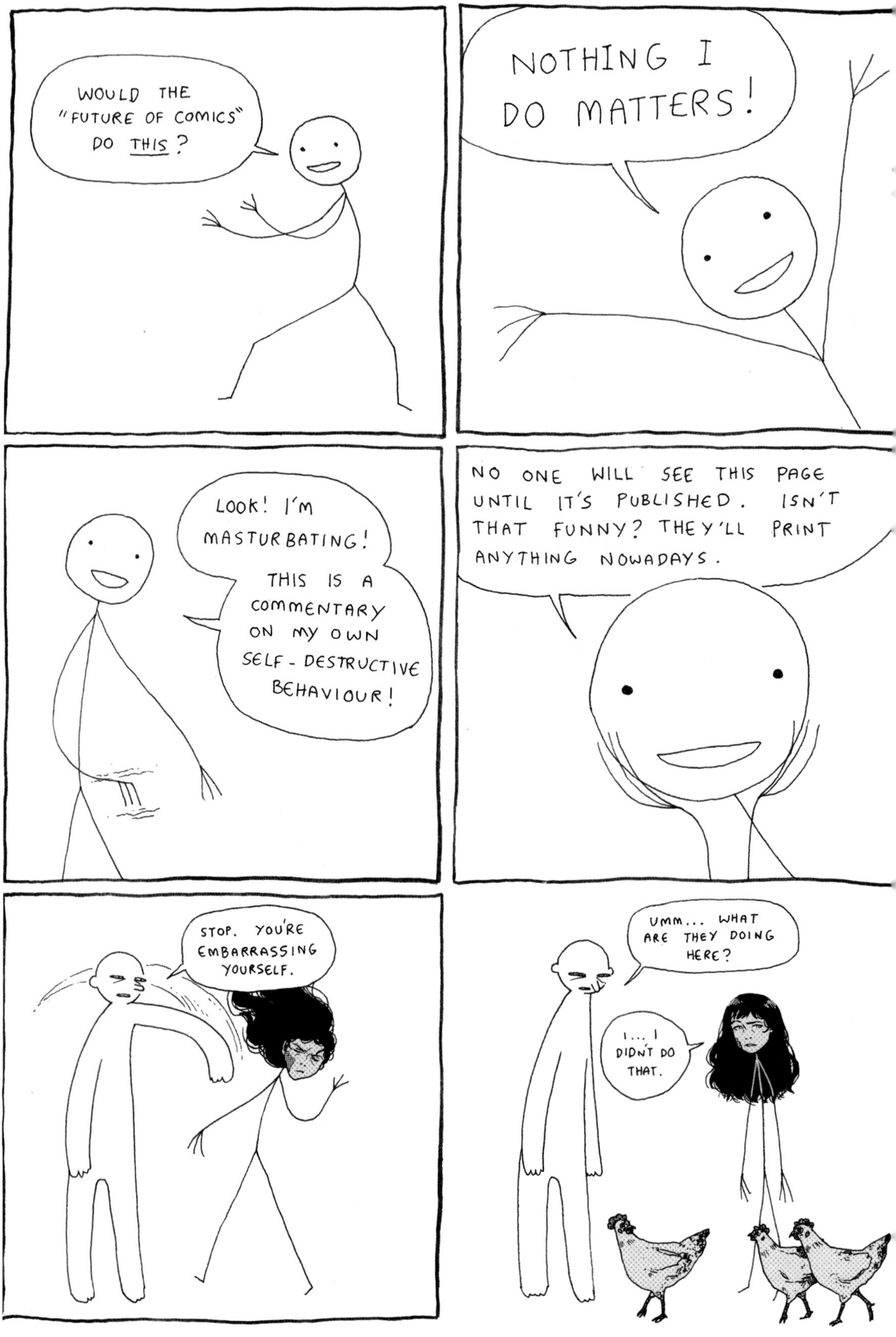

WOULD THE "FUTURE OF COMICS" DO THIS?
NOTHING I DO MATTERS!
LOOK! I'M MASTURBATING!
THIS IS A COMMENTARY ON MY OWN SELF-DESTRUCTIVE BEHAVIOUR!
NO ONE WILL SEE THIS PAGE UNTIL IT'S PUBLISHED. ISN'T THAT FUNNY? THEY'LL PRINT ANYTHING NOWADAYS.
STOP. YOU'RE EMBARRASSING YOURSELF.
UMM... WHAT ARE THEY DOING HERE?
I... I DIDN'T DO THAT.

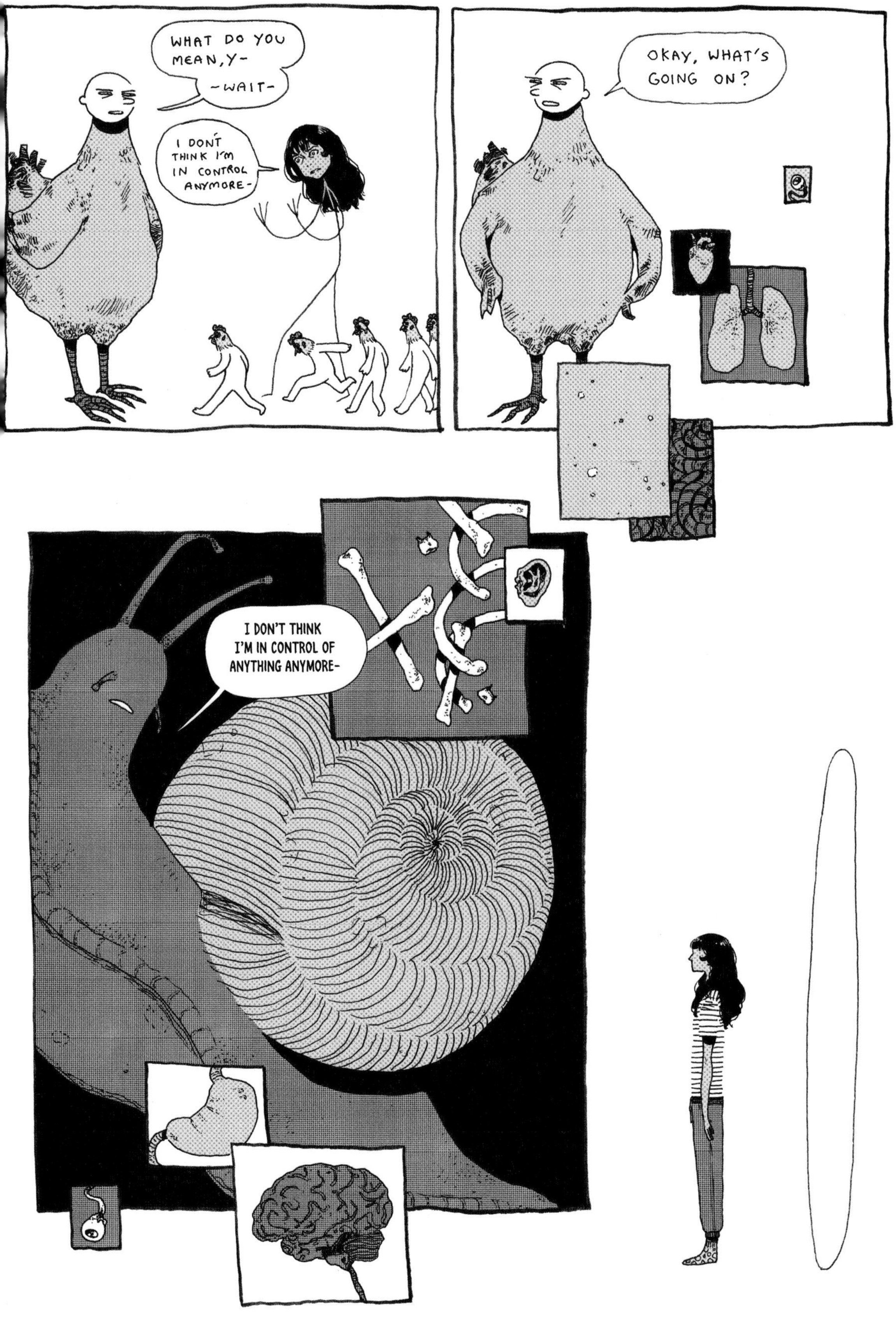
WHAT DO YOU MEAN, Y-
-WAIT-
I DON'T THINK I'M IN CONTROL ANYMORE-
OKAY, WHAT'S GOING ON?
I DON'T THINK I'M IN CONTROL OF ANYTHING ANYMORE-

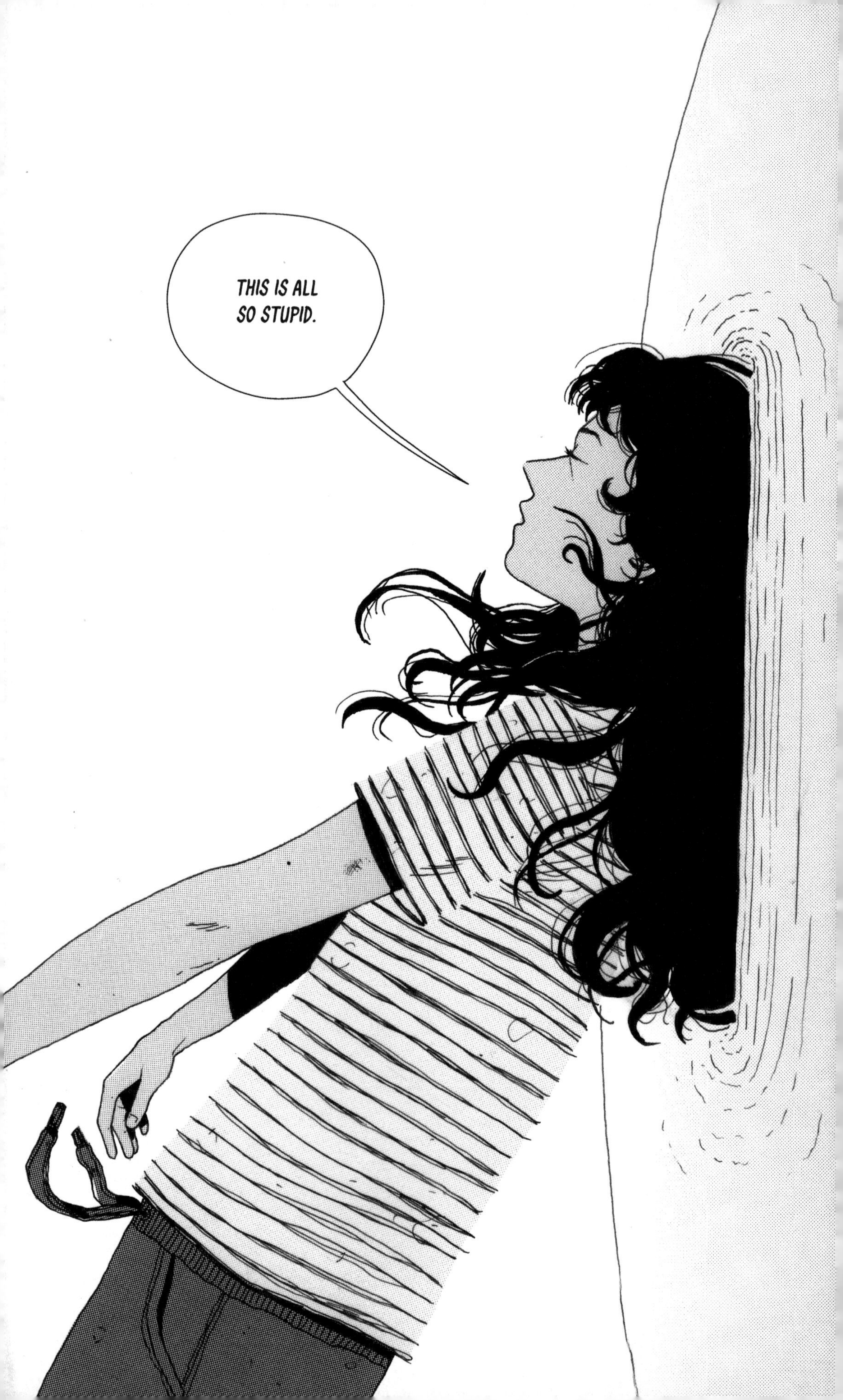
THIS IS ALL SO STUPID.

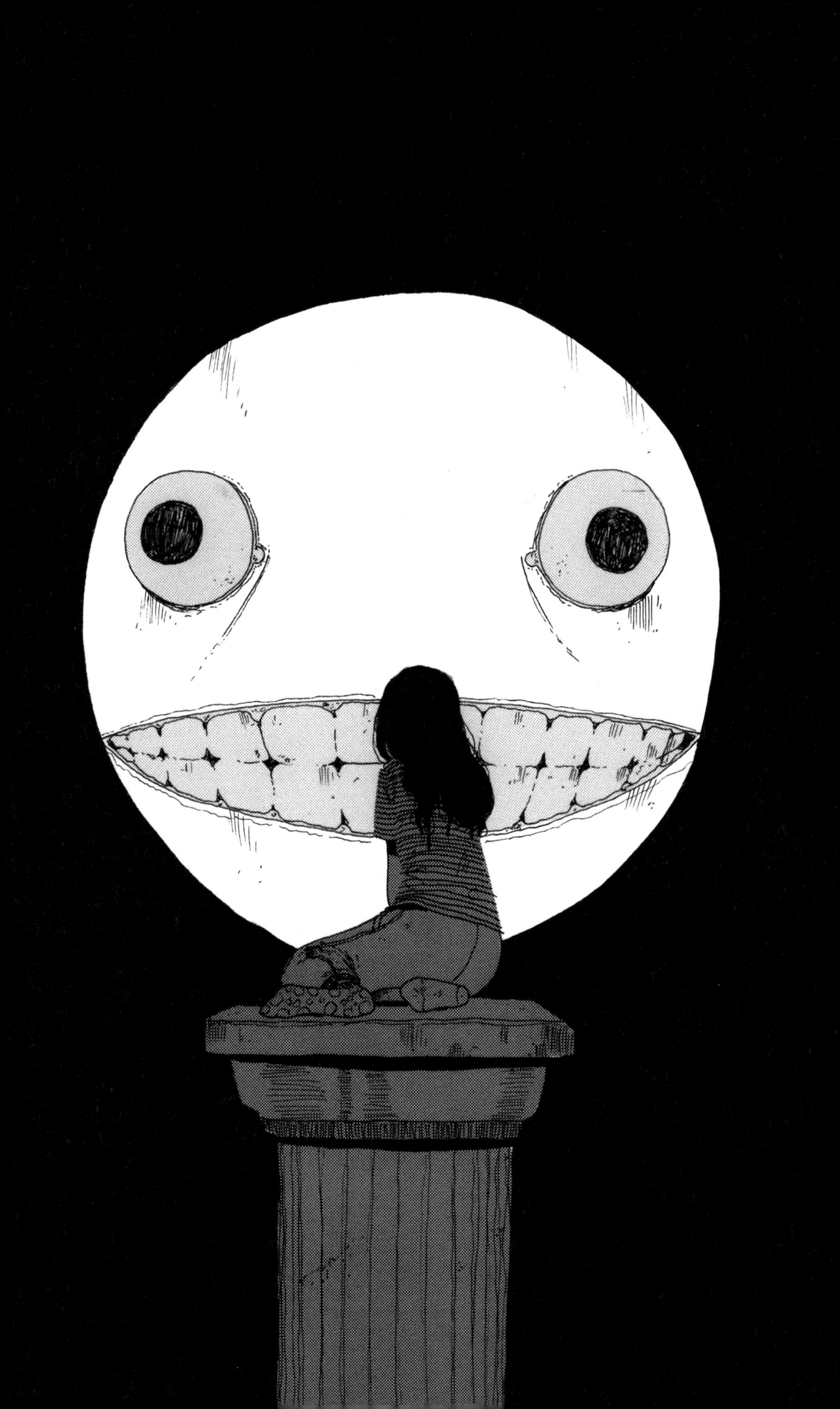

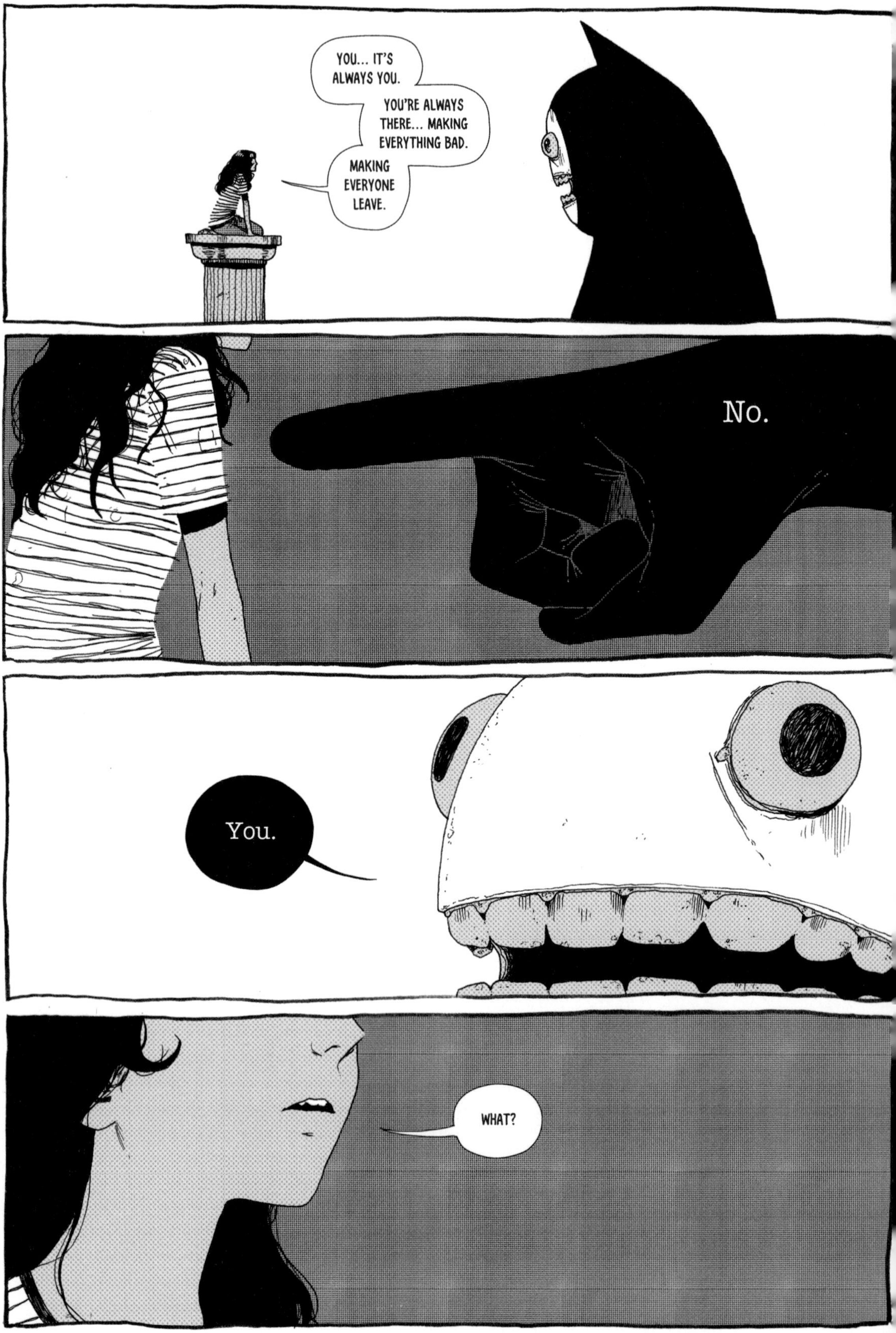
YOU... IT'S ALWAYS YOU.
YOU'RE ALWAYS THERE... MAKING EVERYTHING BAD.
MAKING EVERYONE LEAVE.
No.
You.
WHAT?

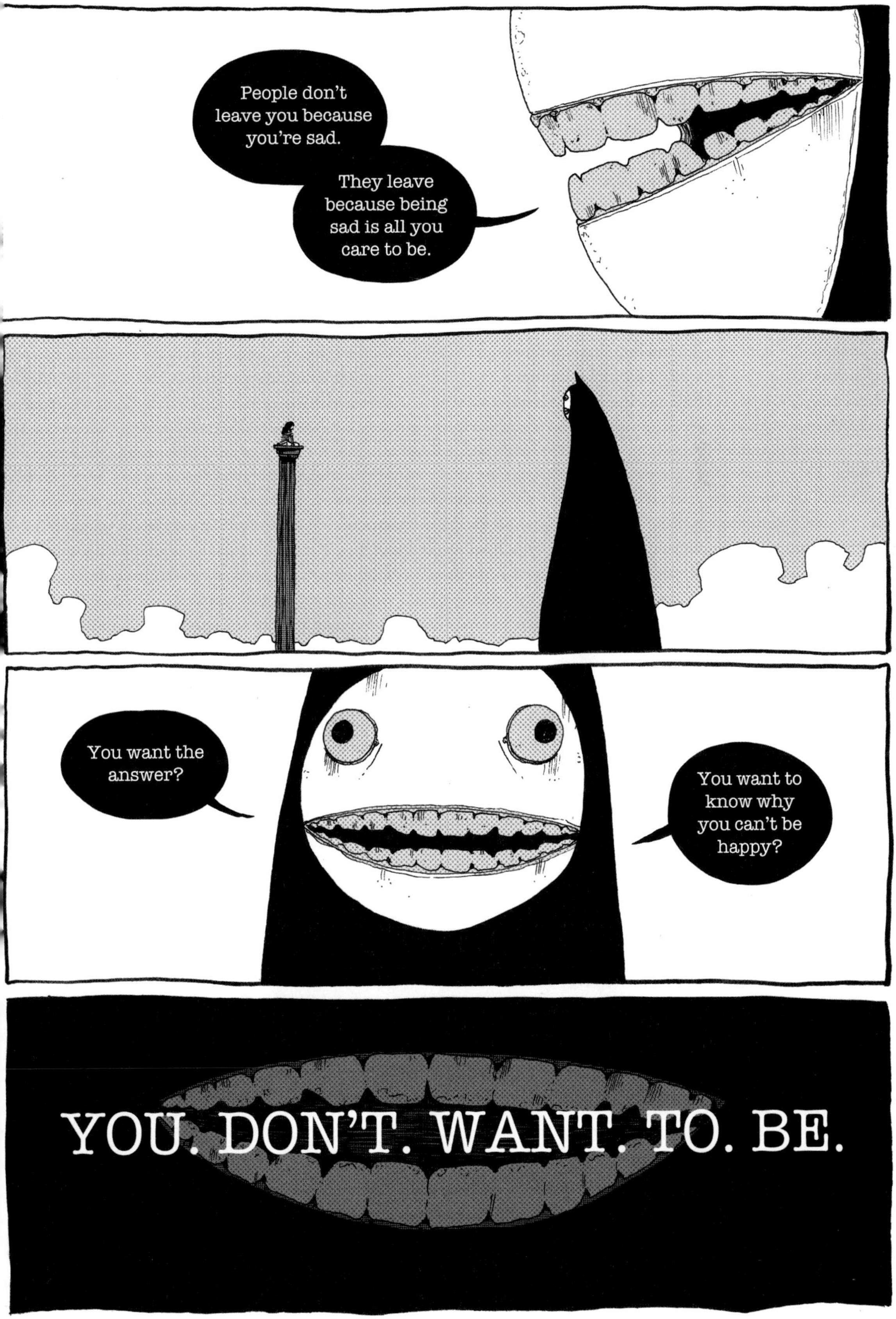
People don't leave you because you're sad.
They leave because being sad is all you care to be.
You want the answer?
You want to know why you can't be happy?
YOU. DON'T. WANT. TO. BE.

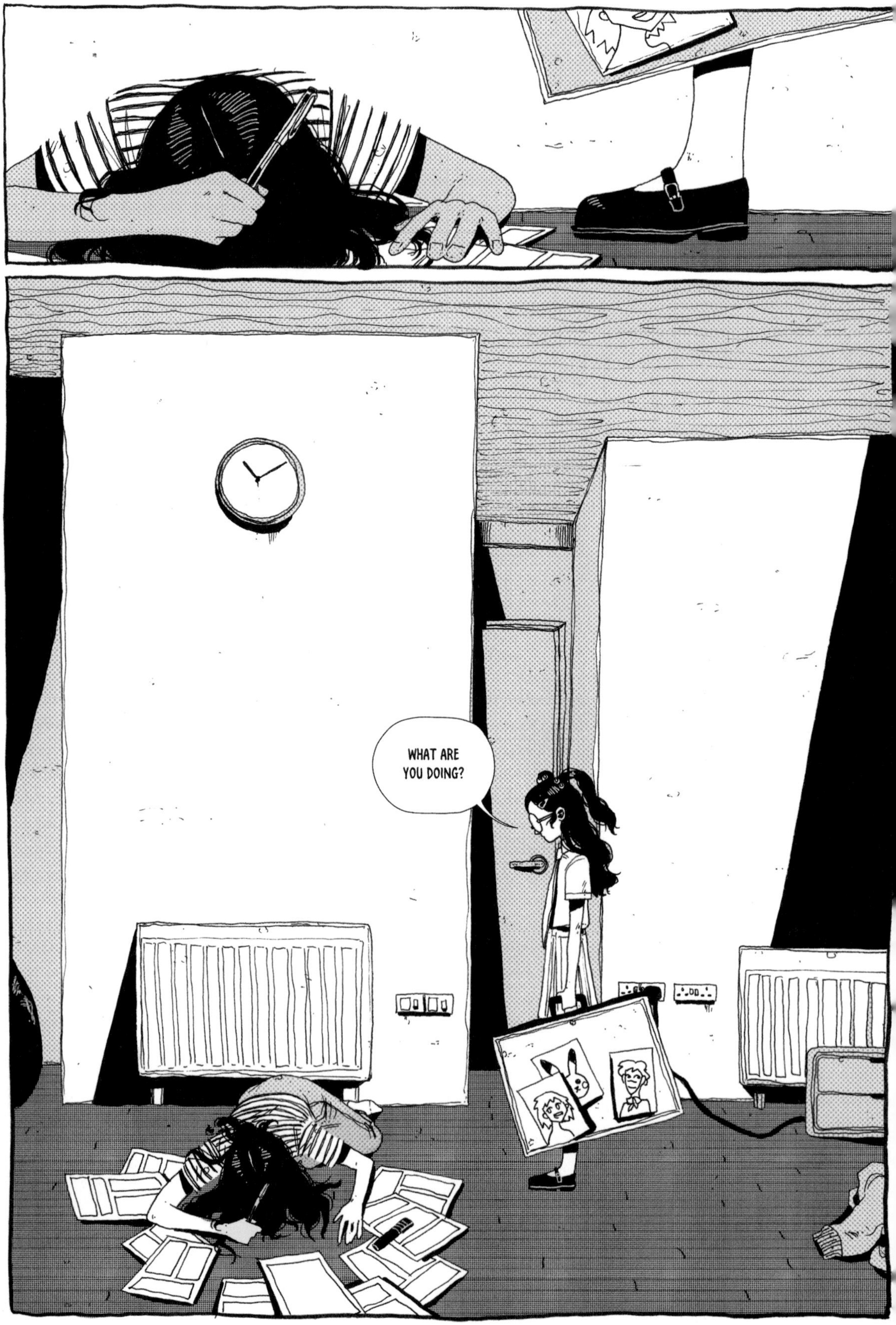
WHAT ARE YOU DOING?

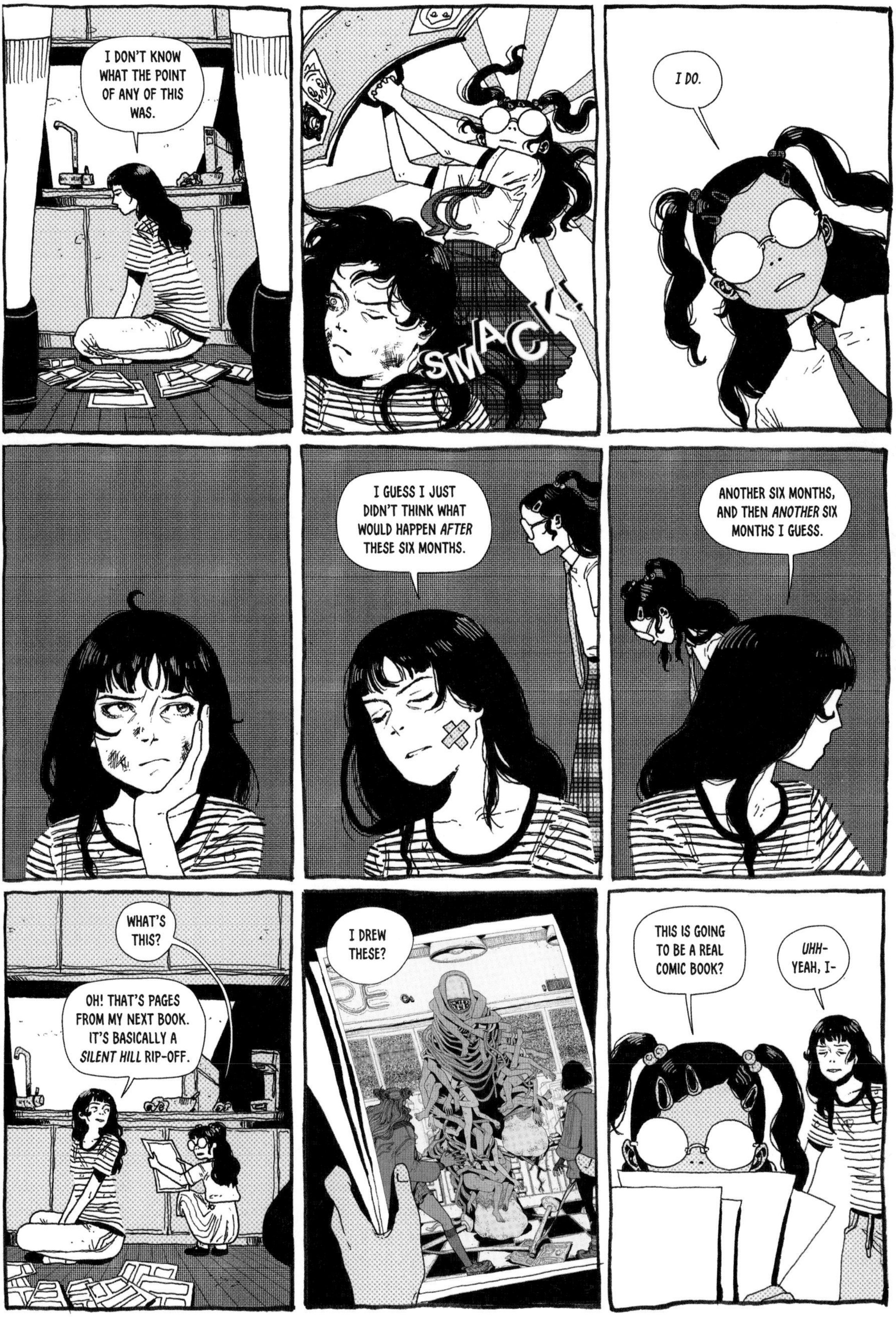
I DON'T KNOW WHAT THE POINT OF ANY OF THIS WAS.
SMACK!
I DO.
I GUESS I JUST DIDN'T THINK WHAT WOULD HAPPEN *AFTER* THESE SIX MONTHS.
ANOTHER SIX MONTHS, AND THEN *ANOTHER* SIX MONTHS I GUESS.
WHAT'S THIS?
OH! THAT'S PAGES FROM MY NEXT BOOK. IT'S BASICALLY A *SILENT HILL* RIP-OFF.
I DREW THESE?
THIS IS GOING TO BE A REAL COMIC BOOK?
UHH- YEAH, I-

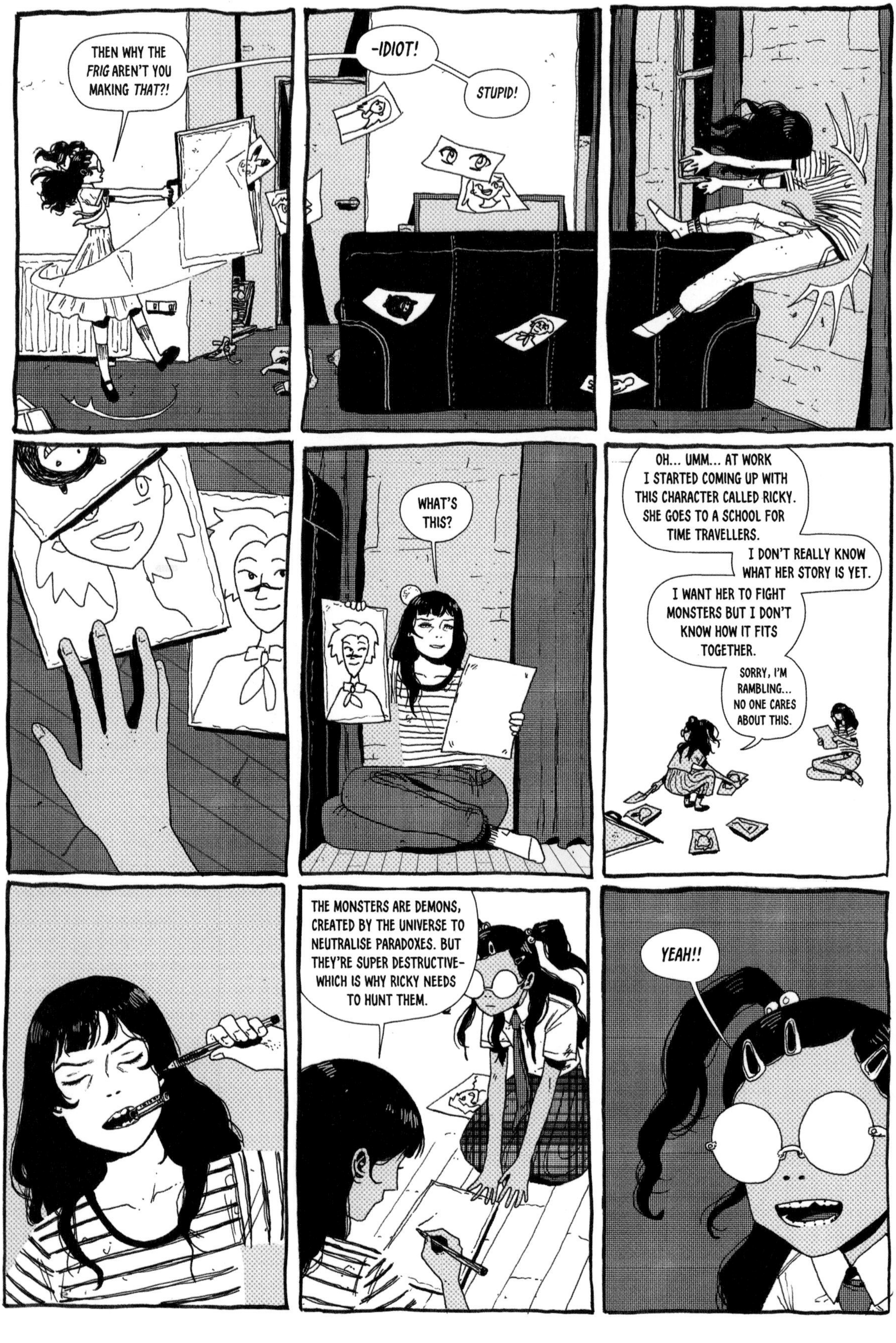

THEN WHY THE *FRIG* AREN'T YOU MAKING *THAT?!*
-IDIOT!
STUPID!
WHAT'S THIS?
OH... UMM... AT WORK I STARTED COMING UP WITH THIS CHARACTER CALLED RICKY. SHE GOES TO A SCHOOL FOR TIME TRAVELLERS.
I DON'T REALLY KNOW WHAT HER STORY IS YET.
I WANT HER TO FIGHT MONSTERS BUT I DON'T KNOW HOW IT FITS TOGETHER.
SORRY, I'M RAMBLING... NO ONE CARES ABOUT THIS.
THE MONSTERS ARE DEMONS, CREATED BY THE UNIVERSE TO NEUTRALISE PARADOXES. BUT THEY'RE SUPER DESTRUCTIVE- WHICH IS WHY RICKY NEEDS TO HUNT THEM.
YEAH!!

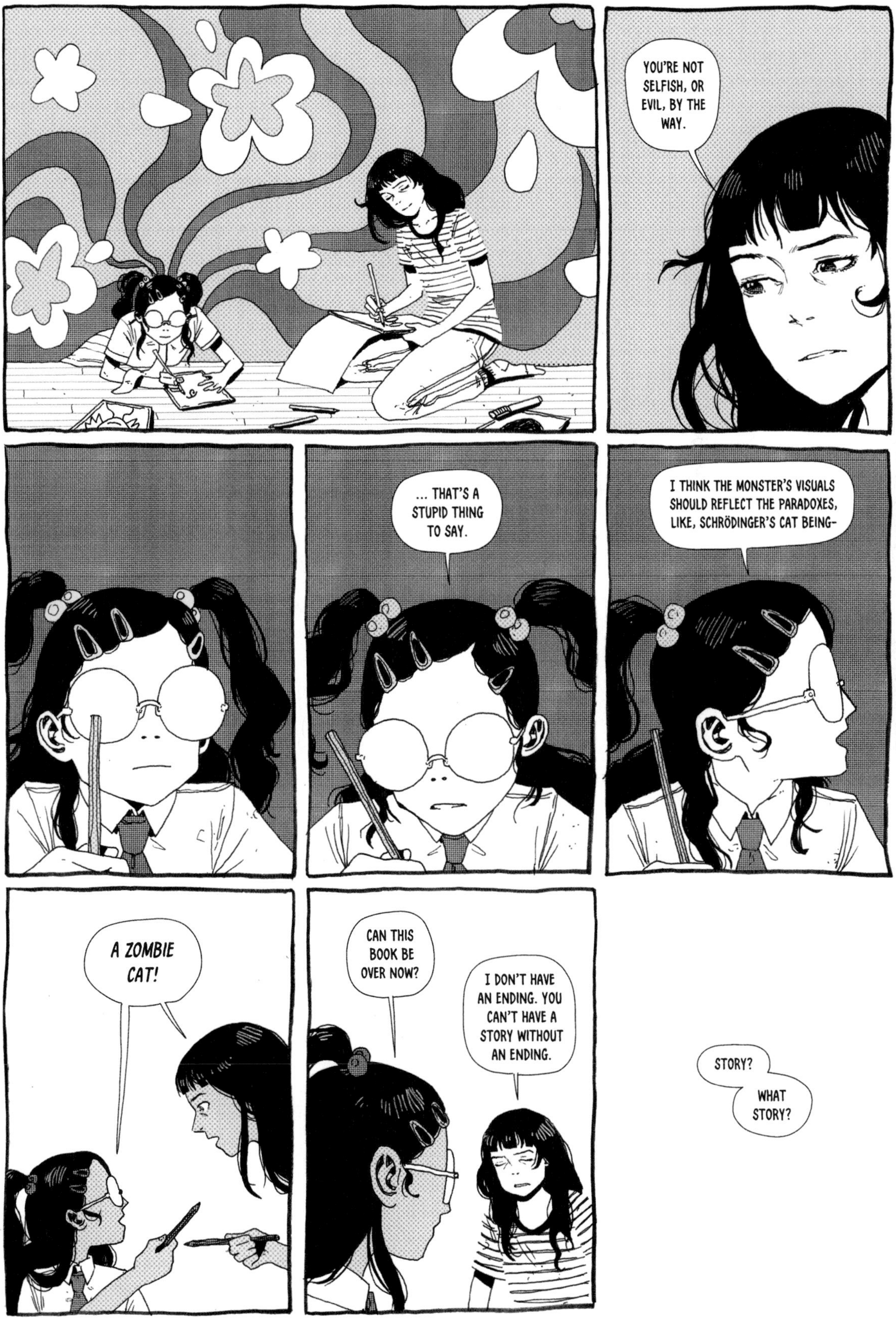
YOU'RE NOT SELFISH, OR EVIL, BY THE WAY.
... THAT'S A STUPID THING TO SAY.
I THINK THE MONSTER'S VISUALS SHOULD REFLECT THE PARADOXES, LIKE, SCHRÖDINGER'S CAT BEING-
A ZOMBIE CAT!
CAN THIS BOOK BE OVER NOW?
I DON'T HAVE AN ENDING. YOU CAN'T HAVE A STORY WITHOUT AN ENDING.
STORY?
WHAT STORY?

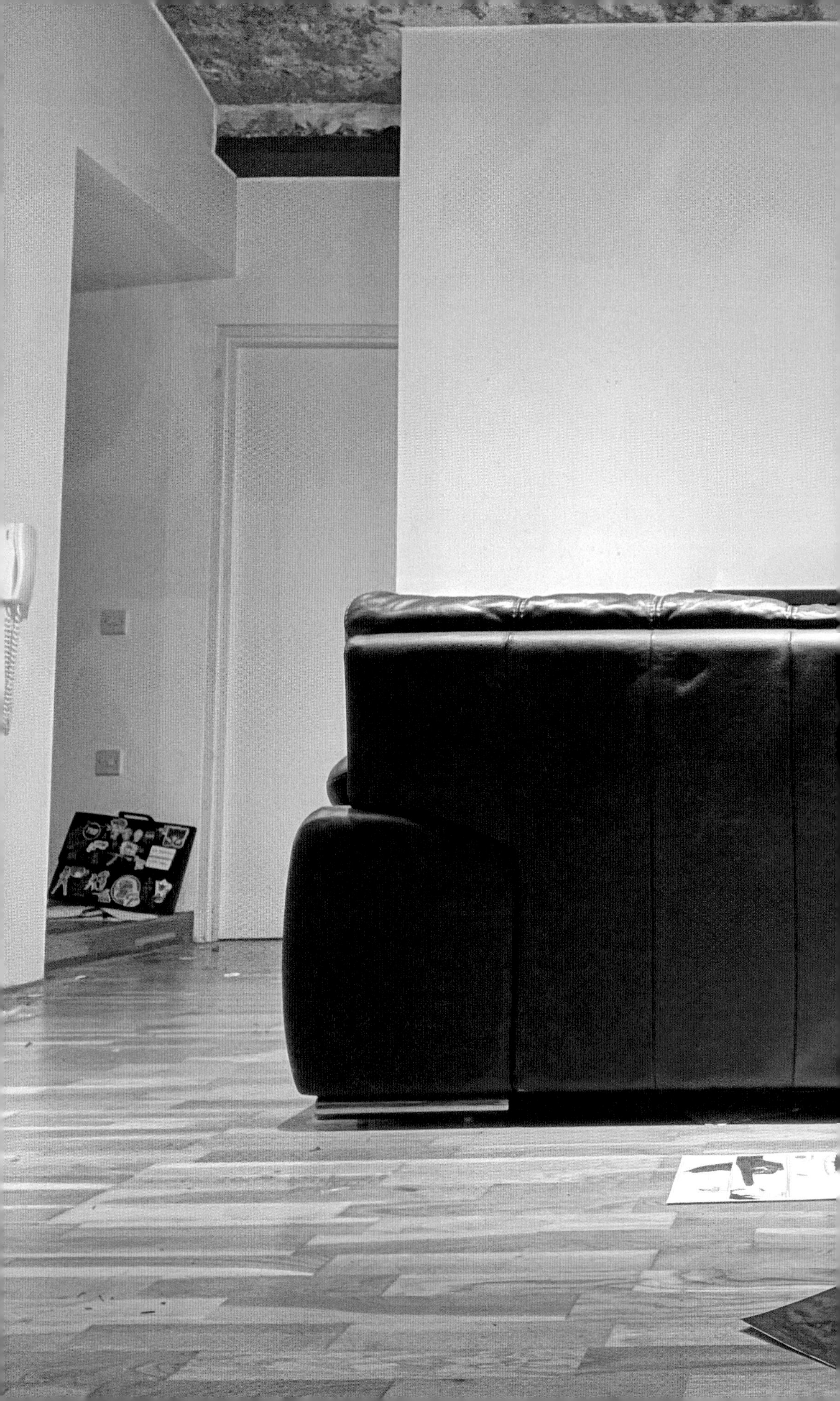

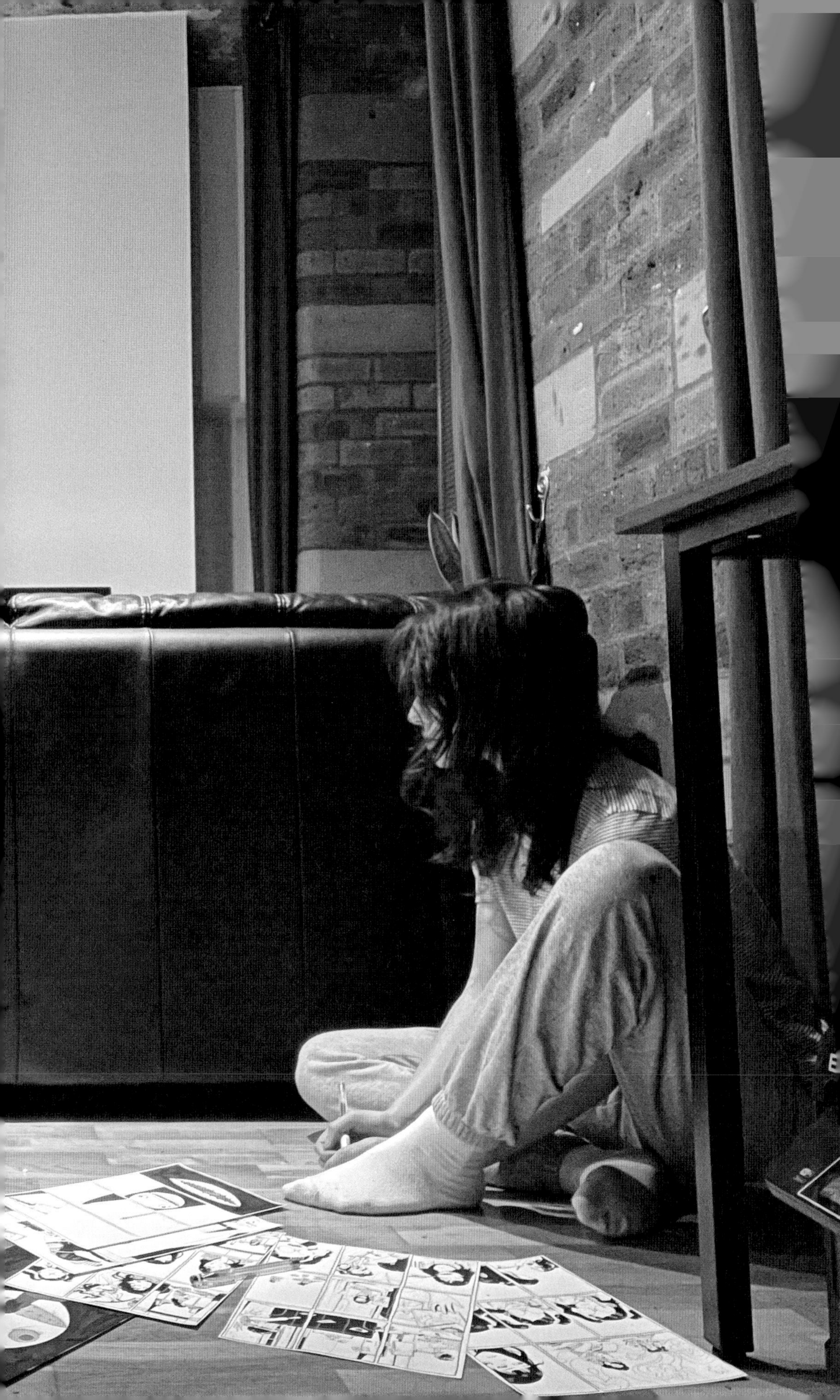

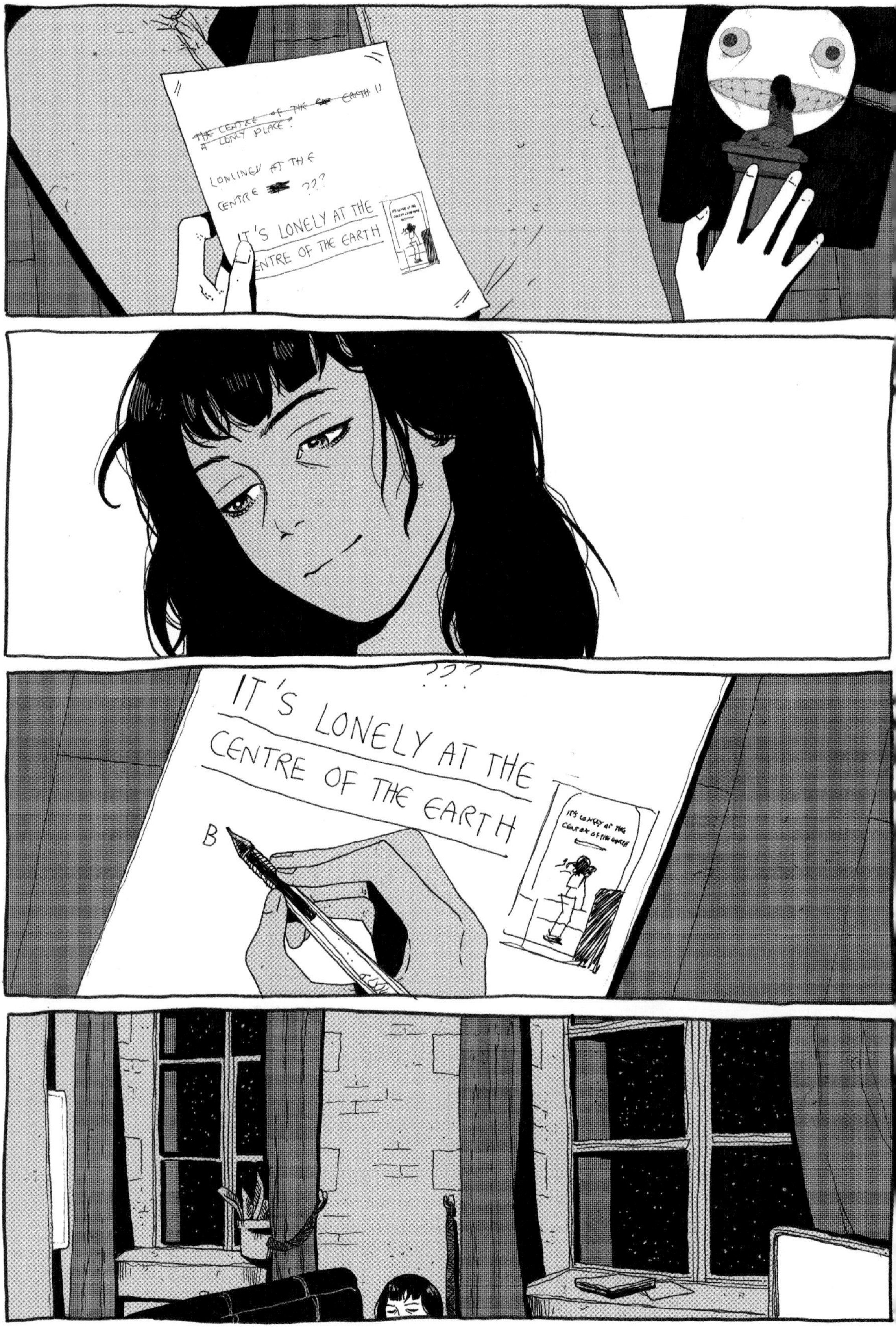
IT'S LONELY AT THE
???
IT'S LONELY AT THE
CENTRE OF THE EARTH
B

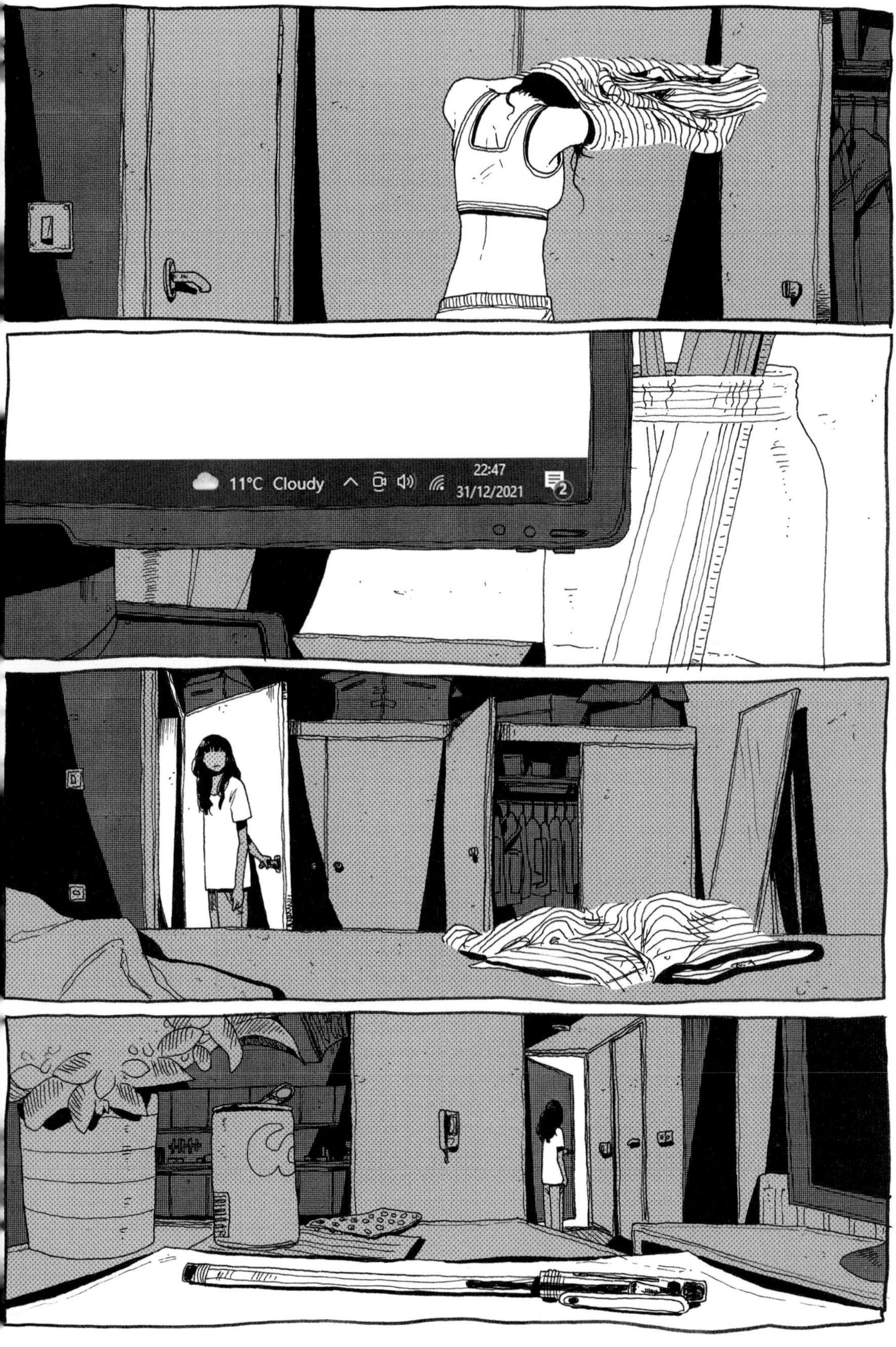
11°C Cloudy
22:47
31/12/2021

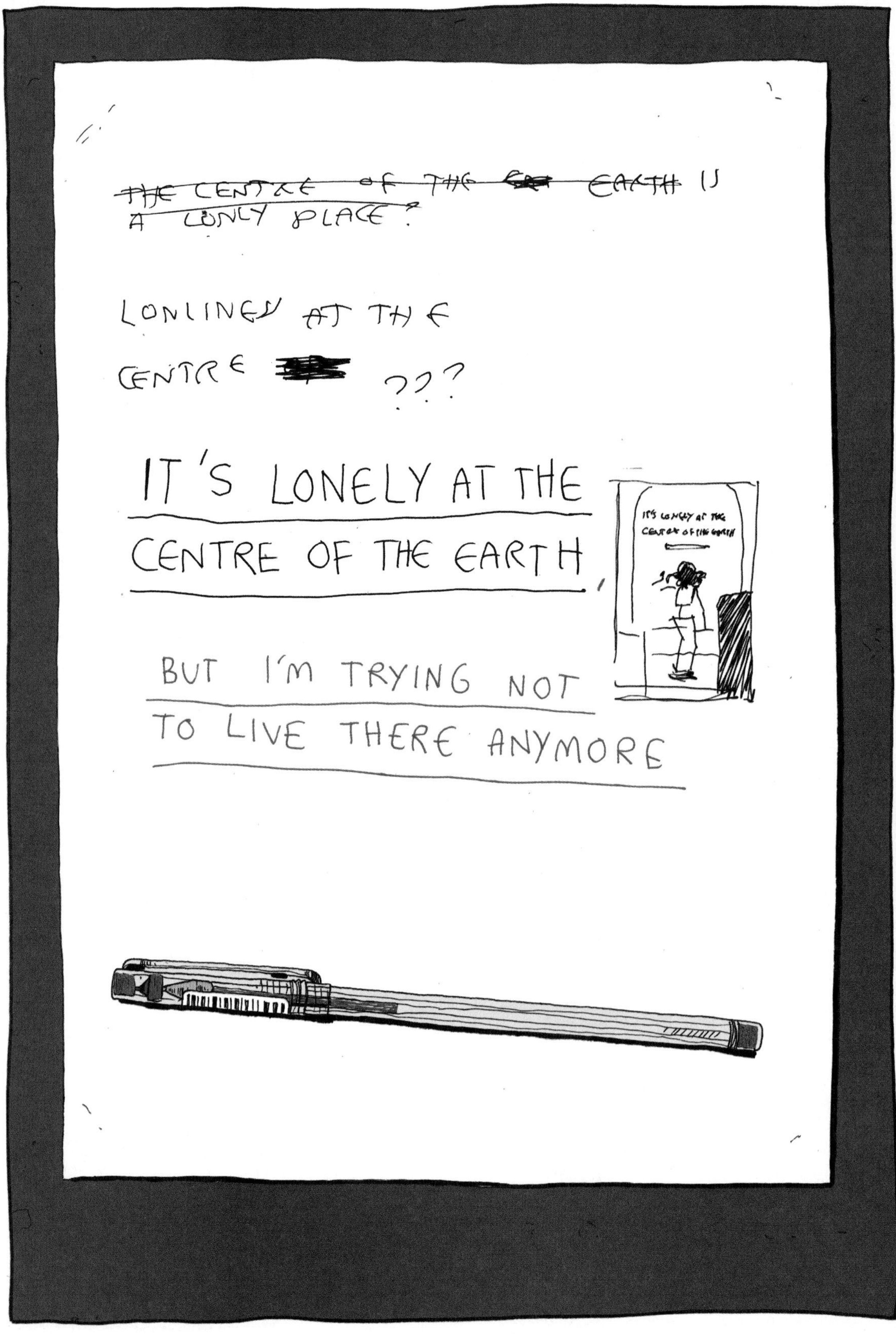
THE CENTRE OF THE EARTH IS
A LONLY PLACE?
LONLINESS AT THE
CENTRE ???
IT'S LONELY AT THE
CENTRE OF THE EARTH
BUT I'M TRYING NOT
TO LIVE THERE ANYMORE

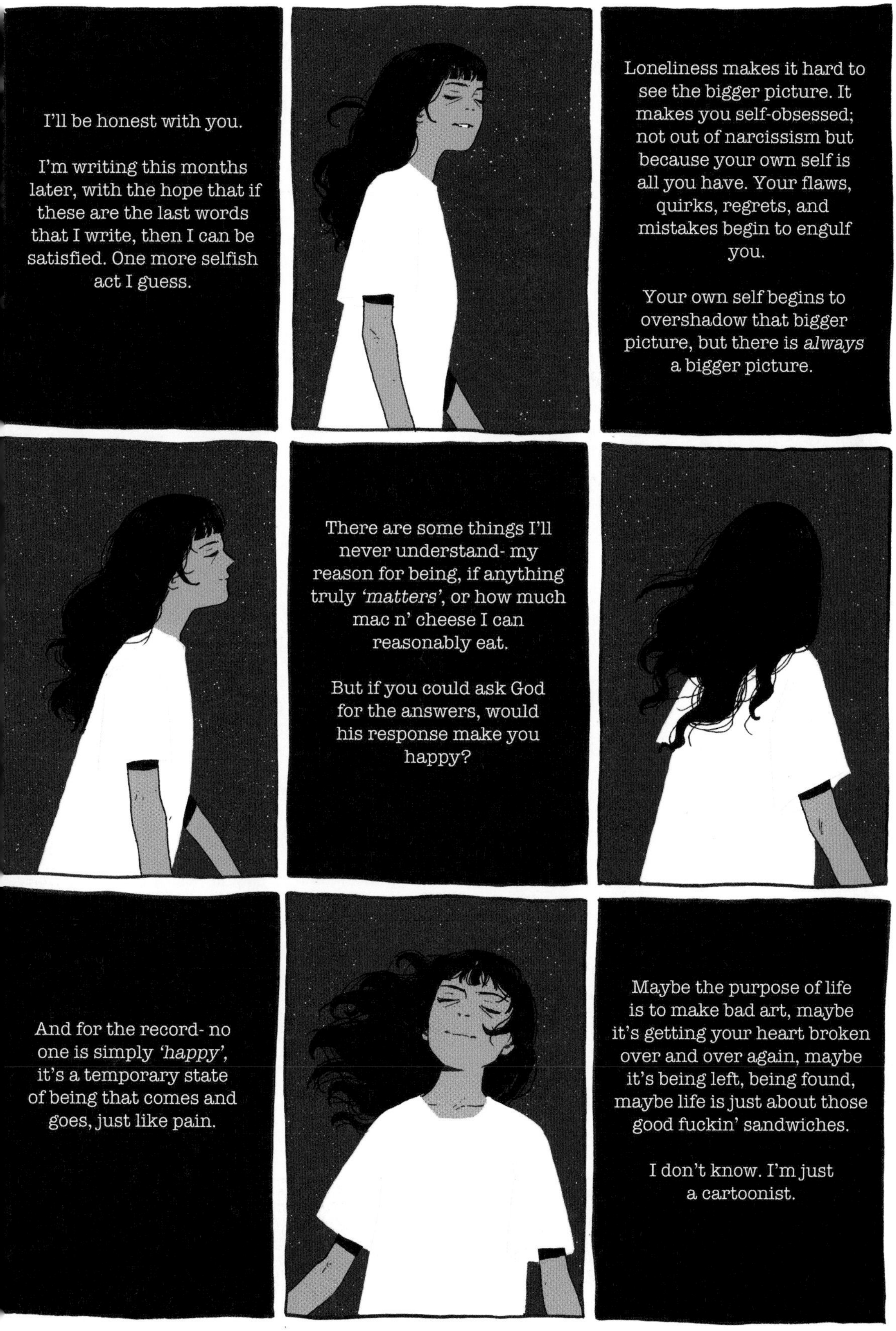
I'll be honest with you.
I'm writing this months later, with the hope that if these are the last words that I write, then I can be satisfied. One more selfish act I guess.
Loneliness makes it hard to see the bigger picture. It makes you self-obsessed; not out of narcissism but because your own self is all you have. Your flaws, quirks, regrets, and mistakes begin to engulf you.
Your own self begins to overshadow that bigger picture, but there is *always* a bigger picture.
There are some things I'll never understand- my reason for being, if anything truly *'matters'*, or how much mac n' cheese I can reasonably eat.
But if you could ask God for the answers, would his response make you happy?
And for the record- no one is simply *'happy'*, it's a temporary state of being that comes and goes, just like pain.
Maybe the purpose of life is to make bad art, maybe it's getting your heart broken over and over again, maybe it's being left, being found, maybe life is just about those good fuckin' sandwiches.
I don't know. I'm just a cartoonist.

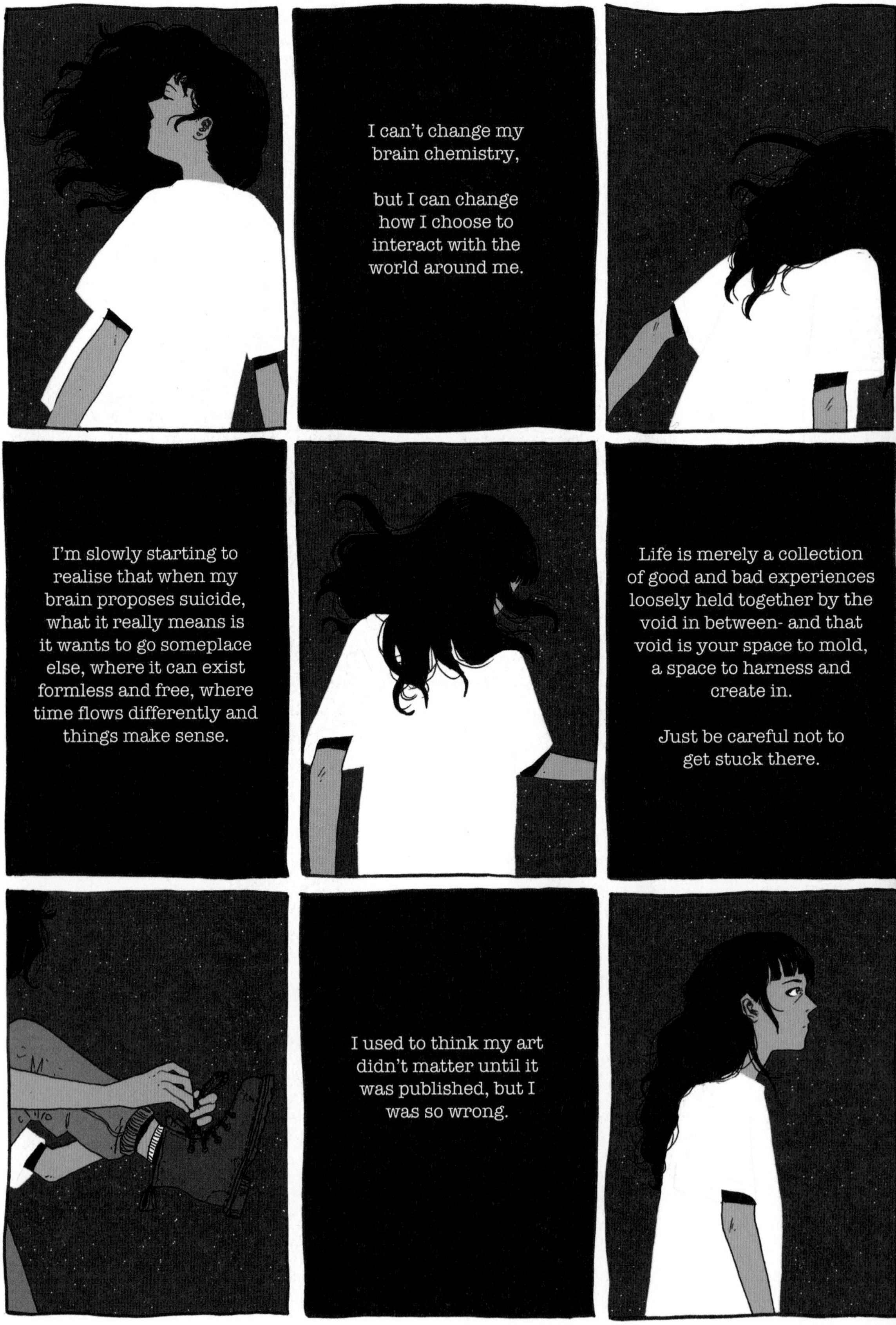
I can't change my brain chemistry,
but I can change how I choose to interact with the world around me.
I'm slowly starting to realise that when my brain proposes suicide, what it really means is it wants to go someplace else, where it can exist formless and free, where time flows differently and things make sense.
Life is merely a collection of good and bad experiences loosely held together by the void in between- and that void is your space to mold, a space to harness and create in.
Just be careful not to get stuck there.
I used to think my art didn't matter until it was published, but I was so wrong.

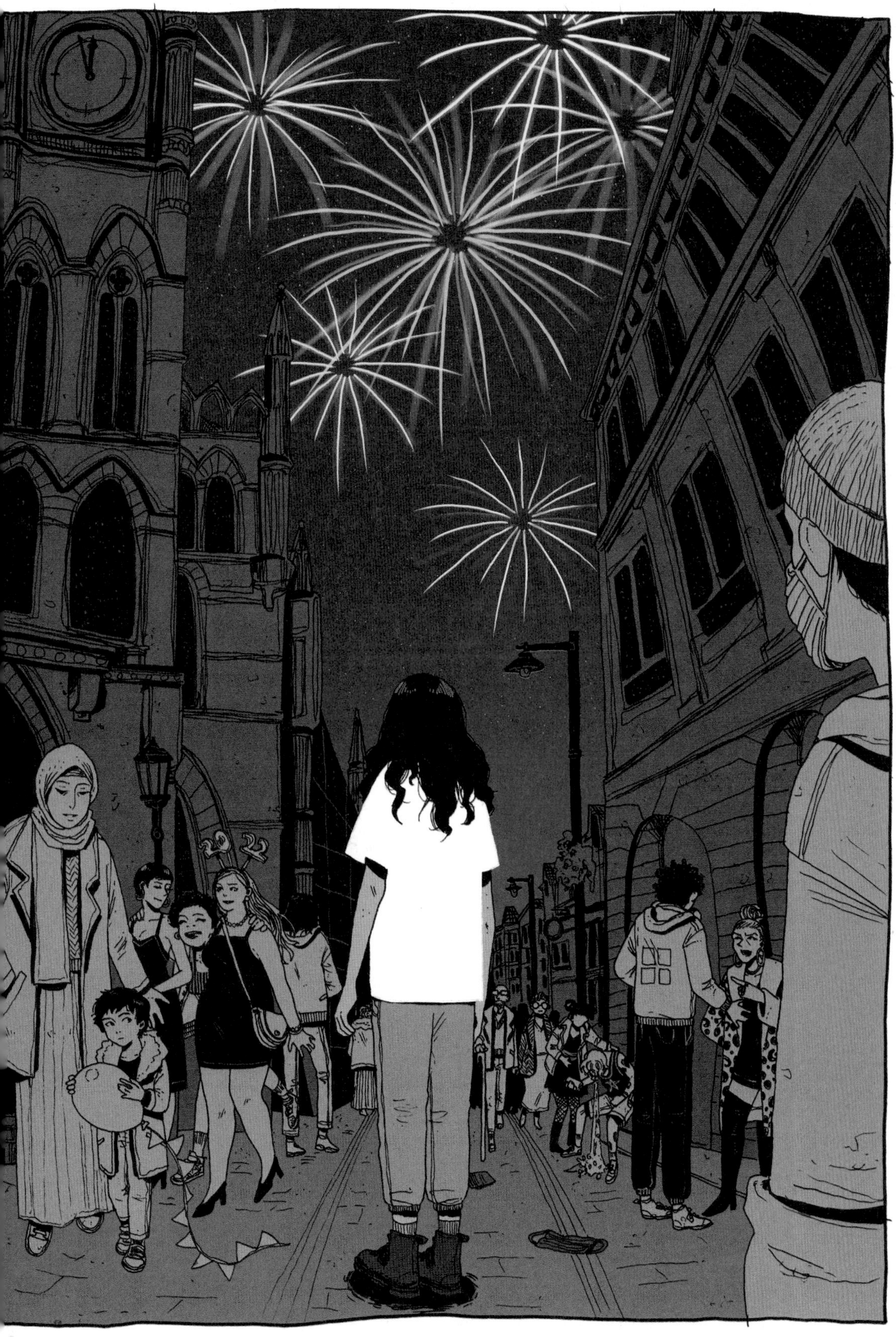
2022

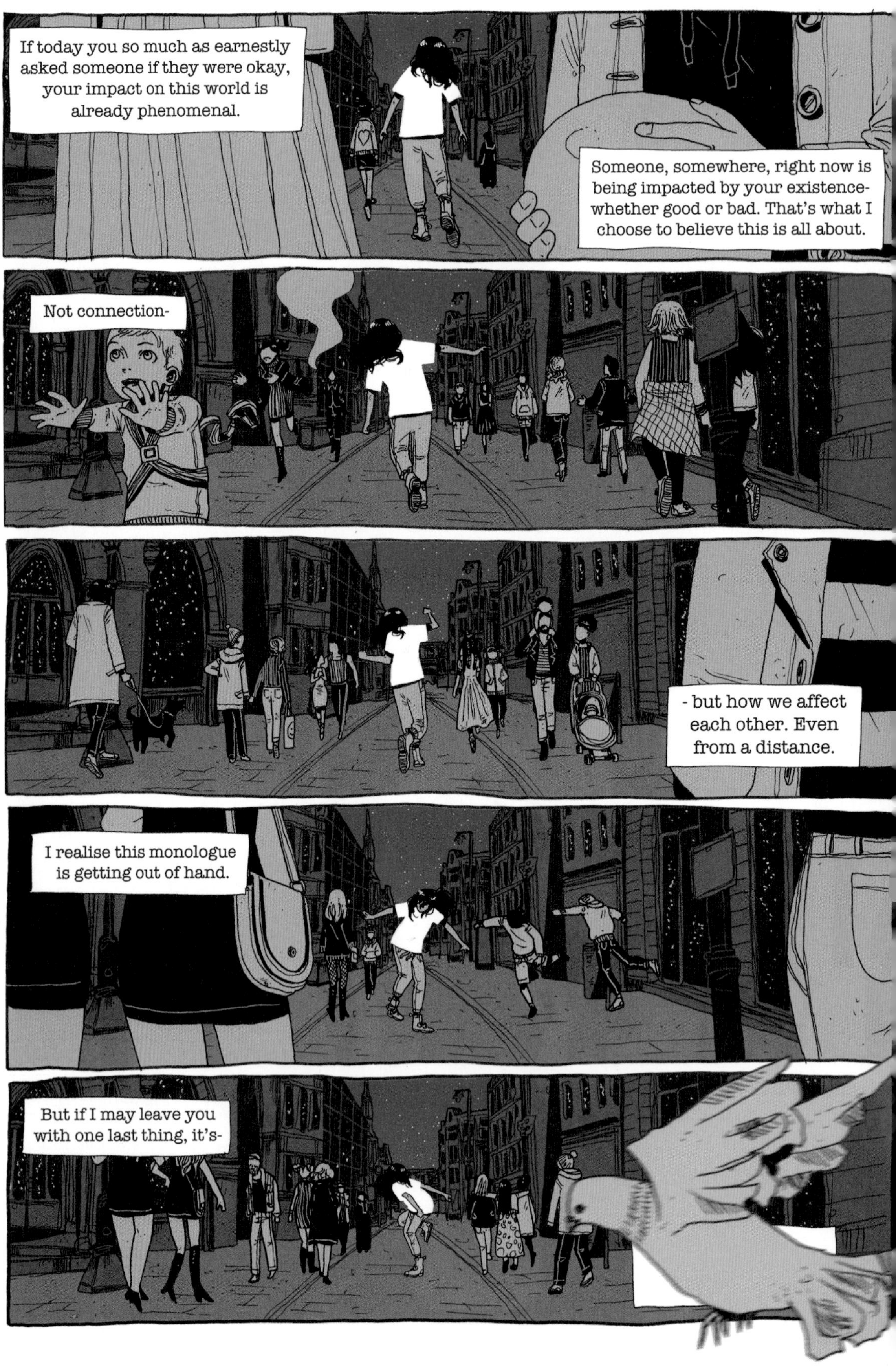
If today you so much as earnestly asked someone if they were okay, your impact on this world is already phenomenal.
Someone, somewhere, right now is being impacted by your existence- whether good or bad. That's what I choose to believe this is all about.
Not connection-
- but how we affect each other. Even from a distance.
I realise this monologue is getting out of hand.
But if I may leave you with one last thing, it's-